*The Campus History Series*

# WILLIAM CAREY UNIVERSITY

## THE FIRST 125 YEARS

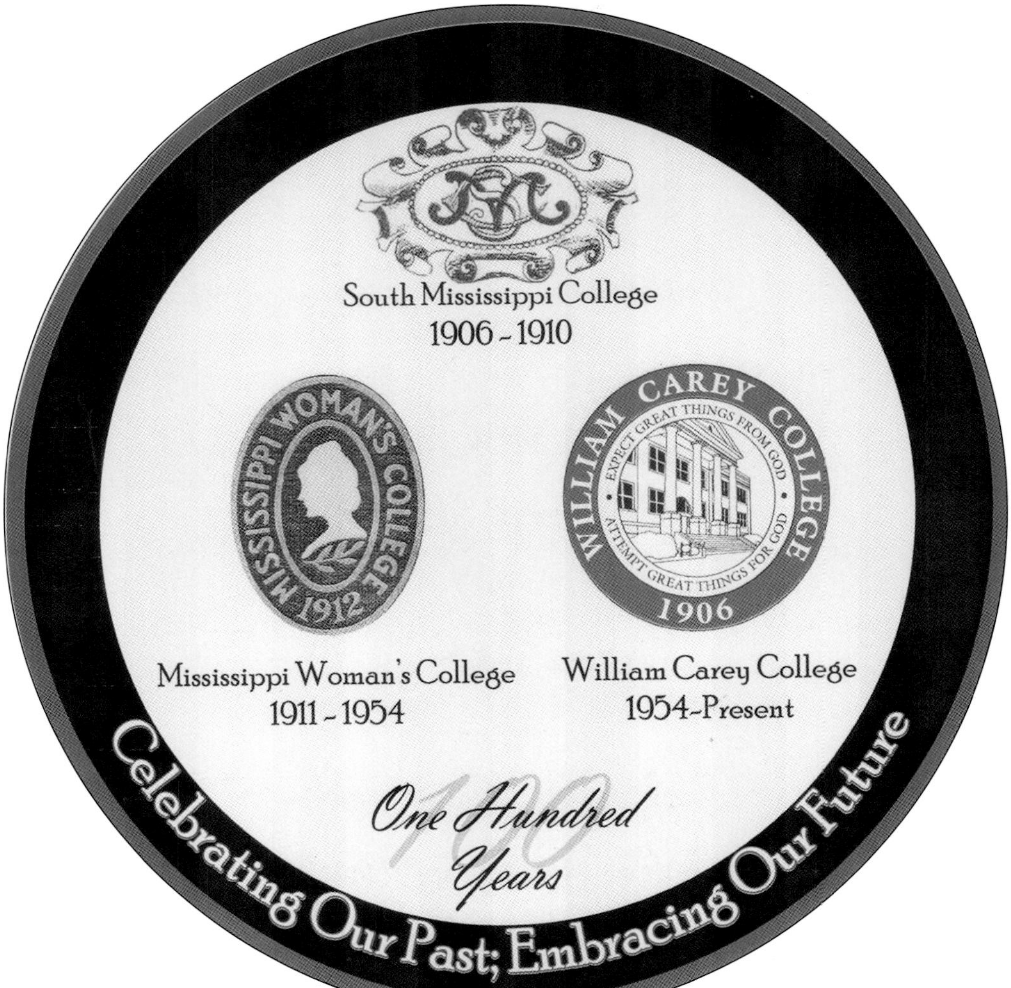


In 2006, William Carey College celebrated its 100th anniversary. A competition was held among the student body in 2005 for a centennial logo design to be used throughout the year. Lacey Walters, a senior communication major, won with this design. The centennial celebration began with homecoming in January 2006, with other events planned throughout the year.

**On the Cover:** *Carey Turns to the World*, a seven-foot, 600-pound statue by sculptor Ben Watts of Columbia, Mississippi, was added to the campus near Smith/Rouse Library in 2011 to celebrate the 250th birthday of William Carey, known as the "father of modern missions." The November statue dedication was the culmination of a year-long celebration of the university namesake's birthday.

**Cover Background:** This 2016 aerial photograph shows the steady growth of the William Carey University Hattiesburg campus, which was established on roughly 10 acres in 1906. The campus has now expanded to more than 170 acres with enrollment surpassing 4,500 students in 2017. An EF-3 tornado devastated much of the campus in January 2017 and destroyed five buildings, including the historic administration building Tatum Court. Rebuilding efforts are currently underway for an anticipated 2018 completion date.

*The Campus History Series*

# William Carey University

## The First 125 Years

Joshua Wilson, Donna Duck Wheeler,
and Barbara Hamilton

Arcadia Publishing

ISBN 978-1-4671-2704-2

Published by Arcadia Publishing
Charleston, South Carolina

Printed in the United States of America

Library of Congress Control Number: 2017946404

For all general information, please contact Arcadia Publishing:
Telephone 843-853-2070
Fax 843-853-0044
E-mail sales@arcadiapublishing.com
For customer service and orders:
Toll-Free 1-888-313-2665

Visit us on the Internet at www.arcadiapublishing.com

# CONTENTS

# ACKNOWLEDGMENTS

Writing this 100-year pictorial history has been both a joy and a challenge. Very few records remain from South Mississippi College. Considerable correspondence and papers remain from Mississippi Woman's College (MWC), but few photographs exist. The college yearbooks are, for the most part, classics, and have provided many of the images used from the MWC era. It was no easy assignment to choose images for the pictorial history from among the thousands that exist from the William Carey College years.

Through the years, most of the photographs were taken by work-study students or those who edited yearbooks and student newspapers. Some names that surfaced merit much gratitude: Jim Hanson, Ron Dyal, Richard Gunther, David Allison, Cecil Rimes, Clyde Davis, Jimmy McFatter, Danny Rawls, Tony Myrick, Milton Wheeler, Mitchell Smith, Jeanna Graves, Allison Chestnut, Lacey Walters, and Emily Wade.

Special thanks go to the Hattiesburg Area Historical Society, the Mississippi Department of Archives, the McCain Library staff at the University of Southern Mississippi, Reagan Grimsley, Jack Rogers, Diane Taylor, Barbara Hamilton, and to those early faculty and staff of Mississippi Woman's College and William Carey College who preserved photographs, scrapbooks, yearbooks, catalogs, papers, and other historic items.

I am indebted to my husband, Dr. Milton Wheeler, professor of history at William Carey College for 42 years, who wrote the introductory history and provided much assistance. Additionally, appreciation goes to Dr. Allison Chestnut, whose skills in editing were invaluable; to the history committee identified on the cover who provided great help and encouragement; and to Pres. Larry W. Kennedy for inspiring this project.

—Donna Wheeler
Hattiesburg, Mississippi
2006

# INTRODUCTION

William Carey College joined the ranks of institutions of higher learning as a product of its age, the Progressive Era, one of the distinctive periods of reform in American history. The first two decades of the 20th century found the nation still in its innocence and bursting with enthusiasm for the future. Political reform flowed like a current: direct election of senators, cleansing of state and local machine governments, and the introduction of new popular measures like the initiative, the recall, the referendum, and primary elections. Nothing could stop the awakened American giant, fresh from a victory over outmatched Spain and flexing its economic muscle along with the energetic foreign policy of Pres. Theodore Roosevelt.

The small town of Hattiesburg felt the same unstoppable drive as the nation. The editor of the Hattiesburg *News,* later to be the *American,* promised readers that the Hub City was destined to be Mississippi's largest city. In 1906, Dr. T.E. Ross pored over plans for his new skyscraper on Front Street. Capt. J.P. Carter pushed his architects to complete the plans for his skyscraper on Front and Main Streets. The new Hotel Hattiesburg opened in October of that

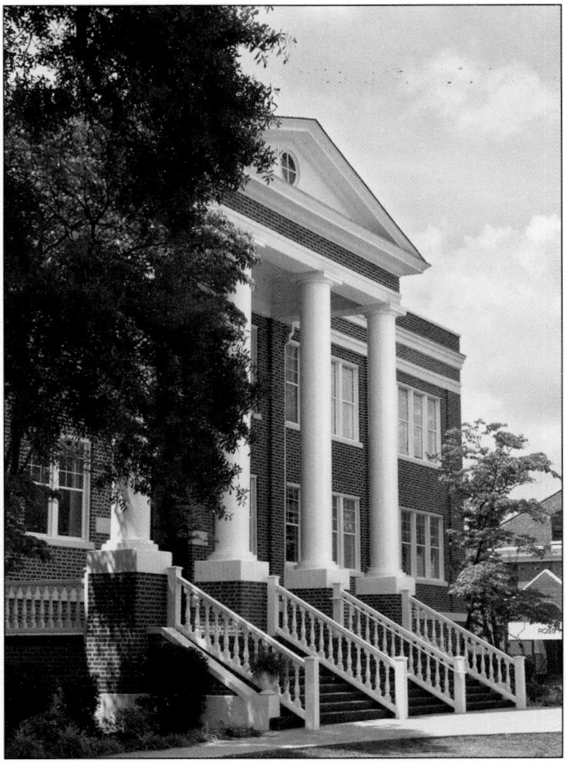

Tatum Court, the oldest and largest of the William Carey College buildings, dates to 1914. It houses administrative offices on the middle floor, classroom space for English, psychology, and art on the third floor, and offices and classrooms for theater and communication on the ground floor. The building was renovated in 2005, as shown in this recent photograph.

year. W.S.F. Tatum, amassing a fortune from lumber, planned a new railroad to the southeast which would have added still another dimension to the town's "Hub City" nickname.

Nationwide the Progressive Era witnessed a spate of new colleges. No one could deny how essential higher education is in a time of growth. As 1906 opened, however, there was no four-year, coeducational liberal arts college in South Mississippi. In fact, there was no school of higher education in Hattiesburg of any kind. Such a situation could no longer be tolerated. Accordingly a group of New Orleans businessmen founded South Mississippi College in 1906. The choice of the name reflected the dearth of liberal arts colleges in South Mississippi.

For a college generation (freshman to senior years), fortune smiled on the fledgling Hattiesburg school. True, just as would happen a hundred years later, a hurricane delayed opening day registration. Students spent their first nights sleeping on mattresses on the floor. But the young college shook off those uneasy weeks and, under the leadership of legendary South Mississippi educator William I. Thames, quickly gained a reputation for a strong faculty, especially in art, music, history, and home economics. It fielded a football team, boasted a marching band, and hosted sessions of an annual Chautauqua, or spiritual retreat.

But in 1910 tragedy struck. A catastrophic fire destroyed the immense administration building, eliminating classrooms, the library, and a large auditorium. The young institution was forced to close. How different would have been the history of William Carey College without that fire. How different would have been the history of higher education in South Mississippi without that blaze.

In 1911, W.S.F. Tatum, wealthy lumberman and Methodist layman, acquired the property and offered it as a gift to the Baptists. The property consisted of two surviving frame buildings and 10 acres of cut-over land. A corporation was organized to own and control the college with nine trustees chosen from Baptist churches in Hattiesburg. In September 1911, the school opened again with a new name, Mississippi Woman's College, under the leadership of Pres. W.W. Rivers, recruited from a similar position in Arkansas. In November 1911, the debt-free college was offered to the Mississippi Baptist Convention and was accepted.

The growth of Mississippi Woman's College was a source of pride for Mississippi Baptists. Under the leadership of Pres. John L. Johnson Jr., from 1912 to 1921, a splendid new administration building was completed in 1914 and named Tatum Court in honor of the college's first major benefactor. New brick dormitories were added (Ross and Johnson Halls) as well as an infirmary and a model home, which was used as a laboratory for domestic science classes. During this period, the campus expanded to 40 acres. Accreditation by the Southern Association of Colleges and Schools was attained in 1926.

The college did not measure its progress simply with physical achievements. An early objective of Mississippi Woman's College was to train intelligent, concerned citizens who could establish Christian homes. Curricula and activities were designed with this primary objective in mind. By 1925, college stationery boldly proclaimed on its letterhead, "Mississippi Woman's College: The School with a Mission." The student body dedicated itself to the mission of the college. Such dedication accounts for Mississippi Woman's College becoming known by the late 1920s as one of the South's outstanding Christian colleges for women. Woman's College ladies still proudly sing from their alma mater "Proud are we of thy fair name! How we love to sing thy praises and to spread abroad thy fame!" Continued growth and an emphasis on missions characterized the presidency of William E. Holcomb from 1932 to 1940.

When the exigencies of the Depression era forced the college to close in 1940, its facilities became available for use as army officers' housing for nearby Camp Shelby. In 1946, Mississippi Woman's College reopened and underwent major renovations. Dr. Irving E. Rouse was elected president in 1946 and served until 1956. In 1953, the Mississippi Baptist Convention voted to convert the college to coeducational status, after more than four decades of admitting female students. This vote necessitated a new name for the institution. In 1954, the board of trustees selected the name William Carey College in honor of the 18th-century English cobbler and linguist whose decades of missionary activity in India earned him international recognition as the "Father of Modern Missions."

Under the leadership of Dr. J. Ralph Noonkester, who was elected president of the college in 1956, William Carey College enjoyed significant growth. In 14 years, a total of 14 new buildings rose on the Hattiesburg campus. The college attracted national attention with baseball, basketball, and tennis teams, the traveling chorale, the theater performance groups, scientific honor societies, student mission efforts (one of the nation's leading colleges in number of mission volunteers), and premedical activities (frequently a leader in percentage of acceptances to medical school).

In 1968, William Carey College entered a new dimension when it announced a merger with the prestigious Mather School of Nursing in New Orleans. Still another dimension opened for the college in 1976 when it purchased the Gulf Coast Military Academy campus in Gulfport. Known as Carey on the Coast, the 20-acre Gulfport campus facing the Gulf of Mexico offers select undergraduate and graduate programs.

Upon Dr. Noonkester's retirement in June 1989, the board of trustees elected Dr. James W. Edwards as the seventh president. Dr. Edwards served until 1997. Under his leadership, student enrollment in church-related vocations increased, the art program at Carey on the Coast was upgraded, the college debt was restructured, salaries improved, a trimester calendar system was inaugurated, and an MBA program in executive leadership was added to the curriculum. The Lucile Parker Gallery on the Hattiesburg campus was opened, and the Sarah Gillespie Art Gallery was upgraded and moved from Fairchild Administration Building to a new and improved location in Parker Hall at Carey on the Coast. A campus beautification project was inaugurated.

Dr. Larry W. Kennedy was appointed interim president in 1997 and became president in 1998. Since that time, the physical facilities on the Hattiesburg and Gulfport campuses have undergone major repair and renovation. The New Orleans nursing program was relocated to the New Orleans Baptist Theological Seminary campus in 1998. The Fail-Asbury School of Nursing building was completed in January 2002, the first new building on the Hattiesburg campus in 25 years. Two soccer fields and an intramural field were dedicated in 2004. The Lorena Roseberry Smith Hall, housing education department programs, was completed in 2004 as well. Donnell Hall opened in 2006, as did Milton Wheeler Field, a new baseball park touted by major league scouts as "the most beautiful baseball park in the nation among small colleges." A new softball park rises next to it and is scheduled for play in 2007. Construction of a new theater is scheduled for 2006, and plans for a new student center have been presented to the board of trustees. In all, 16 buildings have been renovated, 3 new buildings erected, and 4 new sports facilities provided on the Hattiesburg campus in the last eight years. Most remarkably, $17 million in capital improvements have been realized even as the $7.5-million debt was being eliminated. In January 2006, the college announced that it was debt-free 10 months ahead of schedule.

While this physical transformation of the Hattiesburg and Gulfport campuses awed the Carey family, enrollment passed the 3,000 mark in 2005; the debate team won a national championship; the theater students gained national distinction at the Kennedy Center in Washington, D.C.; and programs in art, education, and nursing set standards for their disciplines.

As in its founding a century before, a hurricane of historic magnitude—Katrina in August of 2005—dealt the college a brutal blow during preparations for its centennial. Classes were interrupted for three weeks as repairs proceeded. The Gulfport campus was virtually destroyed, causing classes to meet at a high school and a Baptist church. Although the brand-new nursing building in New Orleans was spared, classes were delayed six months because most of the students were displaced.

But, phoenix-like, the Gulfport campus has taken new life. Drawings of a new inland campus have been presented to the board of trustees. The design harmonizes with the beautiful Hattiesburg campus. Property of at least 50 acres is being sought at publication time. Proceeds from the sale of the valuable beachfront campus have been earmarked for the endowment of the college.

It should thus become apparent that the dramatic developments over the last 100 years demonstrate that William Carey College has accepted the motto of William Carey the man: "Expect great things from God; attempt great things for God."

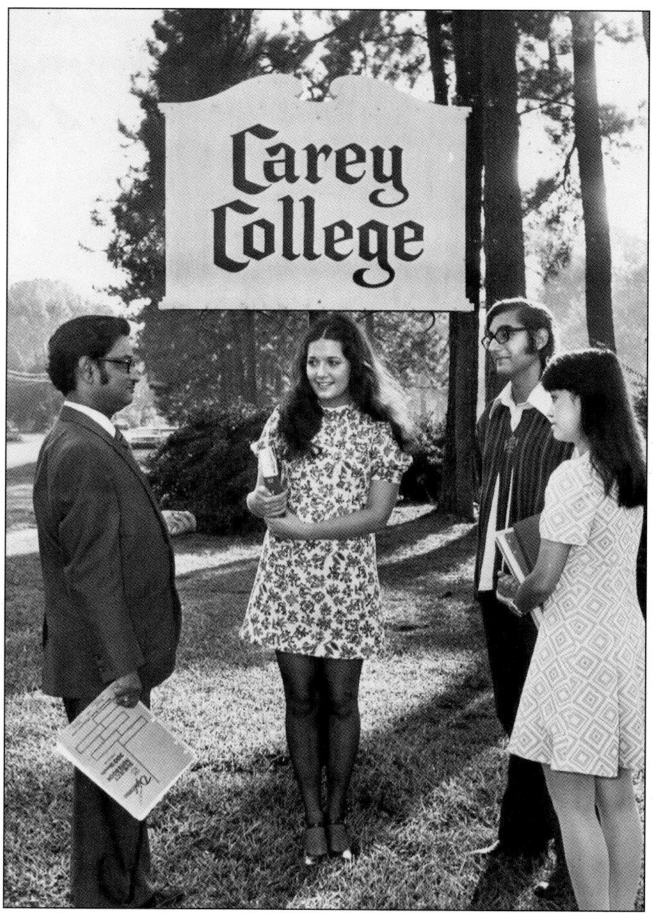


In 1973–1974, H.S. Banerjee, executive secretary to the president of Serampore College of India, founded by William Carey College, spent a year at William Carey College as an administrative intern. He is pictured with, from left to right, students Kathy Smith, David Davis, and Rommanee Hongsirinukul.

# *One*

# South Mississippi College 1906–1910

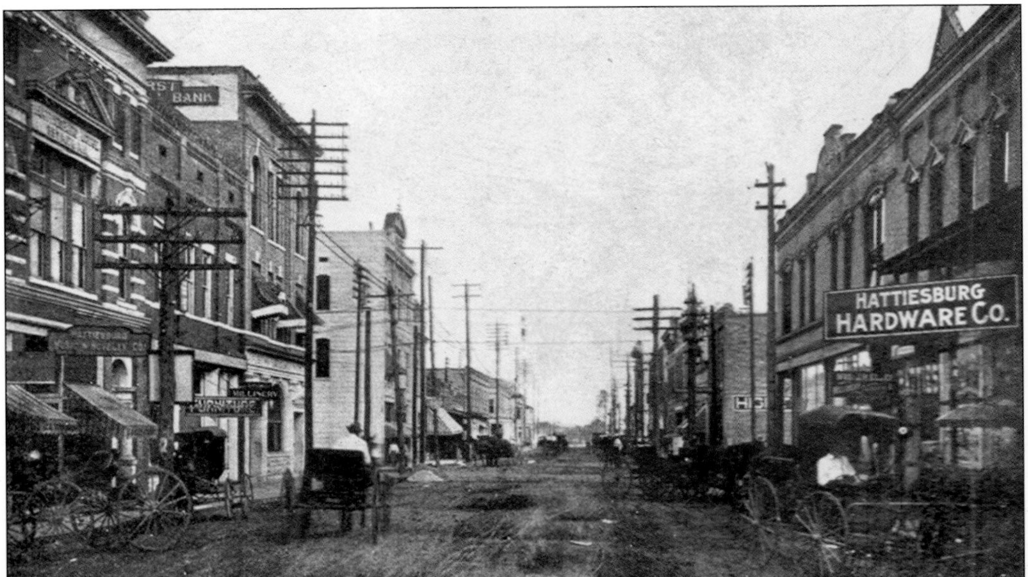


The year 1906 was an exciting time in Hattiesburg. Construction skyrocketed with several new buildings underway. On a 15-acre site in the southwest section of Hattiesburg, a crew of men was framing the three buildings that would house a new college, the first in Hattiesburg. Notices appeared regularly in the *Daily Picayune* of New Orleans. They read: "South Mississippi College (removed from Poplarville) has accommodations for 300 students, with steam heat, electrical lights, sanitary toilets, hot and cold shower baths, and artesian water provided. Primary, intermediate, high school, and college department are offered with an excellent faculty. Sessions open October 2. Send for catalogue."

—W.I. Thames, President
Hattiesburg, Mississippi

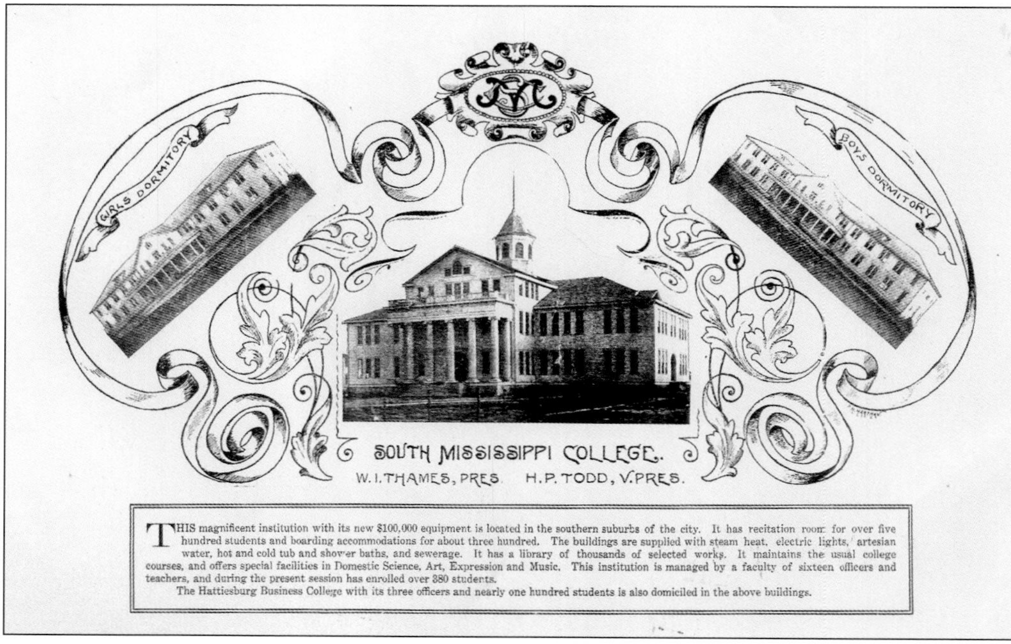


South Mississippi College was the result of efforts by a stock company of New Orleans businessmen from all denominations. The faculty of the college numbered 16, and the college had impressive facilities. The main building of the campus contained 12 recitation rooms to accommodate 500 students, music rooms, a library with several thousand selected works, an auditorium that would seat over 1,000, classrooms, and offices for the administration and faculty of the college. The girls' dormitory had rooms for over 100 women, and the boys' dormitory housed 200 men. The dining hall would accommodate 320 students. (Both, courtesy of the Hattiesburg Area Historical Society.)

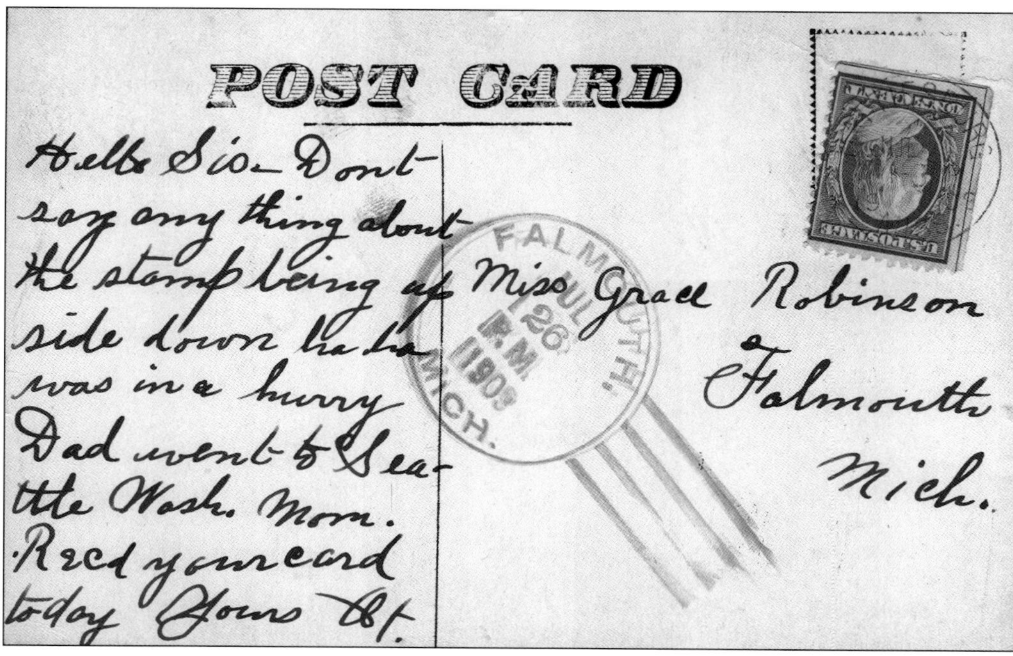

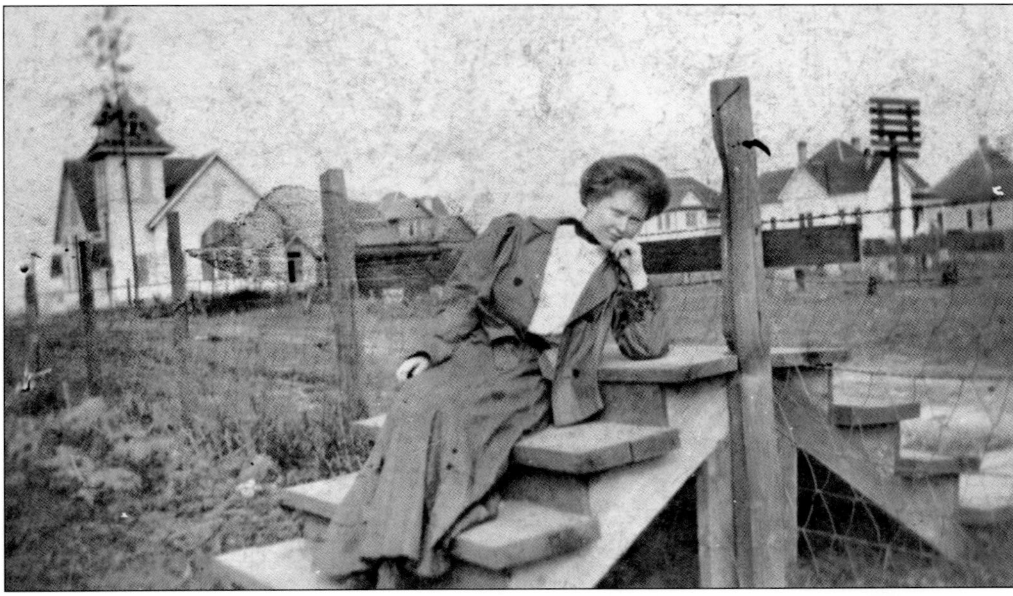

Cora Henry and Cora Henry's report card from South Mississippi College, October 3, 1908, give a glimpse of student academics. (Both, courtesy of the Henry-Rowell-Waldrup Papers of the McCain Library and Archives, the University of Southern Mississippi.)

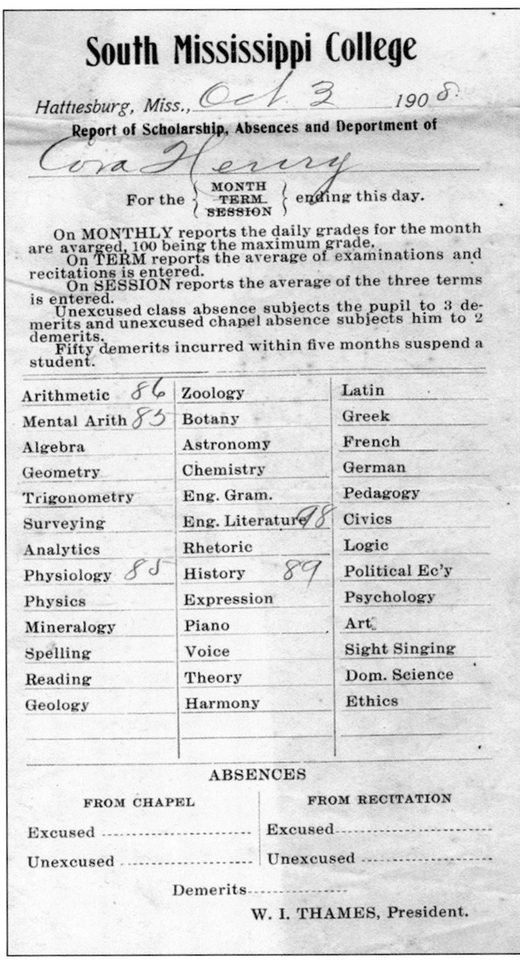

**South Mississippi College**

*Hattiesburg, Miss.,* Oct. 3 190 8.

**Report of Scholarship, Absences and Deportment of**

Cora Henry

For the { MONTH / ~~TERM~~ / SESSION } ending this day.

On MONTHLY reports the daily grades for the month are avarged, 100 being the maximum grade.

On TERM reports the average of examinations and recitations is entered.

On SESSION reports the average of the three terms is entered.

Unexcused class absence subjects the pupil to 3 demerits and unexcused chapel absence subjects him to 2 demerits.

Fifty demerits incurred within five months suspend a student.

| | | | | | |
|---|---|---|---|---|---|
| Arithmetic | 86 | Zoology | | Latin | |
| Mental Arith | 85 | Botany | | Greek | |
| Algebra | | Astronomy | | French | |
| Geometry | | Chemistry | | German | |
| Trigonometry | | Eng. Gram. | | Pedagogy | |
| Surveying | | Eng. Literature | 98 | Civics | |
| Analytics | | Rhetoric | | Logic | |
| Physiology | 85 | History | 89 | Political Ec'y | |
| Physics | | Expression | | Psychology | |
| Mineralogy | | Piano | | Art | |
| Spelling | | Voice | | Sight Singing | |
| Reading | | Theory | | Dom. Science | |
| Geology | | Harmony | | Ethics | |

ABSENCES

| FROM CHAPEL | FROM RECITATION |
|---|---|
| Excused ---------- | Excused ---------- |
| Unexcused ---------- | Unexcused ---------- |

Demerits----------

W. I. THAMES, President.

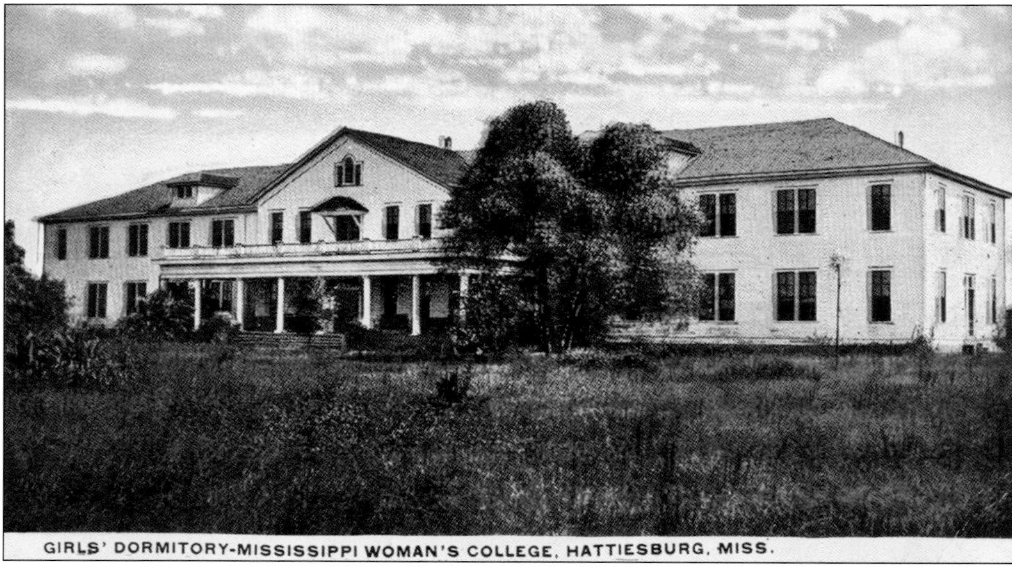


Gale-force wind damage delayed the scheduled beginnings for South Mississippi College until November 8, 1906. About 75 boys had to sleep in the dining hall until repairs were completed. The opening session listed 380 enrolled students. This postcard from the early 20th century shows the girls' dormitory. (Courtesy of Reagan Grimsley.)

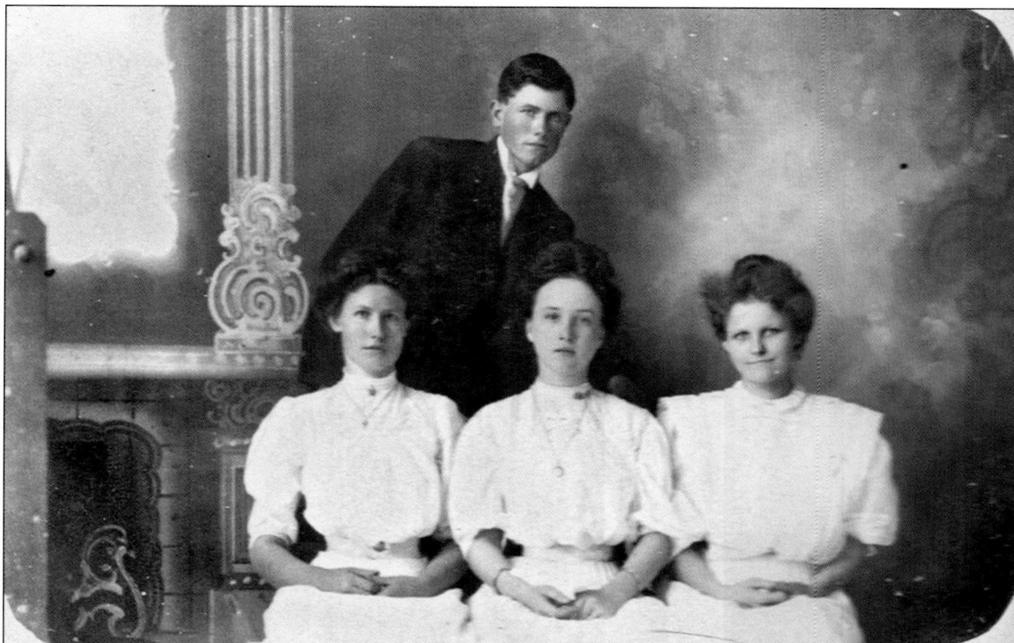

Ira Stockstill, a former student, stated in a 1956 news article in the Hattiesburg *American*, "It (SMC) was nothing but a forest of cut-over pine land covered with stumps. We had a football team and a baseball team. We never had more than 11 men on the football team and substitution was unheard of then. We had demerits for rule-breakers and the penalty was digging stumps. For any offense, the student would be assigned an ax and shovel to dig up a stump. Mr. Thames was a strict disciplinarian." Pictured here is Ira Stockstill as a young man. (Courtesy of Hunter Godsey.)

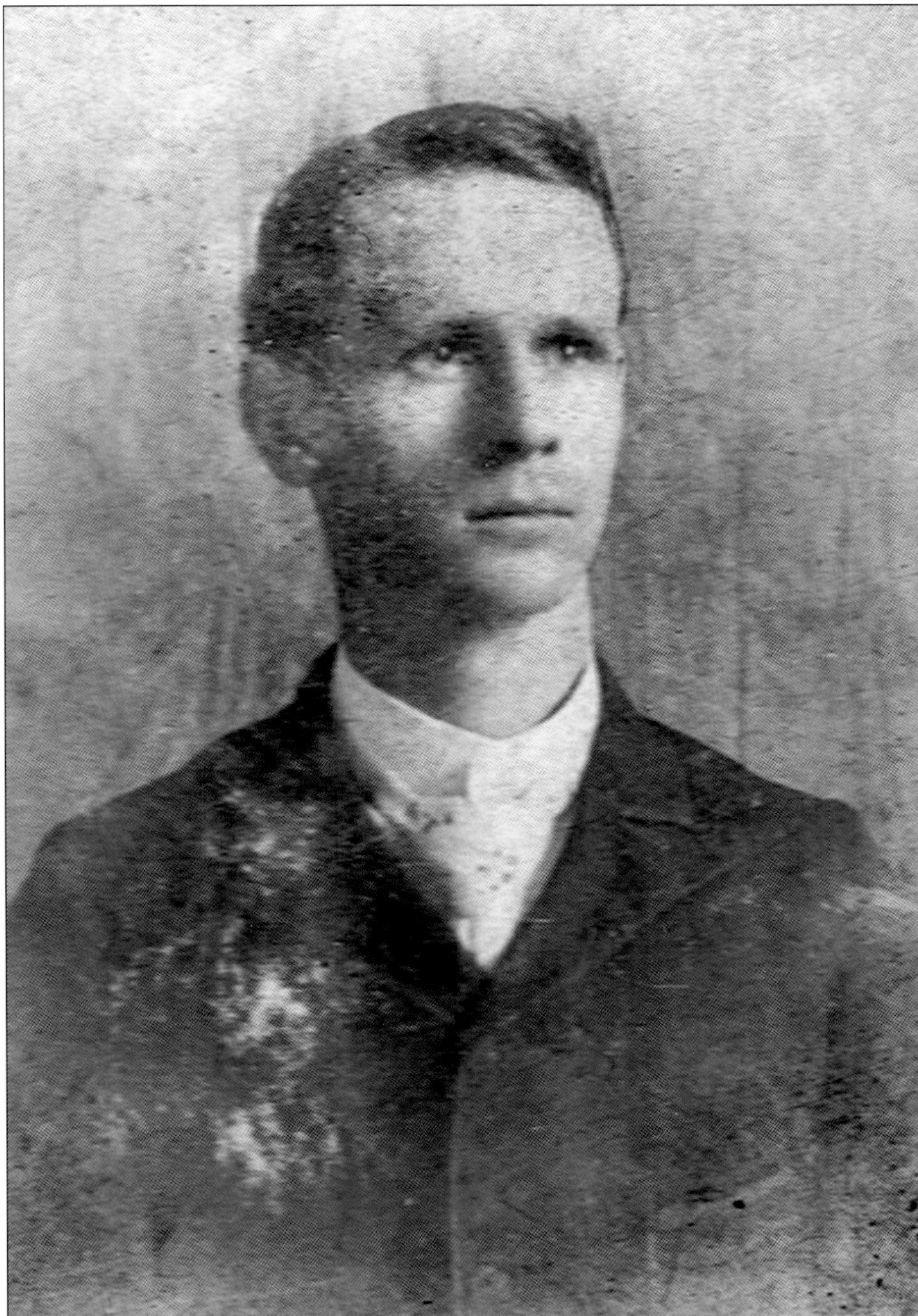

William I. Thames, for whom W.I. Thames Elementary School in Hattiesburg is named, was a pioneer educator with ample qualifications, broad experience, and superior ability. Thames became president of South Mississippi College after serving as principal of the high school in Poplarville for 13 years. After South Mississippi College closed, Thames went on to a further distinguished career in education, serving on the first faculty of State Normal College (now the University of Southern Mississippi), president of Burleson College in Texas, and superintendent of Hattiesburg city schools for 17 years.

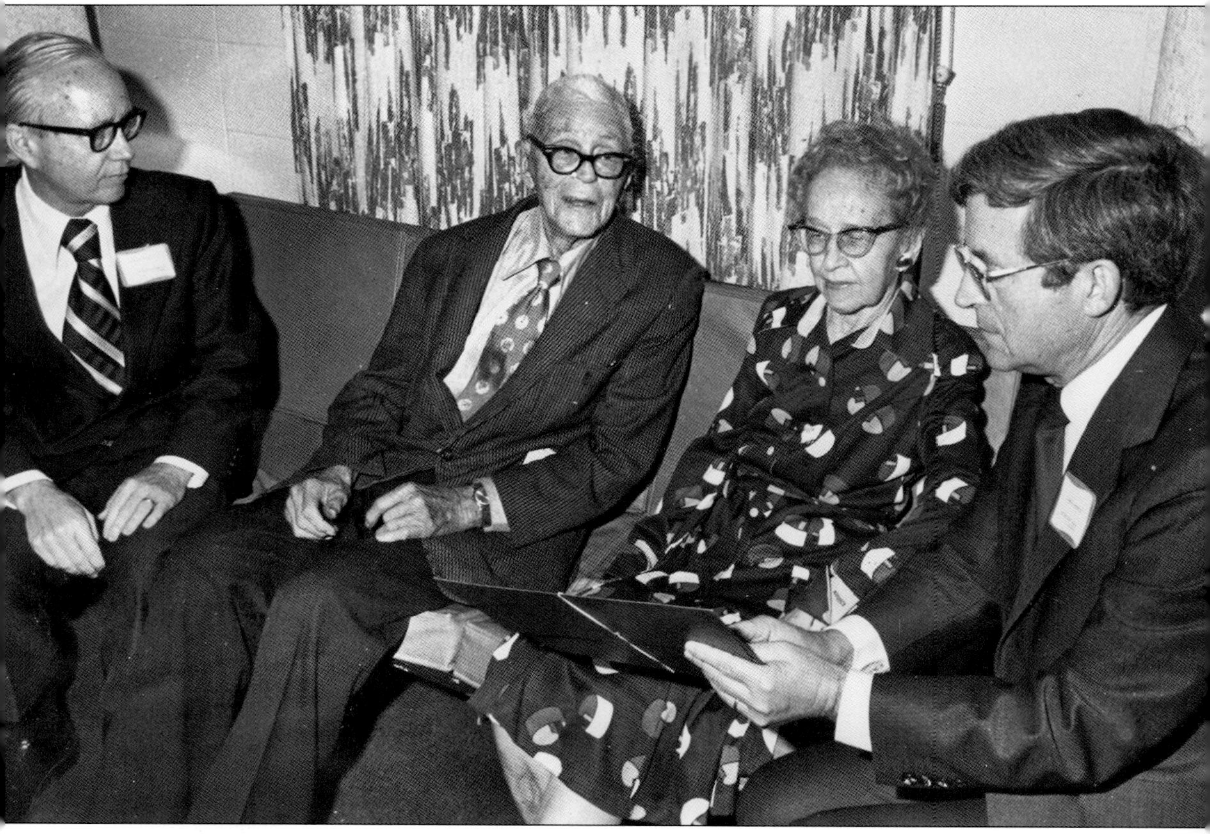

Founders Day guests in 1975 included two Hattiesburg citizens with connections to the school when it was South Mississippi College. At center are H.P. Todd, vice president of the school in 1906–1908, and Lorene Salmond, wife of J.B. Salmond and daughter of W.I. Thames, founder and first president of the school. The two are flanked by Joseph M. Ernest (left), academic vice president of William Carey College, and Ralph Noonkester, president. Salmond stated, "South Mississippi College had good teachers. The departments of art, music, and home economics were especially strong. A home economics department was rare in the early 1900s. The college band was outstanding. They were practicing the night the administration building burned in 1910, and nearly all of the instruments were destroyed in the fire." The devastating fire of February 28, 1910, destroyed the main building, along with its records and accounts. South Mississippi College could not recover and passed from the educational scene in Mississippi. No catalogs or records of South Mississippi College are known to be in existence.

# *Two*

# Mississippi Woman's College 1911–1954

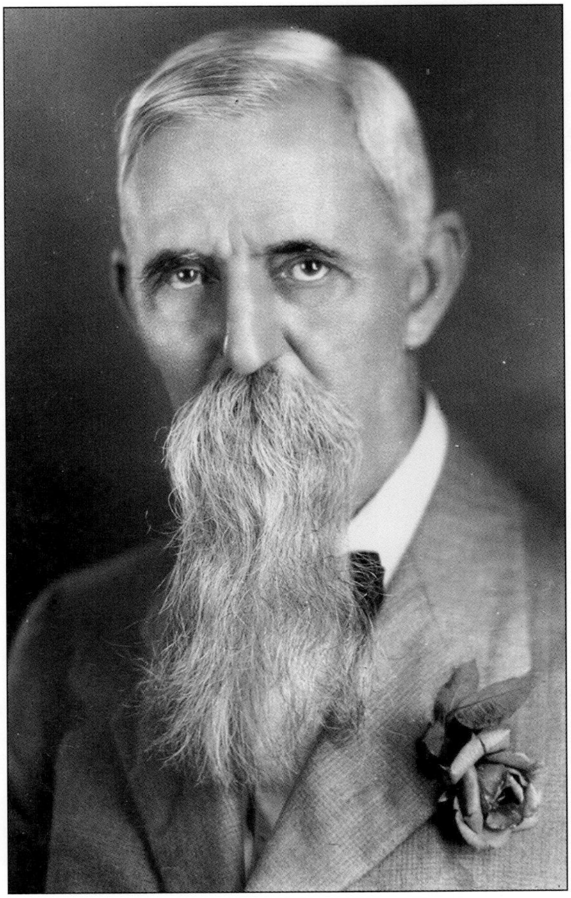

After its closing, the South Mississippi College property was acquired by W.S.F. Tatum, a wealthy Hattiesburg lumberman, businessman, and Methodist layman. After the State of Mississippi declined his offer of the property as the site for the Normal College in Hattiesburg, he offered the property to the Methodists for a college. His fellow churchmen chose not to build another college in the state. He then turned to Mississippi Baptists, who were already making plans for a Baptist college for women in Hattiesburg and who accepted his offer.

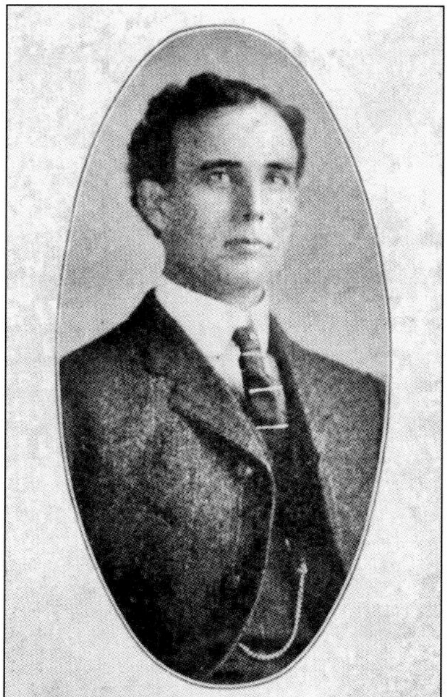

PRESIDENT W. W. RIVERS

The property consisted of two frame buildings and 10 acres of cut-over land. W.W. Rivers, former president of Central Female College in Conway, Arkansas, became president and began putting the two frame buildings in order, securing a faculty, and recruiting students. In 1911, opening exercises were held in the Hattiesburg High School auditorium on Forrest Street, and the new institution became Mississippi Woman's College.

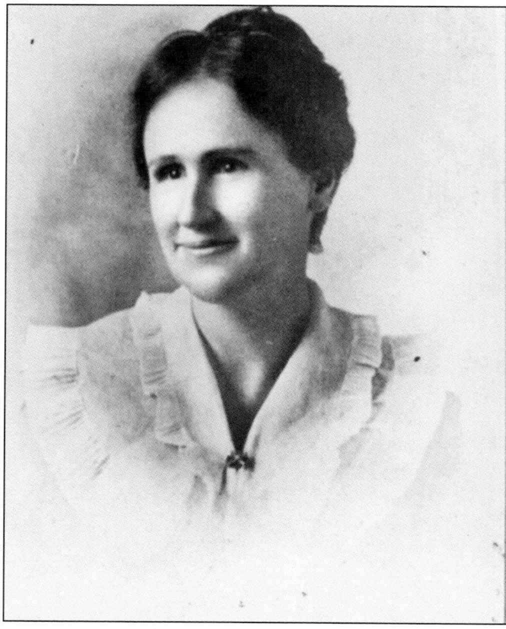

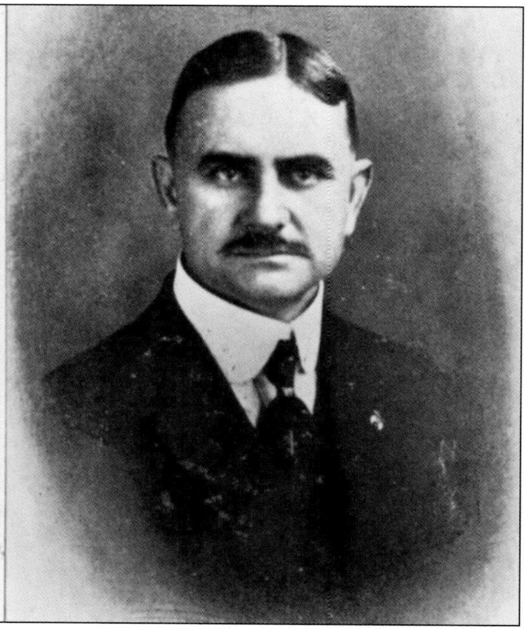

On September 13, 1912, the college opened for its second session with an enrollment of 167 students. John Lipscomb Johnson Jr. assumed leadership. Mae Waller Batson, lady principal, said of Johnson, "Besides being the president, he was also business manager, landscape gardener, teacher, maintenance foreman, and chief solicitor for students and funds. Without official position and without pay, Sue Bell Johnson, wife of Dr. Johnson, labored for 18 years in almost every department. She directed spiritual development of the students and was helpful in fund-raising for the college. Known as a lady of quality and distinction, it was not beyond her to go under dormitories to fix pipes when necessary." Pictured are Sue Bell Johnson and President Johnson.

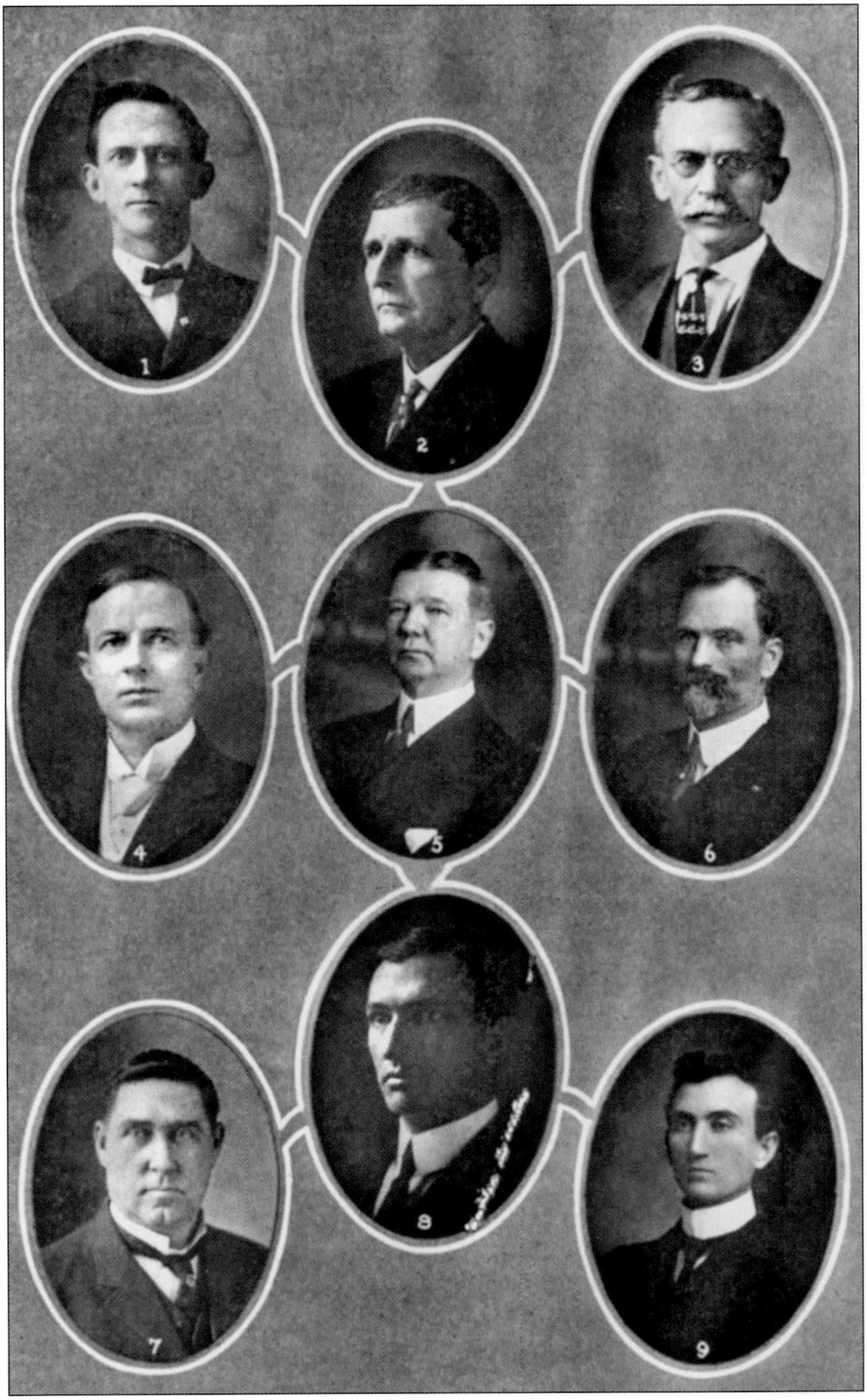

In 1911, nine men from among the Baptist churches in the Hattiesburg area became college trustees. Dr. T.E. Ross, local physician, Christian layman, and benefactor, became the chairman of the board. Included are, in no order, Hon. J.E. Davis, Ellis Hickman, M.P.L. Love, W.L. Pack, Abner Polk (2), Hon. S.E. Travis (6), Rev. A.L. O'Briant, Rev. E.D. Solomon, and Dr. T.E. Ross (7).

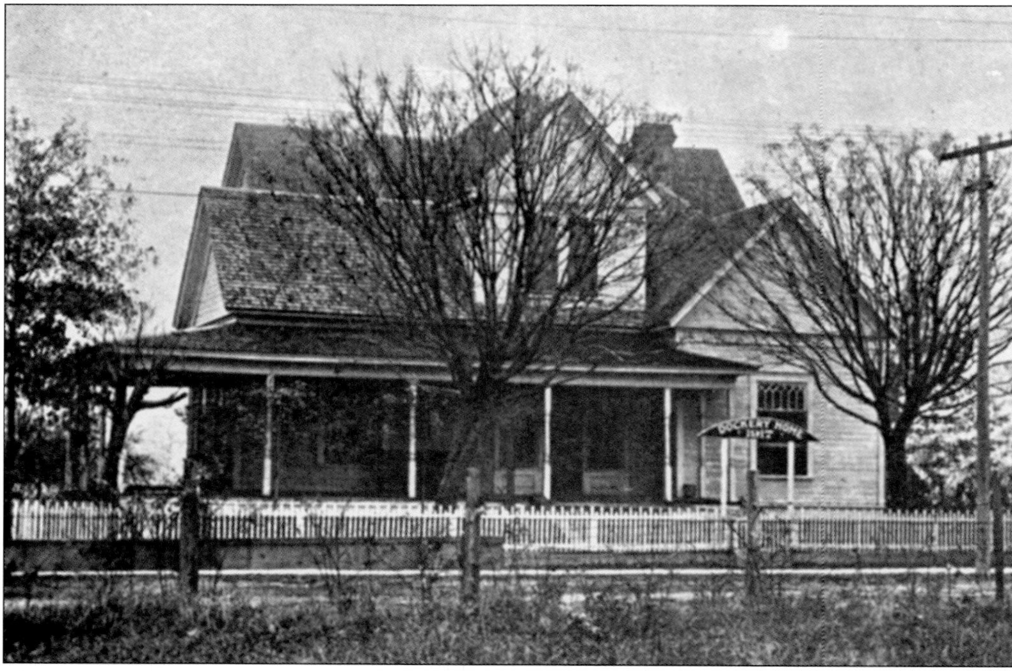

The campus in 1911 consisted of two frame buildings, both used as dormitories by South Mississippi College. This photograph shows Dockery Hall, which housed the president's family, the faculty, a dining hall, a kitchen, a laundry room, and a makeshift auditorium. O'Briant Hall was the administration building, academic building, and housed the Industrial Home, which was run on the cooperative plan with the girls doing all the work, cooking, dishwashing, and scrubbing.

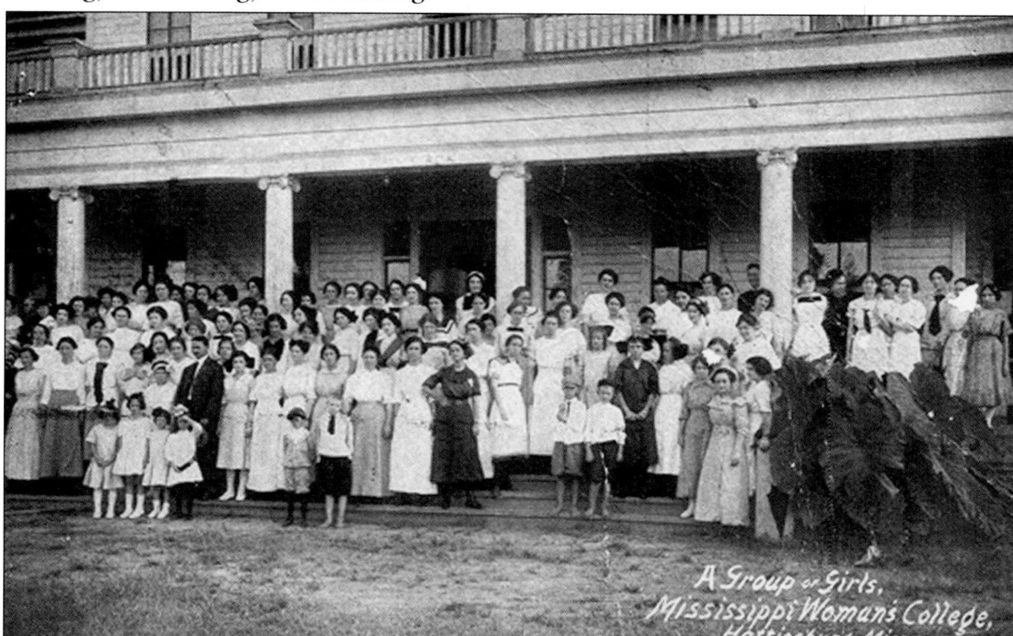


The earliest image archived from Mississippi Woman's College is this 1912 postcard titled "A Group of Girls, Mississippi Woman's College, Hattiesburg, Miss."

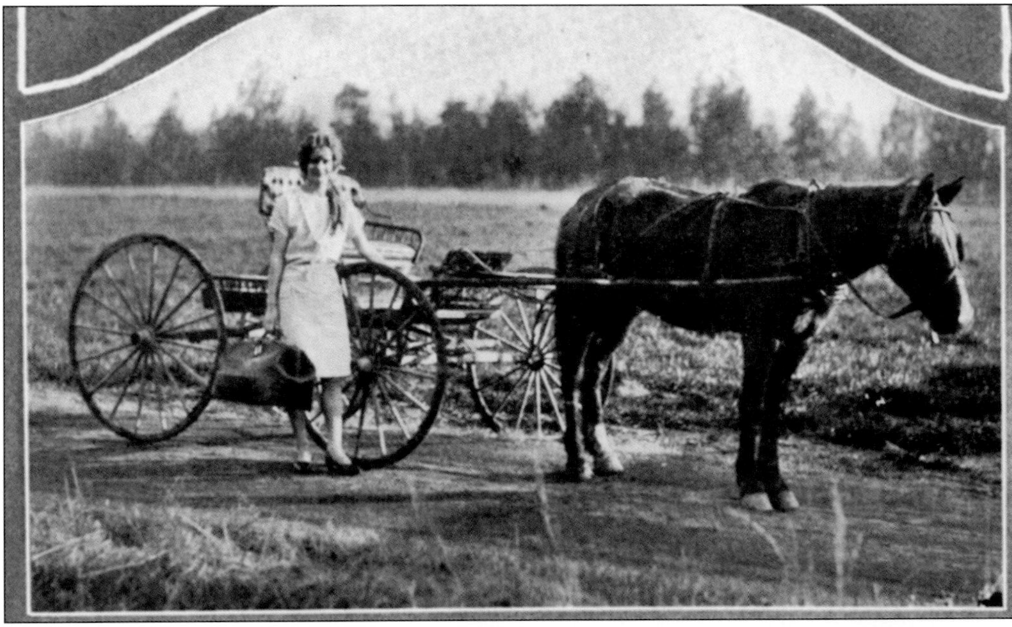

In the early years of Mississippi Woman's College, the Hattiesburg trolley line did not reach the campus. New students and faculty were met at the train station by a horse, fondly called Nellie, and buggy. Soon the automobile arrived in Hattiesburg, and the Johnson family car served as a taxi for the college.

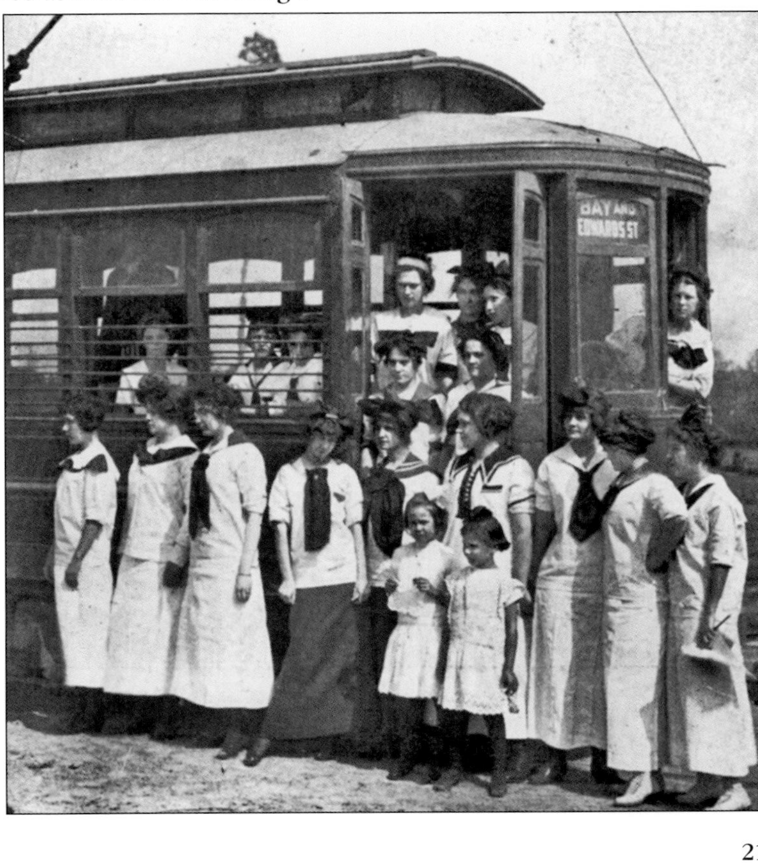


In 1913, the trolley line was extended from downtown Hattiesburg to the campus of Mississippi Woman's College. This group of girls takes advantage of the new mode of transportation.

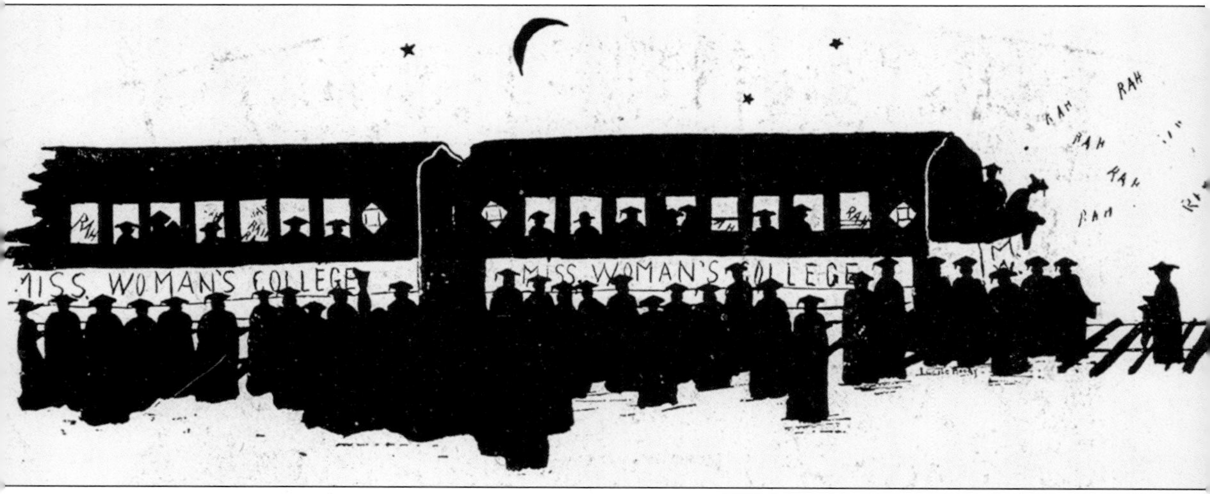


"What was it? What was that sound that floated through the darkened college halls on the morning of November fourteenth? That sound of laughter mingled with exclamations of joy, and that echoed to the rhythm of light foot steps? Had a band of happy spirits taken possession of our Woman's College, or had it suddenly been changed into a palace where fairies romped and played?

These thoughts flashed through the minds of us who were still in the land of dreams. Then we awoke and were half ashamed of our folly—neither spirits nor fairies but the day of all days. Was there a girl who had not dreamed of it? On this day we were going to the state Baptist convention in Jackson and to Mississippi College. Just think 'Little Sister' was really going to visit her 'Big Brother.'

Quickly, we joined the happy throng and when about five-thirty o'clock we assembled at breakfast, a more excited crowd could not have been found.

Then a long line of girls in caps and gowns went to the train, stopping once in town to give our fifteen 'rahs' for Woman's College.

Our train was decorated in all the glory of college colors and huge signs with 'Mississippi Woman's College' painted on them in bold letters. Several of our friends in Hattiesburg went with us and as we passed through different towns we were joined by others.

Finally, about eleven o'clock our train reached Jackson. Then we gave more yells and sang 'We are the girls from the regions of the pines' amid the hearty cheers and welcome given us.

We visited many places of interest in Jackson until about three-thirty, when the train came to carry us to Clinton. When we arrived there, 'whom did we see?' 'All the boys of old M.C.' And it can hardly be called an exaggeration to say, all the people of Clinton.

Time surely had wings that afternoon. After we had spent a few most enjoyable hours on Mississippi College campus and had feasted in the large dining hall it was time to return to Jackson.

Pleasant associations continued until we reached the Convention hall that night.

There the reports of Mississippi's two Baptist schools were discussed and people listened with surprise and delight as an account of our Woman's College, Mississippi's baby, was given by our president.

Train time? Could it be possible? Yes, the face of the honest old clock told us so, and in a short while our friends at the depot waved good bye as our train rolled away loaded with 'girls from the Woman's College in for fun and in for knowledge,' convinced that we had had our share of the former and realizing that we were returning to secure later."

—Lucy Hall Pack
As written in the 1913 *Pine Burr* yearbook

By 1914, enrollment had doubled, and answering the call for an administration building, trustees J. E. Byrd and W.E. Farr raised $50,000 for this purpose. W.S.F. Tatum, the donor of the original property, made another liberal gift of land. The new brick building, which contained administrative offices, classrooms, laboratories, gymnasium, library, and a large auditorium, was named Tatum Court in honor of benefactors Tatum and his wife. In the photograph at right, downtown Hattiesburg can be seen from the front steps of Tatum Court. Below is a front view of Tatum Court in 1918.

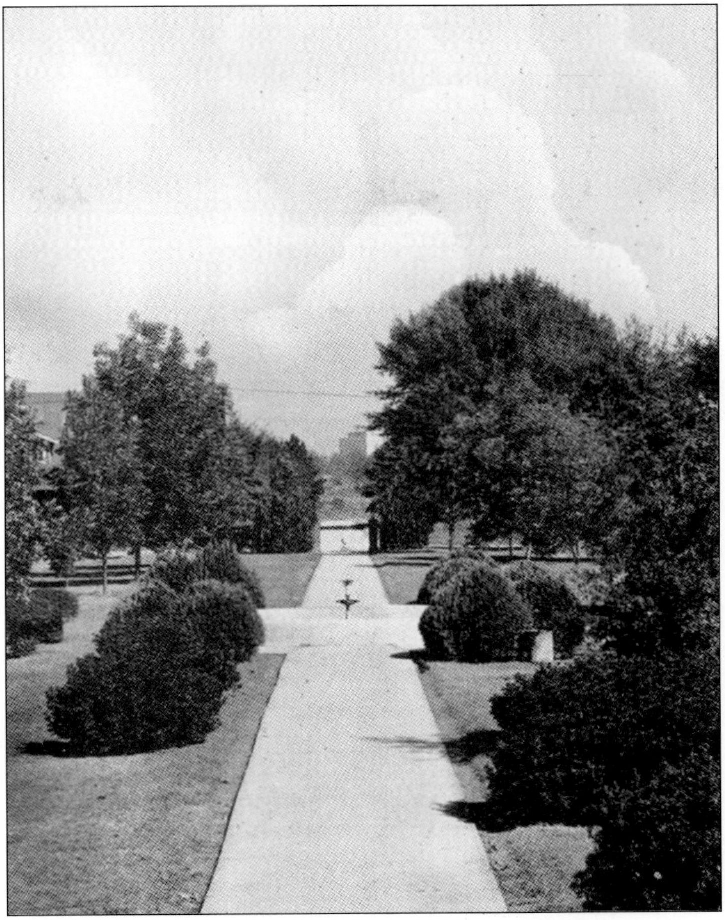

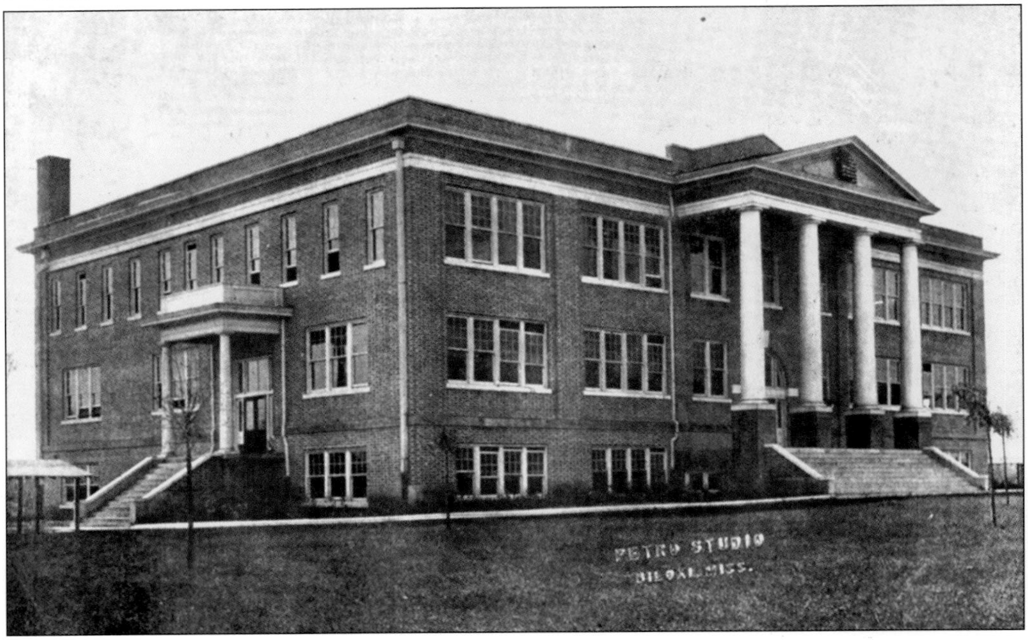

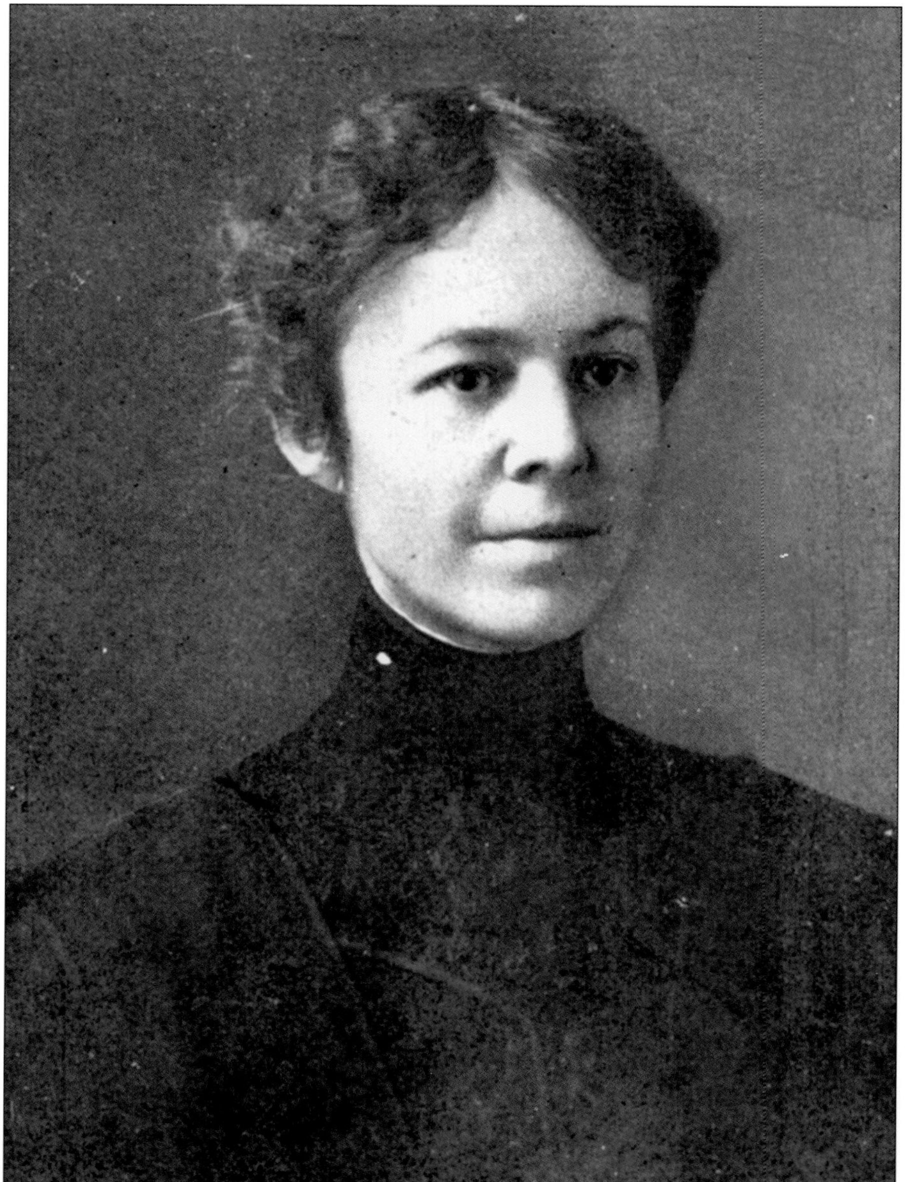

In the early years, Mississippi Woman's College girls followed strict rules. They were allowed to mail four letters per week only to those whose names appeared on a list approved by their mothers. Lipstick and rouge were forbidden for a while, and girls were asked not to cut their hair in short bobs. There were to be "no gentlemen callers" on campus. How did anyone ever get married? Most of the courting was done with the eyes at an occasional Sunday school party. A gentleman who regularly called on teachers and brought supplies to the college reported that he often sneaked a shoebox full of letters back into town for mailing. Customs soon changed, and the idea that when a girl came to college she was a young woman, old enough to know right from wrong, capable of making many of her own decisions, and able, with guidance, to take care of herself became the norm. This is a 1913 photograph of Lady Principal Mae Waller Batson, whose job was to enforce the regulations and to give counsel to the young ladies.

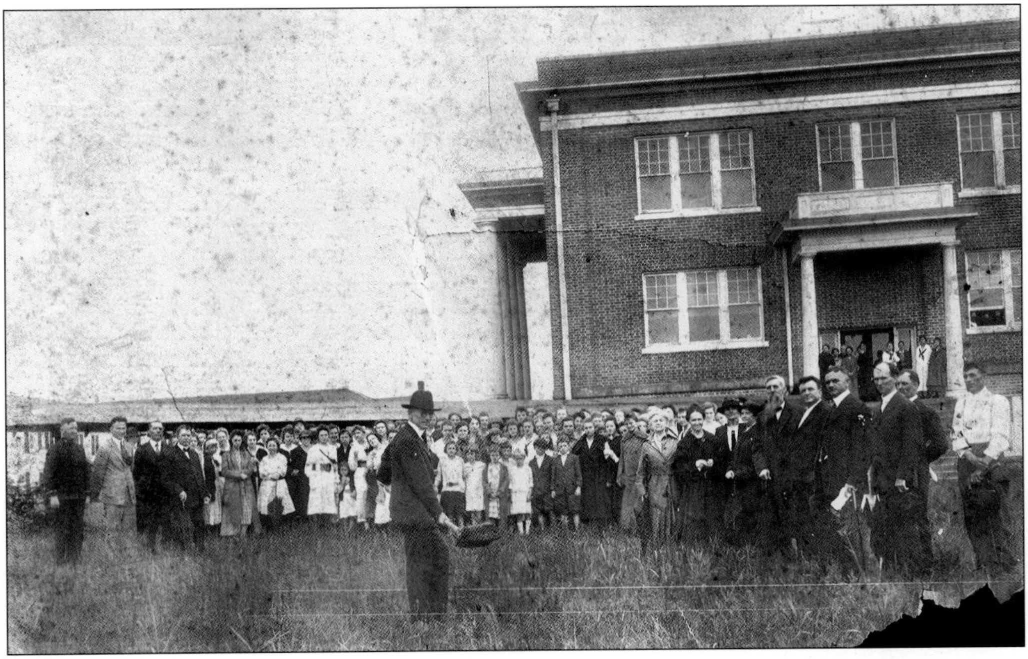

In March 1919, one of the original dormitories, O'Briant Hall, burned. The citizens of Hattiesburg raised $50,000 in cash, and bonds were issued by the Mississippi Baptist Convention to erect two modern fireproof dormitories and a dining hall. The groundbreaking ceremony to begin construction of Ross and Johnson Halls is shown above. W.S.F. Tatum is in the foreground. The new modern twin dormitories, shown below, were called Ross Hall, in honor of local physician and trustee Dr. T.E. Ross, and Johnson Hall for President and Mrs. J.L. Johnson. From left to right are Tatum Court, Ross Hall, and Johnson Hall.

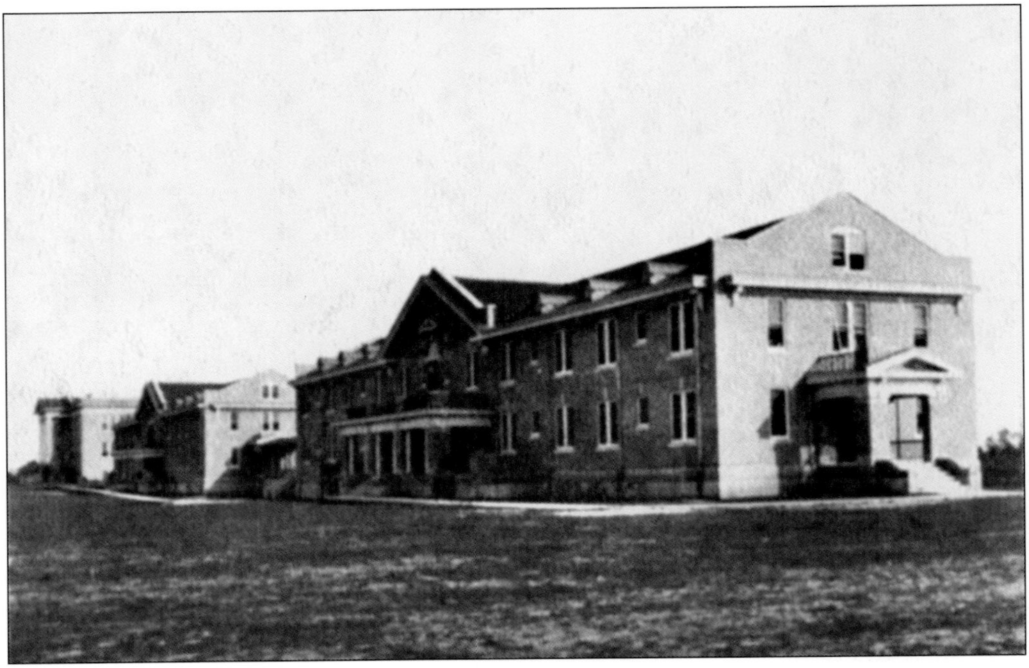

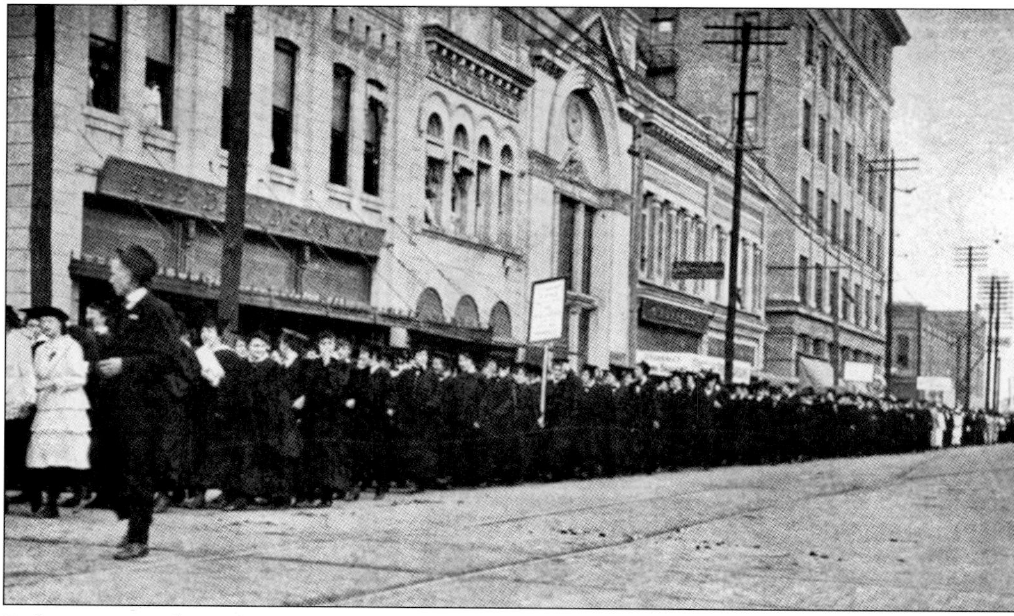

Rules required student attendance at religious services, and the college curriculum included religious studies. Students donned robes and marched to church each Sunday morning, often to Immanuel Baptist Church, located just across the street from the campus. This 1919 photograph shows the students marching through downtown for a special event.

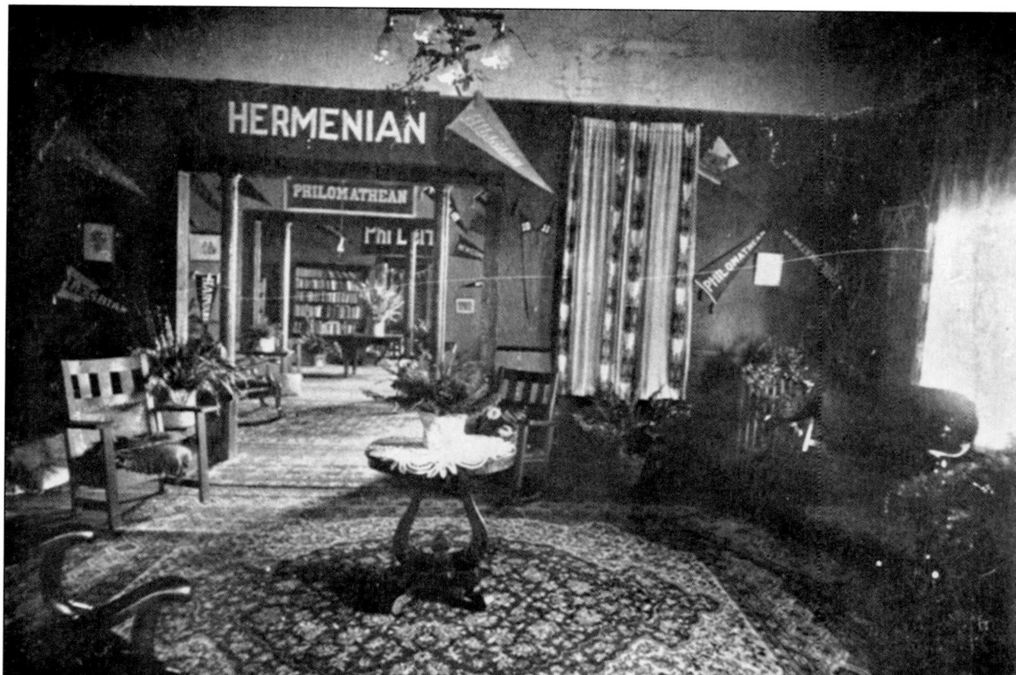


The parlors, or reception rooms, of Ross and Johnson Halls were spacious and well furnished. Two literary societies existed on campus, the Hermenian and the Philomathean. Each organization decorated a parlor room for club activities.

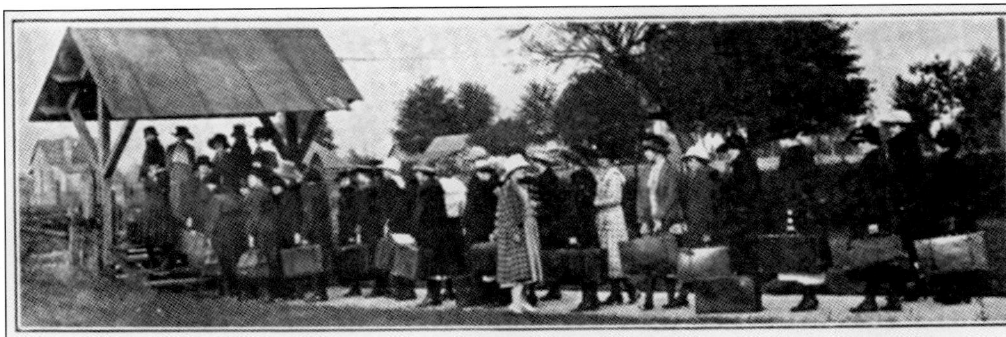

"TURNED AWAY"

Some of the eighty girls who could not find room at the Woman's College.

With the popularity of Mississippi Woman's College growing, the number of girls desiring to live on campus increased as well. In 1919, the college reportedly had 450 students and, according to the yearbook, 80 students were turned away for lack of housing.

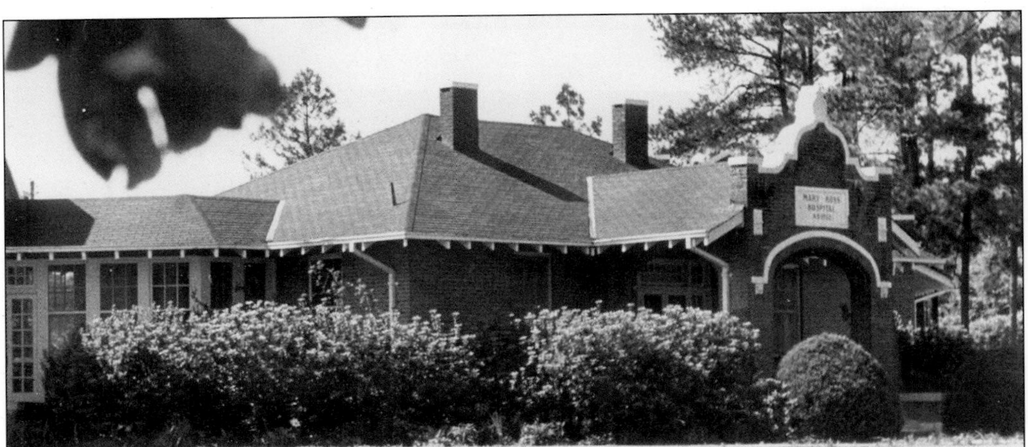

In 1922, Martha Herrin of Laurel donated several thousand dollars to be used in erecting a memorial to her mother, Mary Ross. With this gift as a nucleus, the college built a new brick building called Mary Ross Hospital to meet the health needs of the students. Dr. T.E. Ross served as college physician. The building is currently used as office space for the School of Business.

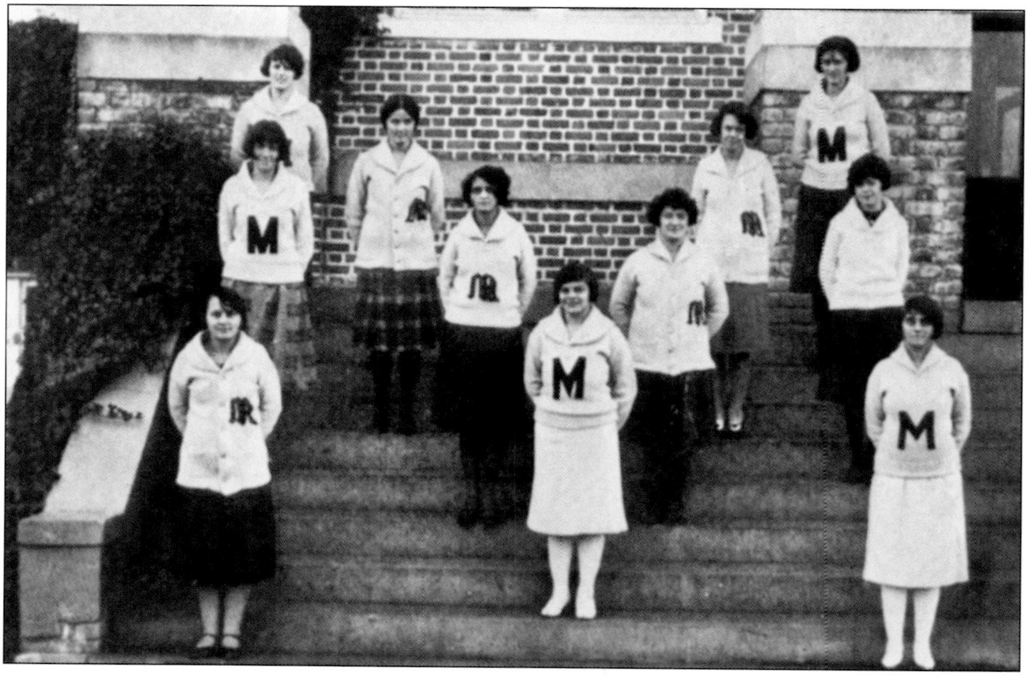

Sports played an important part in college life at Mississippi Woman's College. Basketball, tennis, golf, archery, and swimming were all competitive sports. Pictured is the 1920 cheerleading squad.

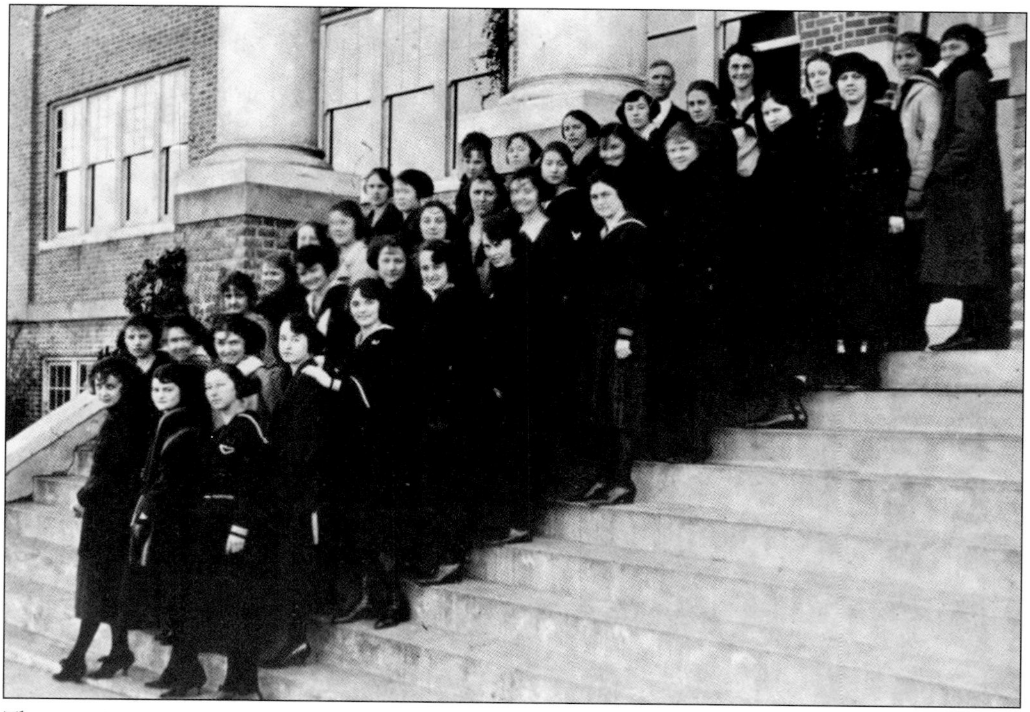

The music program excelled through the years with great participation among students. Concerts were cultural events anticipated by the citizens of Hattiesburg. The Choral Club is shown in 1921.

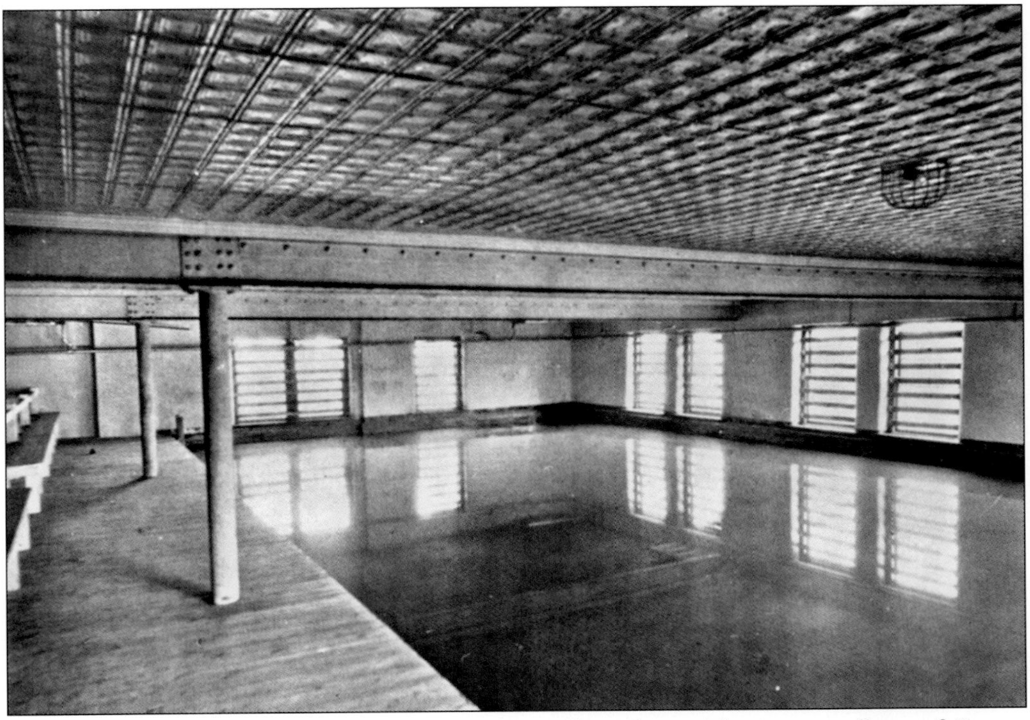

Swimming was a curriculum requirement for all students. The bottom floor of Tatum Court boasted a large swimming pool, pictured above in 1922. In the mid-1960s, the swimming pool became the location for the theater. The photograph below shows the 1922 senior swimming team.

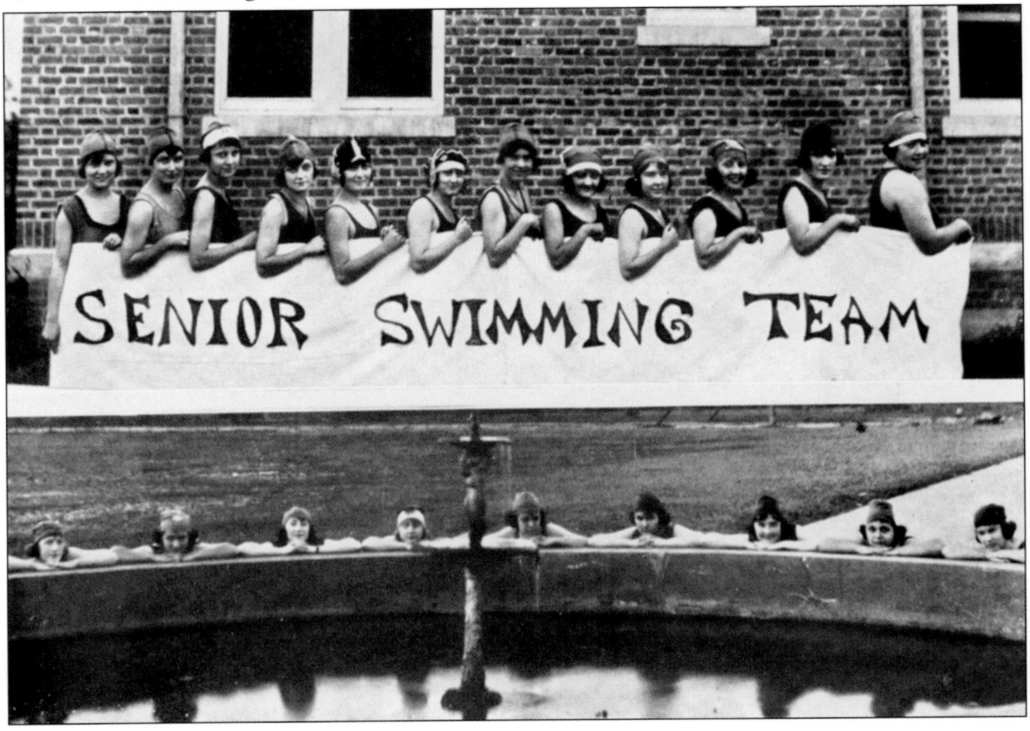

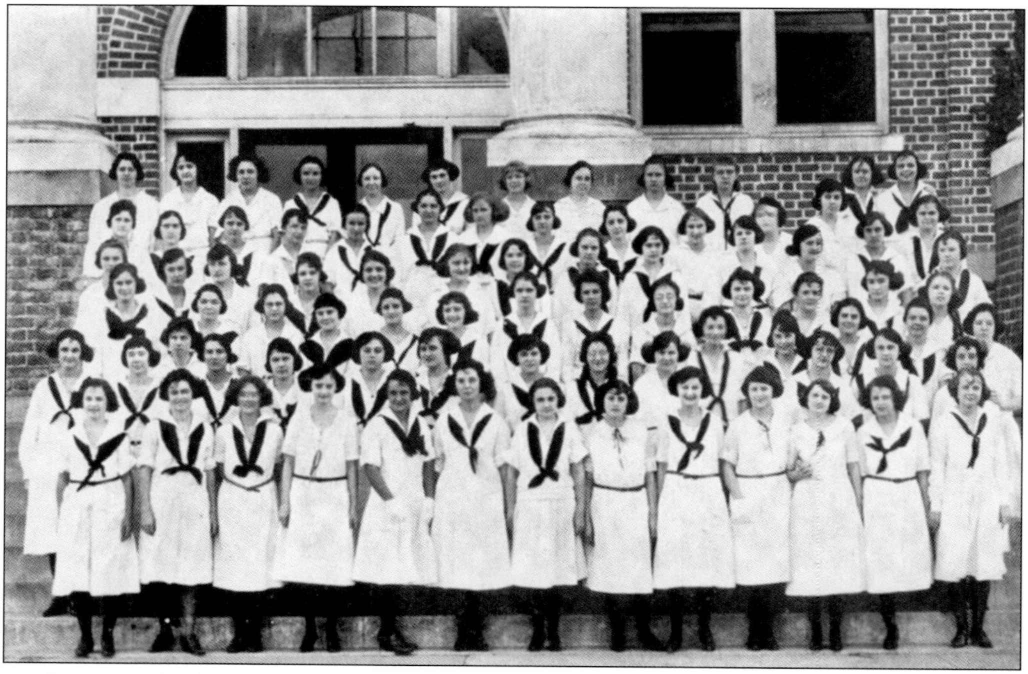

As shown in this 1922 photograph, training in home economics and domestic science was one of the largest academic programs at Mississippi Woman's College.

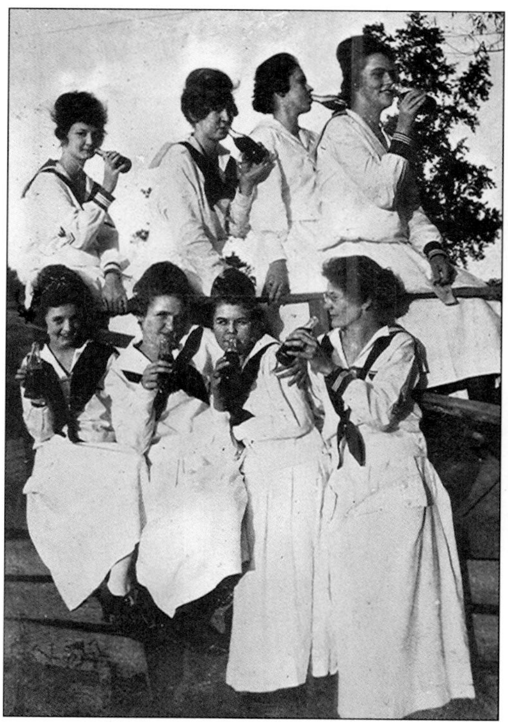

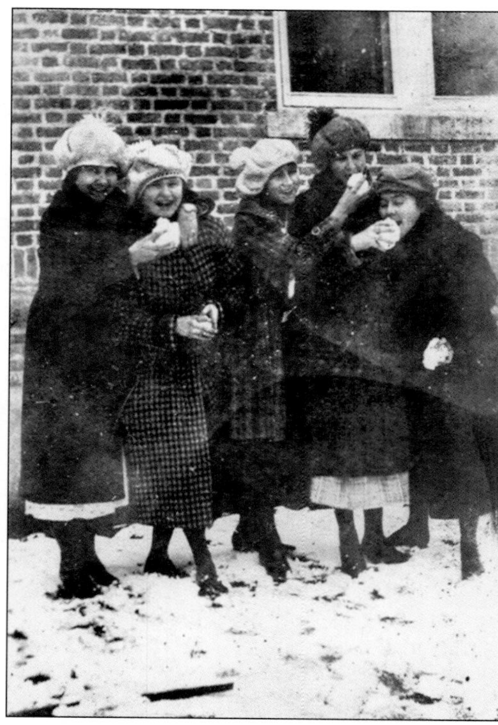

This left 1922 photograph shows a group of girls enjoying a Coca-Cola break, the relatively new beverage of the day. Snow is a rarity in South Mississippi. The girls in the image to the right enjoy the snowfall of 1922.

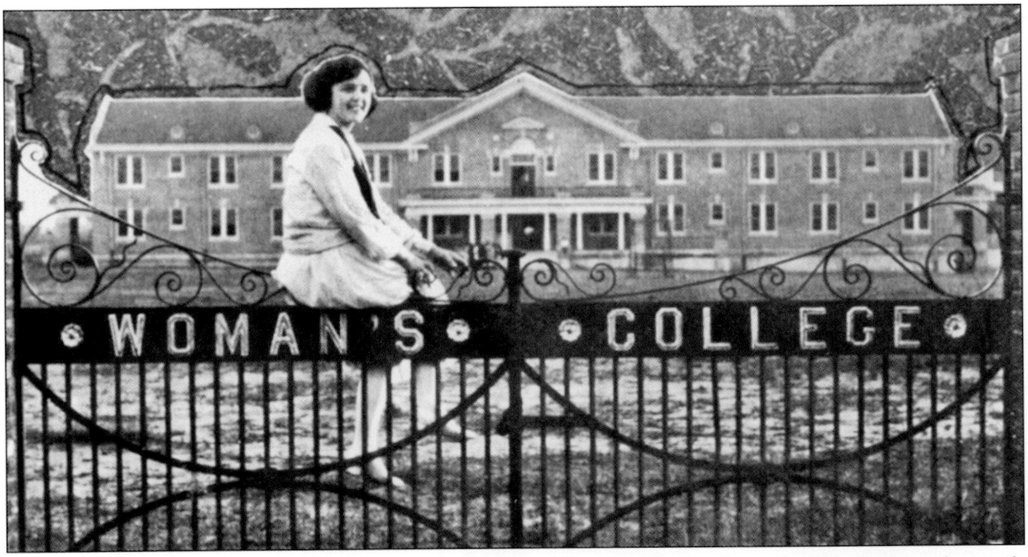


In 1922, the faculty numbered 35. The school served students from kindergarten through college. After consultation with the accrediting board, curriculum changes resulted in the elimination of all classes below college level. President Johnson led the effort to raise the nonexistent endowment of the college to $250,000. When the Southern Association met in Jackson, Mississippi, in 1926, Mississippi Woman's College, with its cash endowment of $300,000 and annual support of $10,000 from the Mississippi Baptist Convention, became a full member. This achievement, more than anything else, was the highlight of Johnson's tenure as president.

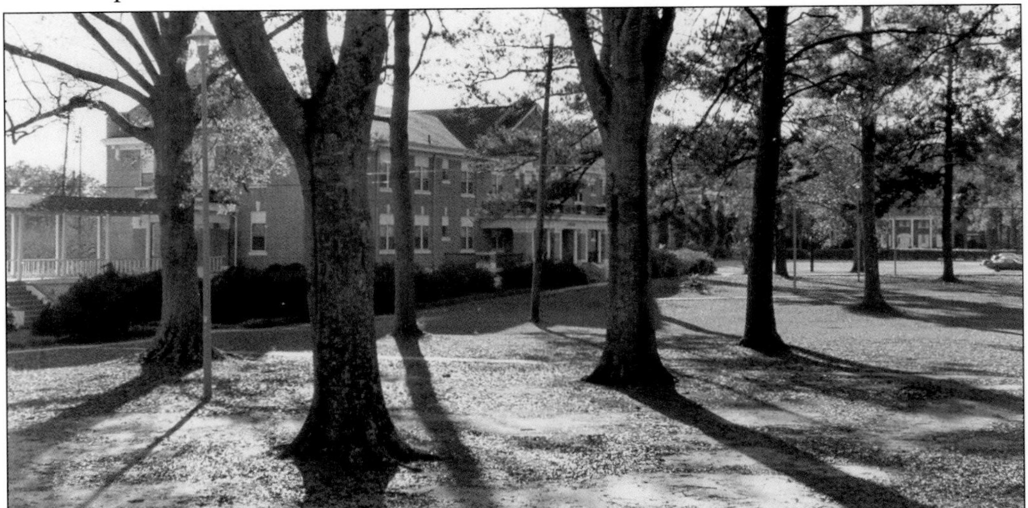

Former lady principal Mae Waller Batson told the story of how the trees on the front campus came to be planted. "I recall one Sunday morning when we were lining up to march to church and the first airplane that any of us had ever seen swooped down and landed on the campus. All that bunch of caps and gowns 'took off' after it like a lot of black crows, surrounded the thing and could not be moved. That was one time we all cut church. And that is why President Johnson ordered the trees be planted on the front campus." This photograph reveals how Johnson's trees grew, discouraging future attempts to use the front campus as a landing strip.

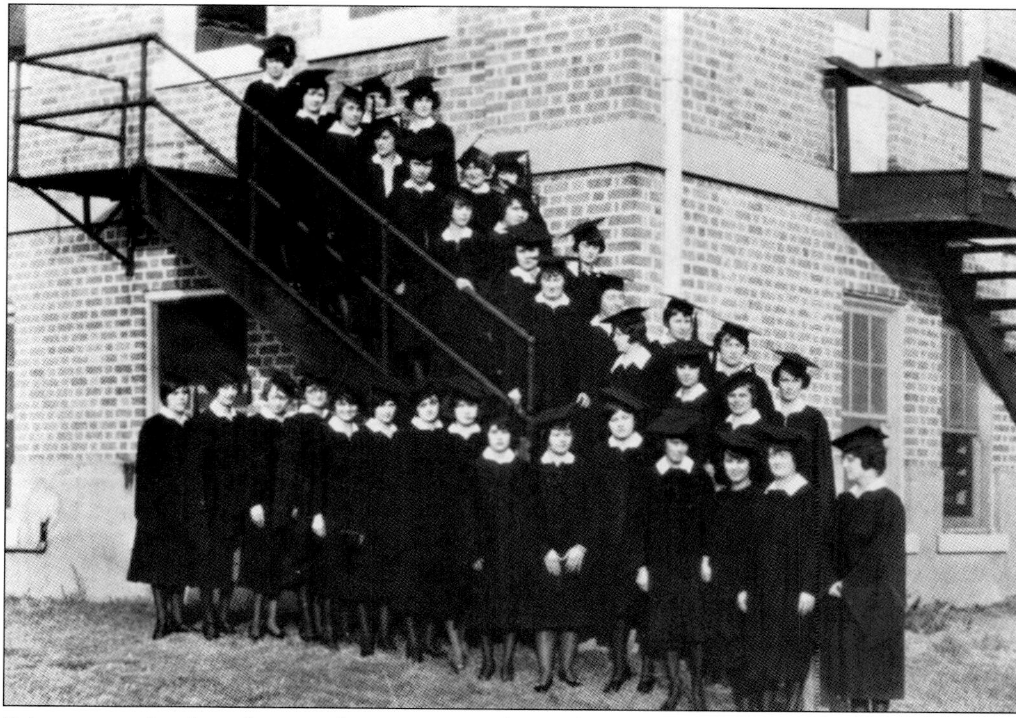

Prior to graduation, future alumnae pose for a photograph on the steps at the back of Tatum Court in 1926. The class listed 49 seniors.

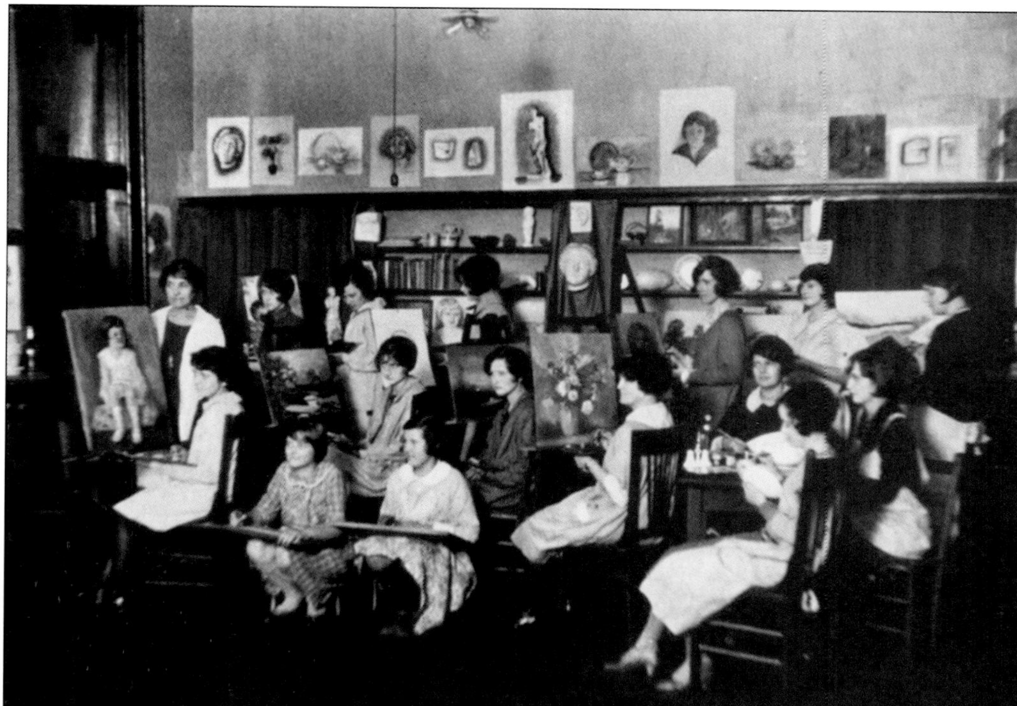

The Sketch Club promoted the arts, and a major in art was offered as a part of the curriculum in 1926.

All indications are that Dean and Professor of English Lucien Quitman Campbell, who served from 1926 through 1936, was popular with students. Alumna Virginia Loftin stated, "He was a dean who taught us that a Christian should be able to excel academically."

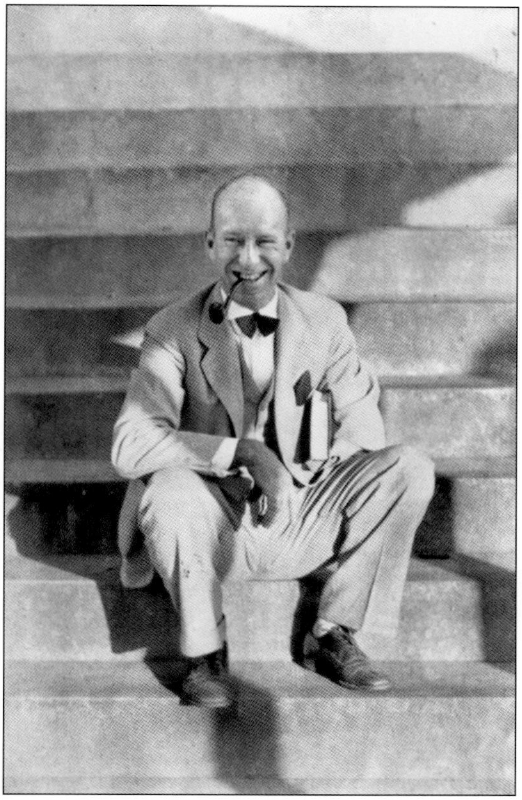

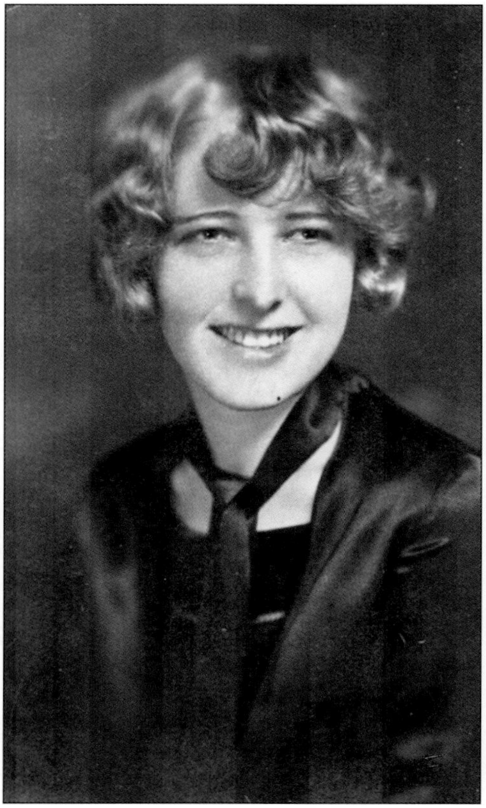

Ethel Ward, class of 1928, a mathematics and chemistry major, is one of many notable graduates. Ward's work as a geophysicist led her to Humble Oil's geological department. The Dallas Geophysical Society states that her career "stands as an example of technical excellence and creative application of theoretical principles. She was an independent scientist who possessed the sharp intellect, personal warmth, and inner strength to achieve her goals." Her contributions to the field of geology were recognized by the Society of Exploration Geophysicists (SEG) who honored her service of over 50 years. The author of numerous scientific publications, she was given a special feature in *Fortune 500* in 1952 and the *Leading Edge*, a publication of the SEG, in 1988.

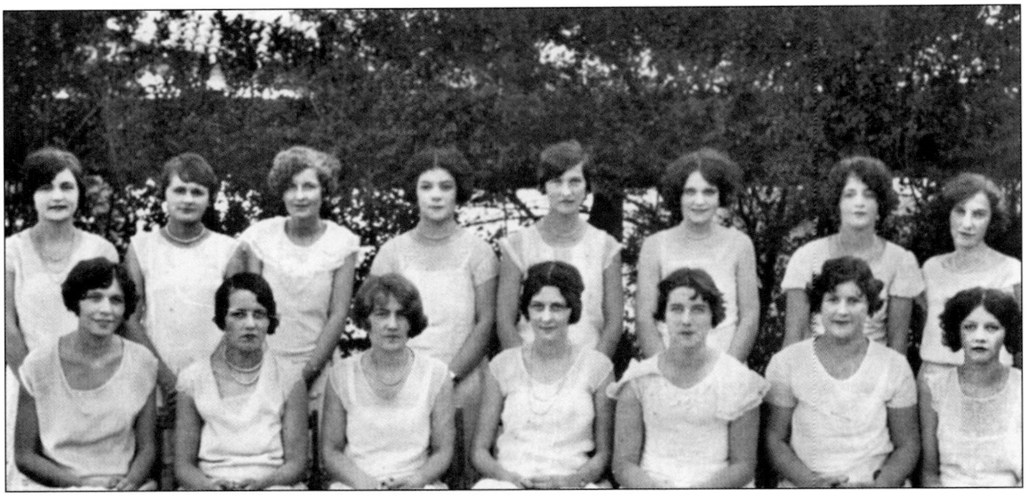

The fine arts program, begun in 1906 with South Mississippi College, was successfully continued during the tenure of Mississippi Woman's College. "Professor E.S. Roeder's piano methods were literally 50 years ahead of his time. Being a music major and now a teacher, I realize his vision and wisdom," stated alumna Virginia Loftin. A Glee Club and a school orchestra formed the core of the program in 1927. Loftin also reported that she "thrilled" to hear at the college "a big symphony play great music," that she "wept tears of joy at hearing the great Madame Schuman Heinck sing, even in German," and was amazed "at the visit of Franco-American pianist and composer E. Robert Schmitz."

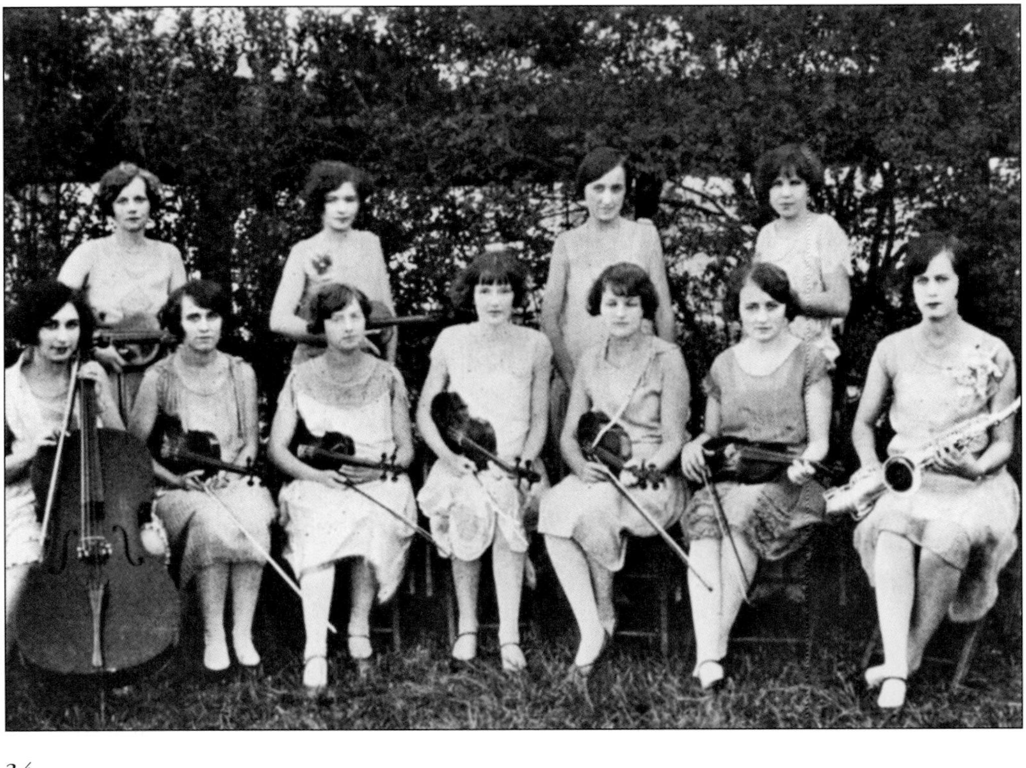

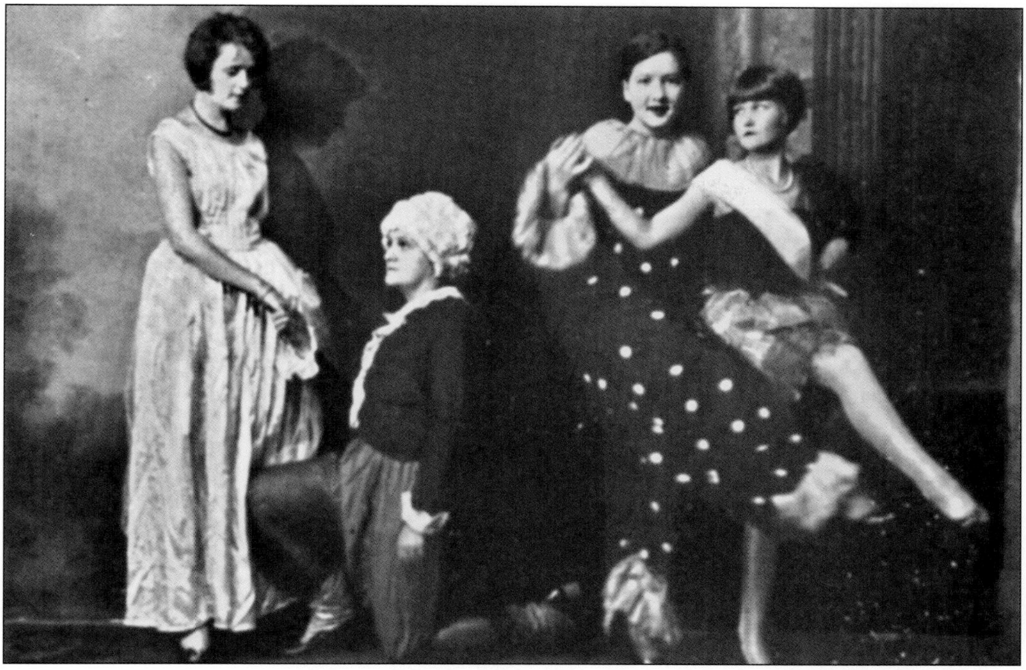

Expression, theater, and drama contributed to the cultural life of both the college and the Hattiesburg community. Edna Phillips taught expression at the college in 1912–1913, and the local newspaper reported that a Christmas drama was presented titled *The Creole Belles* in which there was "some good acting and splendid chorus work." Kate Downs P'Pool joined the faculty of the college in 1915 to chair the department. The scene above is from the 1928 play *Makers of Dreams*.

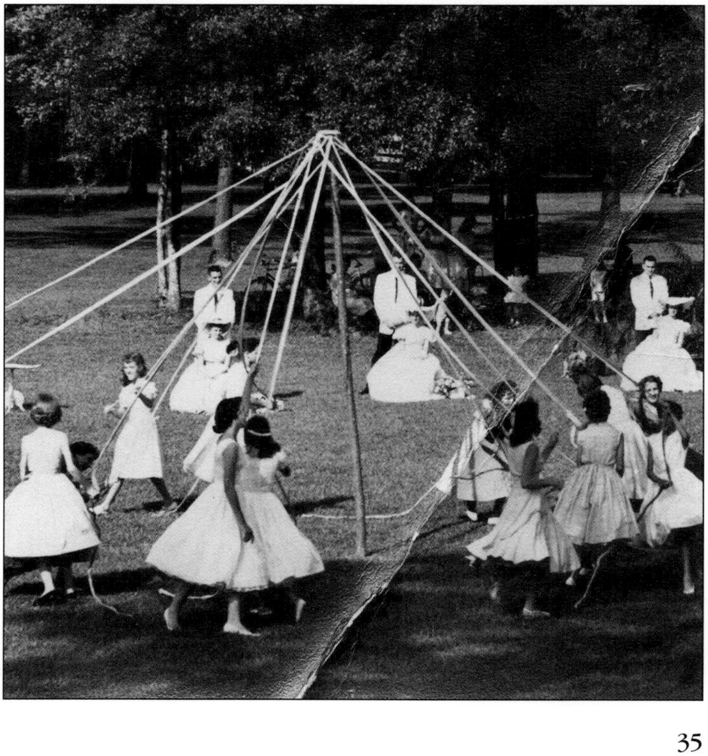

Annual May Day festivities were a much-anticipated community event at Mississippi Woman's College, with pageantry, dance, and music. The May Pole dance is shown in this photograph. The May Day tradition was continued into the 1970s.

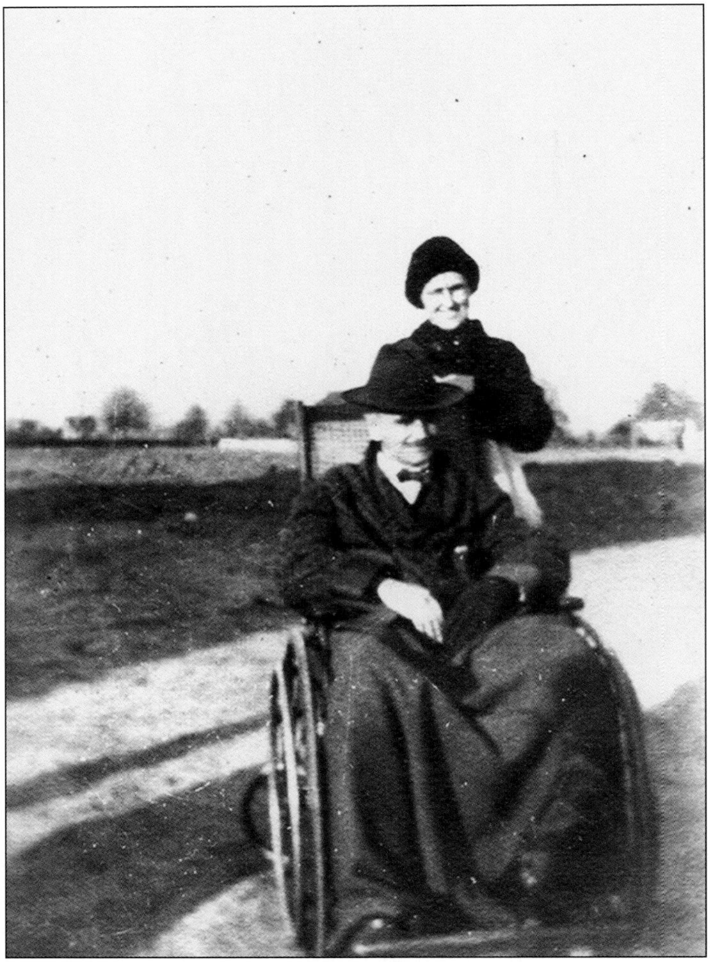

Although confined to a wheelchair during the latter months of his presidency, Johnson spoke eloquently to the graduates as he awarded their diplomas in 1931. Johnson died in 1932 and is remembered as a beloved president.

As I sit by the fire at evening when the work of the day is done.
And the cares that infest the daylight have gone with the setting sun,
I look in the glowing fireplace as the flame around it curls
And I see the smiling faces of my Woman's College girls.
The grey clouds of the storm king high in the heavens ride,
And the rain of the winter evening beats hard on the pane outside;
But in the wind with many voices that through the chimney whirls
I hear the merry laughter of my Woman's College girls.
So I gaze and see in fancy the girls that shall leave these walls.
And I think of the gladsome accents that are ringing throughout these halls
Then the glory of their future before my eyes unfurls
And I see the truest women in my Woman's College girls.
And all of their homes shall be better and all of their lives we find
Shall make this old world sweeter for the use of all mankind;
And their price is greater than rubies and their value is more than pearls
For heaven is brought around us by my Woman's College girls.

—J.L. Johnson, President

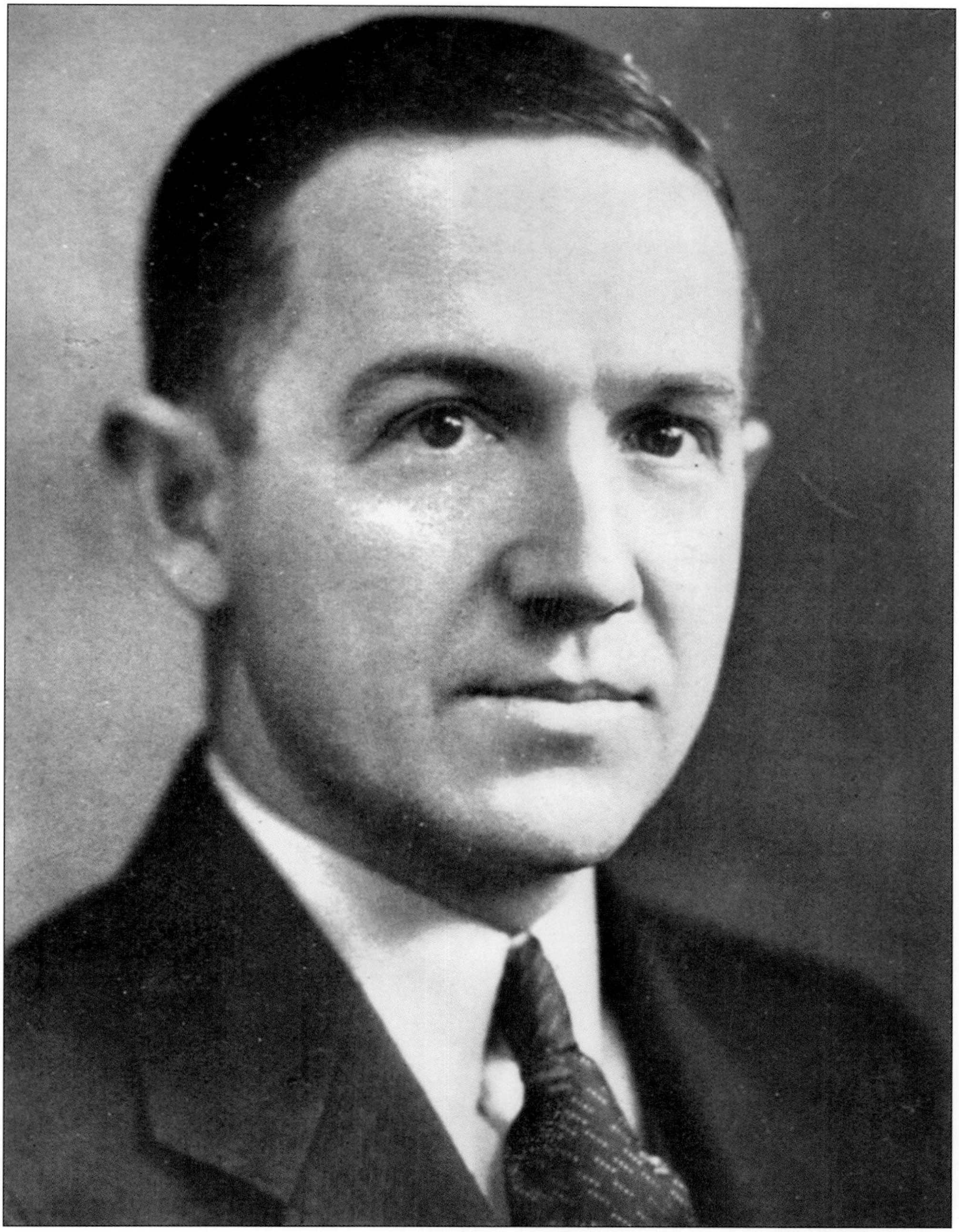

Upon the death of Johnson, Dr. William Edgar Holcomb, who served as college vice president, assumed the presidency. His was no easy task, for in addition to the financial Depression of the 1930s, the college dining hall burned in 1936, and the cut in support from the Mississippi Baptist Convention threatened the accreditation of the college. In a report to the board of trustees in May 1935, Holcomb reported "our registration for the year has been approximately 230. From the standpoint of scholarship of our faculty and the work required, we are looked upon as more strict and exacting than many institutions. Our primary problem is financial." In 1935, the college business manager reported paying the faculty only half of the proposed salary scale.

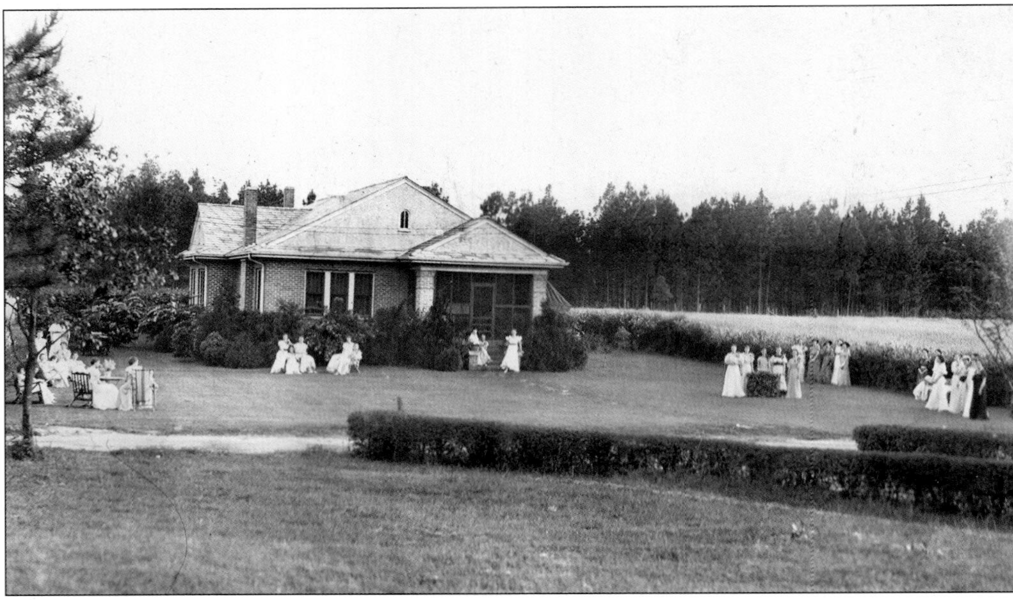

Through a generous gift of L.O. Crosby of Picayune and the gifts of other supporters, the model home for the home economics department was erected in 1936. This building later served as the president's home in the mid-1950s, in the 1960s as housing for the home economics department, and today as the center for the Baptist Student Union.

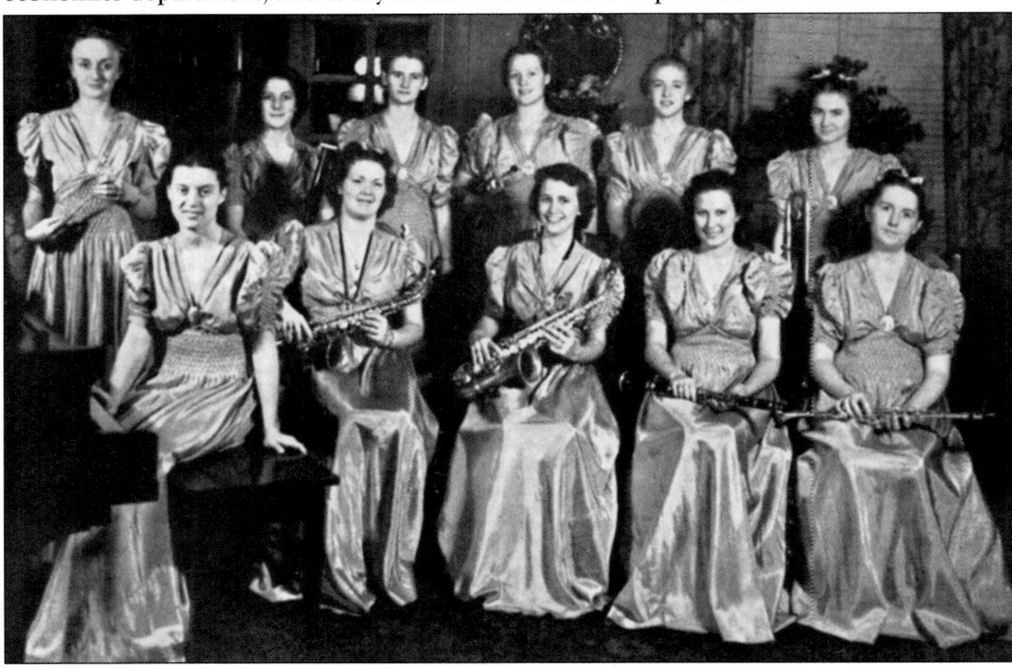

Although the later 1930s were difficult years for the administration and trustees, a high spirit continued among the Woman's College girls. College yearbooks depict a full circle of student activities, clubs, organizations, and camaraderie. Athletics and recreation received high priority, the Players' Guild provided a high level of dramatic productions, and the Glee Clubs performed locally as well as in nearby towns and cities. The 1939 Swing Orchestra appears in this photograph.

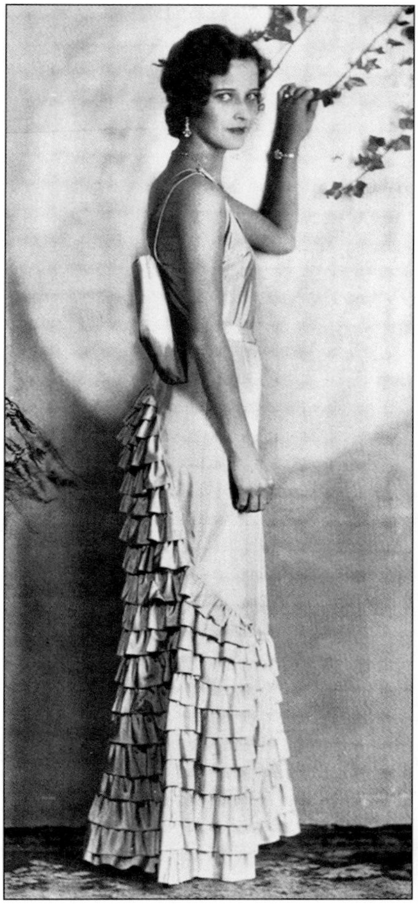

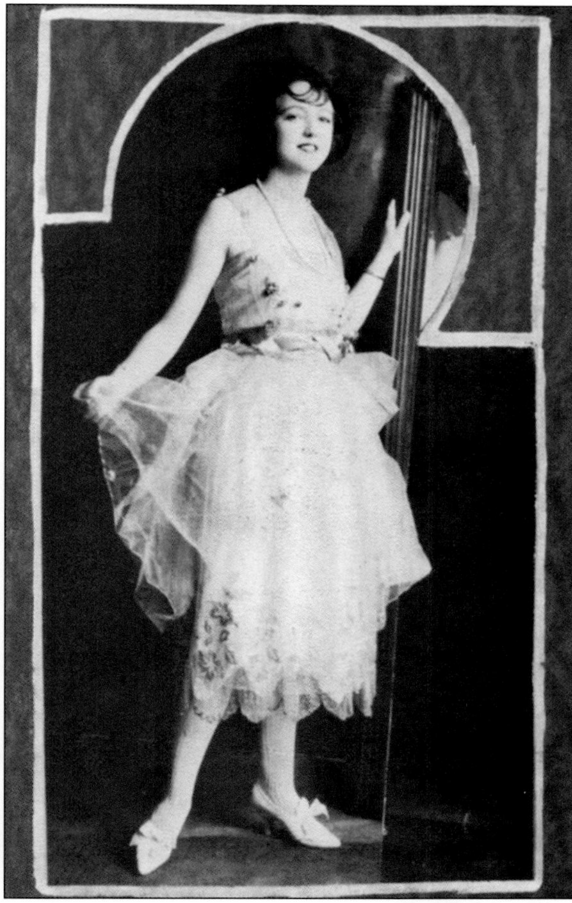

The Mississippi Woman's College girl exuded intellect, beauty, charm, and athleticism. Pictured are, from left to right (above) Maurine Dale, 1932 Most Charming; Norma Williams, 1921 Mlle. Vogue; (below) Virginia Cooper, 1935 Miss MWC; and Mildred Breland, 1935 Most Athletic.

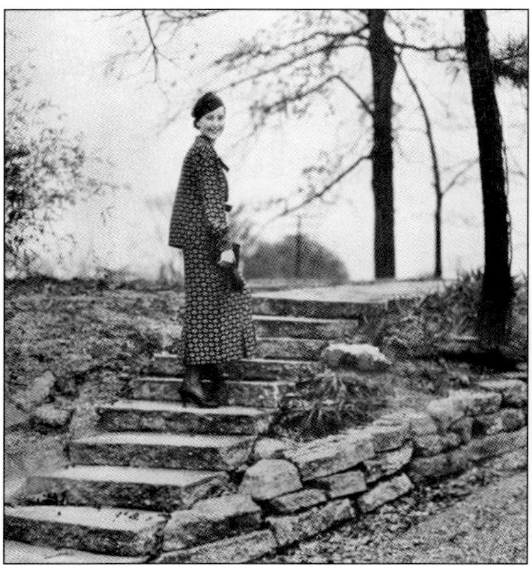

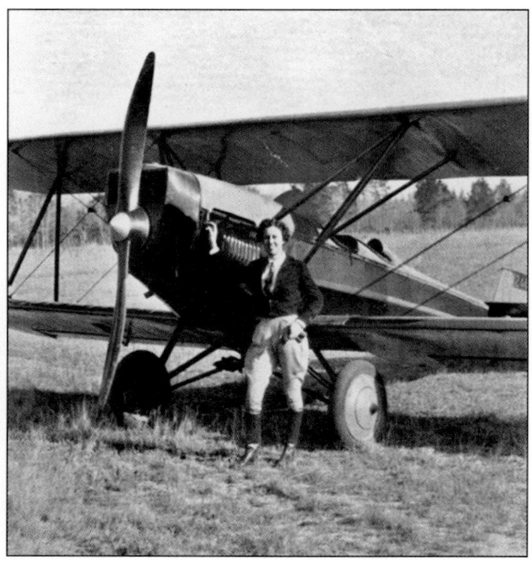

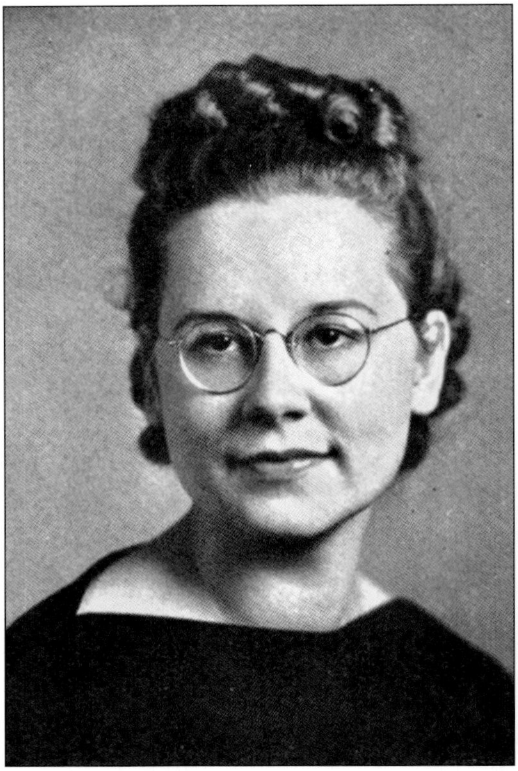

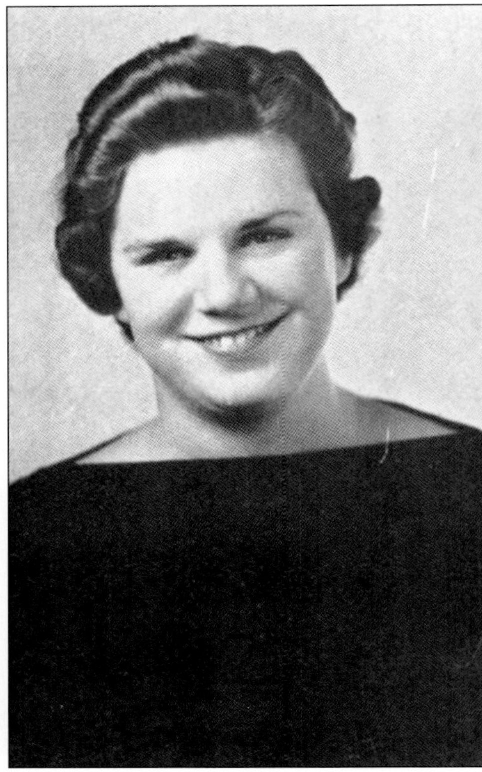

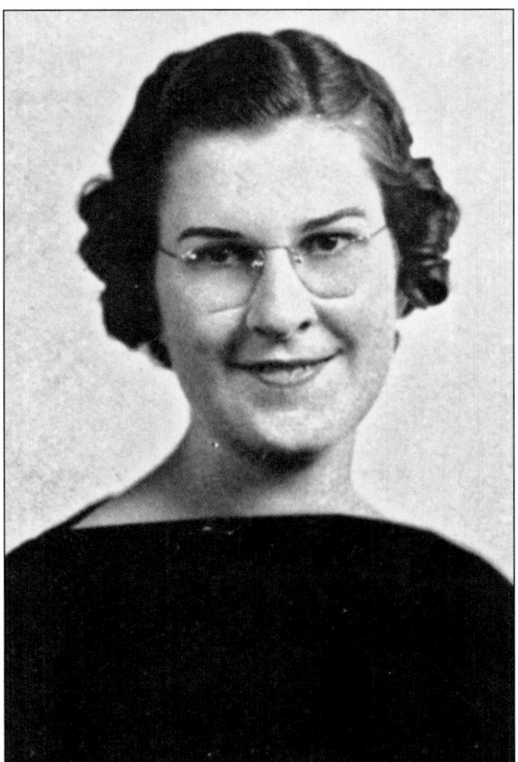

Math and chemistry were strong academic programs at Mississippi Woman's College. In 1939, three students competed in the national William Lowell Putnam Mathematical Competition, finishing third behind Brooklyn College and MIT. They beat Harvard, Rutgers, Berkeley, UCLA, and 33 other teams, thus demolishing a number of stereotypes, being from a small female college in the South. Pictured above from left to right are Louise Tate and Mary Emma Fancher; to the left is Nina Pearl Byrd.

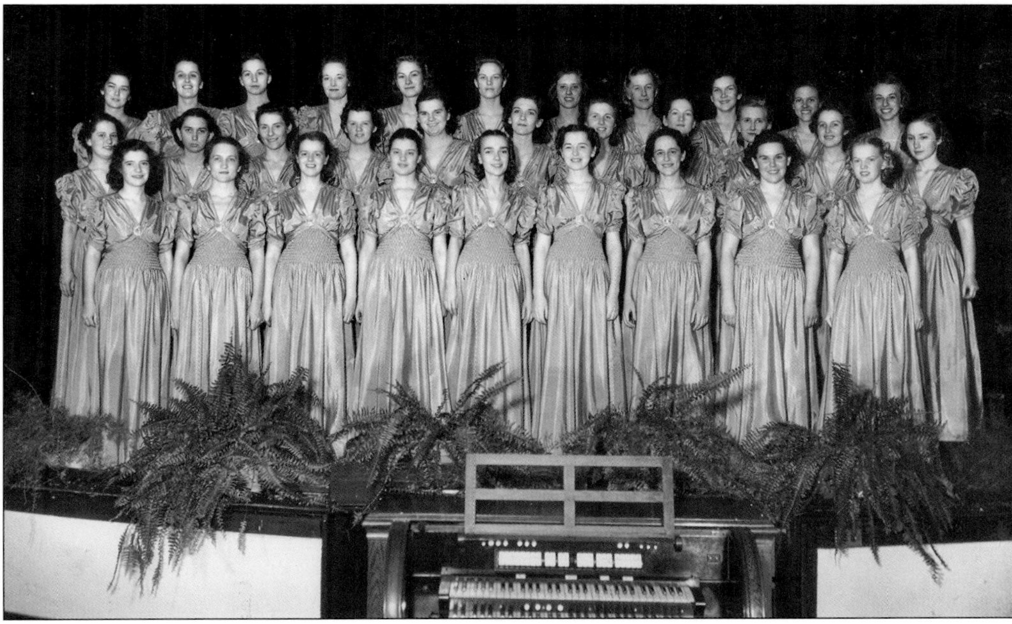

The music program of the college continued to excel and provide delightful programs for the college as well as the Hattiesburg community. Pictured above in this 1938 photograph are members of the Glee Club. Pictured below are members of the quartet in 1939 who sang in churches and at school programs, helping in the recruitment efforts of the college.

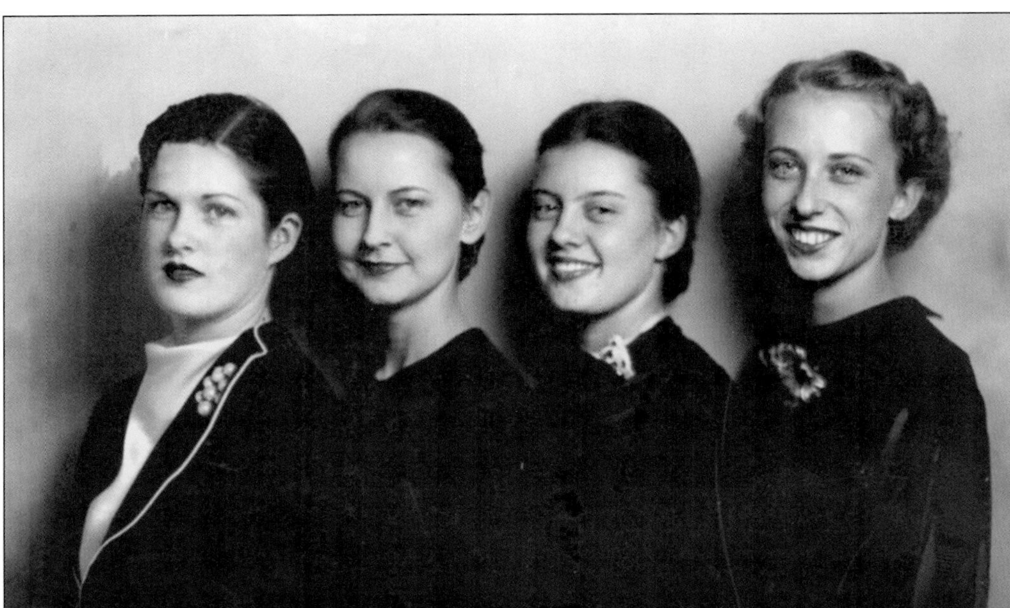

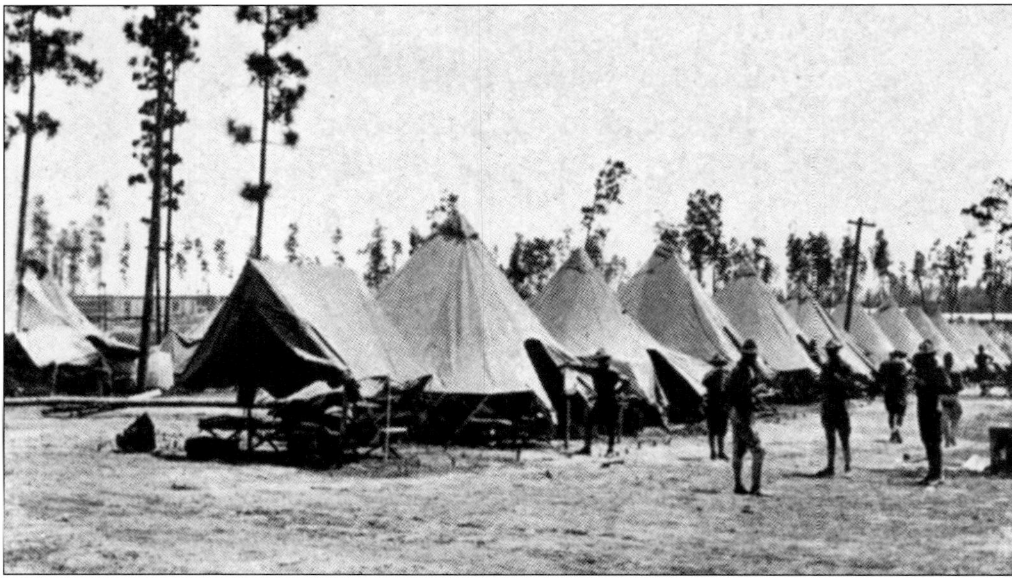

Despite his heroic efforts, the latter years of Holcomb's presidency proved difficult. The Depression led to a gradual decline in enrollment, which dropped to 176 students in 1936. With salary cuts, budget cuts, and lower student enrollment, the trustees went to the Mississippi Baptist Convention and requested funds in order to remain accredited. With no funds available, the college was dropped from the accredited list in 1939. Trustees tried every means available, through a campaign and further cutbacks, to keep the college open, but in November 1940, the Mississippi Baptist Convention voted to close Mississippi Woman's College. World War II brought an influx of thousands of soldiers to Camp Shelby, located south of Hattiesburg. A critical housing situation developed, and the college trustees offered the buildings and equipment of the college to the federal government for housing and supplemental hospital facilities. From 1941 to 1946, Camp Shelby used the campus. This resulted in liquidation of the college debt and the accumulation of a cash reserve, but a loss of much equipment and records in the process.

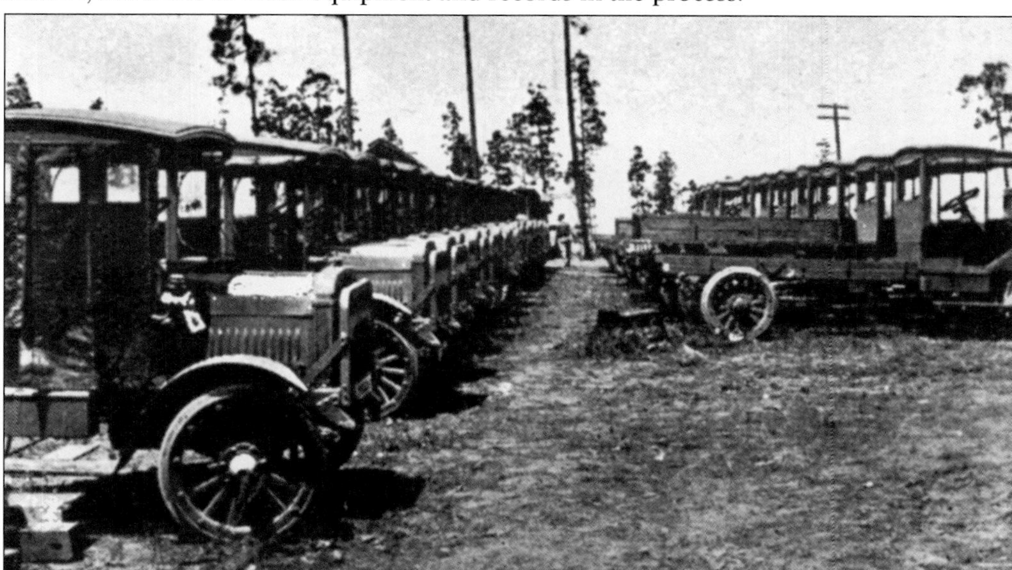

In 1945, the Mississippi Baptist Convention resurrected Mississippi Woman's College and instructed the trustees to reopen the school as of September 1947. Dr. Irving E. Rouse, pastor of Fifth Avenue Baptist Church in Hattiesburg, was unanimously elected president in 1946 and was charged with renovating and refurbishing the college plant, securing a Christian faculty, and enlisting a student body to begin a new chapter in Christian education. The college reopened its doors on September 9, 1947, with a registration of 76 students. Sarah Rouse, wife of the president, served the college as dean of women.

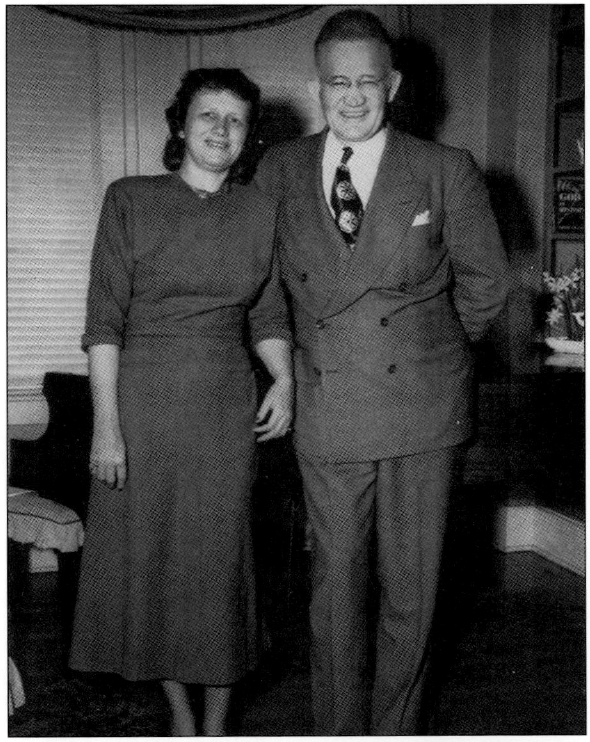

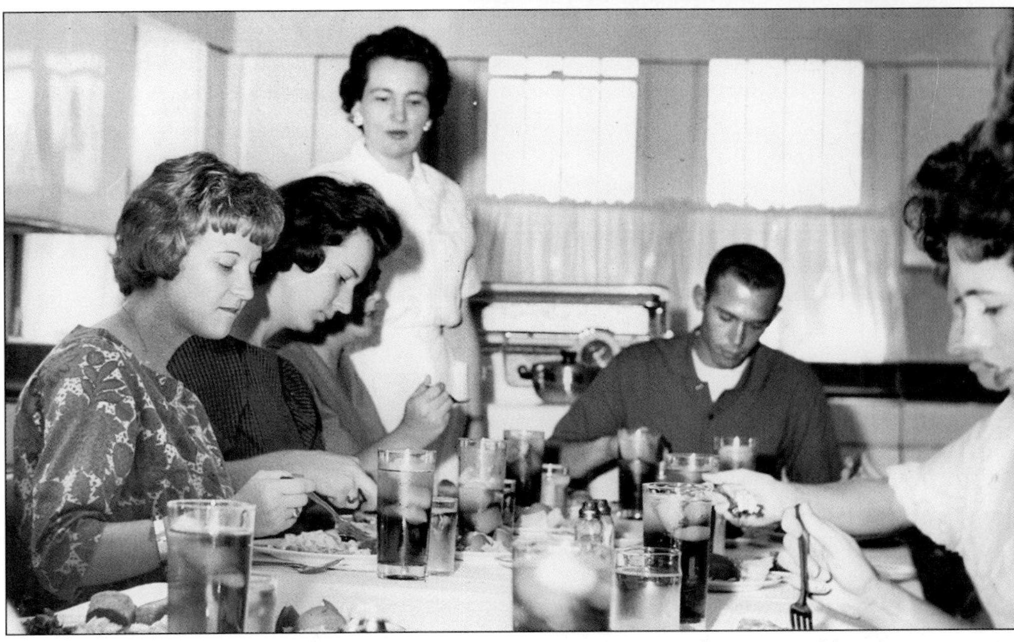

Evelyn McClure joined the faculty in 1946 as head of the department of home economics and yearbook sponsor. Labs and classes were located in the basement of Tatum Court until 1961, when the program relocated to the domestic science building (now Crawford Hall). The curriculum included cooking, home management, and sewing. This photograph shows an early 1960s food preparation class. McClure taught home economics at the college for 37 years.

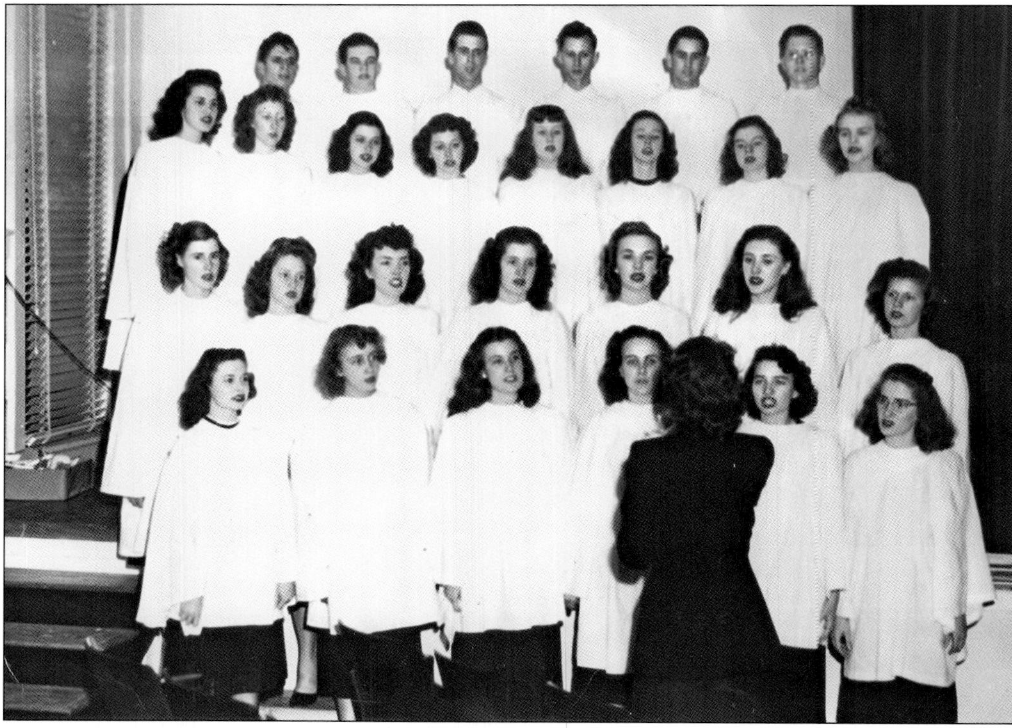

After the reopening of the college in 1947, the music program once again provided an important link to the community. The choir presented programs in the Hattiesburg area, and smaller ensembles sang in churches and schools, again helping to recruit students for the college. The 1948 choir, under the direction of Julia Guess, is shown in this photograph.

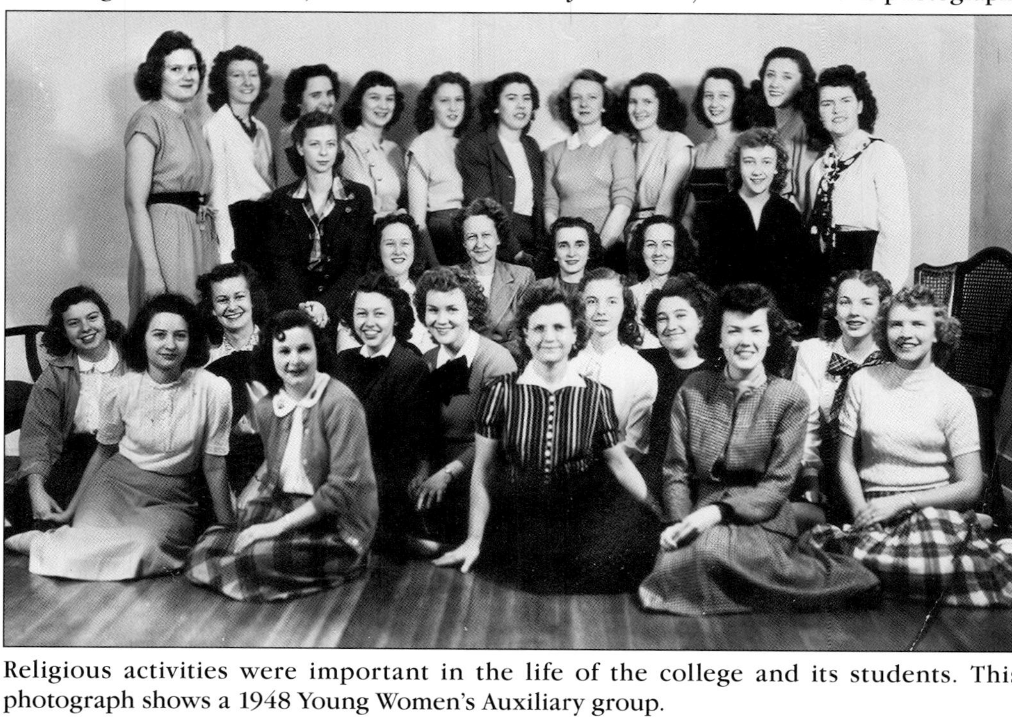

Religious activities were important in the life of the college and its students. This photograph shows a 1948 Young Women's Auxiliary group.

Dr. Rouse made a "cornstalk fiddle" at the request of music professor Eloise Quackenboss. Here he demonstrates the fiddle to the students of the music department.

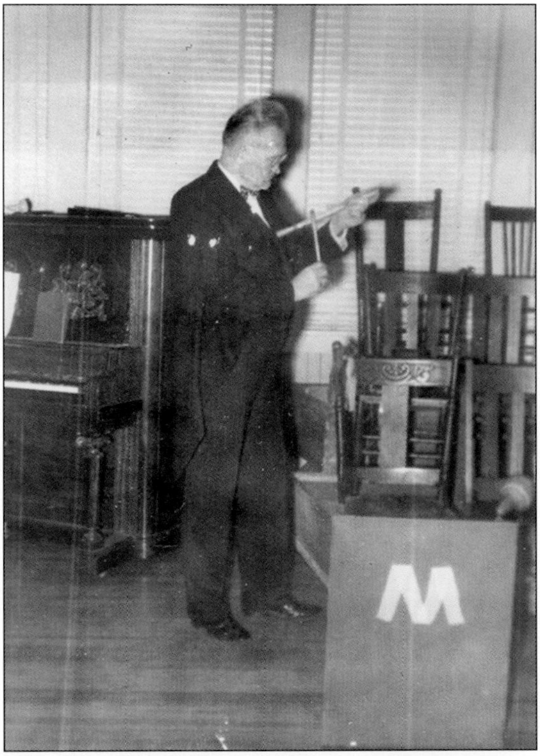

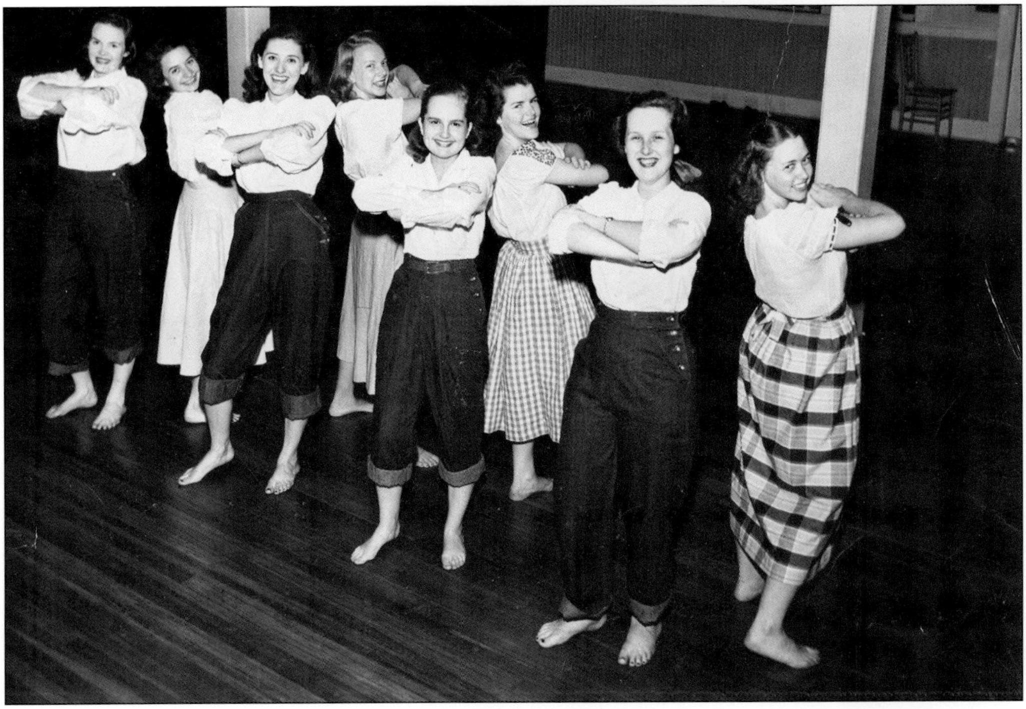

Physical education classes were popular and enjoyable. Under the direction of Mary Helen Chappell, classes offered a wide variety of activities, including the Virginia reel. This photograph is from 1949.

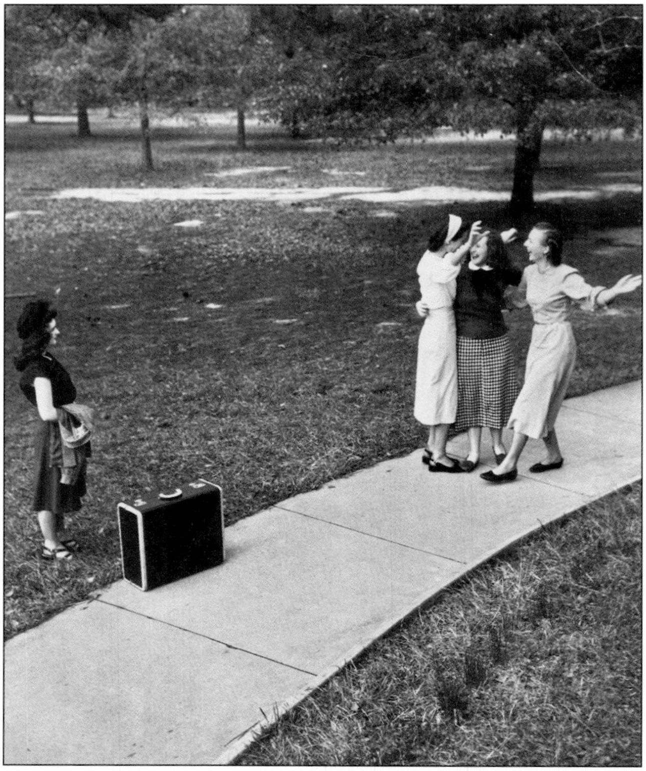

Mississippi Women's College (MWC) girls formed lasting friendships. Shown from left to right are Rose Crumby Downs, Annie Vera Oden Major, Jeanette Bilbo Larrimore, and Helen Toney Thornton in 1949.

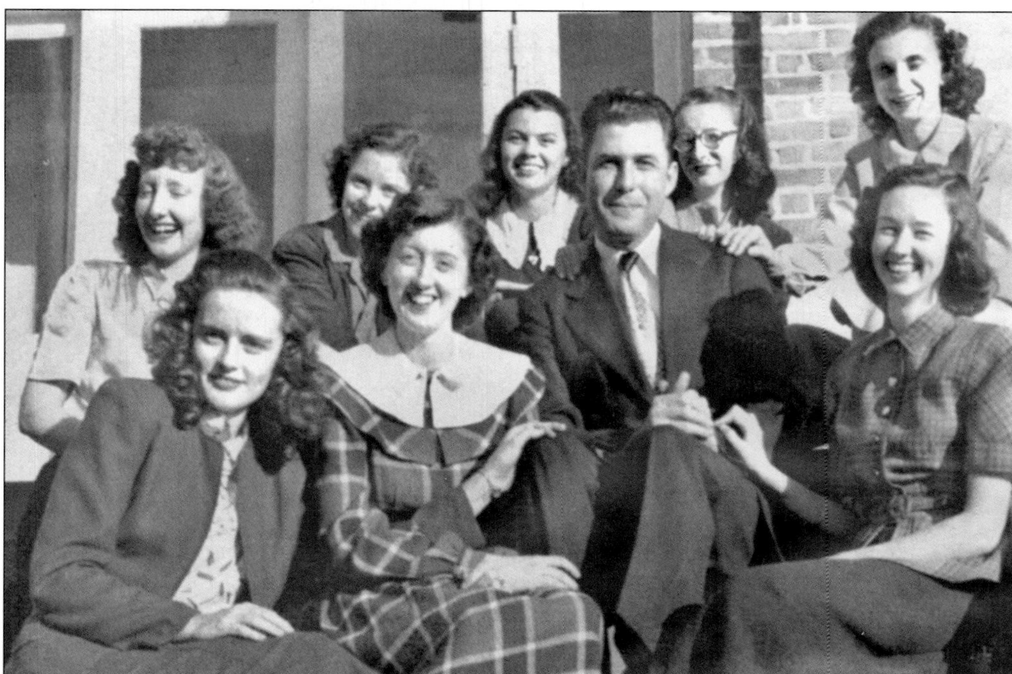

A few males, called "special students," attended Mississippi Woman's College in the late 1940s and early 1950s; they were mostly ministerial students taking day classes. Ralph Davis, pictured in this 1948 photograph, was the one male among the senior class.

In 1952, a young couple from Virginia joined the Mississippi Woman's College administration. Dr. Ralph Noonkester, a Phi Beta Kappa graduate of the University of Richmond, was on the faculty in the religion department and soon became dean of instruction. He is shown advising three sisters attending Mississippi Woman's College, Nancy (bottom left), Carolyn (top left), and Bernice McIntosh. His wife, Naomi Noonkester, pictured below, served as registrar and helped ease the transition from an all-girls school to a coeducational institution. She admitted shock at the differences in manners between the refinement of Woman's College ladies and the brusqueness of the men students who entered in 1954.

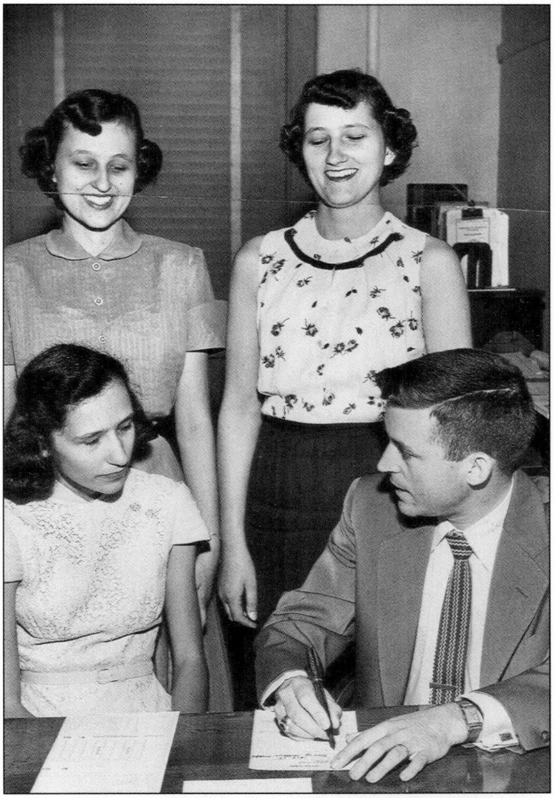

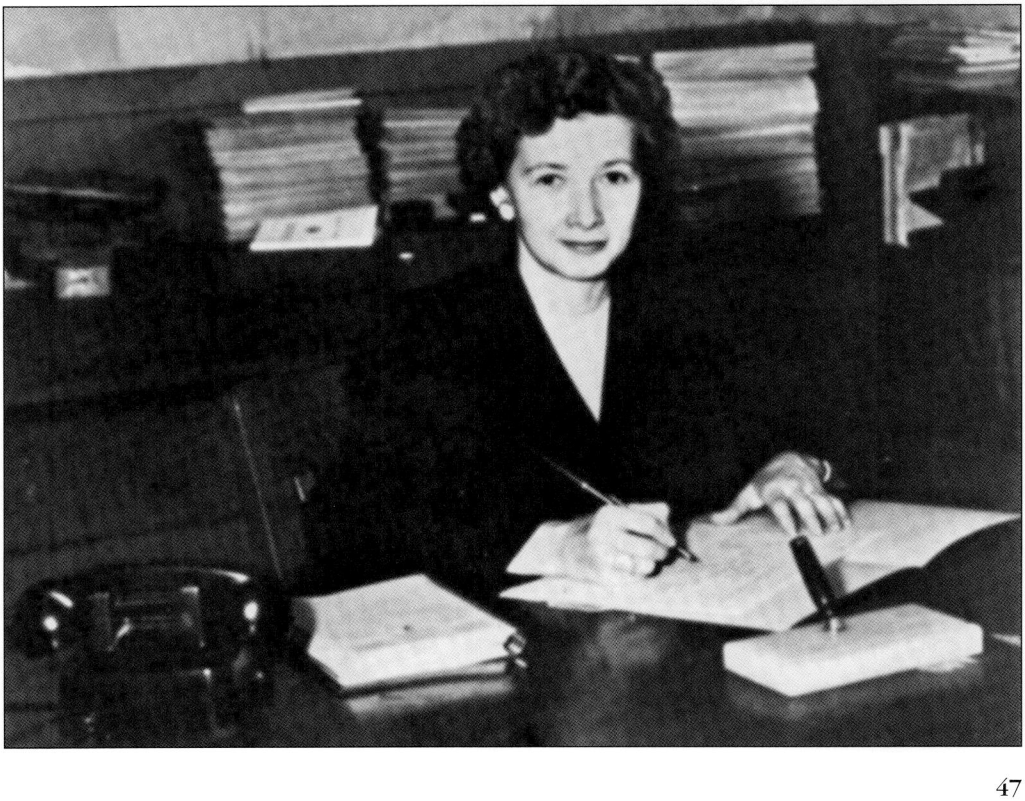

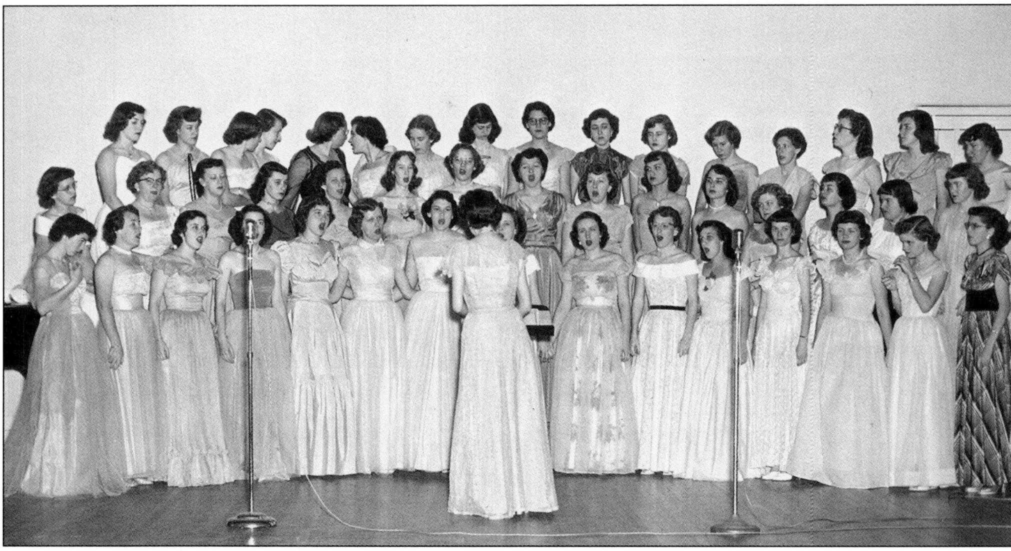

Music was one of the most visible and largest academic programs of the college. The Hattiesburg community continued to enjoy the performances of the Glee Club and ensembles. The 1953 Glee Club is shown in this photograph.

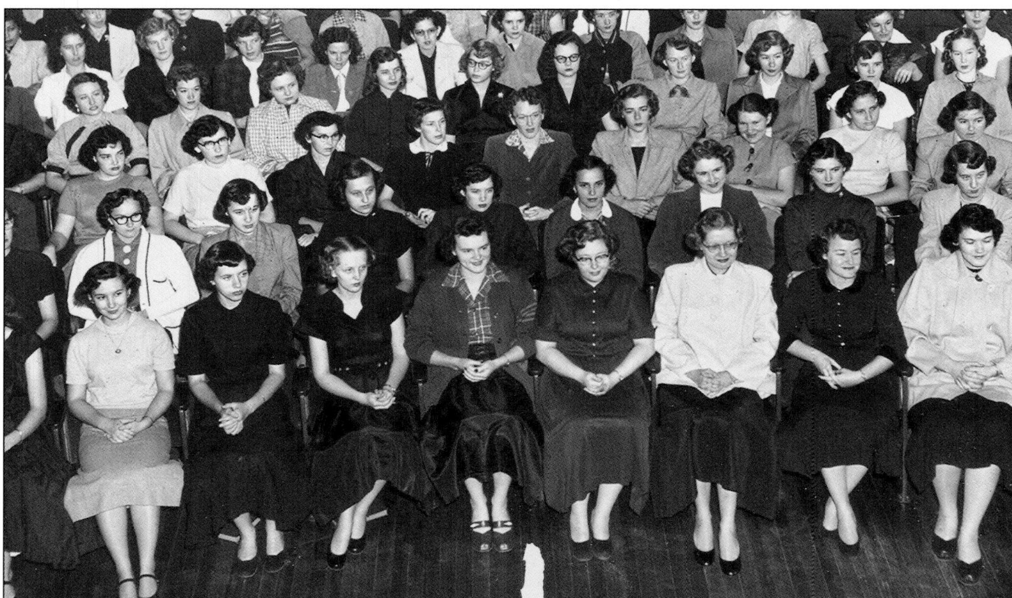

In 1950, the Mississippi Baptist Convention brought the college under review. According to Sue Bell Johnson, wife of former president Johnson, the faction wanting to close the college had all the "cold facts" on their side. A lone dissenter, Dr. Zack Huggins, filed a minority report. As he rose to speak, Johnson prayed, "Lord, if Woman's College can help bring in the Kingdom, save it." By the narrowest of votes, Woman's College remained alive. The students had formed a prayer chain, and President Rouse, after the vote, called the campus and instructed student Rachel Monk to play "Praise God From Whom All Blessings Flow" on the organ to let the students and the neighborhood know that Mississippi Woman's College lived. Above, the student body attends a 1949 chapel service in Tatum Court.

# *Three*

# William Carey College 1954–1980

After three years of careful study, the Mississippi Baptist Convention of 1953 voted a coeducational status to Mississippi Woman's College and authorized a new name in harmony with her new status. According to tradition, President Rouse meditated in the forest adjacent to the campus and felt inspired to name the college William Carey in honor of a brilliant 18th-century English cobbler-linguist (1761–1834) who went to India as the pioneer of the modern missionary movement. In April 1954, the name William Carey College was approved, and with the name change, the college inherited a challenging motto of the man himself who dared to do the unusual: "Expect great things from God; attempt great things for God."

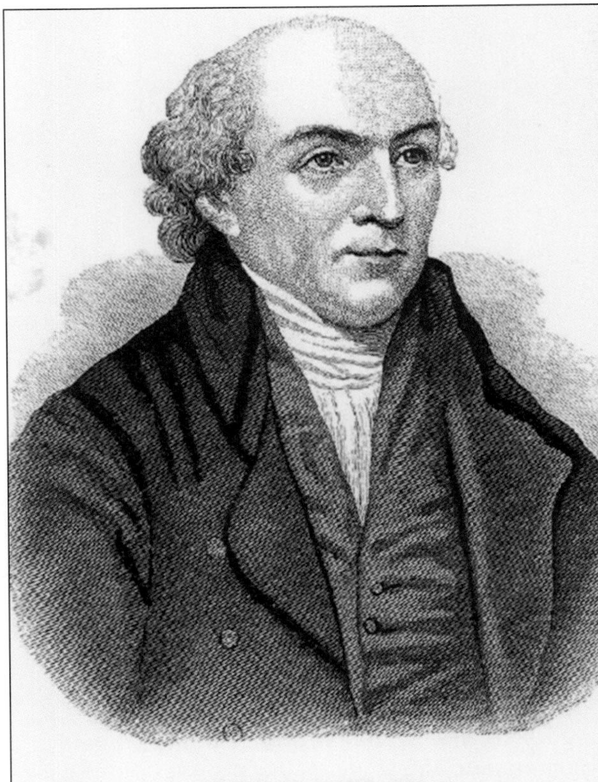

WILLIAM CAREY, D.D.

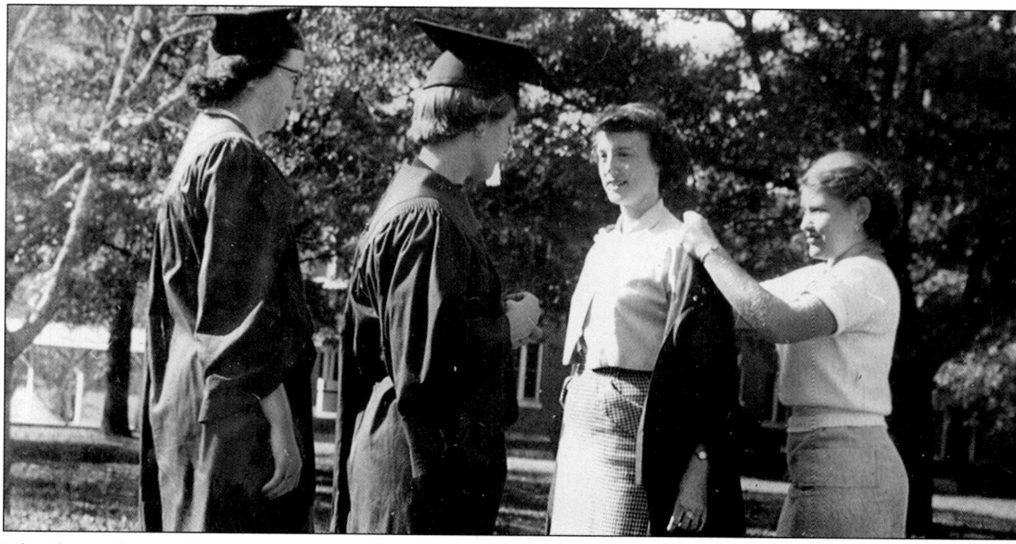

The last class of Mississippi Woman's College graduated in May 1954, with 13 receiving degrees. The graduates were given the choice of having either Mississippi Woman's College or William Carey College on their diplomas. In this graduation photograph are, from left to right, Doris Barth, two unidentified, and Mary Lou Baygents.

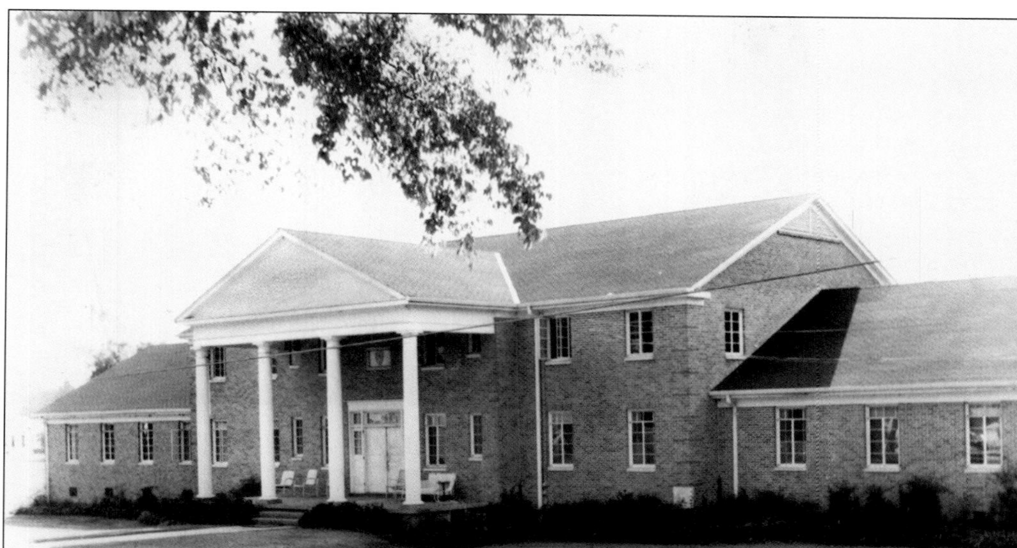

Coeducational status required male housing. Lawrence Hall opened in 1954 to accommodate 102 students. Furnishings did not arrive until after classes began, and for a few weeks, students slept on mattresses without beds or other furnishings.

In 1954, before the name change was officially approved by the Mississippi Baptist Convention, the trustees and administration knew that a quick way to bring in male students was the creation of an athletic program. Les De Vall (right), head coach at Hinds Junior College in Raymond, was hired to coach teams in football, baseball, basketball, and track. Many of the recruits came from Hinds and other junior colleges in the area. Glenn Daughtrey (left), head coach at Soso High School, was named assistant football coach.

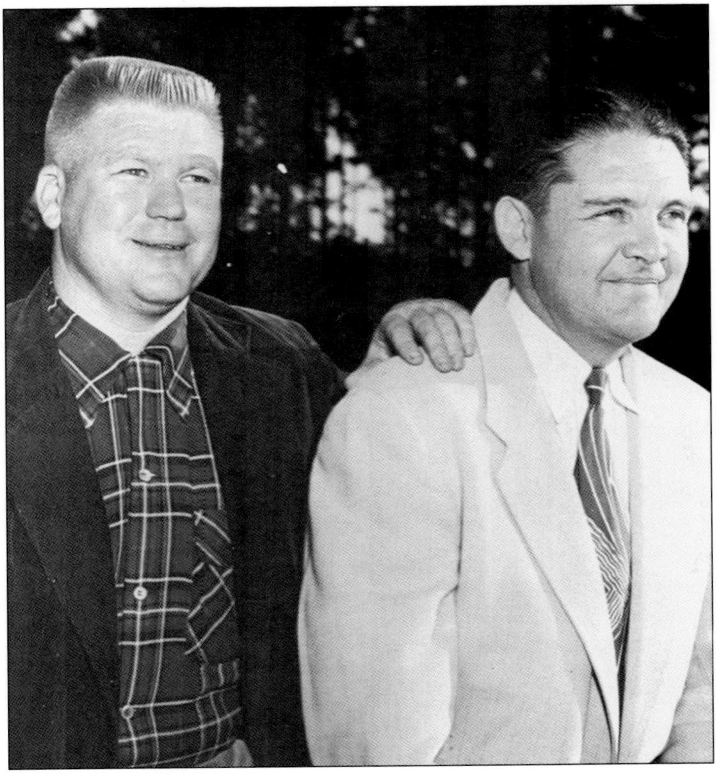

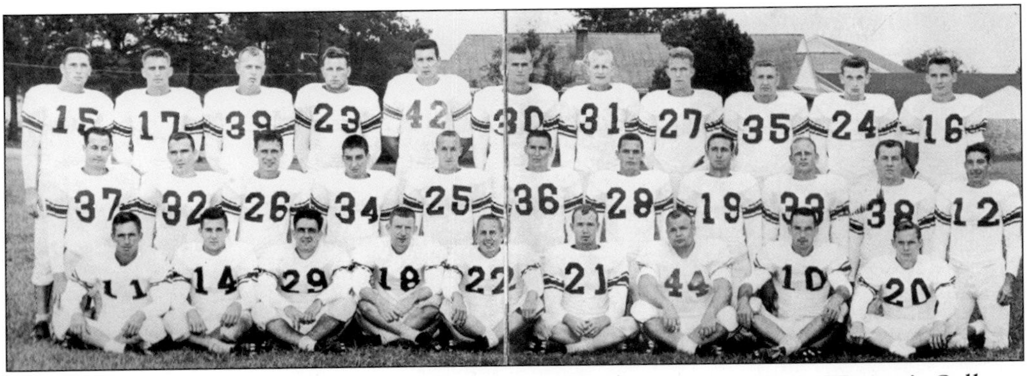

Many of the football players were recruited under the name Mississippi Woman's College. Billy Crosby, member of the football and baseball teams, said that one day President Rouse asked if he would be interested in playing for Mississippi Woman's College, "I could just see the headlines: 'The Skirts Lose Again.'" Nevertheless, on August 30, 1954, Billy appeared on the campus of the then-renamed William Carey College along with approximately 35 other players. The team posted winning seasons in both years of intercollegiate competition, 1954 and 1955.

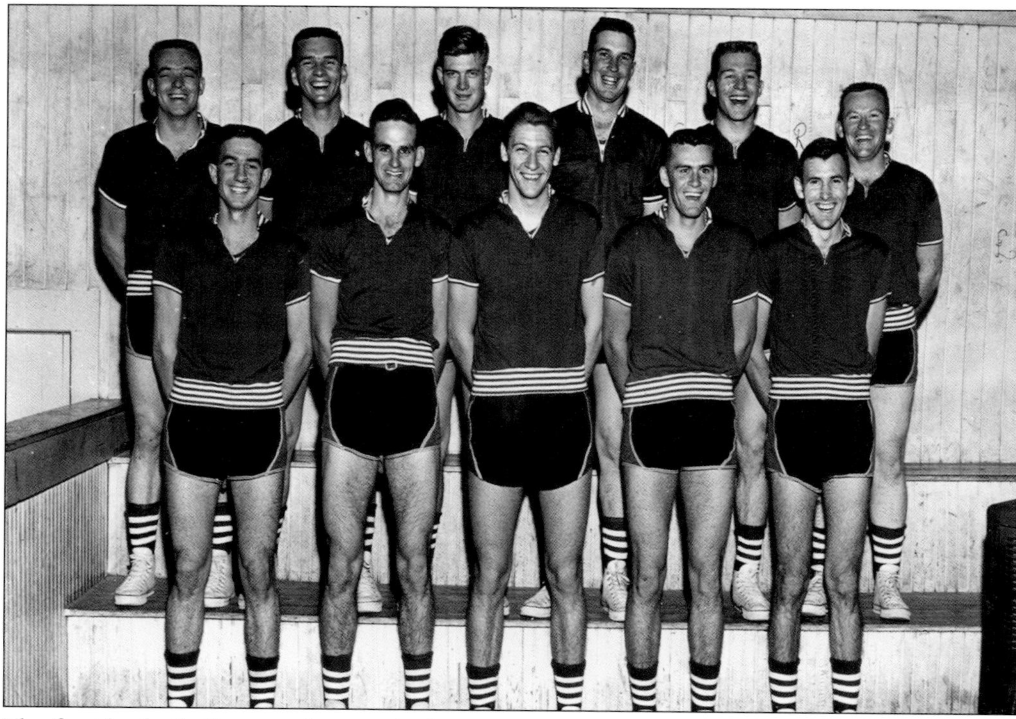

The first basketball team also notched winning records in 1954 and 1955. Playing in local high school gymnasiums, the Crusaders had a home of their own in 1960 when Clinton Gymnasium was built. Coach John O'Keefe was hired in 1955 to coach basketball. The 1956 basketball team members are, from left to right, (first row) Bob Finn, Howard Moore, Bill Payne, M.L. Faler, and Richard Madden; (second row) Doyle "Sleepy" Wheat, Leon Lucky, Billy Harold Smith, Hershel Ladner, Donice Knight, and Joe Carmichael. (Courtesy of Joe Carmichael.)

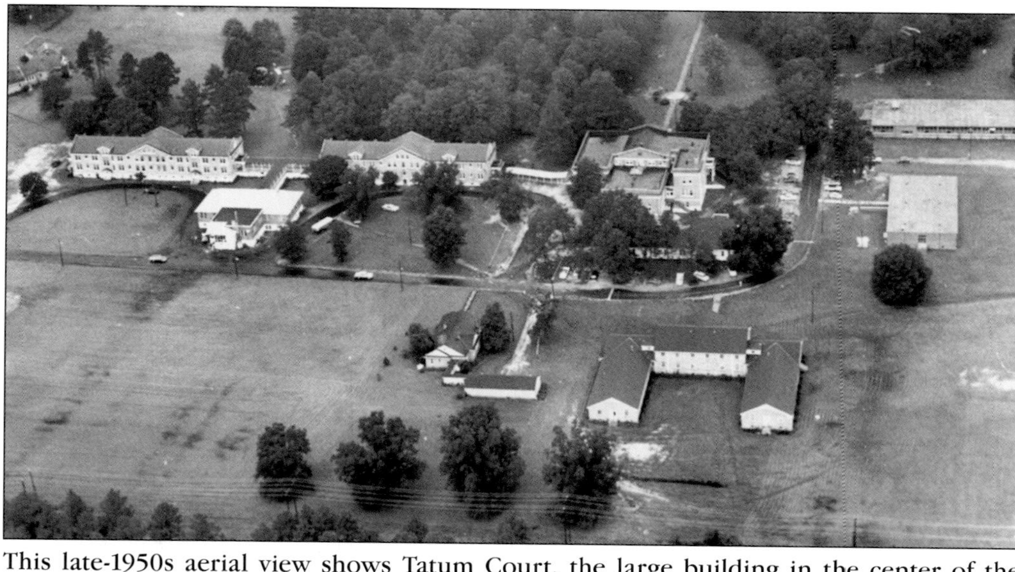

This late-1950s aerial view shows Tatum Court, the large building in the center of the photograph, with twin dormitories Ross and Johnson Halls on the left side. The U-shaped building in the lower right-hand corner is Lawrence Hall.

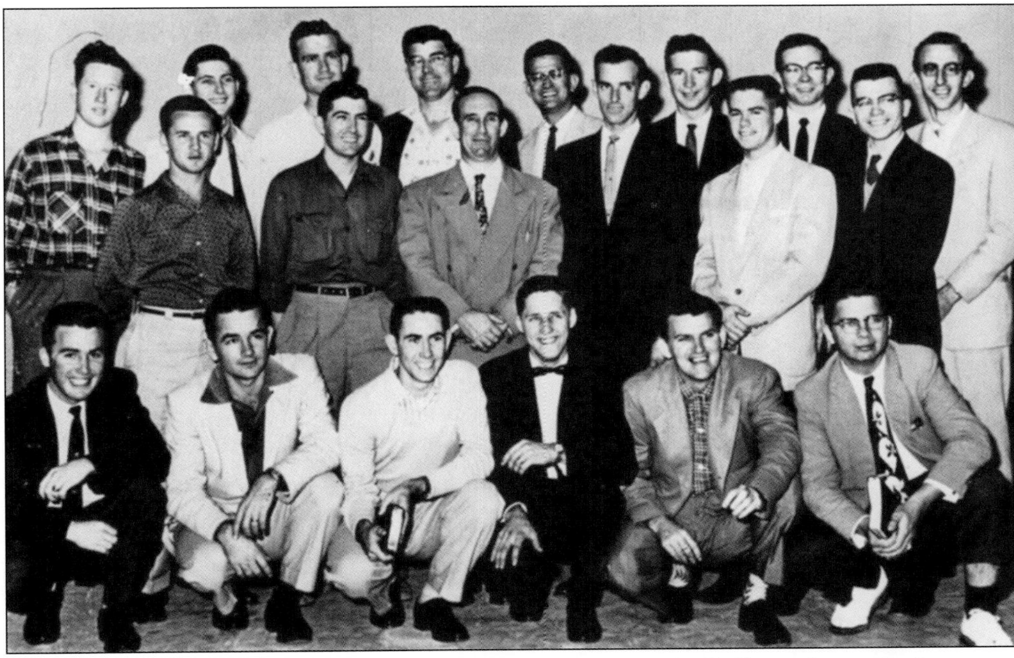

A few ministerial students attended Mississippi Woman's College through the years, but in the 1950s, the growth of the department of Biblical studies accelerated. After Dr. Andy Tate, dean of men, led several of the football players to become Christians, a revival occurred on campus, and over 100 professions of faith were made. Some of the athletes became ministers. Above is a group of ministerial students in 1958. Below are four football team members known as the Touchdown Quartet. From left to right are Bob Harris, Billy Crosby, Glynn Watts, and Billy Mitchell. (Courtesy of Bob Harris.)

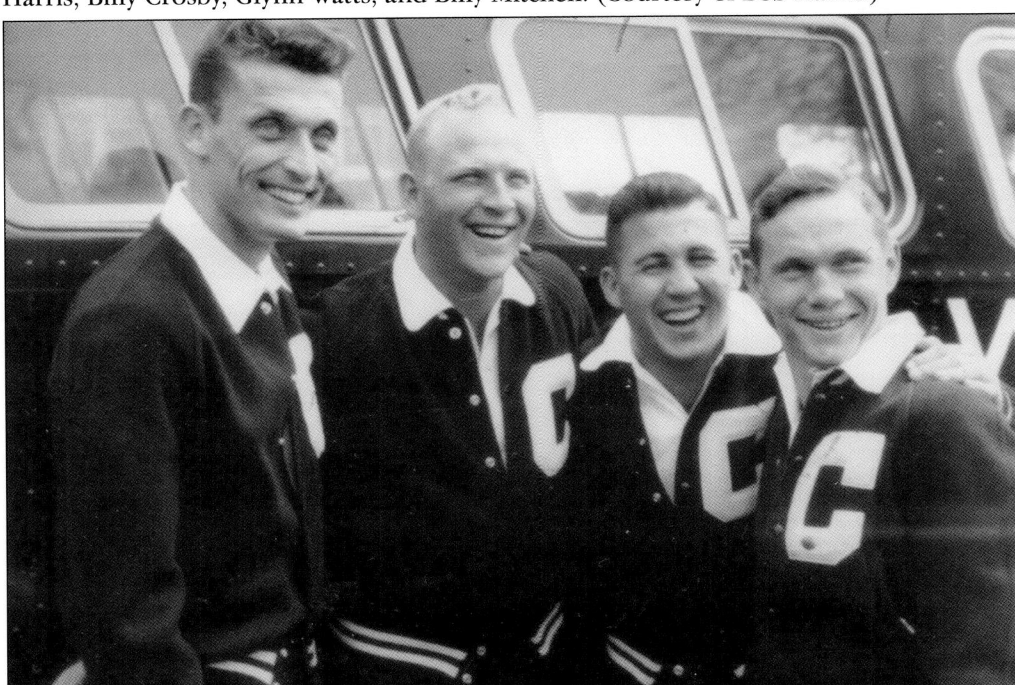

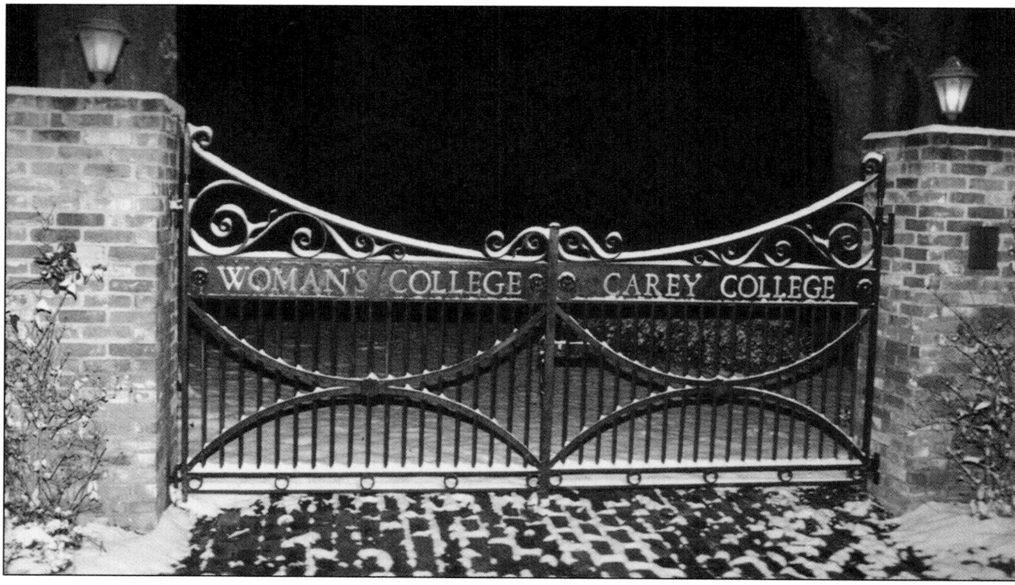


In a news article, Dr. Noonkester stated, "Dr. Rouse didn't want to change half-heartedly to a coeducation institution, so he started a football team to get more men in the college. The plan worked. During the 1953–1954 year, Mississippi Woman's College had less than 100 students. In 1954, the enrollment had increased to 324, 173 men and 151 females. We had a $38,000 operating deficit. We had gone all-out for football and coeducation." This photograph shows the original gate that was located on the front of the fenced Mississippi Woman's College campus. It was preserved by the J.D. Sims family and returned to the college in 1992. The gate was modified to include the "Carey College" name.

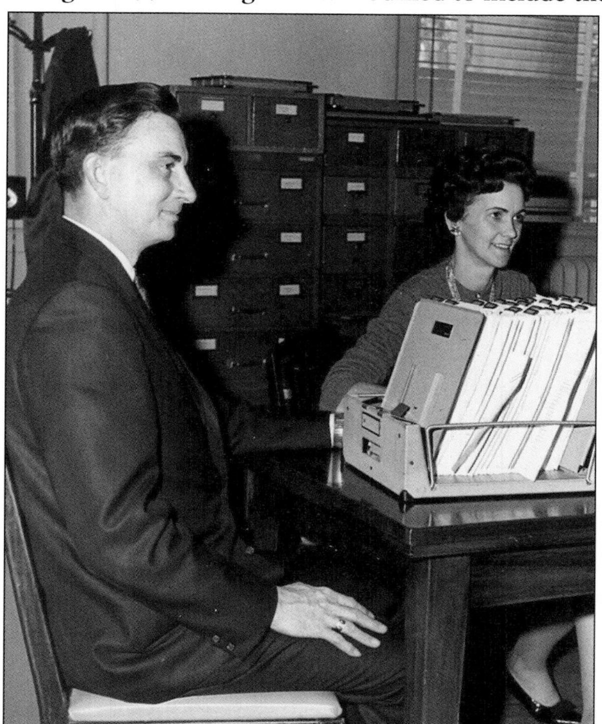

J.D. Sims became business manager at a time when the college was struggling, operating on a budget of only $127,000. A college official stated, "Two years later, a balanced budget was accomplished and now in 1981, in the 25 years since, the college never again exceeded its budget." Sims is pictured here with his wife, Mary Lou, an assistant in the business office.

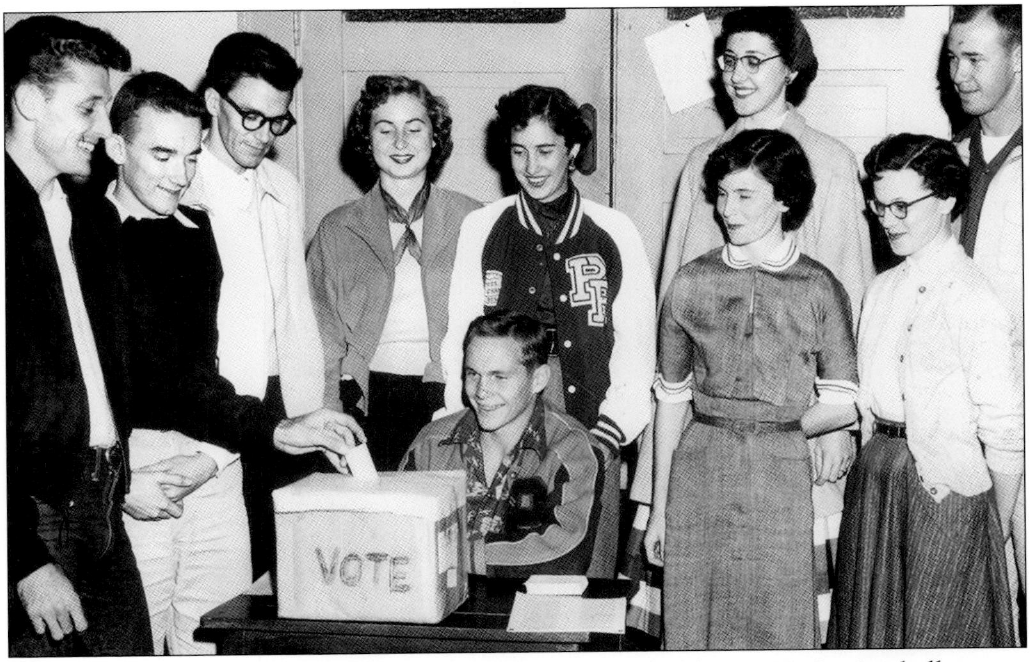


The first student election at William Carey College was held in 1955. Casting ballots are, from left to right, (first row) Billy Mitchell, Bobby Harris, Don Stewart, David Larrimore, Sylvia Lee, Betty Mitchell, Dorcas Hudgins, and Jane Brigance; (second row) Hanieth Jefcoat and Bill Davis. (Courtesy of Bob Harris.)

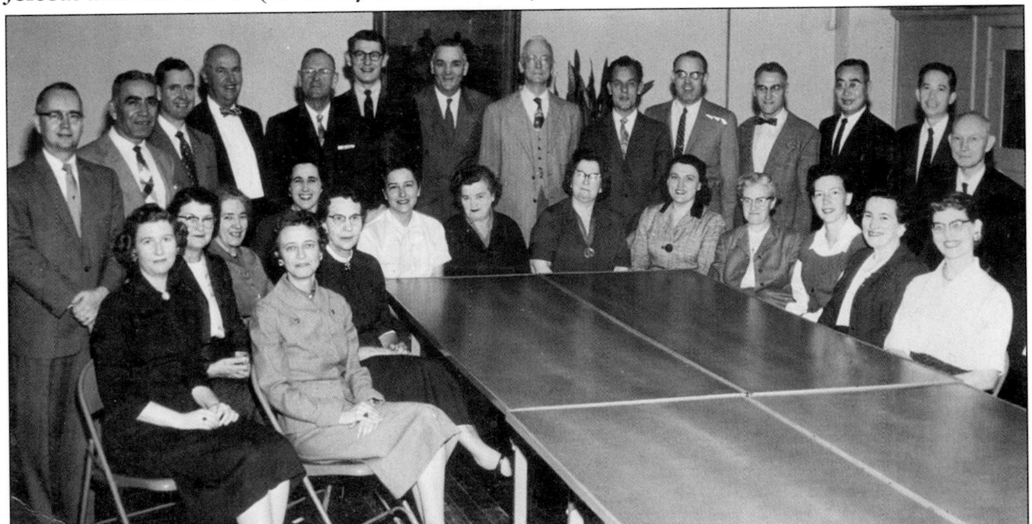

The student population grew, and so did the number of faculty and staff. This photograph shows the faculty of the college in 1958. From left to right are (first row) Fay Eubanks, Julia Loper, Mary Treser, Ruth Duncan, Clarice Robinson, Edith Boushy, Lillian Weidenhammer, Grace Walker, Evelyn McClure, and Helen McWhorter; (second row) Ruth Randle, Gertrude Smith, Ruth Sanders, and Elizabeth Jenkins; (third row) Joe Ernest, Theodore Boushy, George M. Jenkins, Judson Chastain, B.F. Smith, James Miller, Roy Hood, Burney L. Parkinson, Cecil Crawford, Donald Winters, Donald Packard, David Yang, Charles Calkins, and W.G. Gregory.

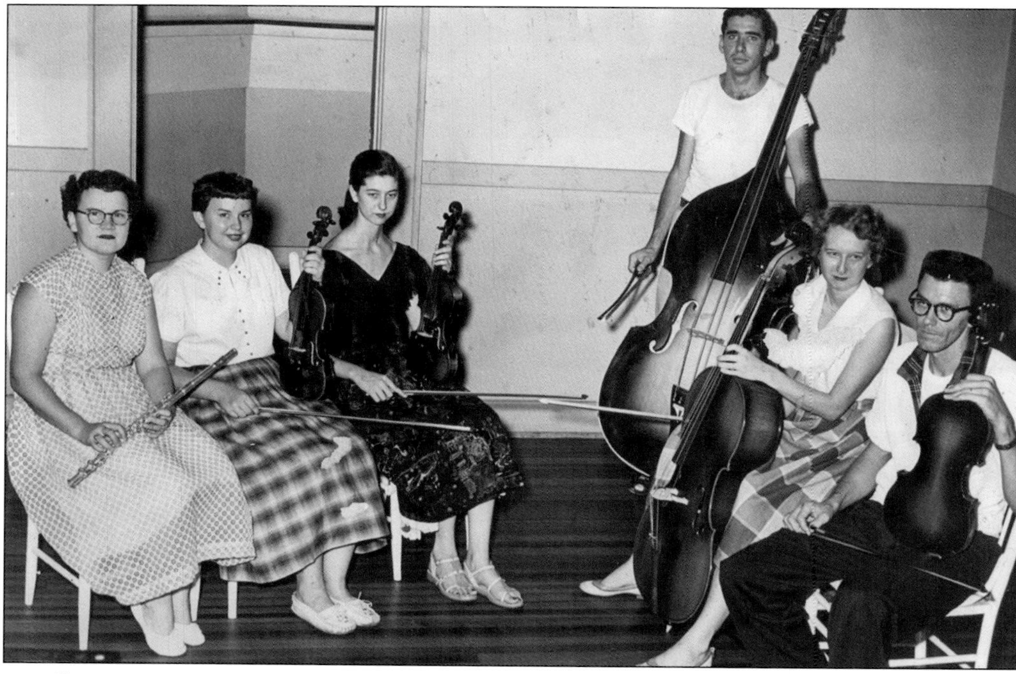

Excellence in music and drama, established at Mississippi Woman's College, was continued when the college became coeducational. Members of the chamber music ensemble in 1955 are, from left to right, Betty Jo Flowers, Vivian Smith, Ellen Davis, Bill Collins, Mary Ella Smith, and David Larrimore.

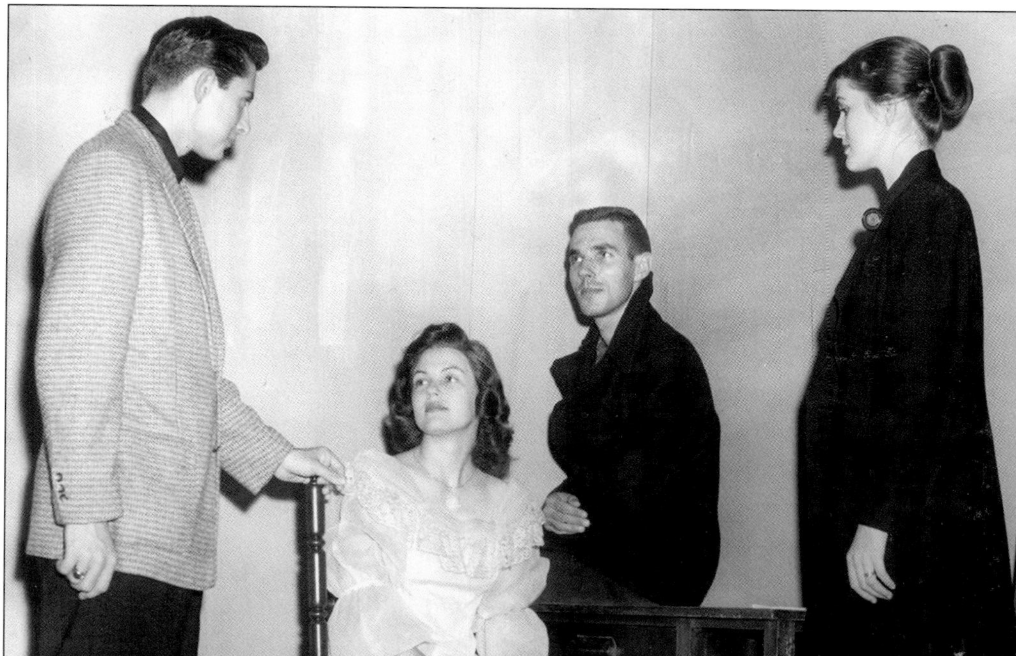

The drama department's Theatre Guild in 1957 performed Tennessee Williams's *The Glass Menagerie*. The cast members are, from left to right, David Scarborough, Mary Gayle Smith, Joe Patrick, and Marjorie Smith.

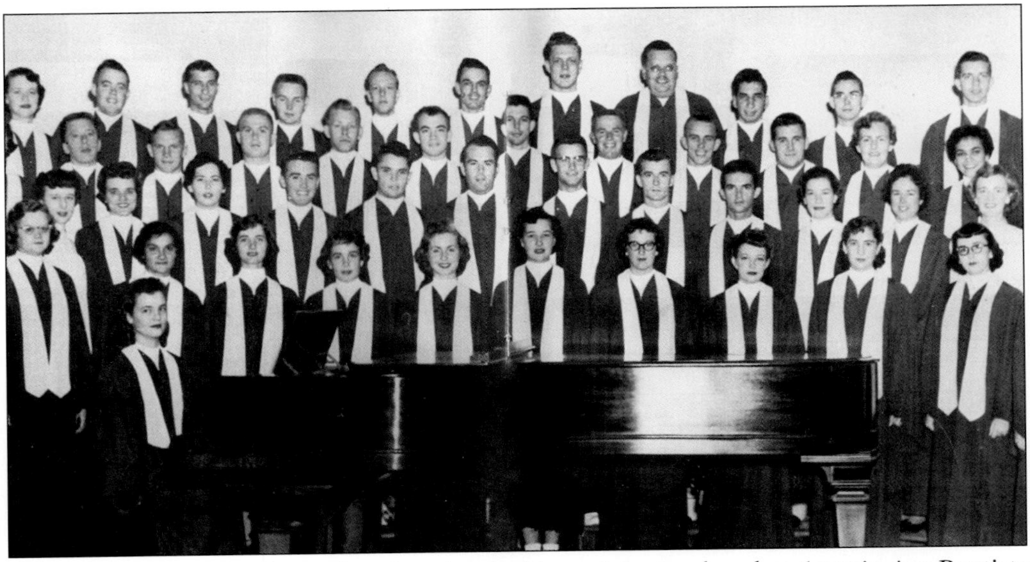

The William Carey College Chorale gained wide acclaim in churches (convincing Baptists that they still had a college in South Mississippi) and in schools, recruiting future students for the college. The chorale, under the direction of Jack Lyall, received widespread attention in 1955 when it was selected by the National Broadcasting Company (NBC) to furnish 30 minutes of special Easter music.

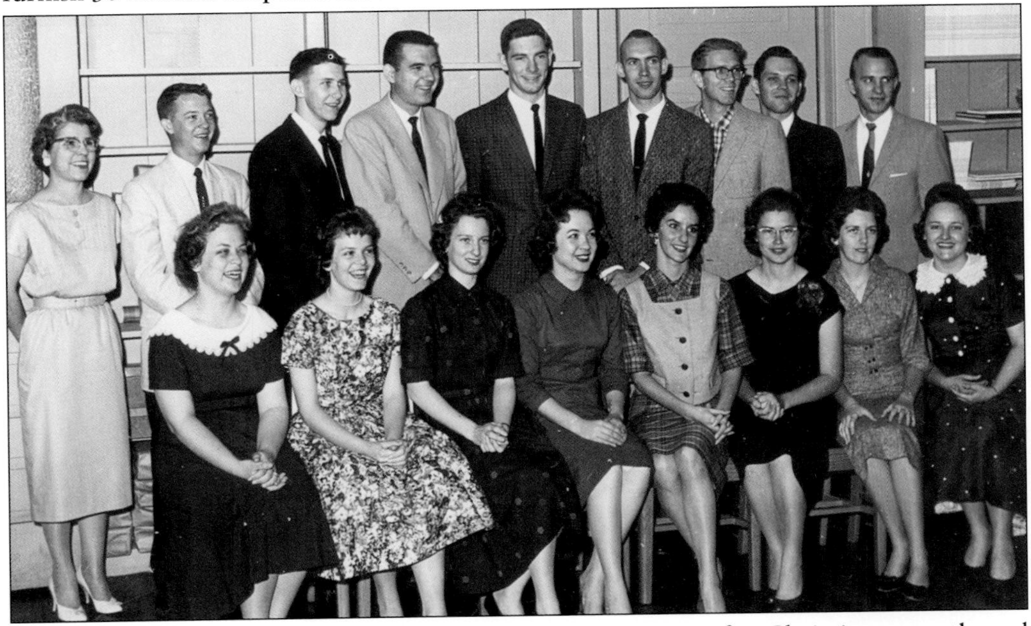

The Baptist Student Union (BSU) provided opportunities for Christian growth and service. Bible study, Young Women's Auxiliary, visits to nursing homes, jail ministries, and vacation Bible schools flourished in the 1950s and 1960s under the guidance of Jewell Hannah. With her encouragement, many students served as summer missionaries all across the nation and abroad. Other students spent their summers on staff at Mississippi's Baptist assemblies. In 1956, the student newspaper reported that 143 places of service in churches and mission points were served by Carey students. The 1960 BSU Executive Council is shown in this photograph.

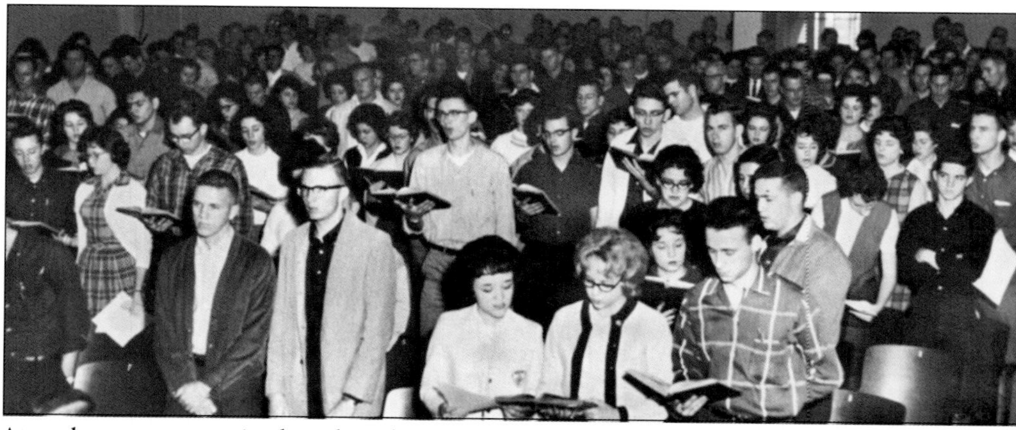

Attendance was required at chapel services held each day during the Mississippi Woman's College era. Chapel requirements were reduced to three days a week in the 1960s and to one service a week in the 1980s.

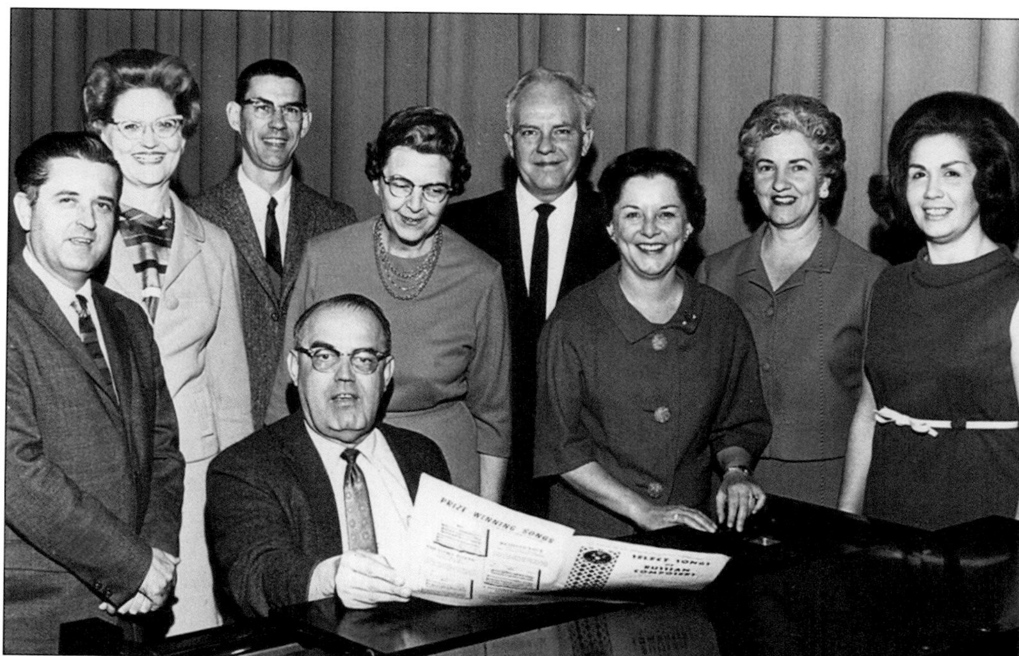

President Rouse and Dean Noonkester chose Donald Winters of the University of Indiana to head the fine arts department of the college in 1956. Winters had served for seven years both as organist-choir master of the Broadway Baptist Church and as the administrative head of church music at Southern Baptist Theological Seminary in Louisville, Kentucky. Frances Winters joined her husband on the faculty of the music department in 1958. Dr. Winters's tenure continued for 25 years, and the music department is now known as the Winters School of Music. The music faculty in 1970 included Donald Winters (seated) and, standing from left to right, alumnus Jim Downey, Helen McWhorter, James Casey, Frances Winters, Benjamin Dunford, Nancy Dunford, Jennie Lou Breland, and alumna Josephine D'Arpa.

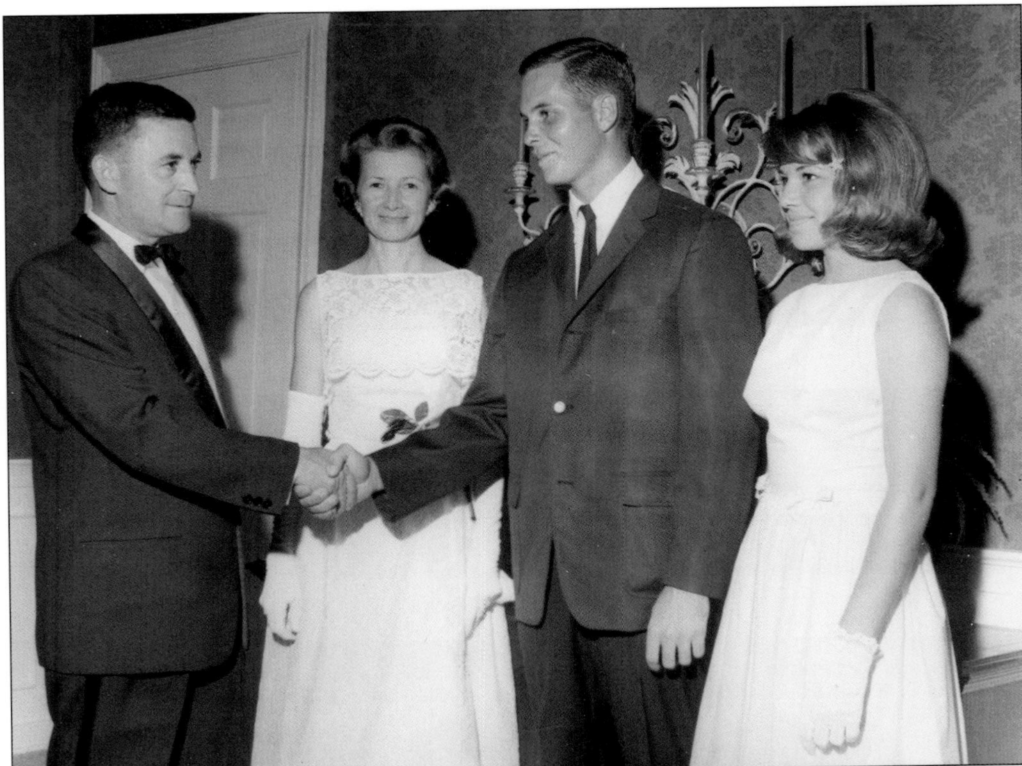

Ralph Noonkester arrived at Mississippi Woman's College planning to stay only a couple of years and then return to his much-loved home in Virginia. The small, somewhat bleak campus had been ravished by fire, war interruptions, financial strains, and academic limitations. In 1956, with the resignation of President Rouse, Noonkester was chosen as president. He was 32 years old, the youngest college president in the nation. Naomi Noonkester resigned her position as registrar to serve as Carey's first lady. Welcoming new and returning students became an annual event under the leadership of the Noonkesters.

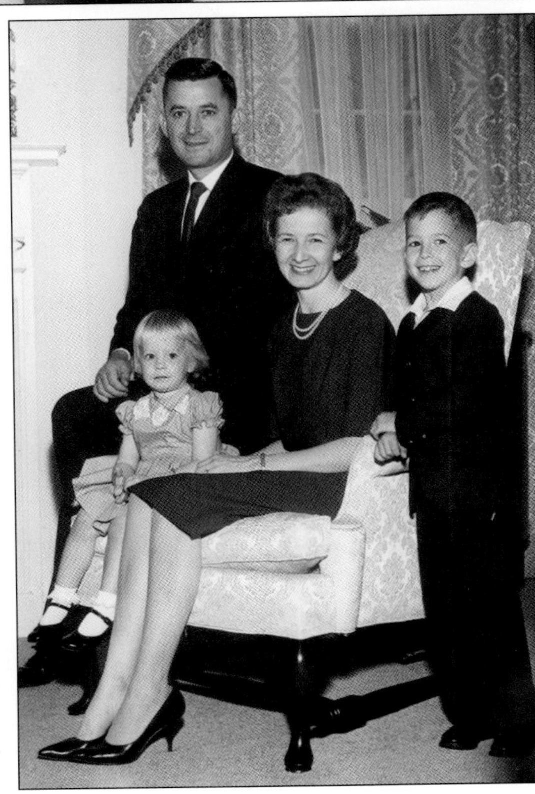

The Noonkester family grew with the birth of a son, Myron, in 1957 and a daughter, Lila, in 1961. Myron is now a professor of history and dean of the School of Arts, Humanities, and Sciences at William Carey College, and Lila is a professor of music at Lander University in South Carolina.

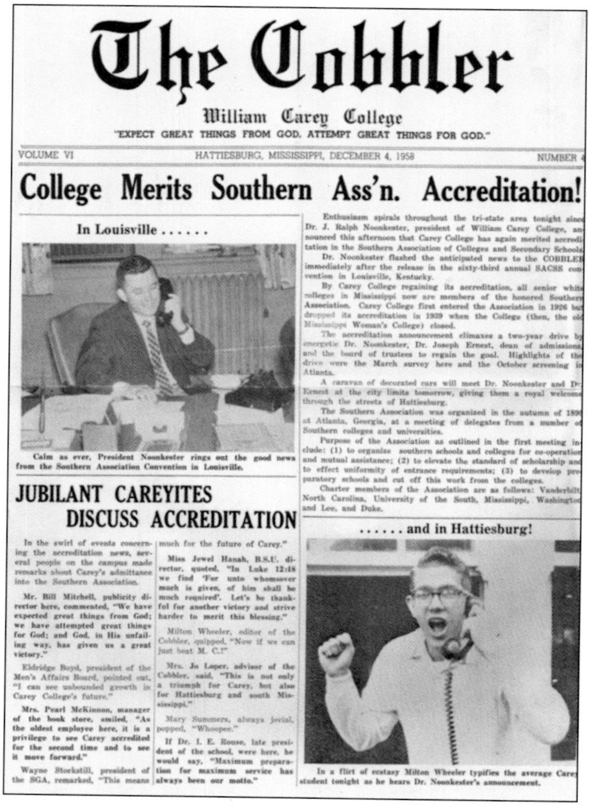

# The Cobbler

William Carey College

"EXPECT GREAT THINGS FROM GOD, ATTEMPT GREAT THINGS FOR GOD."

VOLUME VI HATTIESBURG, MISSISSIPPI, DECEMBER 4, 1958 NUMBER 4

## College Merits Southern Ass'n. Accreditation!

In Louisville . . . . . .

Calm as ever, President Noonkester rings out the good news from the Southern Association Convention in Louisville.

Enthusiasm spirals throughout the tri-state area tonight sinc[e] Dr. J. Ralph Noonkester, president of William Carey College, an[-]nounced this afternoon that Carey College has again merited accredi[-]tation in the Southern Association of Colleges and Secondary School[s].

Dr. Noonkester flashed the anticipated news to the COBBLER immediately after the release in the sixty-third annual SACSS con[-]vention in Louisville, Kentucky.

By Carey College regaining its accreditation, all senior whit[e] colleges in Mississippi now are members of the honored Souther[n] Association. Carey College first entered the Association in 1926 bu[t] dropped its accreditation in 1939 when the College (then, the ol[d] Mississippi Woman's College) closed.

The accreditation announcement climaxes a two-year drive b[y] energetic Dr. Noonkester, Dr. Joseph Ernest, dean of admissions, and the board of trustees to regain the goal. Highlights of th[e] drive were the March survey here and the October screening i[n] Atlanta.

A caravan of decorated cars will meet Dr. Noonkester and D[r.] Ernest at the city limits tomorrow, giving them a royal welcom[e] through the streets of Hattiesburg.

The Southern Association was organized in the autumn of 189[5] at Atlanta, Georgia, at a meeting of delegates from a number o[f] Southern colleges and universities.

Purpose of the Association as outlined in the first meeting in[-]clude: (1) to organize southern schools and colleges for co-operation and mutual assistance; (2) to elevate the standard of scholarship and to effect uniformity of entrance requirements; (3) to develop pre[-]paratory schools and cut off this work from the colleges.

Charter members of the Association are as follows: Vanderbilt, North Carolina, University of the South, Mississippi, Washington and Lee, and Duke.

## JUBILANT CAREYITES DISCUSS ACCREDITATION

In the swirl of events concerning the accreditation news, several people on the campus made remarks about Carey's admittance into the Southern Association.

Mr. Bill Mitchell, publicity director here, commented, "We have expected great things from God; we have attempted great things for God; and God, in His unfailing way, has given us a great victory."

Eldridge Boyd, president of the Men's Affairs Board, pointed out, "I can see unbounded growth in Carey College's future."

Mrs. Pearl McKinnon, manager of the book store, smiled, "As the oldest employee here, it is a privilege to see Carey accredited for the second time and to see it move forward."

Wayne Stockstill, president of the SGA, remarked, "This means much for the future of Carey."

Miss Jewel Hanah, B.S.U. director, quoted, "In Luke 12:48 we find 'For unto whomsoever much is given, of him shall be much required'. Let's be thankful for another victory and strive harder to merit this blessing."

Milton Wheeler, editor of the Cobbler, quipped, "Now if we can just beat M. C.!"

Mrs. Jo Loper, advisor of the Cobbler, said, "This is not only a triumph for Carey, but also for Hattiesburg and south Mississippi."

Mary Summers, always jovial, popped, "Whoopee."

If Dr. I. E. Rouse, late president of the school, were here, he would say, "Maximum preparation for maximum service has always been our motto."

. . . . . . and in Hattiesburg!

In a flirt of ecstasy Milton Wheeler typifies the average Care[y] student tonight as he hears Dr. Noonkester's announcement.

President Noonkester's first priority became the reaccreditation of the college. The day in 1958 when the president phoned from Louisville, Kentucky, the news that the college had been granted full accreditation by the Southern Association of Colleges and Schools, created much excitement for the students. Editor Milton Wheeler and the staff of the *Cobbler,* the student newspaper, had their presses ready. Immediately every class was interrupted with a news "Extra."

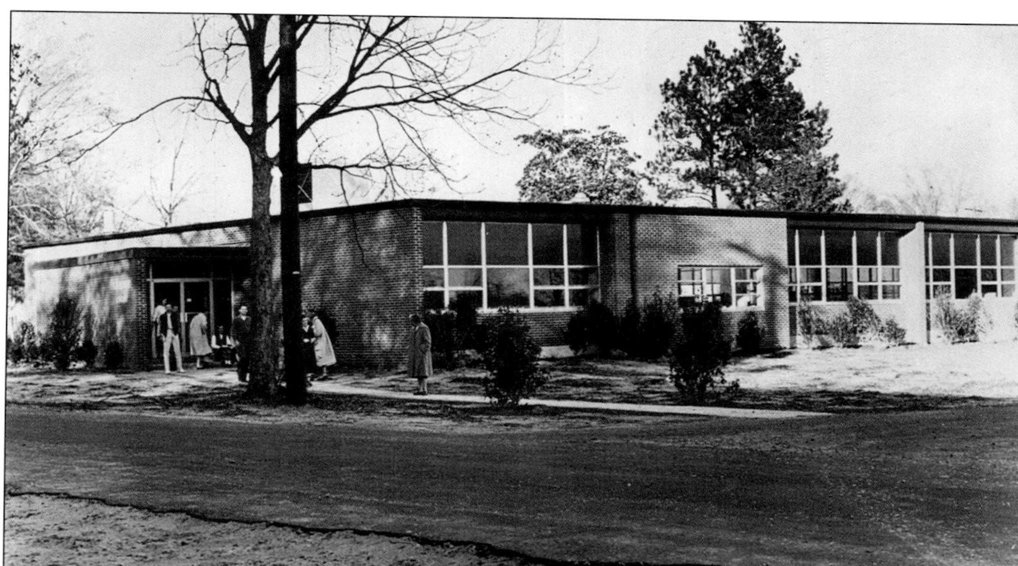

The library in 1954 was located in the crowded Tatum Court administration building. A new library was constructed in 1957, and in 1958, the college dedicated it in honor of former president I.E. Rouse. Space was quadrupled in the new library, and holdings were substantially increased.

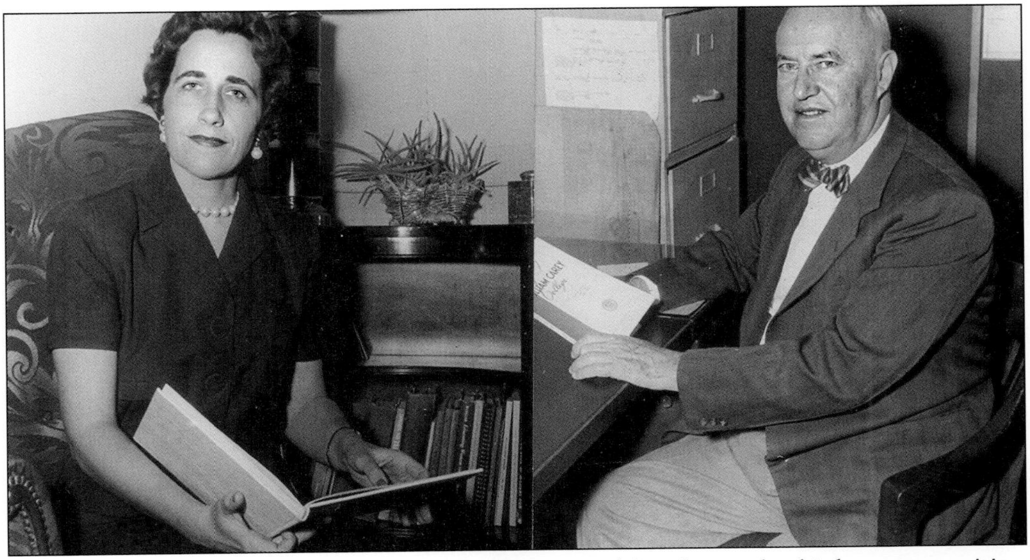

Since 1957, the Jenkins-Chastain Citizenship Award has been the highest recognition given each year at Honors Day. Named for Elizabeth Jenkins, dean of women, and Judson Chastain, dean of men, the award is given to both a male and female student who best represent outstanding citizenship.

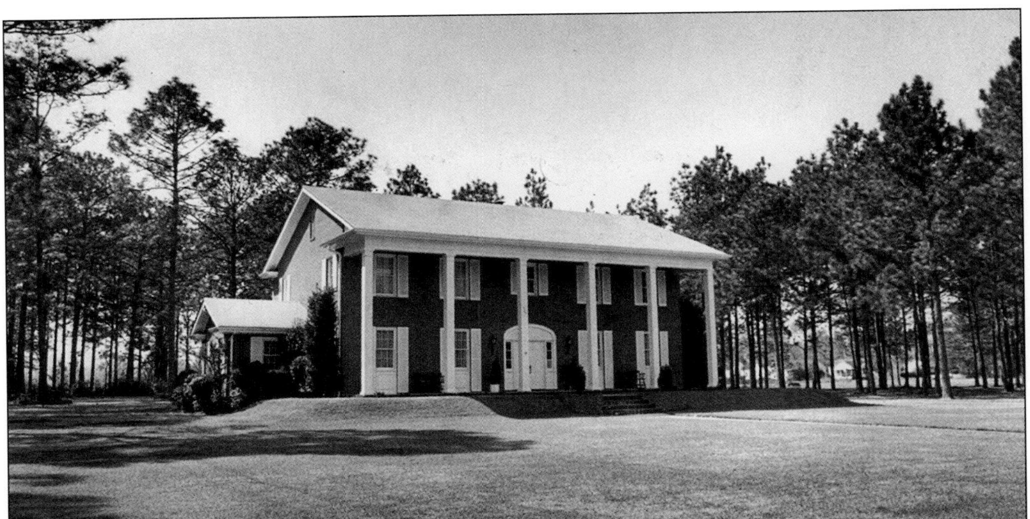

The 1960s brought many changes to the appearance of the William Carey College campus, as 10 new buildings were built in the first 10 years of Noonkester's presidency. Only six buildings existed in 1956. I.E. Rouse Library opened in 1958; Green Science Hall in 1959; Thomas Apartments in 1960; Clinton Gymnasium in 1961; the president's home in 1962; Polk Hall for men in 1962; Bass Hall for women in 1963; McMillan Student Center in 1964; Thomas Hall in 1966; and Bryant Hall for men in 1966. Pictured here is the president's home.

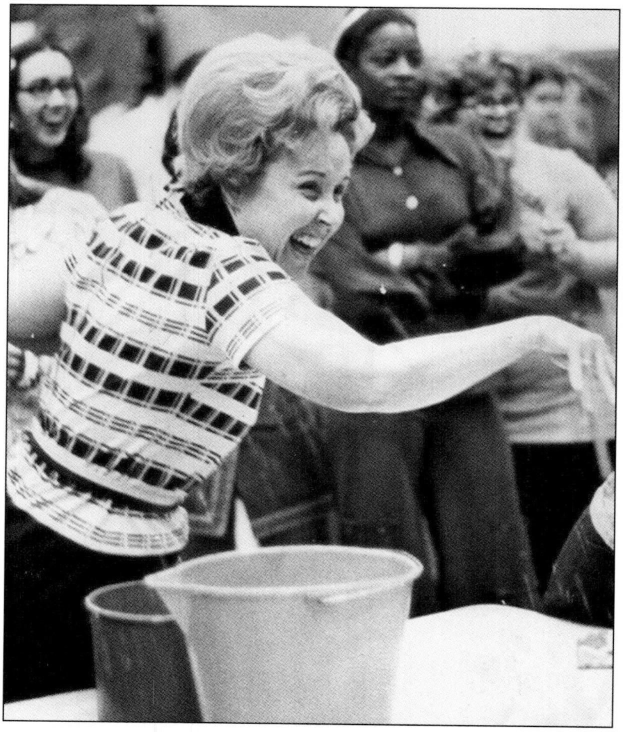

Marjorie Rowden became director of public relations and alumni affairs in 1962. Under her direction, the alumni association membership greatly increased, alumni chapters were formed, homecomings were scheduled on an annual basis, and the first alumni magazine was published in the spring of 1964. The magazine reported an enrollment of 683 students with 50 full-time faculty members. A popular administrator, Rowden takes aim in a sponge-throwing student event.

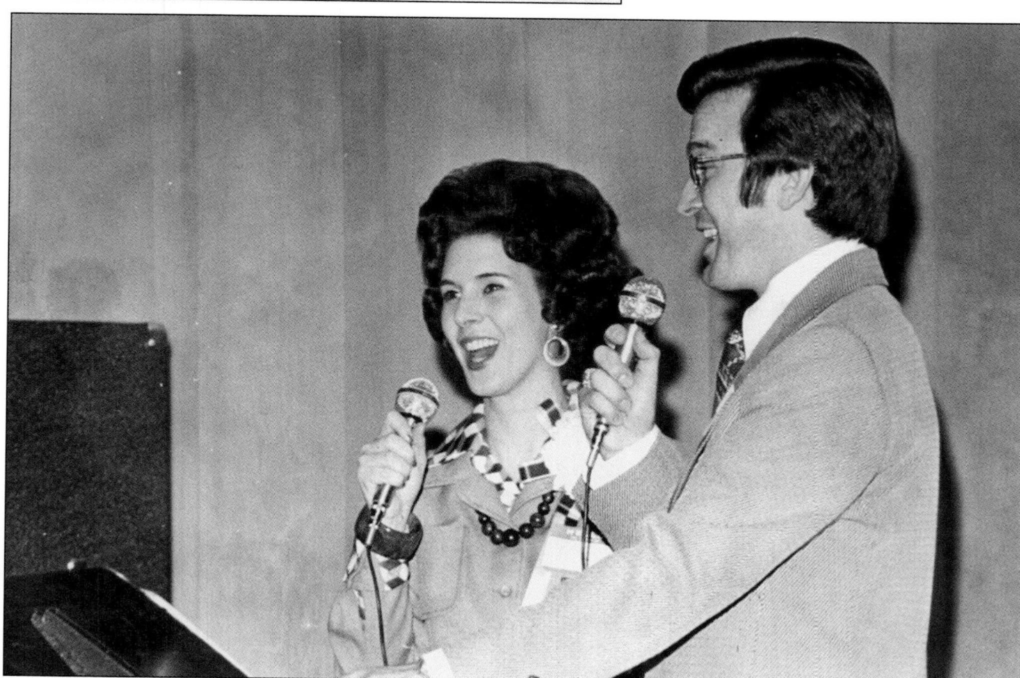

In 1964, William Carey College led all Southern Baptist colleges in the number of alumni serving as missionaries. Among many others from both Mississippi Woman's College and William Carey College, John and Kathy Lee McNair left in 1975 for missionary service to India, the home of William Carey. They later served in Spain and spent the greater part of their career in Uruguay. John served in medical missions and Kathy in music.

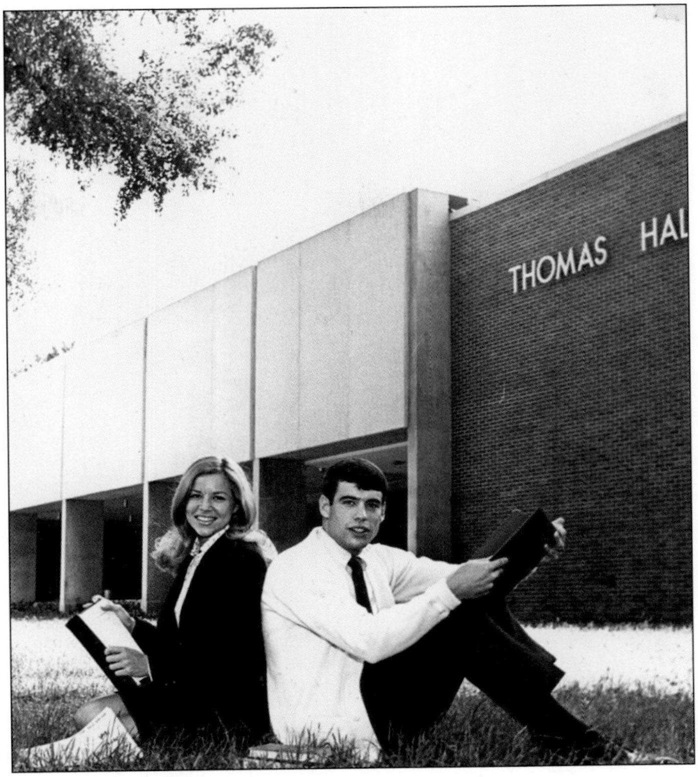


One of William Carey College's "finest hours" occurred in 1963, when a development campaign successfully raised $700,000 for the construction of Thomas Hall. Named in honor of Mr. and Mrs. R.B. Thomas, it housed music offices, practice rooms, and an auditorium that would seat 1,200, providing space to hold graduation on campus rather than in local churches. In 1985, the auditorium was completely refurbished and was named in honor of trustee and donor Dumas L. Smith. Linda Waldon and Randy Read pose in front of the new Thomas Hall in 1966.

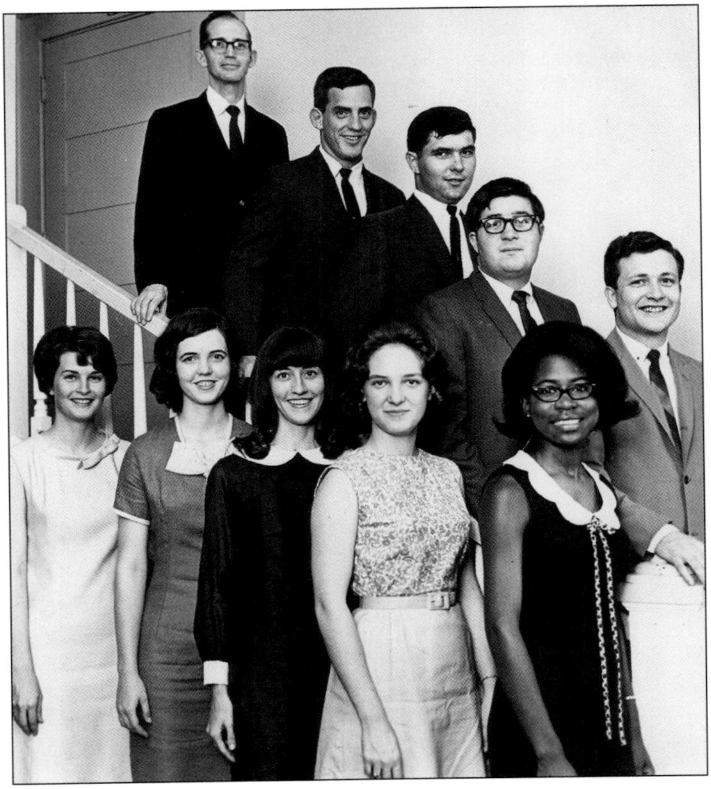

A significant event to occur in the life of the college was the signing in 1965 of the Civil Rights Compliance Act of 1963. The decision to integrate the college brought both praise and protest. A cross was burned on the lawn of the president's home. William Carey College was the first private school in Mississippi to sign the act and to integrate. Two honor graduates of Rowan High School, Vermester Jackson and Linda Williams, were the first African American students at William Carey College in 1966. Jackson, a mathematics major, is shown in this photograph with other math majors.

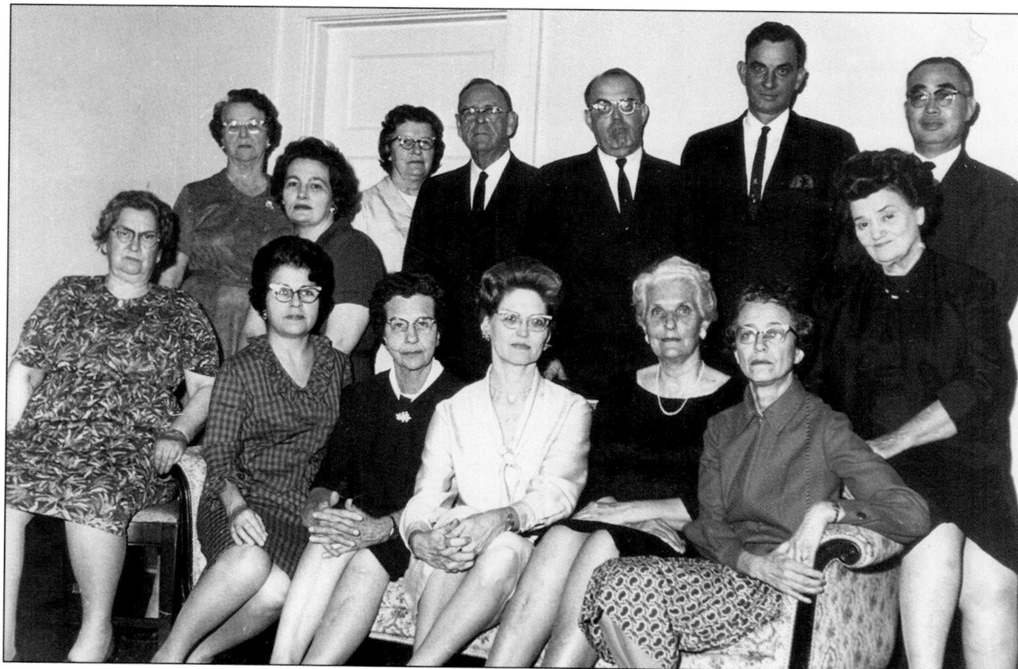

In 1966, 14 faculty and staff of the college celebrated 10-year anniversaries. From left to right, they are (first row) Jewell Hannah Conniff, BSU director; Julia O. Loper, journalism; Helen McWhorter, music; Florence Lambert, school nurse; and Fay Eubanks, French; (second row) Clarice Robinson, business; Maude Hedrick, food service manager; Evelyn McClure, home economics; Gertrude Smith, botany; B. F. Smith, religion; Donald Winters, music; J.D. Sims, business manager; Ruth Duncan, librarian; and David Yang, education.

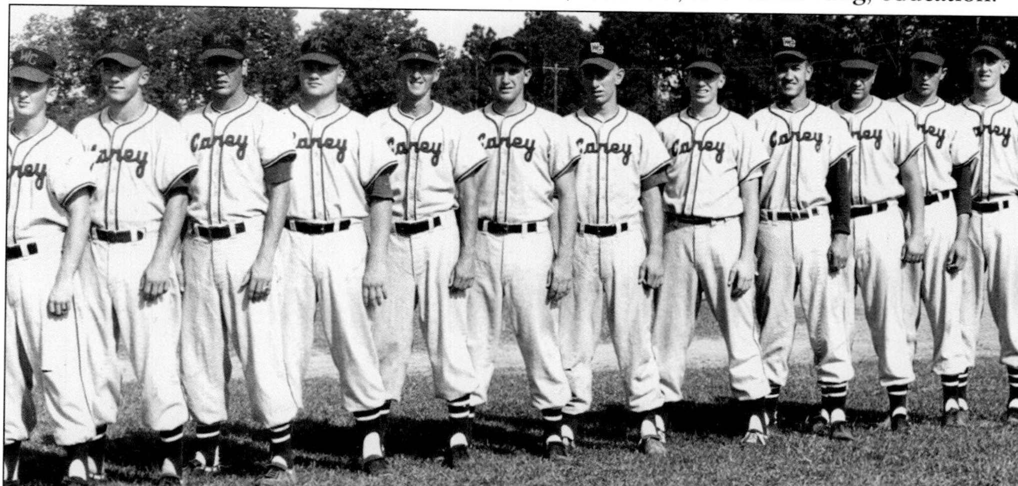

John Stephenson of South Portsmouth, Kentucky, became the first athlete to be drafted from William Carey College by a professional baseball team. He signed with the New York Mets organization in 1963 and spent 10 years as a catcher with the Mets, Chicago Cubs, San Francisco Giants, and California Angels. Stephenson later had a successful career as a coach at his alma mater and at Southeastern Louisiana College. Since 1963, approximately 40 players have signed professional contracts. This photograph shows the 1960 baseball team, with Stephenson sixth from the left.

In May 1968, 168 students received diplomas. President Noonkester is shown with three sisters who graduated that year: from left to right, Jean and Jane Clinton, seated, and Carolyn Clinton, standing. A fourth sister, Joyce Clinton, graduated in 1956. During Noonkester's 33-year tenure as president, 7,445 degrees were awarded to graduates.

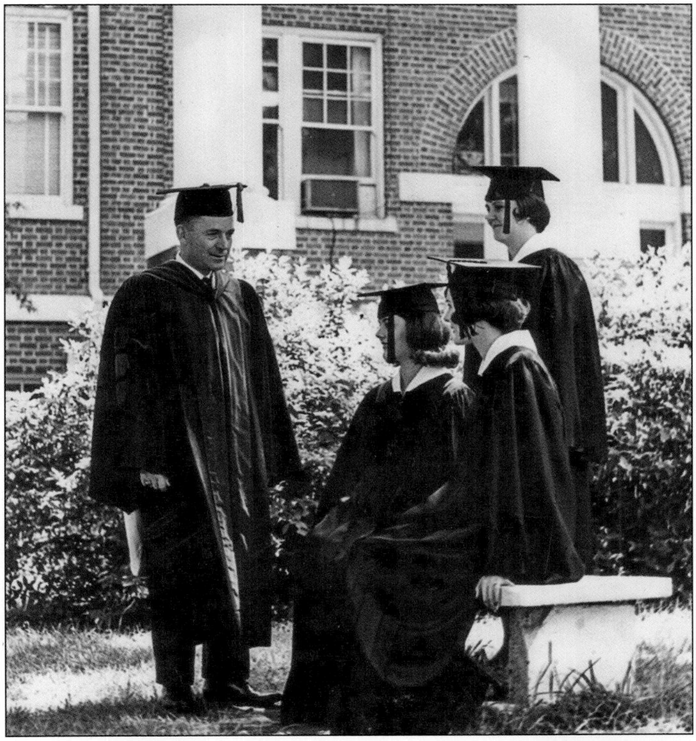

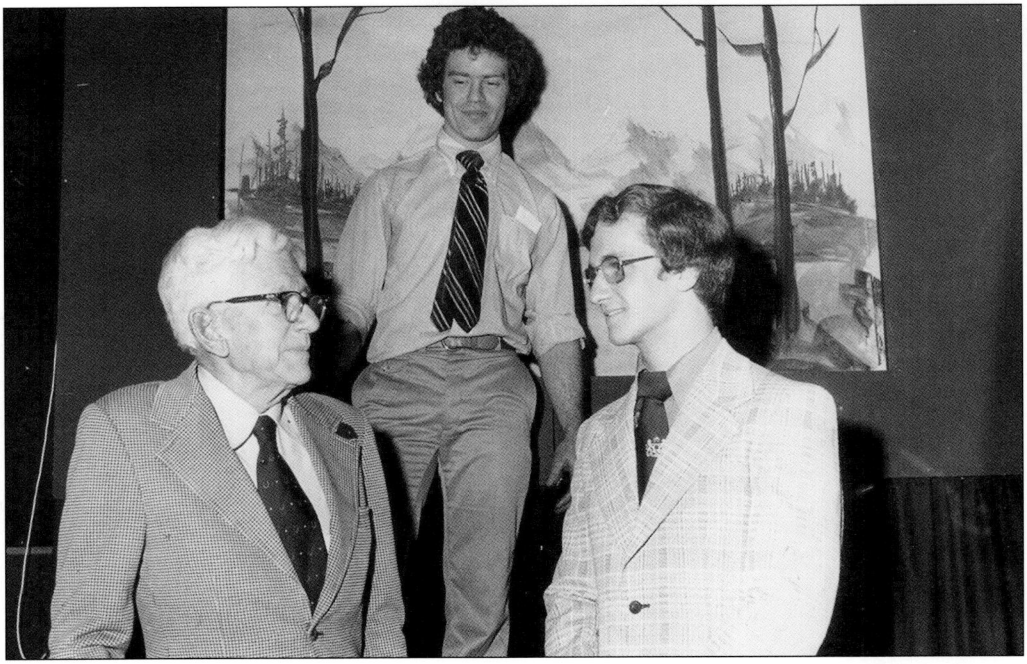

The annual Spiritual Emphasis Week brought noted speakers and authors to the campus. Some of the distinguished visitors included Clifton Allen, Elton Trueblood, Roland Q. Leavell, Chester Swor, Lewis Myers, Buryl Red, and Grady Nutt. A favorite with students, Swor returned to the campus annually for lectures. In this mid-1970s photograph are Swor (left), unidentified, and Al Fike (right).

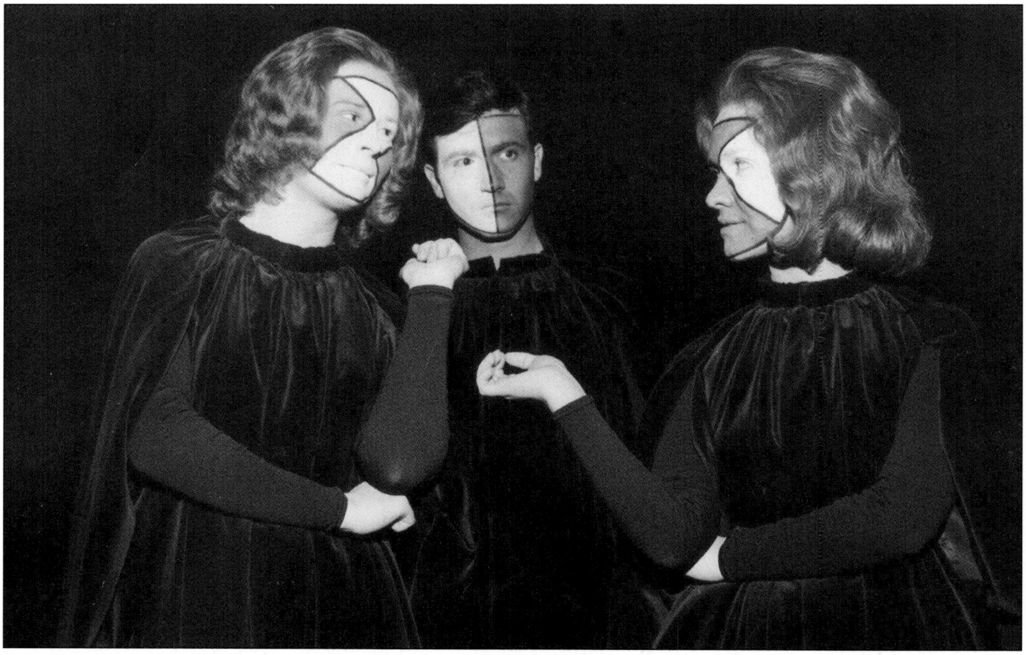

In the 1960s, the Theatre Guild became the Serampore Players, in honor of the city where William Carey lived and worked in India, and an annual touring production was begun that continued for 13 years until the energy crisis of 1973. This 1965 photograph shows a scene from the touring drama *Christ in the Concrete City*. Memorable venues included the US Military Academy at West Point, New York, an international student conference in Texas, a military base in Illinois, and the federal penitentiary in Atlanta. Pictured from left to right are Peggy Bell, Jim McDill, and Linda Harvill.

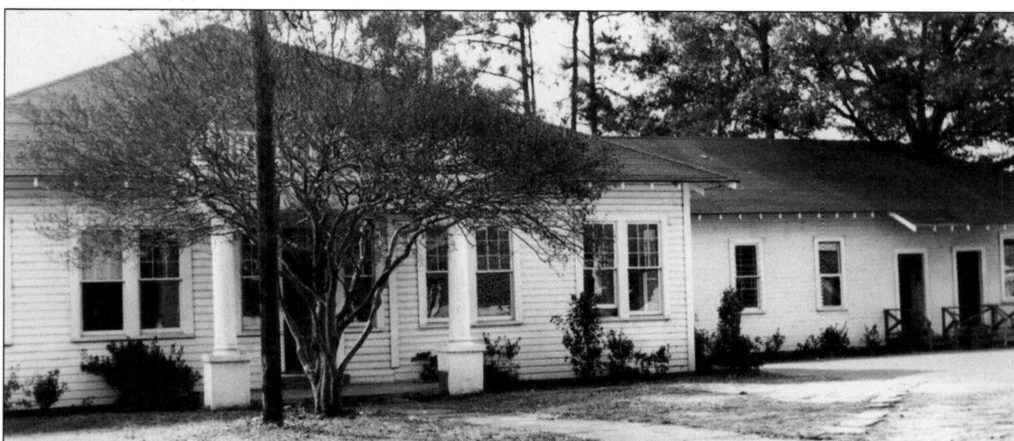

In June 1963, a fire completely destroyed the building, shown above, that housed the speech and theater department. Everything was lost—library, lighting equipment, costumes, properties, scenery, and tools. The department was soon relocated on the ground floor of Tatum Court with the theater itself occupying the area that had once been a swimming pool. In 1972, the theater was named in honor of Obra Quave, chairman of the department. With a recent lead gift of $500,000 from Joe and Virginia Tatum, a new theater building is in the planning stages in 2006. Joe is the grandson of W.S.F. Tatum, who gave the original property to the college.

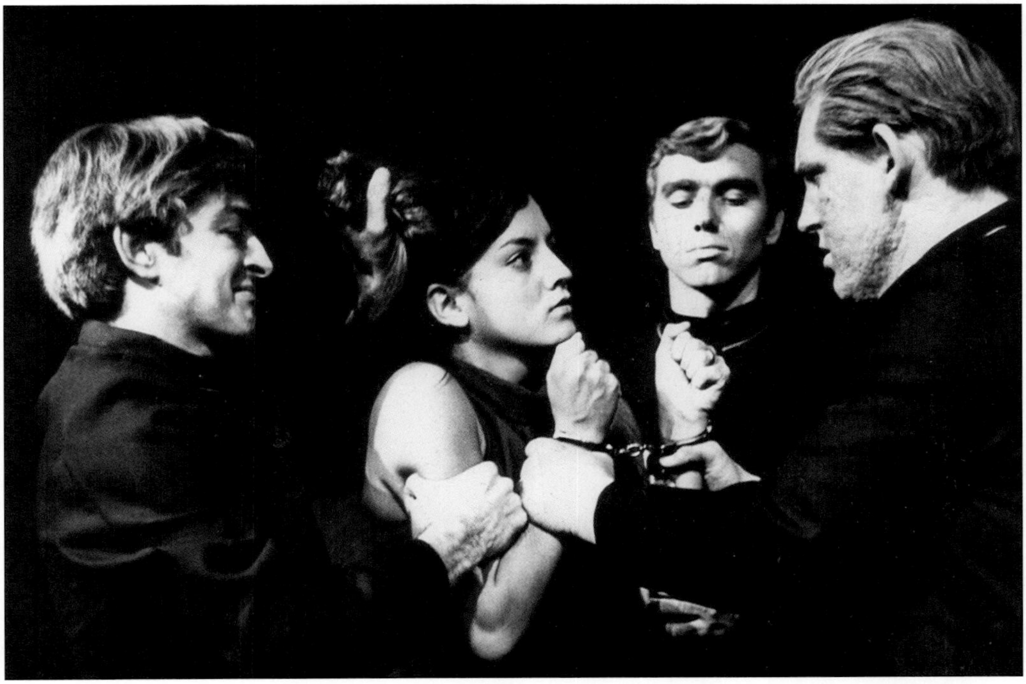

In the last four decades, theater productions have drawn praise and delighted audiences from Mississippi and beyond. The program produced distinguished alumni who are now teaching in colleges and high schools and performing across the country. The 1960s saw many productions, including *Antigone*, *Cave Dwellers*, *Harvey*, *Scrooge*, *Under Milkwood*, *The Lark*, and the touring drama *Christ in the Concrete City*. A scene from *Antigone* is shown in this photograph. From left to right are John Davis, Pam Blakeney, Grayson Bottom, and Ken Johnson.

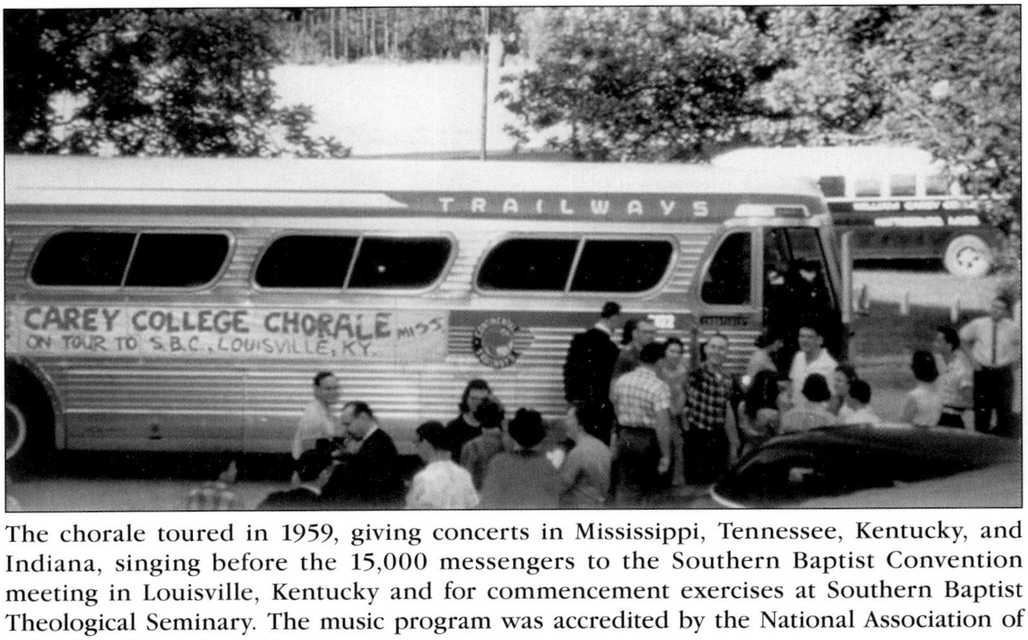


The chorale toured in 1959, giving concerts in Mississippi, Tennessee, Kentucky, and Indiana, singing before the 15,000 messengers to the Southern Baptist Convention meeting in Louisville, Kentucky and for commencement exercises at Southern Baptist Theological Seminary. The music program was accredited by the National Association of Schools of Music in 1966.

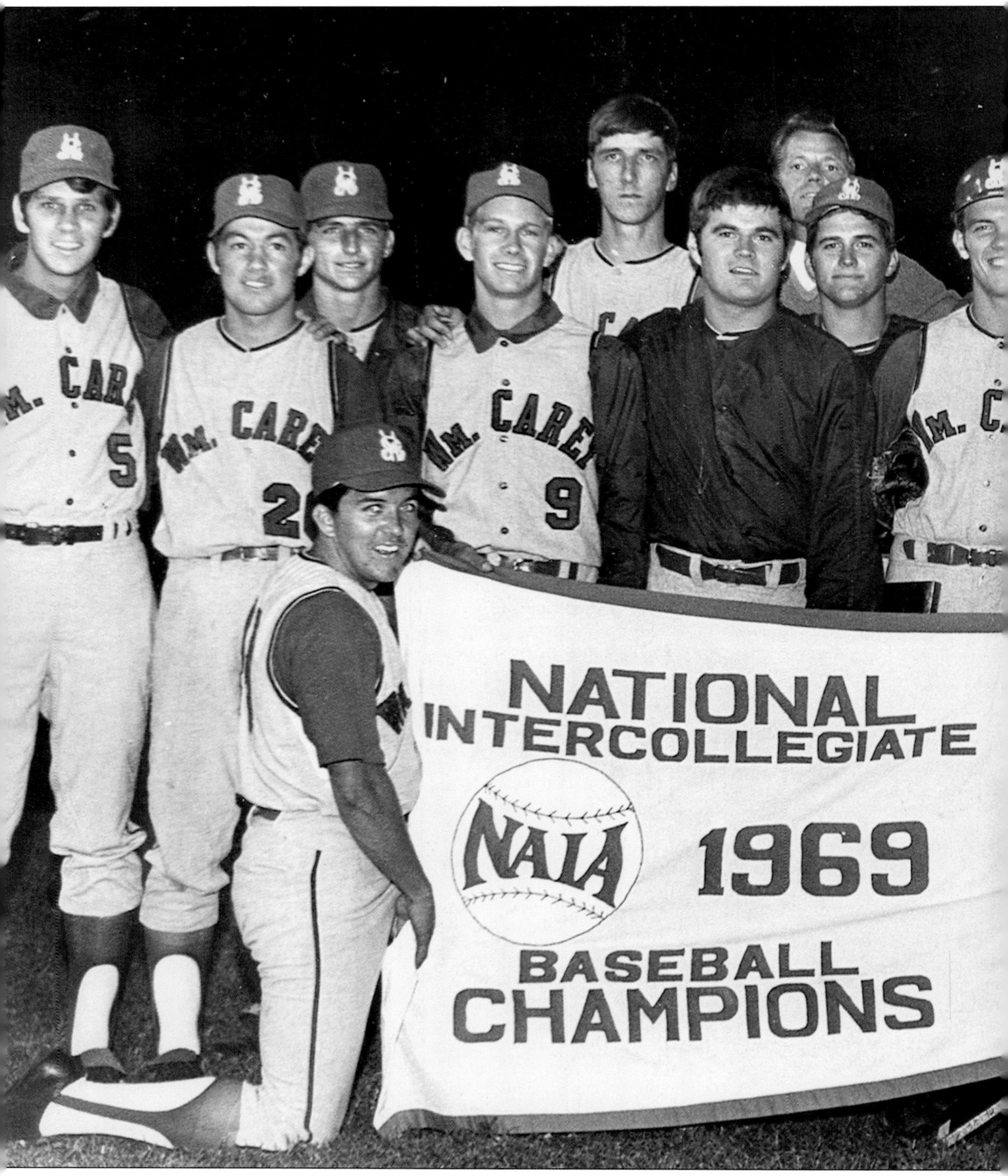


The highlight of all time for Carey's athletic program came in 1969, when the little-known William Carey College Crusader baseball team defeated team after team to win the NAIA National Baseball Championship in St. Joseph, Missouri. Upon their return to Hattiesburg, the team was met with a 30-car motorcade, a police escort, the Hattiesburg Fire Department, the state highway patrol, fellow students, and fans from across the region.

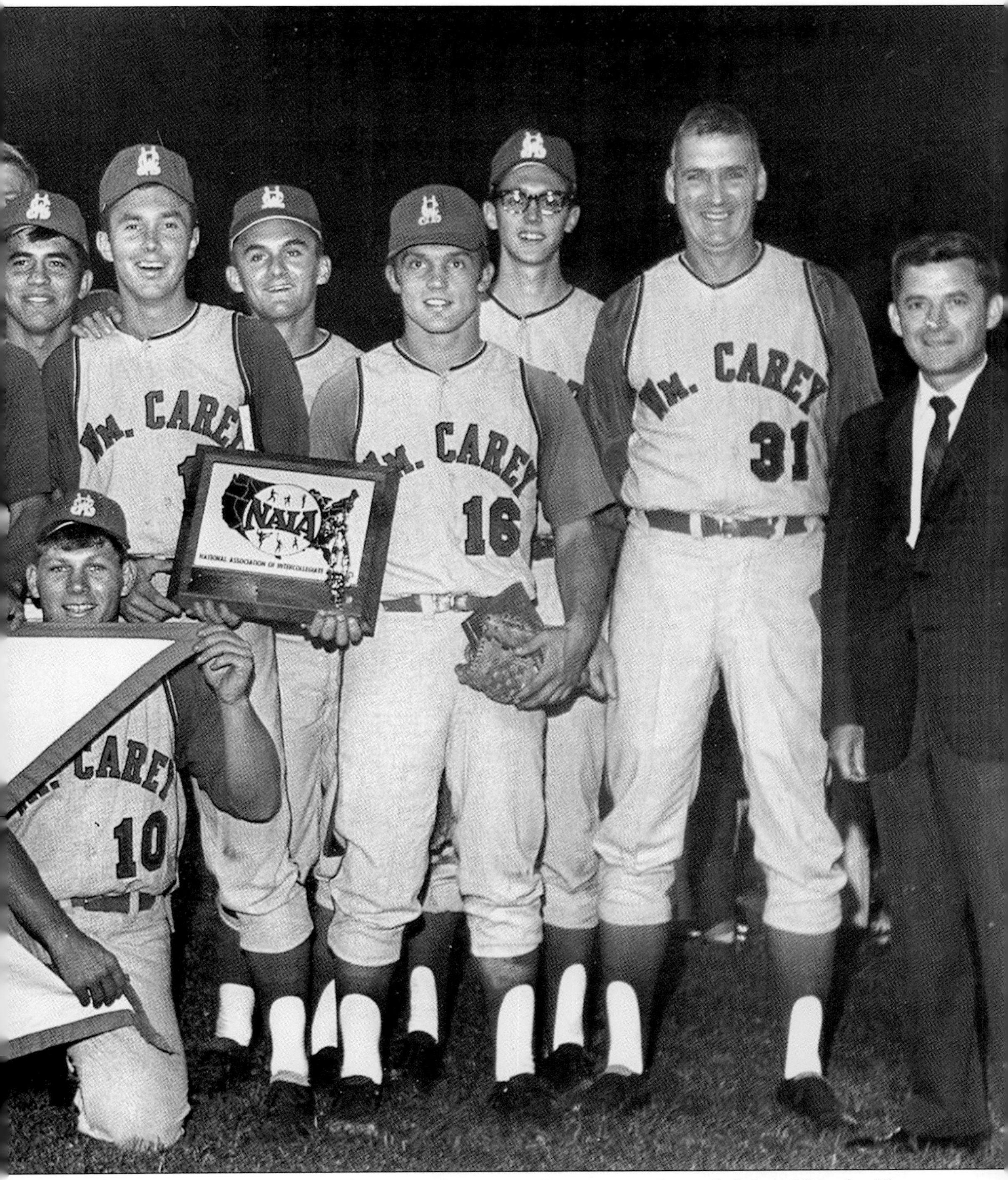


City officials presented a proclamation honoring the team and coach John O'Keefe. The 1969 champs are, from left to right, (holding banner) Leon Tingle and Clyde Dearman; (standing) Monk Burns, Junior Broome, Harold Sealy, Claude Yarborough, Jim Smith, Steve Proffer, Ed Shelton, Forrest Stevenson, Mike Harris, Bill Collins, Tony Ladner, Bobby Eades, Jim Arnold, Dale Willis, Chuck Harlan, Coach O'Keefe, and President Noonkester.

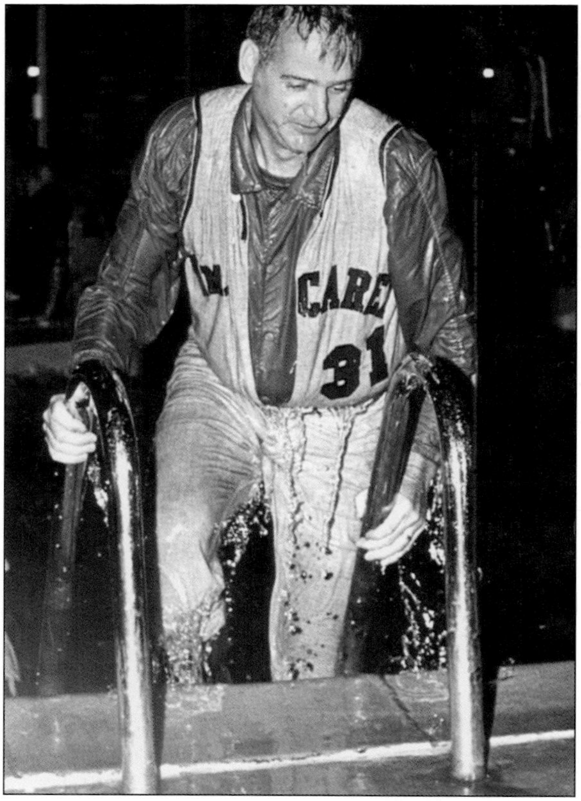


The coach was one of the first to be thrown in the pool at the Holiday Inn where the team celebrated. President Noonkester expected to be tossed and dressed for the occasion with his swim trunks on under his pants.

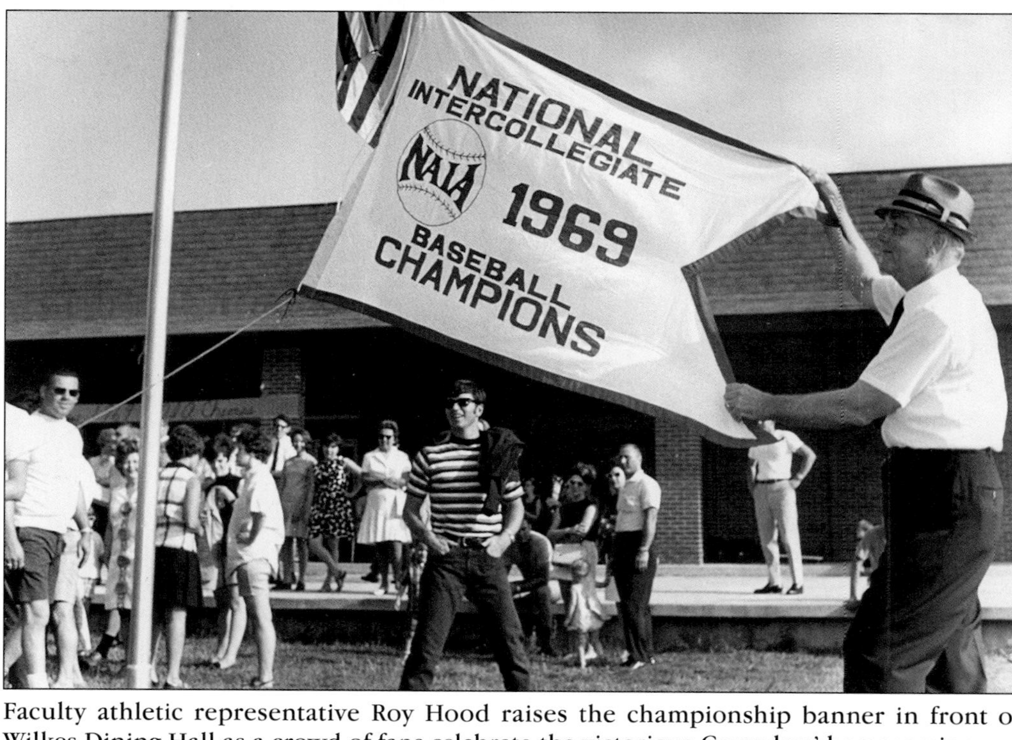


Faculty athletic representative Roy Hood raises the championship banner in front of Wilkes Dining Hall as a crowd of fans celebrate the victorious Crusaders' homecoming.

William Carey College entered the Miss America competition with the selection of Linda Waldon as the first "Miss Carey" in 1967. She placed as second alternate in the Miss Mississippi Pageant, beginning a long tradition of success in the state pageant. Since her graduation, Waldon has had a successful career in children's radio and television programming.

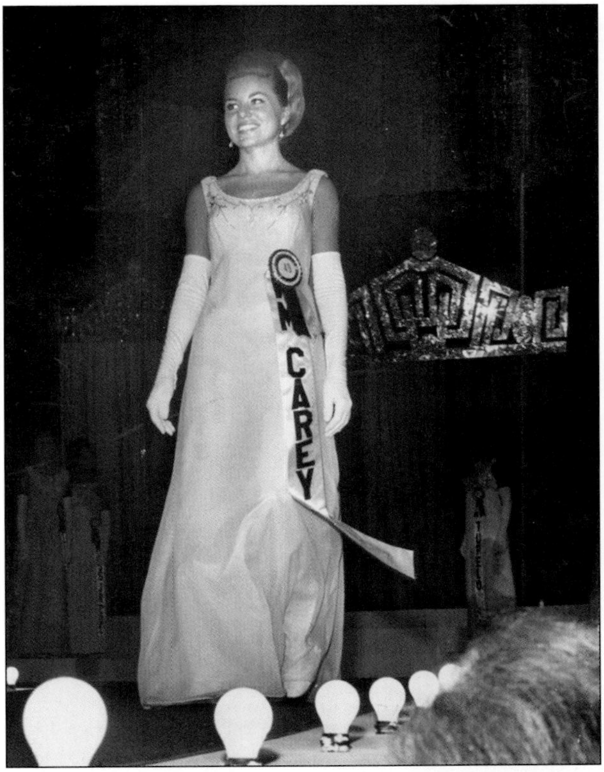

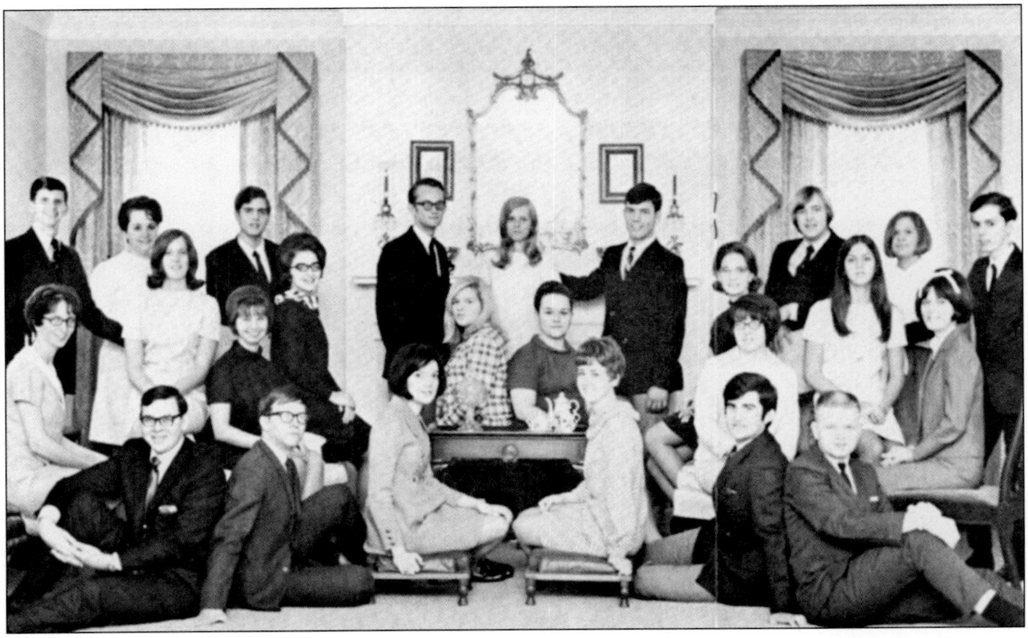

Established in 1968 under the direction of Milton Wheeler, the Freshman-Sophomore Honors Program brought to the campus 27 highly qualified students, all scoring in the top 10 percent in the nation on the ACT or SAT and graduating in the top 5 percent of their high school classes. The students took honors classes, participated in monthly cultural or scholarly programs, took field trips, and began preparation for graduate school.

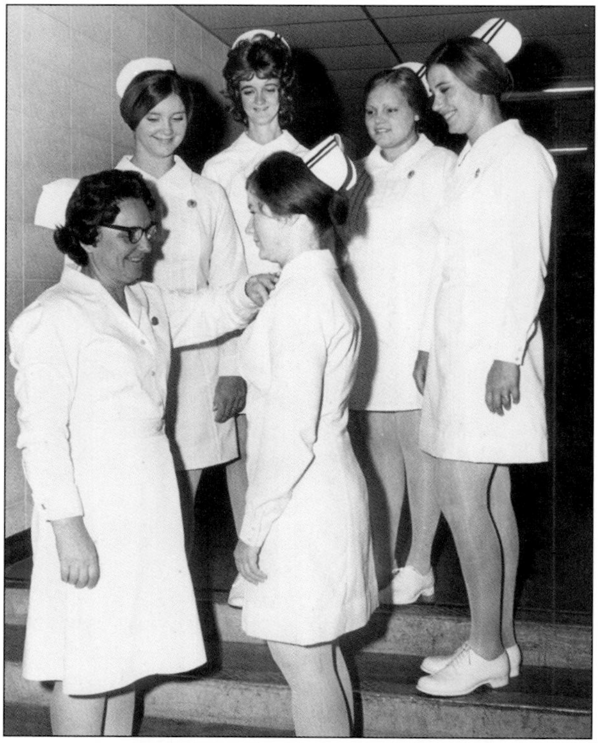

In 1969, the college took a bold step when it crossed state lines to acquire the prestigious Mather School of Nursing in New Orleans. In the early years of the program, students were required to spend two years studying core courses in Hattiesburg, then transferring to New Orleans for two years of clinicals. A four-year baccalaureate degree program in nursing is now available in New Orleans, Gulfport, and Hattiesburg. A master's program in nursing was added at Carey on the Coast in 2003. Pictured with Dean Shirley Morrison are five of the six first nursing graduates in 1972 (not in order) Sandra Brice, Georganne Faith, Lynda Havens, Judy Morris, Alicia Rawls, and Judy Roberts.

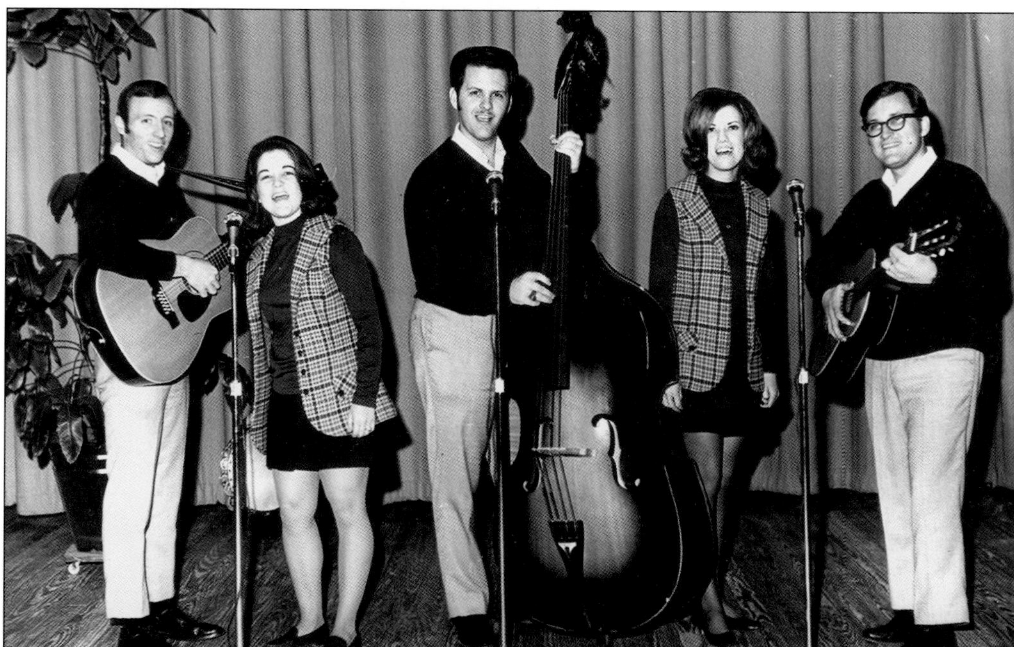

A group of music students wanted to sing more contemporary musical selections and formed the ensemble Carpenter's Wood in the late 1960s. Today, the group performs in churches and schools throughout Mississippi, Alabama, and Florida and has participated in mission trips to Korea and India. The original members are, from left to right, Tim Thomas, Beverly Rush, J.E. Sims, Mary Hayes, and Carl Bridgman.

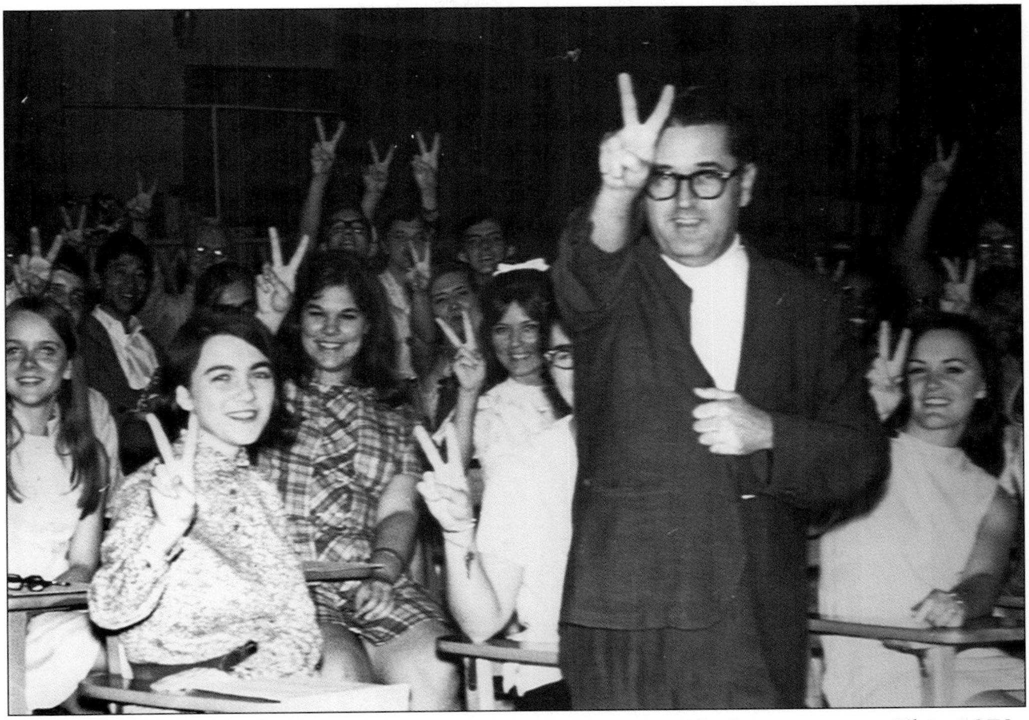

The academic program in 1969 offered 23 majors in 12 departments. This 1970s photograph is the classroom of Dr. James Downey, music professor.

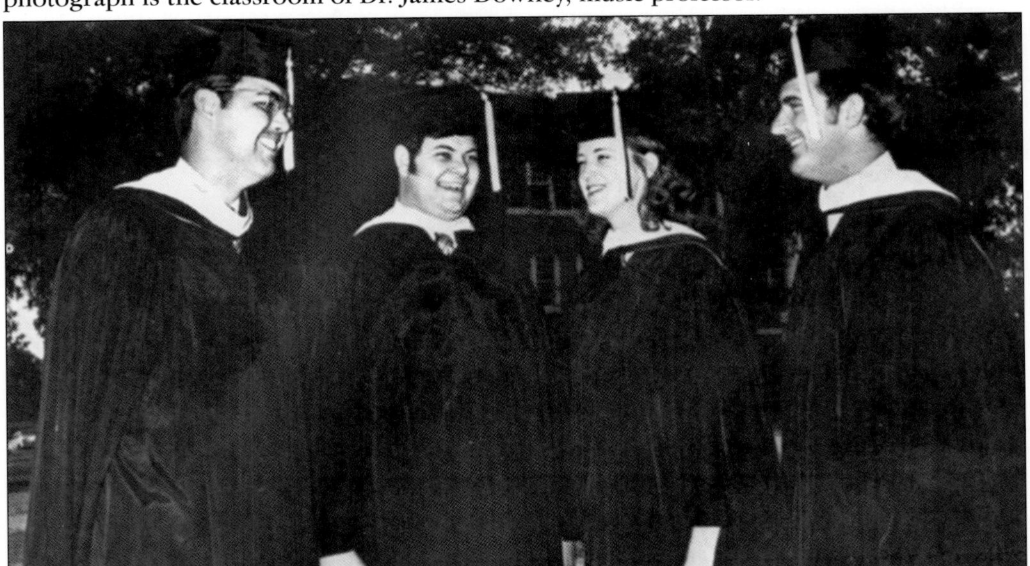

The college obtained approval for the granting of master's degrees in 1970, and the first graduate degrees were presented in music to four students in 1972. In the spring of 1975, 24 students received the master of education degree. While the master of music degree has been discontinued, the graduate program in education has grown annually with an enrollment of 708 students in the summer of 2005. The first four students to receive master's degrees in 1972 are, from left to right, Gene Winters, Clark Adams, Patti McCarty, and Ronnie Parker.

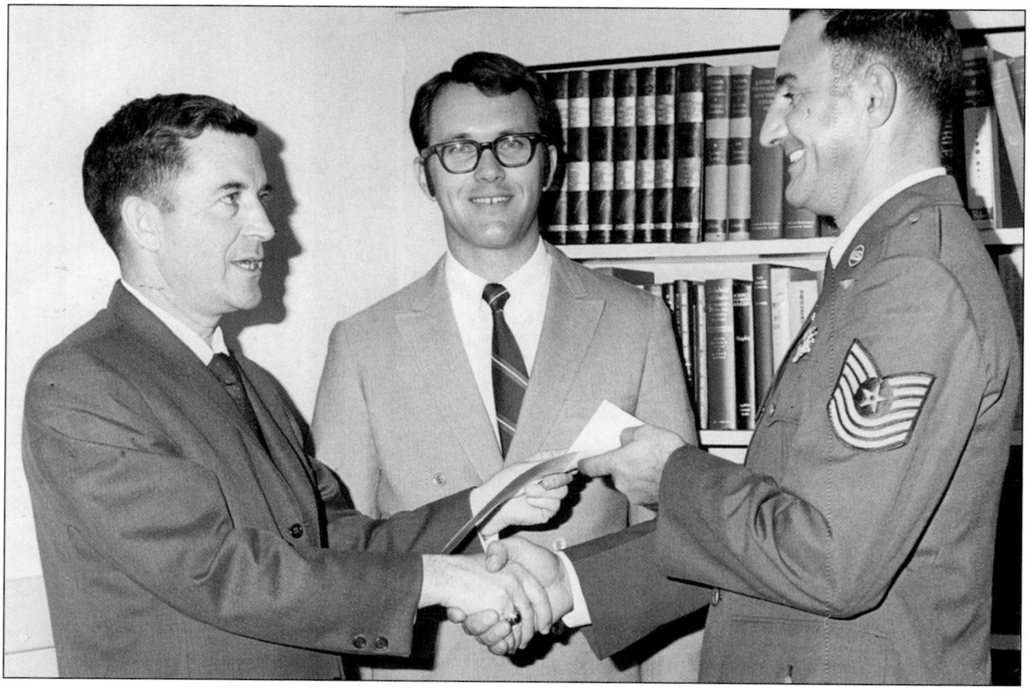

In the early 1970s, the student body took on a different flavor when military service personnel enrolled at the college. Carey became a leader in actively recruiting these military men and women to complete bachelor's degrees through the "Bootstrapper" program. Pictured above are, from left to right, President Noonkester, alumnus and director of admissions Bryan Brand, and Tony Pascale, who was the first bootstrapper to graduate from Carey. Pascale later served as the director of military affairs and as admissions director for 20 years. Below, Sen. John C. Stennis addressed the graduating class in 1974, which included more than 40 bootstrappers.

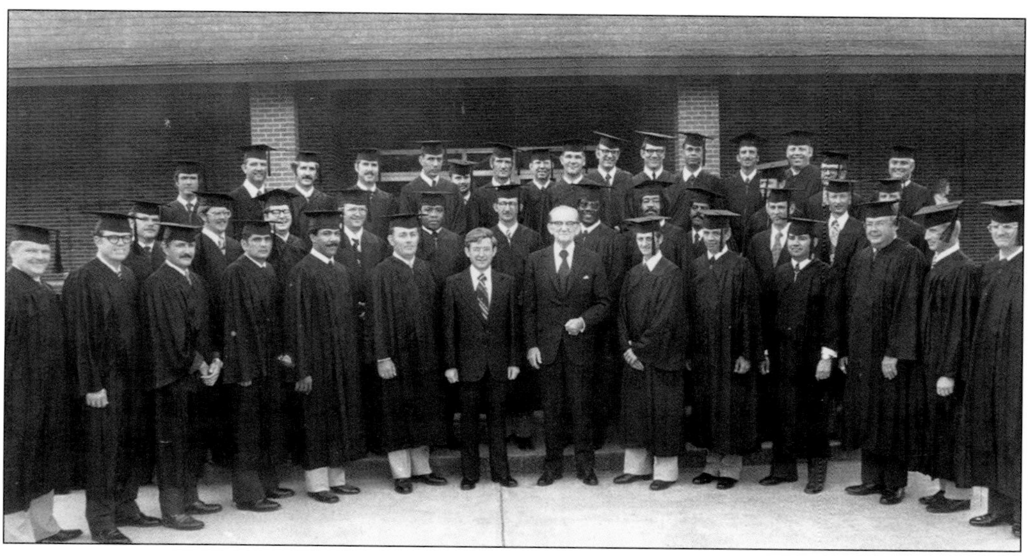

The education department in 1973 saw a dual opportunity: to prepare students as teachers and to provide a much-needed service to the community. An Early Childhood Development Laboratory opened on campus with approximately 40 children in attendance the first year. Education Specialist Iris Brantley served as director, and education students provided learning experiences for the four- and five-year-old preschoolers.

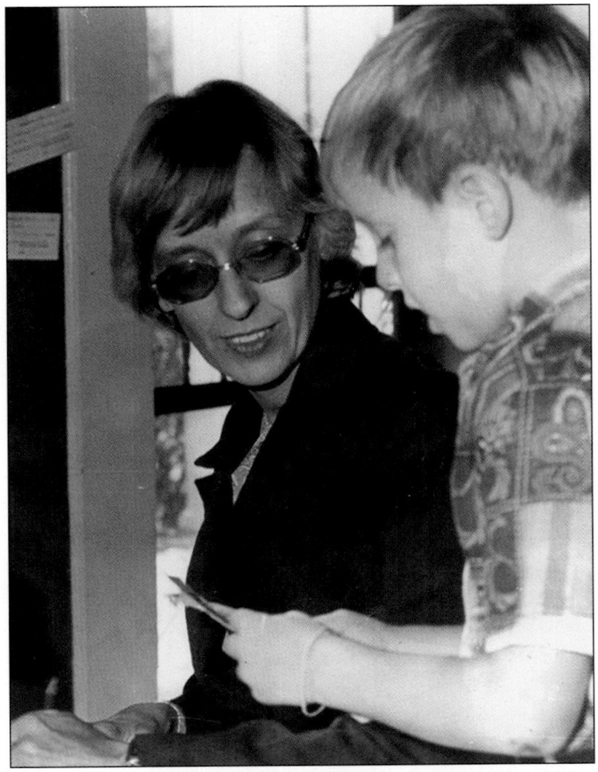

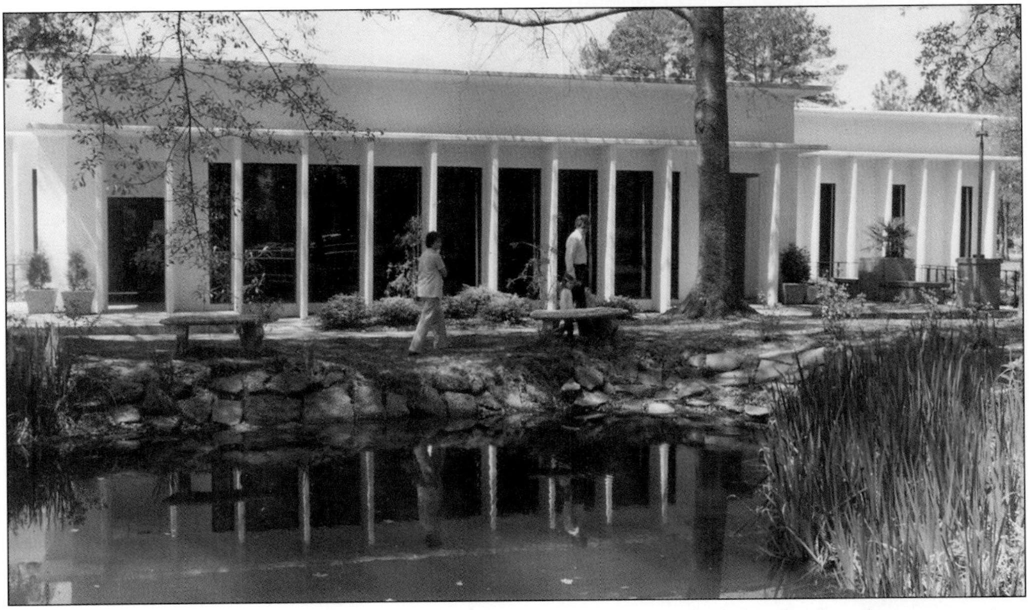

The Million Dollar Development Campaign in 1973 provided funds for the renovation of Tatum Court and the construction of a new business building. Other 1973 milestones included the first mid-year commencement in December, graduating 66, along with 306 graduates in May, and a new major in music therapy was offered. Thomas Business Building, above, became a reality in 1974 and was named for generous benefactors John D. and Ollie Thomas.

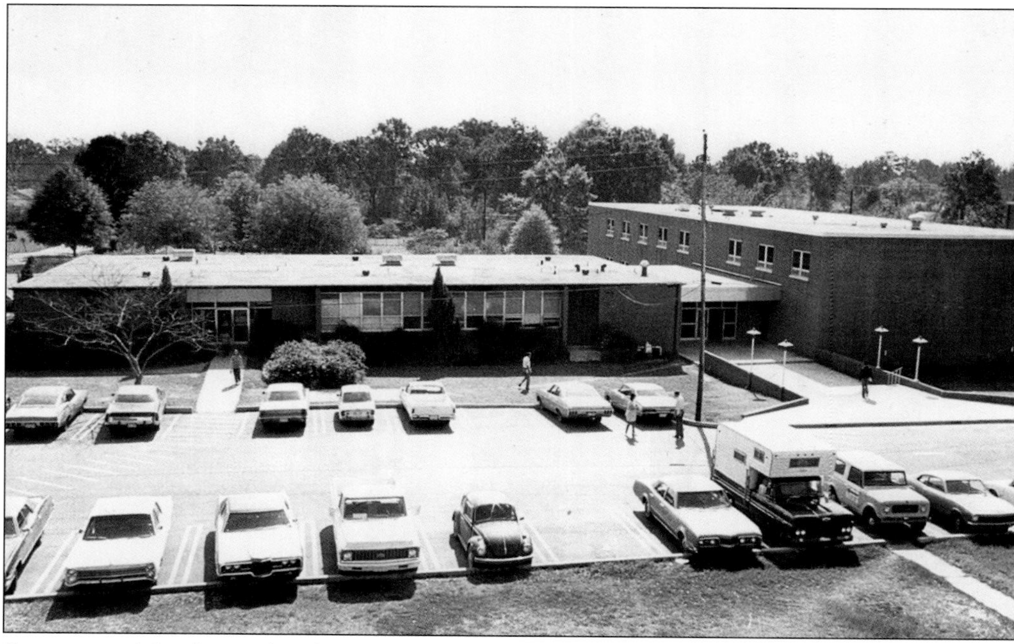

Constructed in the mid-1960s, Green Science Hall, named in honor of longtime trustee Benjamin Green, was more than doubled in space in 1973 to house not only the sciences, but also history and psychology. The son and grandson of Benjamin Green, Dr. Earl Green and Dr. John Green, have continued the tradition of service on the board of trustees.

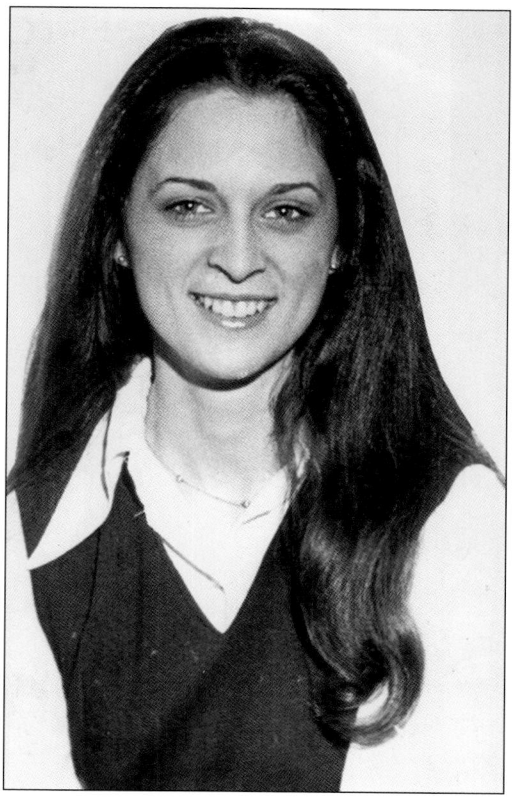

William Carey College in 1973 became the only Mississippi institution to offer a degree in music therapy. Helen Driskell was the first graduate of the program. She graduated at the top of her class with a 4.0 grade-point average and studied music therapy at the University of London as Carey's first Rotary Ambassadorial Scholar.

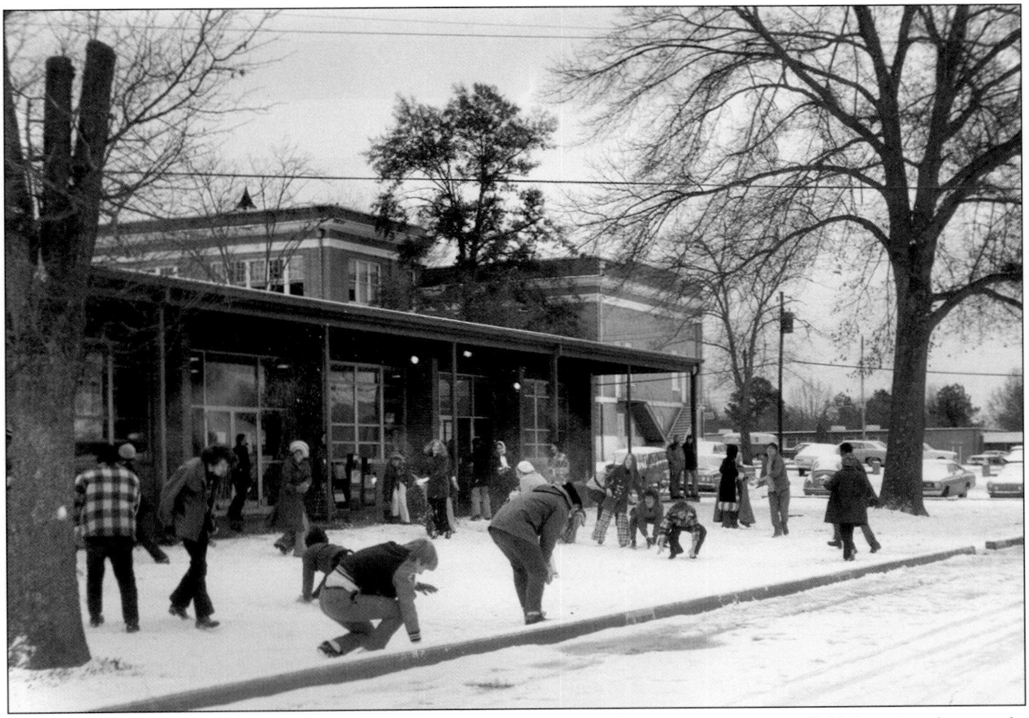

Students play in front of McMillan Student Center when a rare snowfall hit in the early 1970s. Tatum Court can be seen in the background.

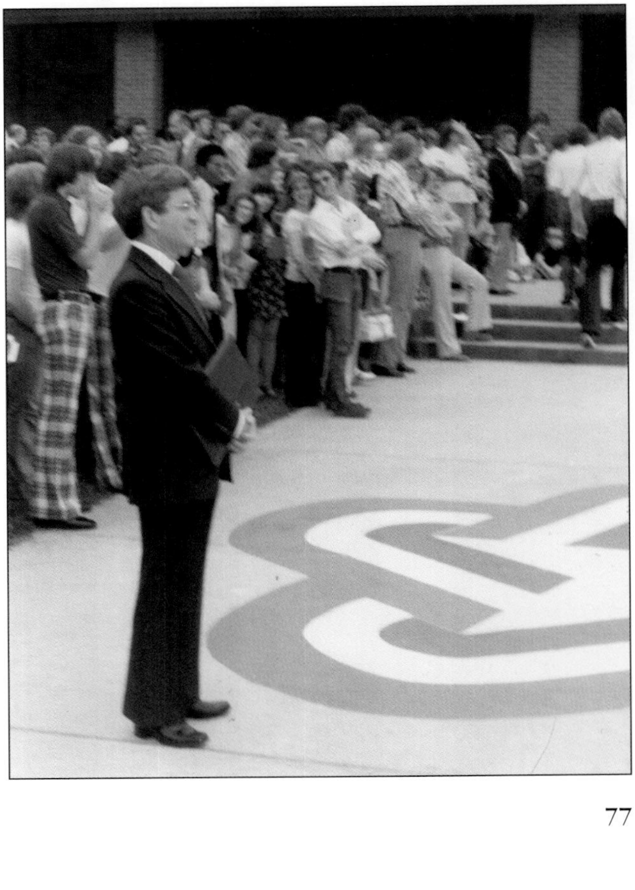

William Carey College was declared a bicentennial campus in 1976, and celebrations were held throughout the year. The symbol for the nation's celebration was painted on the porch of Wilkes Dining Hall, as can be seen in this 1976 photograph. The occasion was a concert by the Keesler Air Force Band of the Gulf Coast.

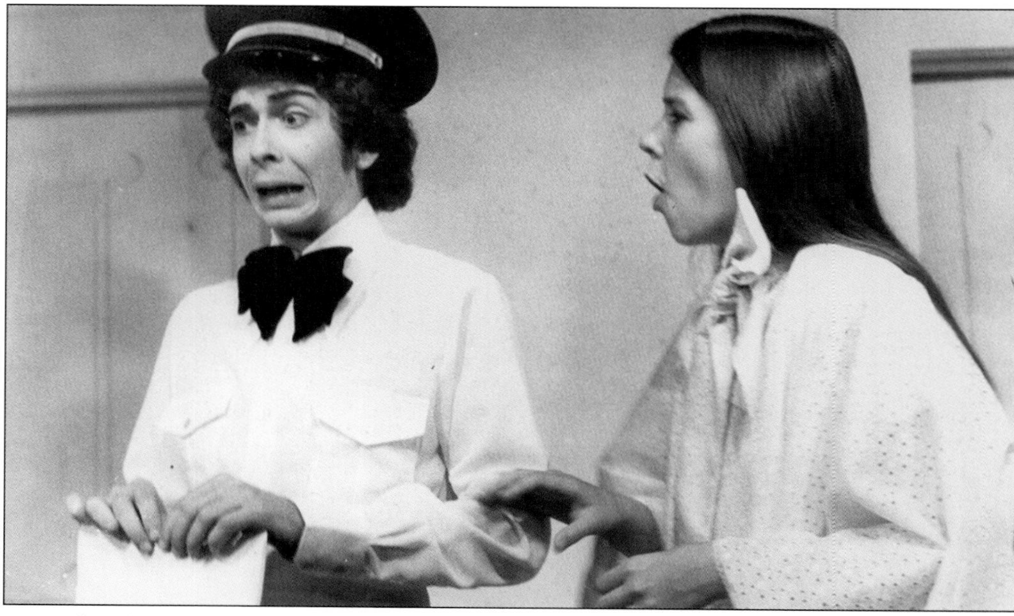

Out of a desire to give young performers a professional yet educationally sound opportunity to express their talents in a unique format and to provide public family entertainment, Carey Dinner Theatre was born. Following a 30-year tradition of excellence in entertainment, CDT has earned its title as Mississippi's unique dinner theater. Two students, Keith Thompson and Jay Rogers, were interested in writing and composing for musical theater. This desire resulted in *It's Make Believe,* a musical produced in 1975, the first season of what was then called Carey Summer Showcase. Jay Rogers and Jane Lindsey perform in this scene from *It's Make Believe.*

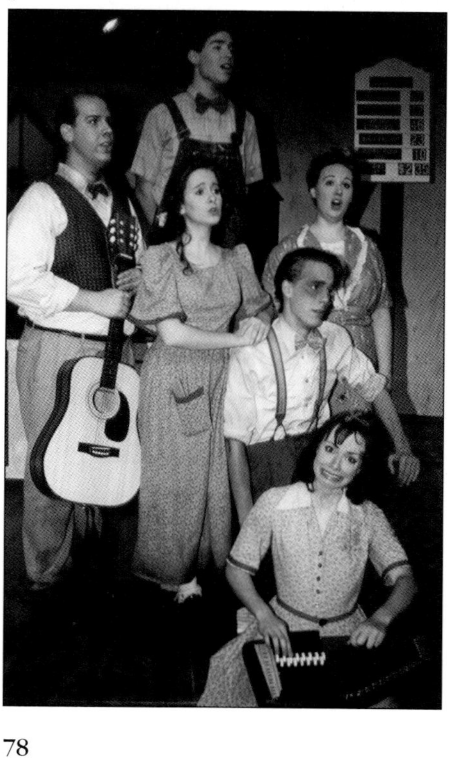

Carey Dinner Theatre has become the most popular ticket for summer entertainment in Hattiesburg. A paid company of performers and staff is selected each spring for two musicals. Not only do students perform, but they also serve dinner, thus creating personal contact with the audience. Over 50 schools, including Juilliard, Wake Forest, Duke, and Eastman School of Music, have been represented by members of the CDT company. Alumni of CDT can be found in professional theaters across the country. *Smoke on the Mountain* was a CDT production in 2005.

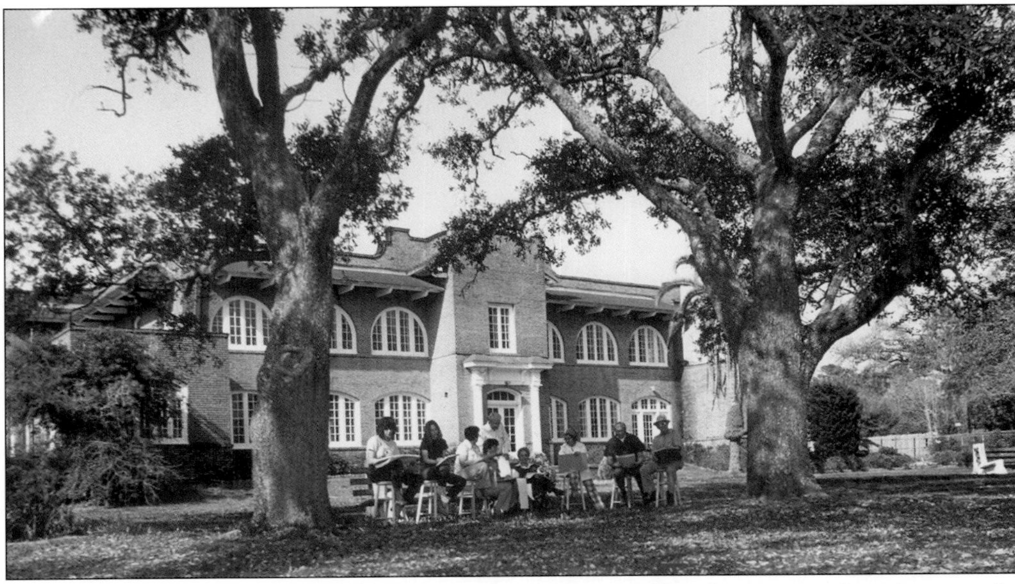

To have a permanent location for classes already being offered at various locations on the Mississippi Gulf Coast, in 1976 William Carey College purchased the former Gulf Coast Military Academy, 20 acres of beautiful beachfront property in Gulfport. The campus lies in the fastest-growing industrial and recreational area of Mississippi. Enrollment was 313 when Carey on the Coast opened.

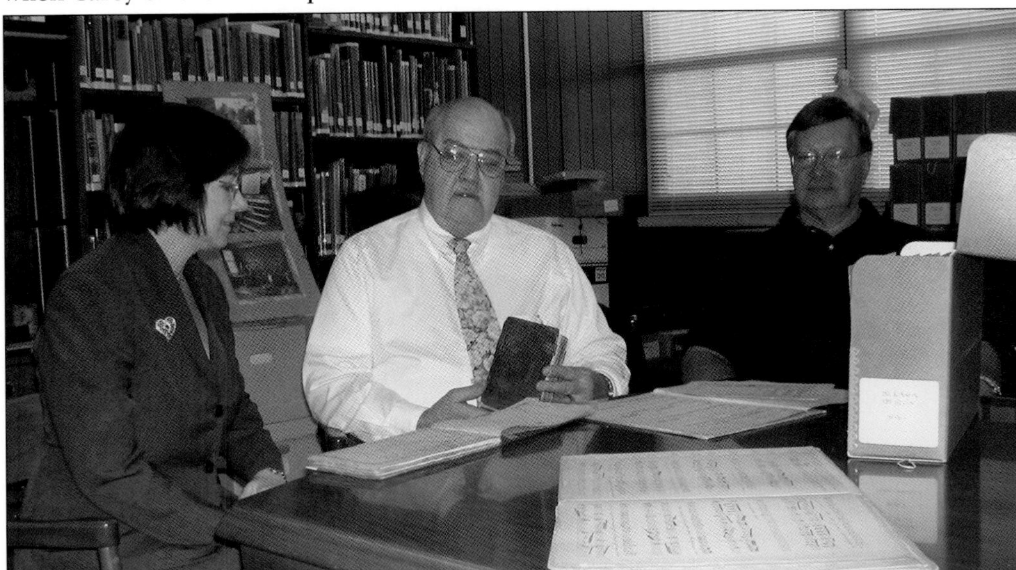

In 1974, the Winters School of Music received a prize collection of books, musical scores, and other memorabilia from Dr. and Mrs. Clarence Dickinson. A founding member of the American Guild of Organists and the Hymn Society of America, Dickinson was dean of the school of sacred music of Union Theological Seminary in New York. A beautifully carved mahogany piano, outstanding paintings, and items that belonged to Emily Dickinson, a cousin, are part of the collection. Cousins of the Dickinsons, Elizabeth Keithcart (left) and John Haydon (right), visit Dr. Gene Winters, alumnus and interim dean of the school of music.

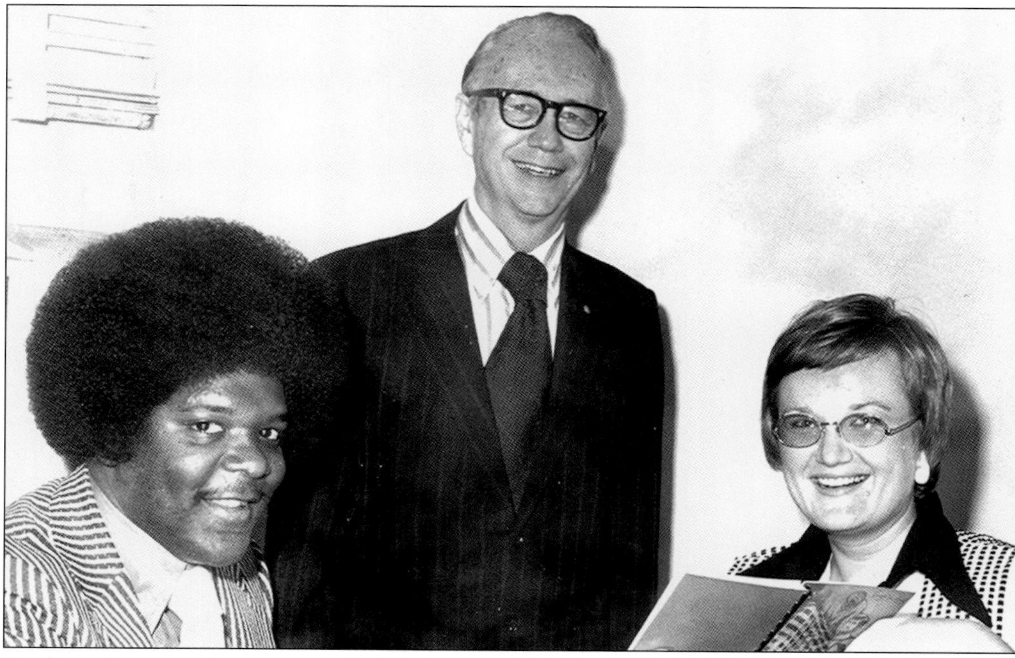

Student Support Services, a federally funded TRIO program, has offered, since 1975, assistance to first-generation college students, those who are eligible for financial aid at a level established by the US Department of Education, or to students with a documented disability. The program currently assists 135 eligible undergraduate students. Pictured in 1975 are, from left to right, staff member Eddie Holloway, academic vice president Joe Ernest, and director Dr. Rebecca Thompson.

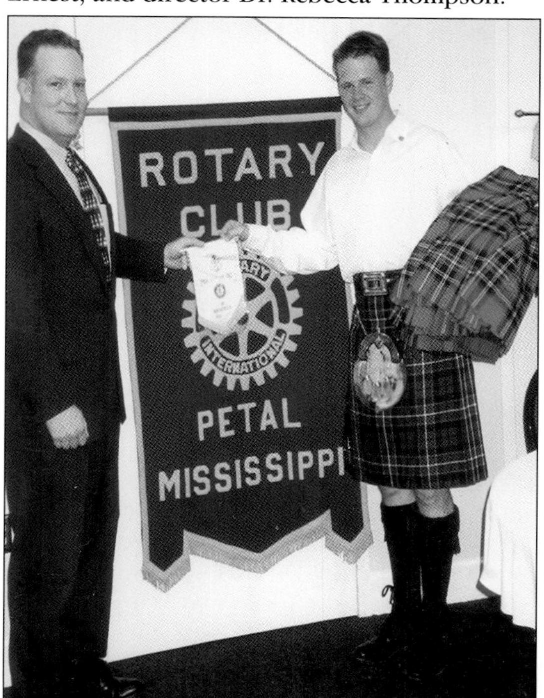


Since 1975, William Carey College has had more Rotary Ambassadorial Scholars than any other college in the state. Fifteen students have won scholarships that provide funding for one year of study anywhere in the world. In addition, three faculty members have been awarded Rotary Teaching Grants to teach abroad, and eight alumni have participated in Rotary Goodwill Study programs. Scholar James Mitchell, after his return from Scotland, gave a report of his experiences to the Petal, Mississippi, Rotary Club.

In 1976, Bobbye Wood (right) became Miss Carey and was the first Carey student to win the title of Miss Mississippi at the pageant in Vicksburg. Her talent, spirit, and obvious good looks led her to sweep the competition. Bobbye was treated with a royal reception by the student body and the city of Hattiesburg when she returned to Hattiesburg. The first alternate in the Miss Carey Pageant, Dorothy Roberts (left), was crowned Miss Carey.

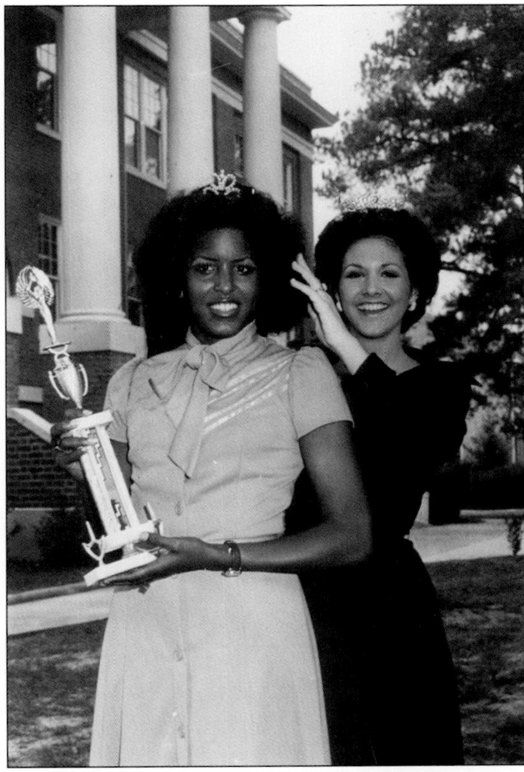

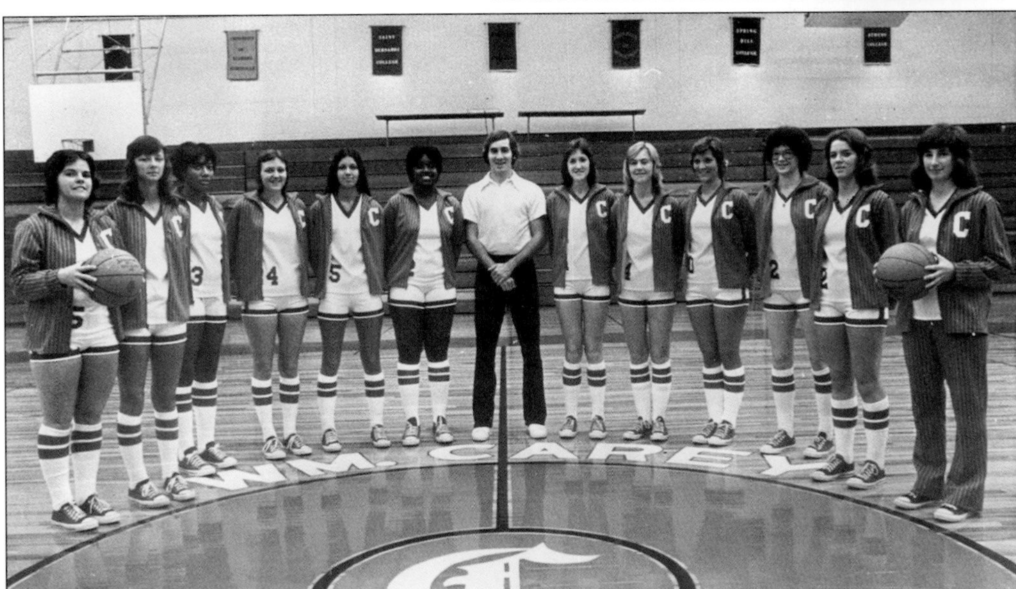


Basketball was the first intercollegiate sport for women. The program began in 1975, and Kathy Swilley of Lumberton High School was the first female student to receive an athletic scholarship. Alumnus Bobby Halford, who coached women's basketball for nine seasons, is pictured in this photograph with the original team. The centennial team of Lady Crusaders, under coach Tracy English, brought honor to the college by earning a berth in the NAIA national championship.

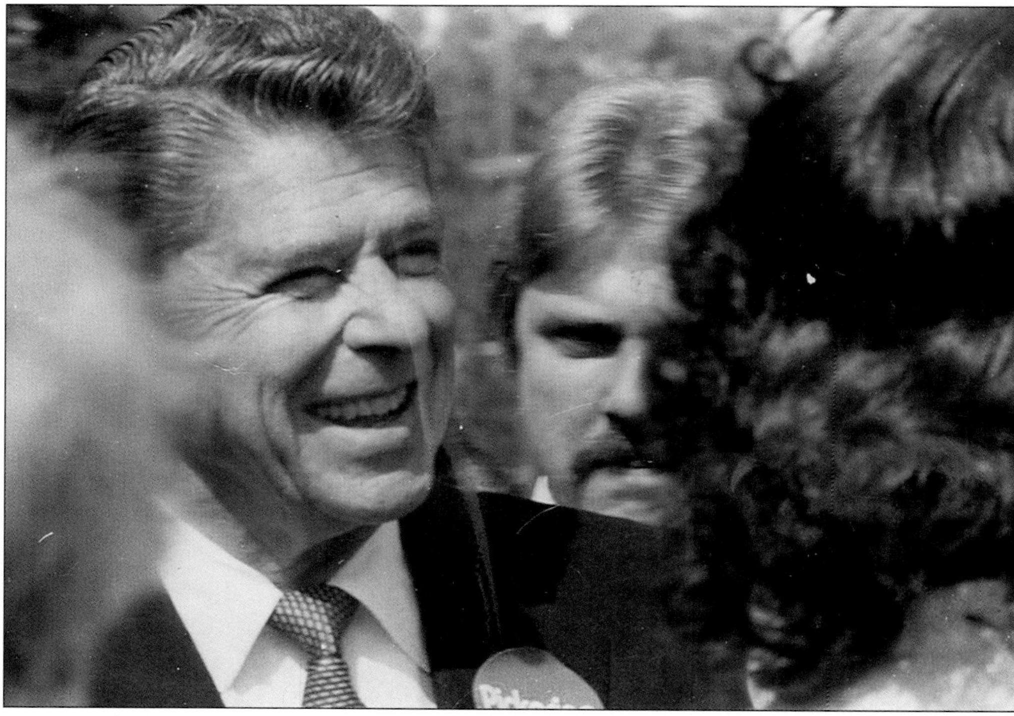

A sense of excitement filled the city when Ronald Reagan came to the Hattiesburg campus in 1979. The future president was the guest speaker at a fund-raiser luncheon for Charles Pickering, who was running for attorney general.

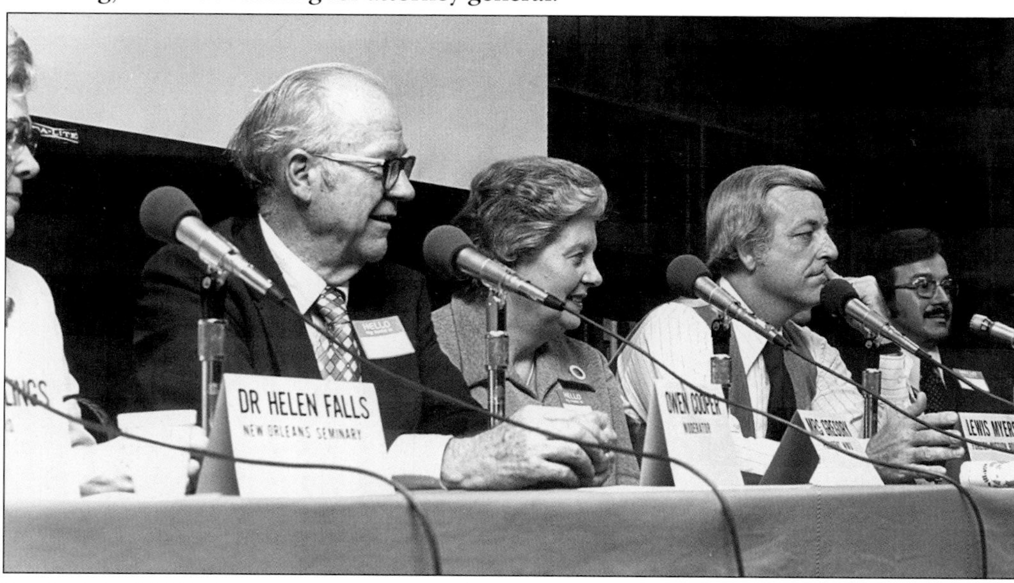


In 1978, Bold Mission Day at Carey brought to the campus many leaders of the Southern Baptist Convention (SBC) to dialogue with the task of making Bold Missions work, the thrust of the SBC in the 1970s. Moderated by Mississippi layman and SBC president Owen Cooper, the program challenged hundreds of South Mississippians to consider service as "volunteer missionaries" for one or two years. From left to right are Helen Falls, Owen Cooper, Christine Gregory, Lewis Myers, and alumnus John McNair.

# *Four*

# William Carey College 1981–2006

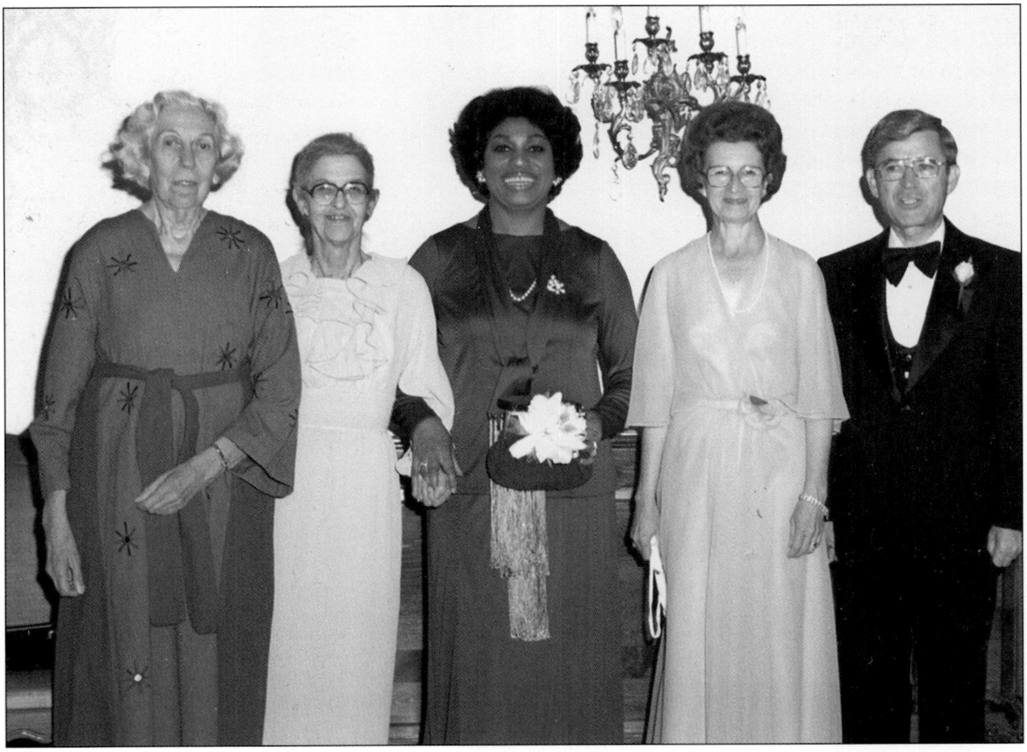

William Carey College celebrated its 75th anniversary in 1981. A convocation paid tribute to Mississippi Woman's College and honorary doctoral degrees were awarded to three leading Mississippi women in the arts. Attending the Hattiesburg Country Club reception are, from left to right, Pulitzer Prize–winning author Eudora Welty, wildflower and portrait artist Lucile Parker, internationally acclaimed opera star Leontyne Price, Naomi Noonkester, and President Noonkester.

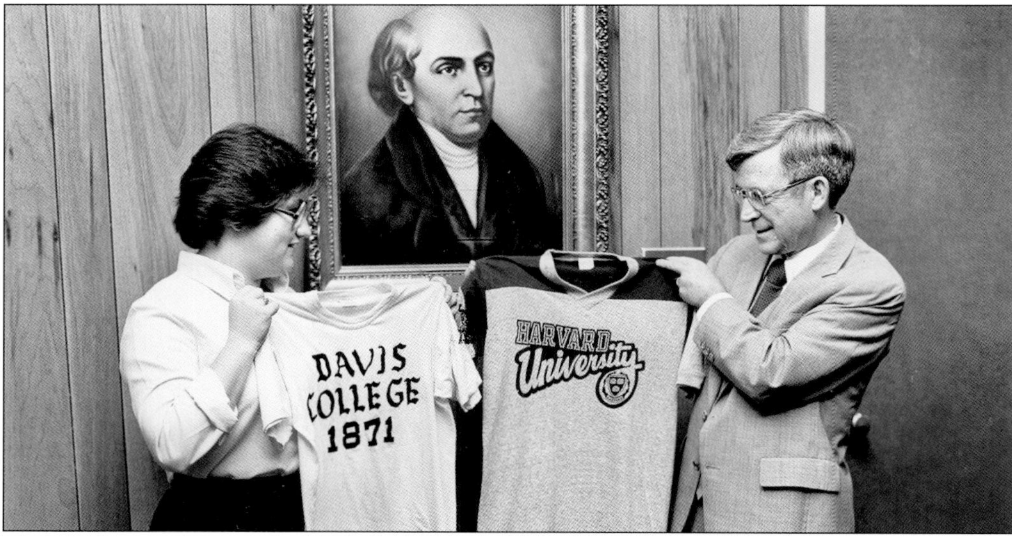


In President Noonkester's 1981 annual report, Carey was cited as the second largest private college in Mississippi, the leader of all schools in the number of graduates enrolled at New Orleans Baptist Theological Seminary, the leader of all colleges in Mississippi in the percentage of students admitted to medical or dental school, the winner of Chi Beta Phi's Grand Chapter Award seven of the last nine years, and the prototype college chosen by Harvard University for a case study examining alternative educational programs for small colleges, thus creating a fictitious model known as Davis College. Student Government president Karla Hatchett and President Noonkester show off a shirt from the so-called Davis College.

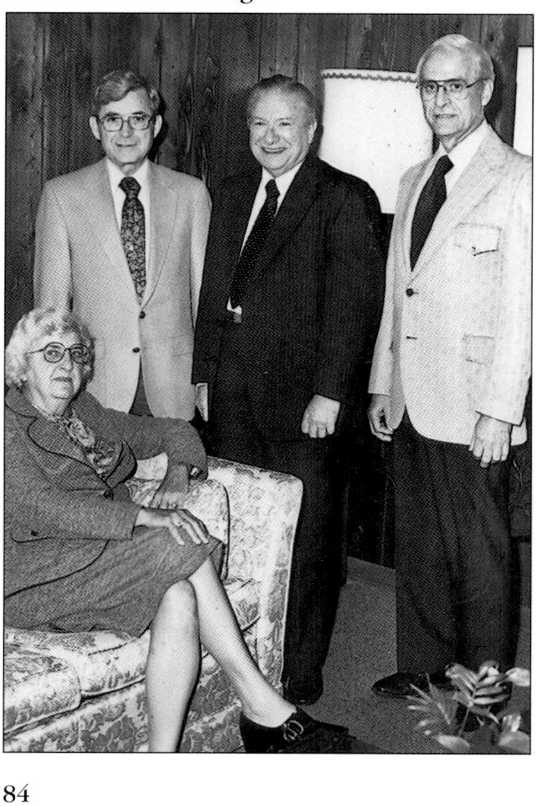

Sarah Gillespie began donating artwork to the college in 1982, giving what is considered to be the most complete collection of works by Mississippi artists from the 1920s to the present. The holdings include paintings by Marie Hull, Walter Anderson, Wyatt Waters, and many other artists. Established in 1982, the Sarah Gillespie Art Gallery was relocated from Fairchild Administration Building to Parker Hall in 1999. Pictured from left to right are Sarah Gillespie, President Noonkester, trustee chairman Bruce Aultman, and Charles Ambrose, well-known Mississippi artist and chairman of the art department at Carey on the Coast from 1982 to 1988.

Three renovated buildings at Carey on the Coast campus were officially dedicated in 1981 and named for prominent benefactors of the college—the administration building for the W.R. Fairchild family, the Learning Resource Center for the W.P. McMullan family, and the classroom building for the Richard Parker family. In 1986, 96 apartment units were built at the Coast campus, changing the campus from primarily an evening school to a residential campus offering a day program.

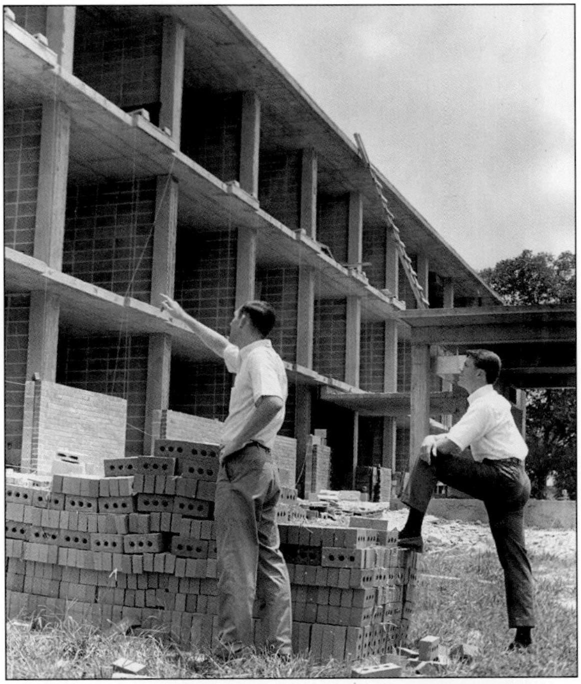

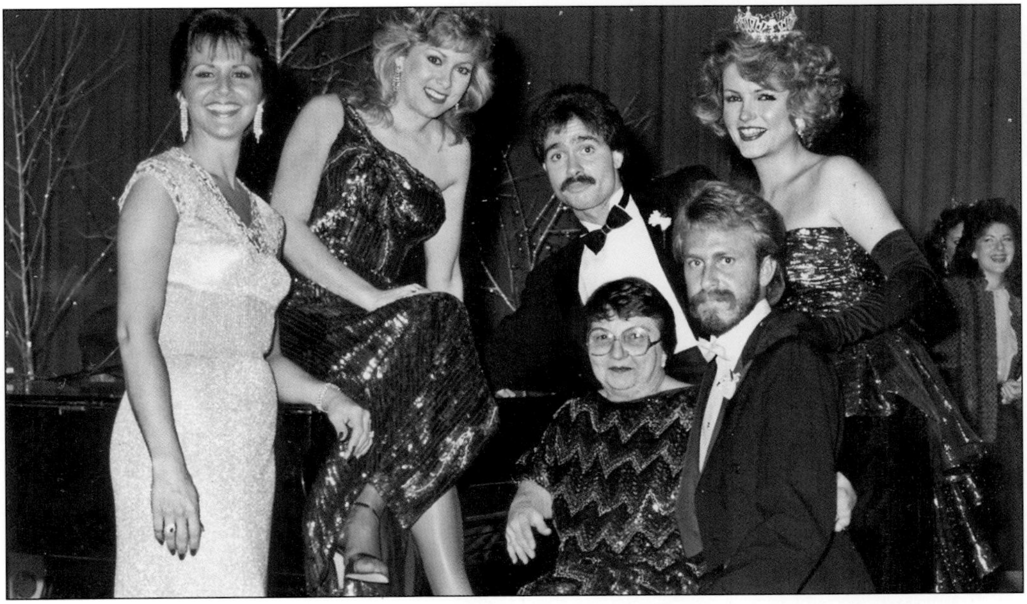

William Carey College claimed back-to-back Miss Mississippis in the early 1980s. Carey student Dianne Evans became Miss Mississippi in 1982 and won second alternate to Miss America in the national pageant. Wanda Geddie, Miss Mississippi 1983, placed as third alternate to Miss America. Carey's three Miss Mississippis, along with alumni Philip Fortenberry and Keith Thompson, returned to the campus to present a musical concert in 1984. The Miss Carey pageant was begun in 1969 by Rita Goodbread, dean of women, and continued by Virginia Scott, who served as its popular director from 1972 to 1985. Shown in this photograph are, from left to right, Bobbye Wood, Dianne Evans, Keith Thompson, Virginia Scott, Philip Fortenberry, and Wanda Geddie.

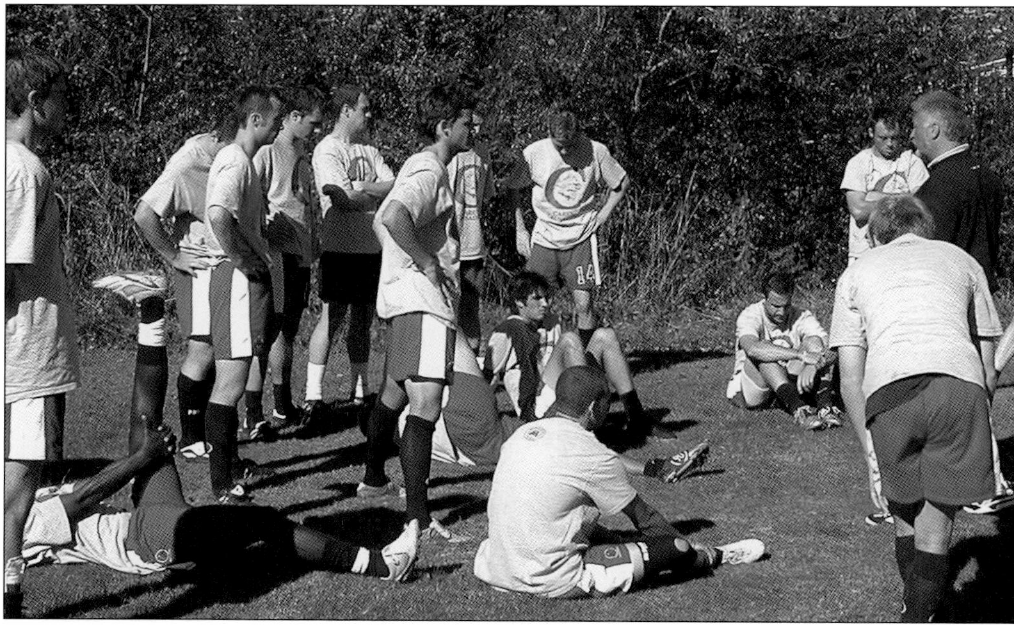

The men's soccer program began at Carey on the Coast in 1985 and has never had a losing season. Women's soccer was added in the late 1980s. Both the men's and women's programs have been rated consistently in the top 25 NAIA rankings. Numerous players have been selected as All-Americans. The program moved to the Hattiesburg campus in 2003.

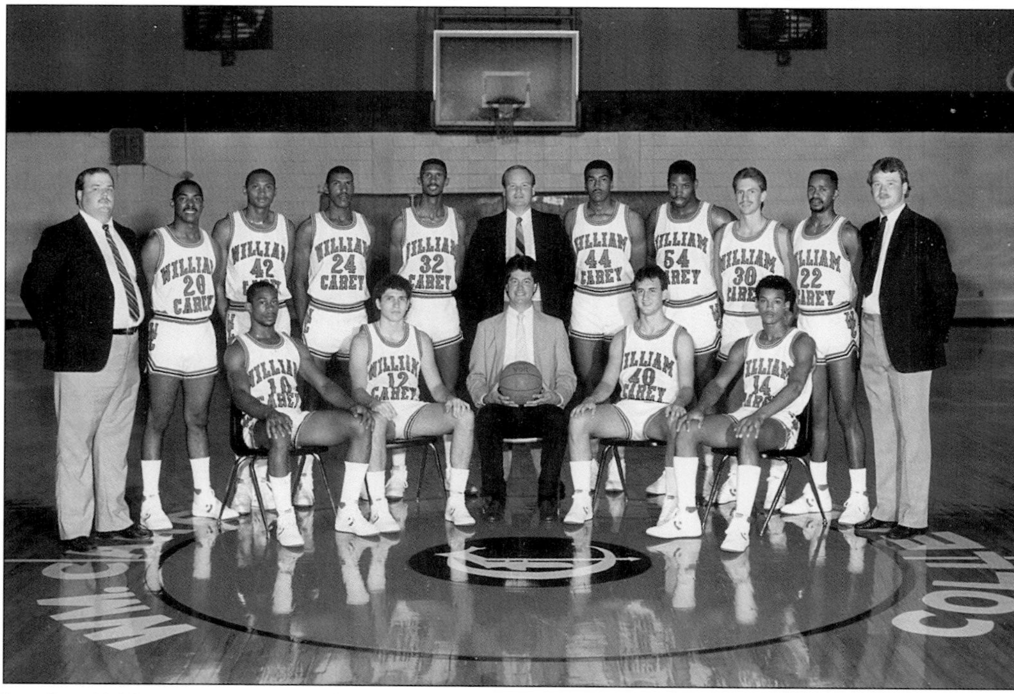

In the 1980s, six Carey basketball teams made it to the national tournament held in Kemper Arena in Kansas City. Teams have won six Gulf Coast Athletic Conference titles, six NAIA District 30 championships, and have produced eight NAIA All-Americans. Coach Steve Knight is seen holding the basketball in the center of this 1987 team photograph.

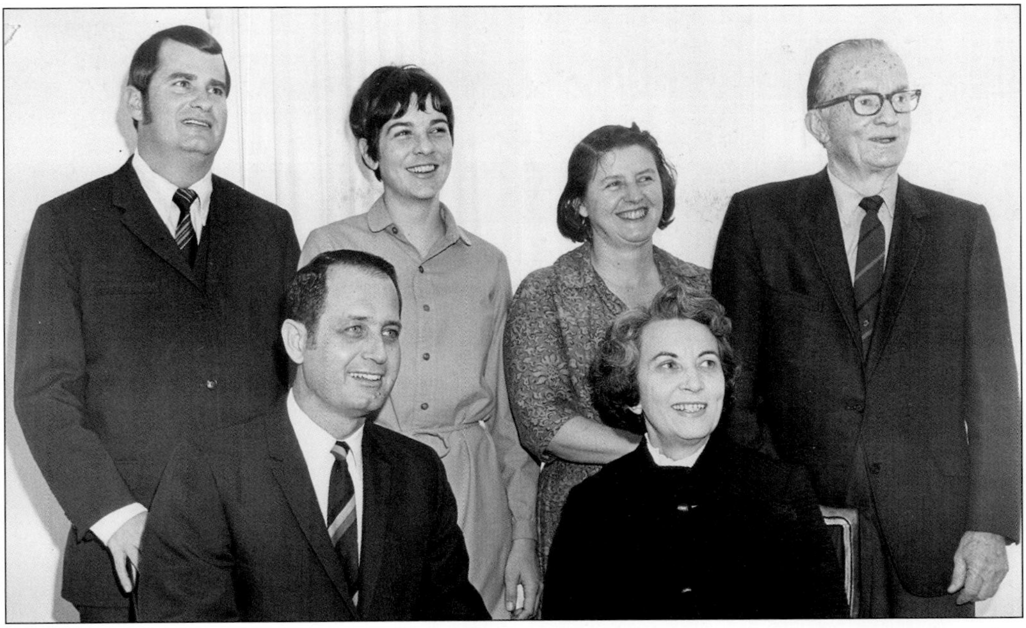

Dr. Hugh Dickens served Carey as administrative vice president, vice president for development, and secretary to the board of trustees from 1971 to 1990. He was the guiding force in the development of the graduate education program. Under his leadership, 1,795 teachers and administrators received advanced degrees. The faculty of the education department is shown in this early 1970s photograph. From left to right are (first row) Dickens and Elma McWilliams; (second row) Ron Paddack, Carol Doumas, Frances Smith, and Roy Bigelow.

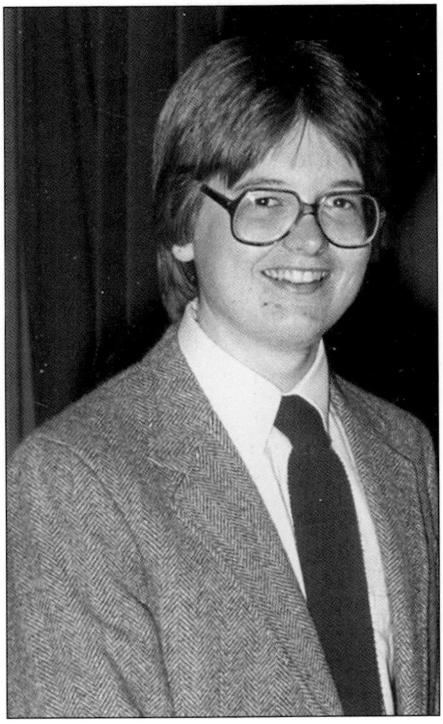

Dr. Rose West served as chairman of the chemistry department from 1968 until 2003. Under her tutelage, Carey students ranked among the highest in acceptance to graduate schools throughout the United States. In 1989, Daniel Edney (pictured) graduated first in his class at the University of Mississippi Medical Center. He is a physician in Vicksburg and broadcasts a syndicated radio show titled *OnCall*. In 2005, he was part of a disaster relief team that travelled to Indonesia to provide medical assistance.

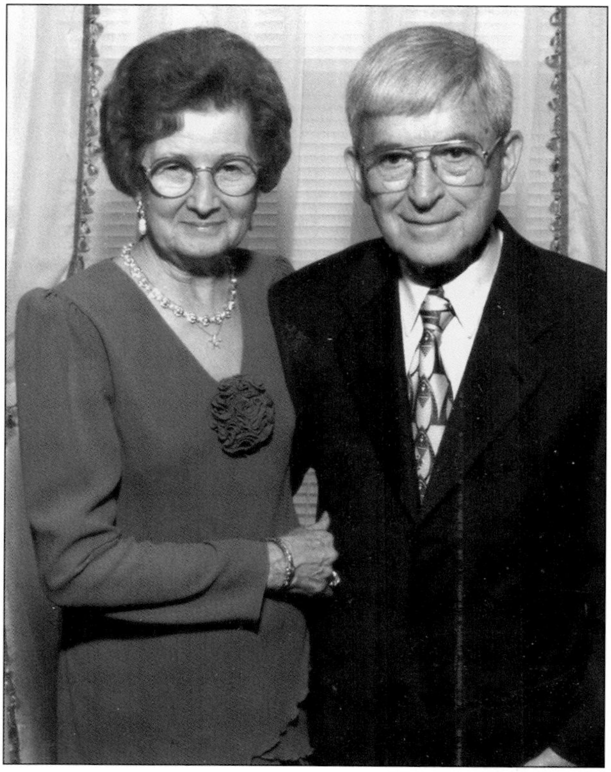

President Noonkester retired in 1989 after serving as president for 33 years. Among other accomplishments, his long tenure witnessed the construction of 19 new buildings, the reaccreditation of the college, the admission of African American students, and the addition of two regional campuses.

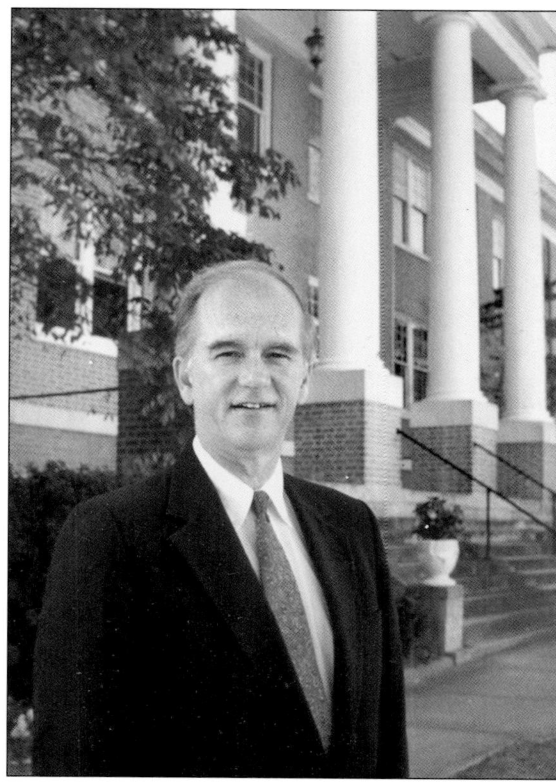

Dr. James Wyatt Edwards was inaugurated as the seventh president of William Carey College in 1990. He immediately began intense student recruitment efforts, a work-service program for students and faculty, a Wall of Honor to recognize major donors, a restructured college debt, and a new academic calendar based on the trimester system.

In 1990, the Lucile Parker Gallery opened on the Hattiesburg campus, named in honor of former professor and art department chair Lucile Parker, who was known for her wildflower paintings and portraits. The gallery exhibits works of well-known artists, including an annual showing of works of Parker. In this photograph, she is fourth on the right in the front row, surrounded by her students.

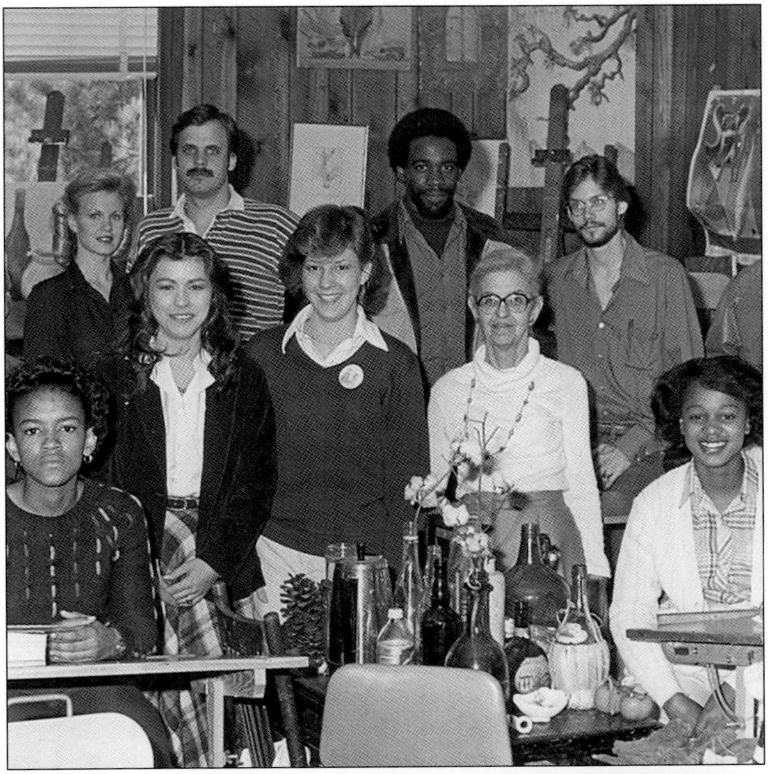

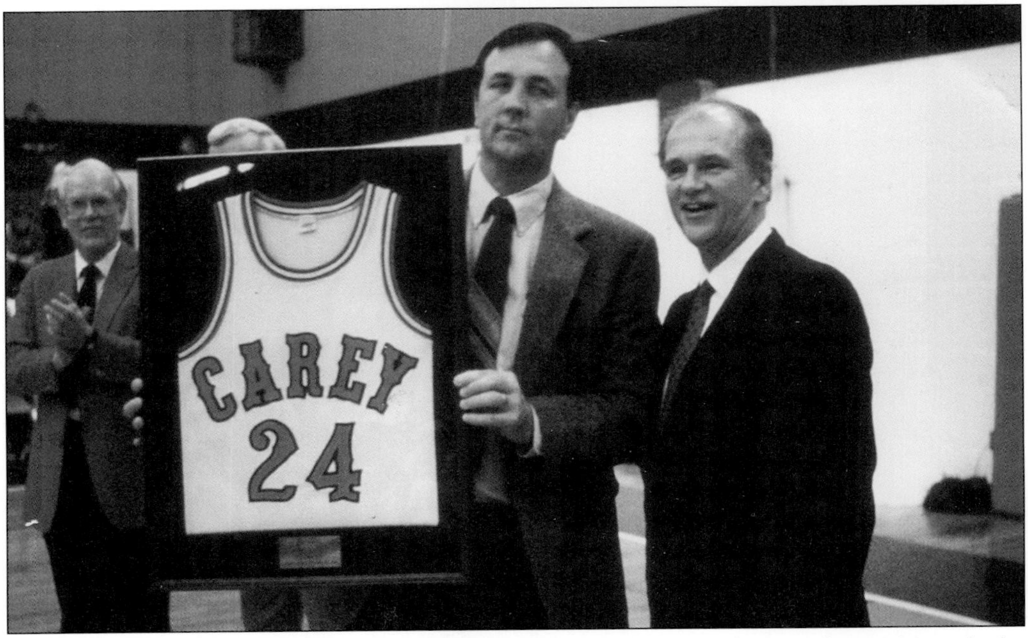


All-American basketball player Mike Necaise, class of 1971, was honored in 1990 with the retiring of his jersey, No. 24. He was the Crusaders' all-time leading scorer with 2,064 career points, the first Carey basketball player named to the NAIA All-American team, and the first player drafted by the NBA. Dexter Pugh scored 2,146 career points in 1998, ending Necaise's long-standing career record.

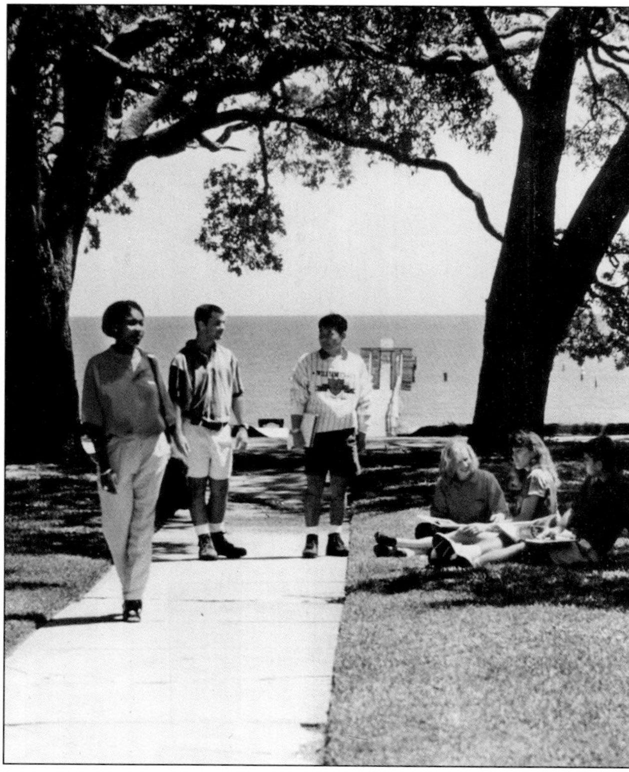

Under the leadership of alumnus Dr. Bill Payne, the Coast campus grew substantially in the 1990s. Full occupancy of the apartment units occurred in 1995, the enrollment swelled to an all-time high of 692, the college staff numbered 45, and the annual budget reached $2.5 million.

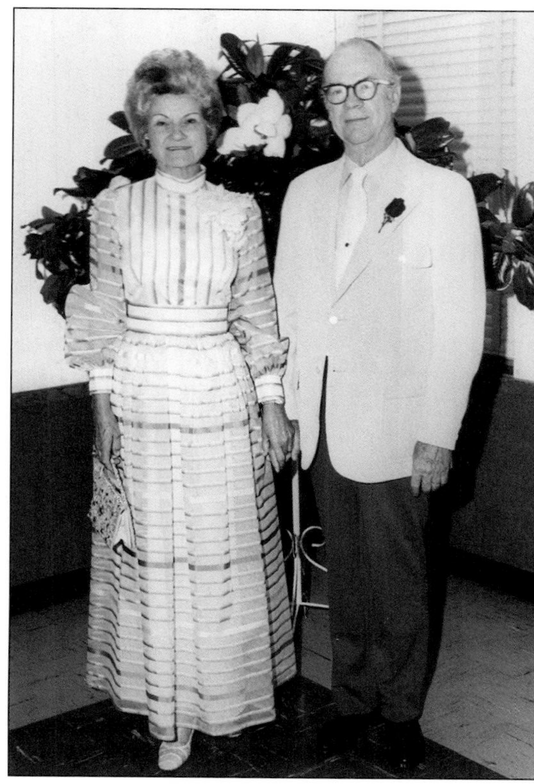

In 1991, the Cooper School of Missions and Biblical Studies was established and named for Owen and Elizabeth Cooper, humanitarians, business leaders, and SBC lay leaders. Elizabeth served on the Carey board of trustees.

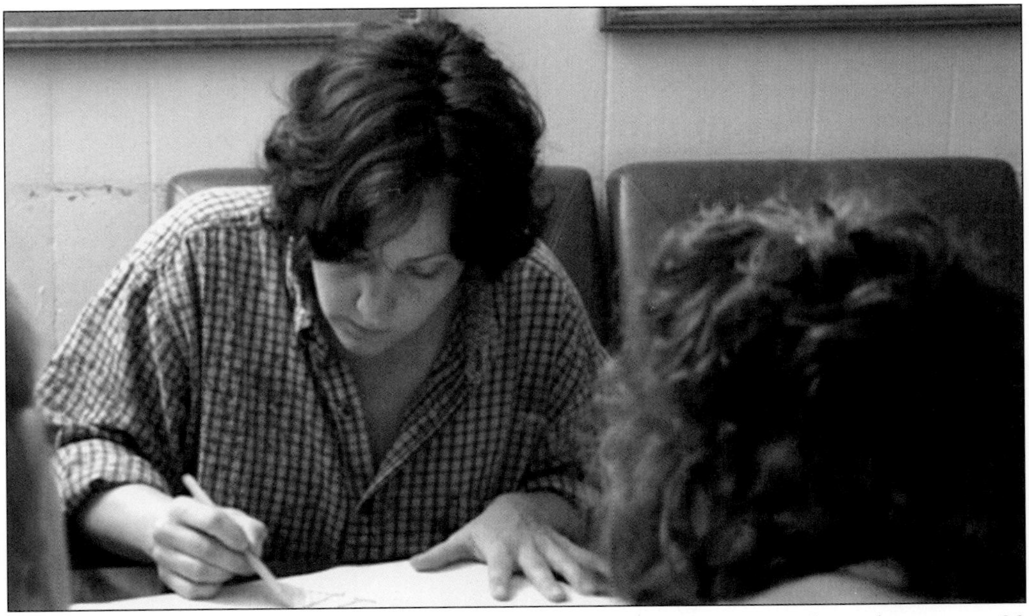

Under the direction of alumna Shannon Robert, theater design students have won 20 regional awards and have brought home three national first-place awards from the Kennedy Center American College Theater Festival. In 2004, Robert wrote the docudrama *In His Shoes,* a play about William Carey's life. The drama was performed for the 50th-anniversary celebration of the renaming of the college.

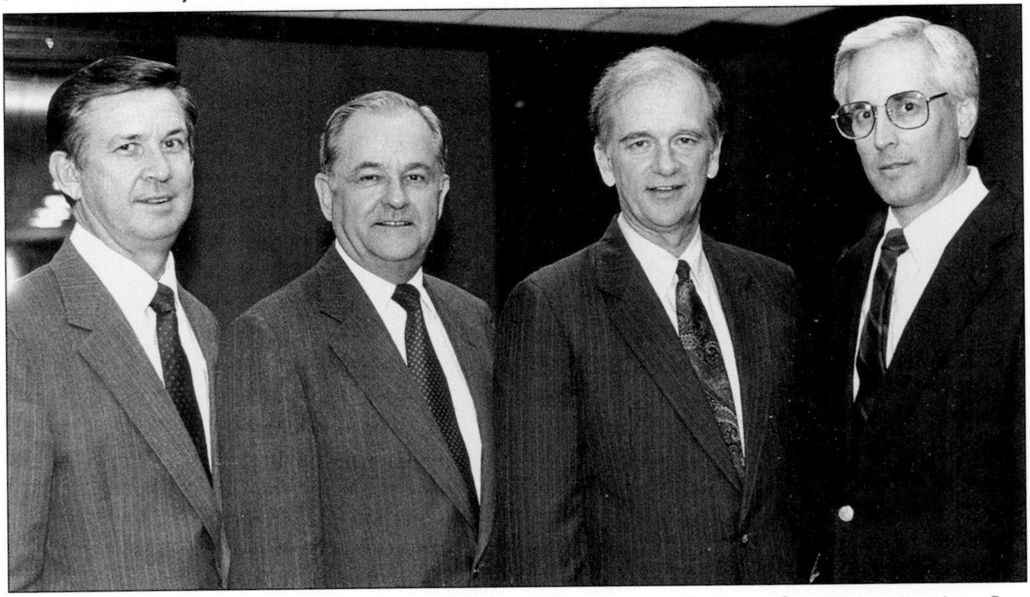

Named in honor of Laurel businessman and former professor of communication Joe Roberts, the Small Business Leadership Award recognizes the contributions of small businesses to the economic, social, and cultural life of the community. A committee chooses one Hattiesburg area small business leader as the recipient each year. Jack Simmons of Simmons Furniture Company was the first recipient in 1990. This photograph, from left to right, shows Judge Charles Pickering; speaker Harmon Born, president of Beaudry Ford Company, Atlanta; President Edwards; and Jack Simmons.

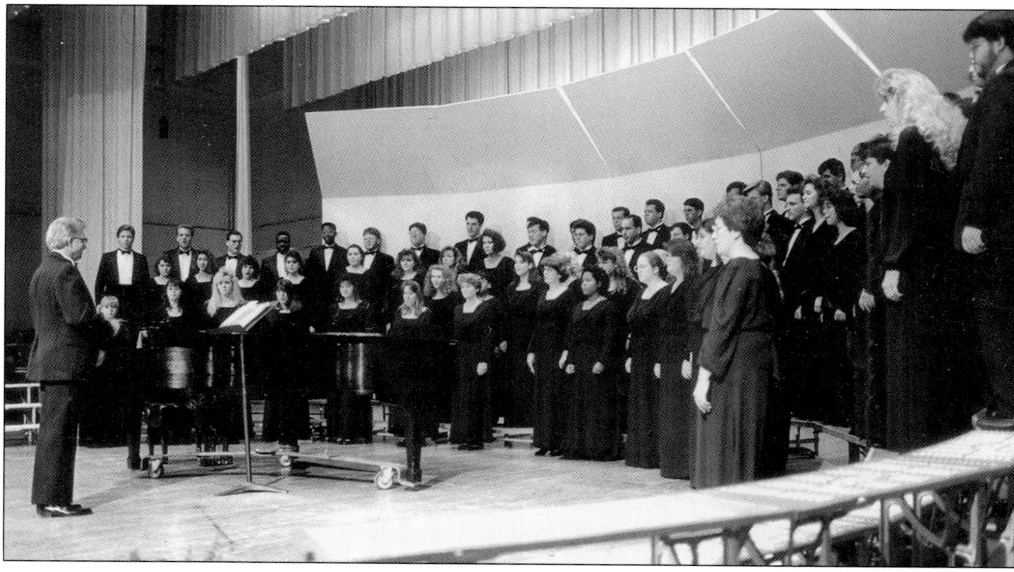

The chorale in the 1990s gave concerts, sang in churches, and traveled to England, visiting the area where William Carey lived until his move to India. Dr. Milfred Valentine directs the chorale in this 1993 photograph.

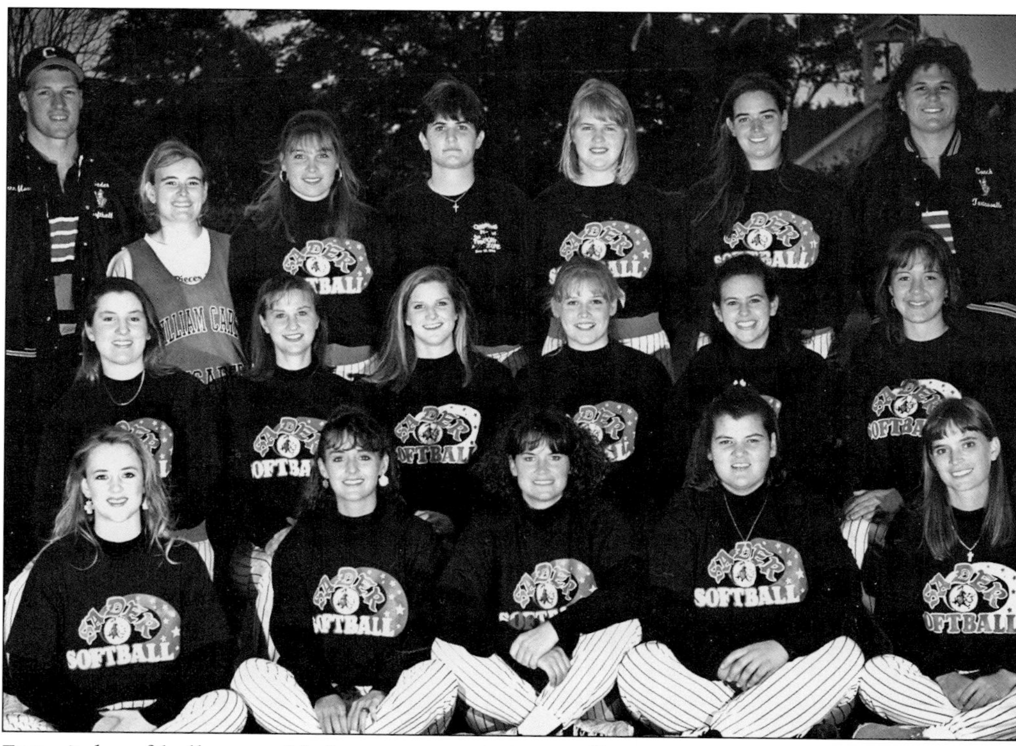


Fast-pitch softball was added as a women's intercollegiate sport in 1995. A new softball complex is under construction in 2006. Wendy Hogue, pictured on the front row at far right, played on the first team and in 2004 became coach of women's softball.

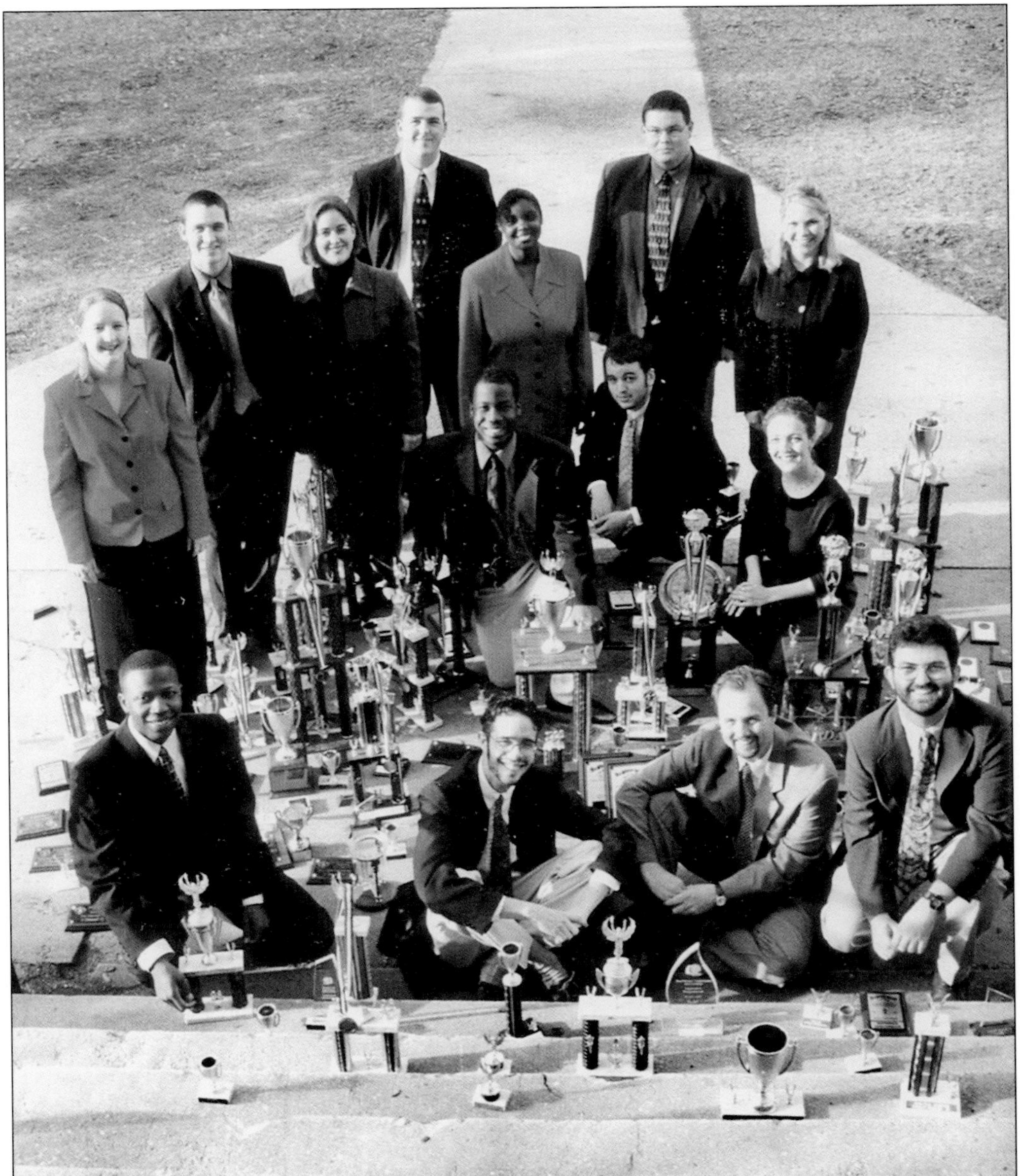

The forensics program met with success in the 1960s and early 1970s but was dropped due to the high costs of travel. Reinstated in 1994, it has been a major contender in national tournaments, consistently ranking among the top schools in the nation. Debate teams have won a championship and a second place in the national tournament. Team members in 1999 show the many trophies captured in tournaments. Since 1995, the speech and debate team has ranked in the top 10 every year, according to Pi Kappa Delta National Honor Society.

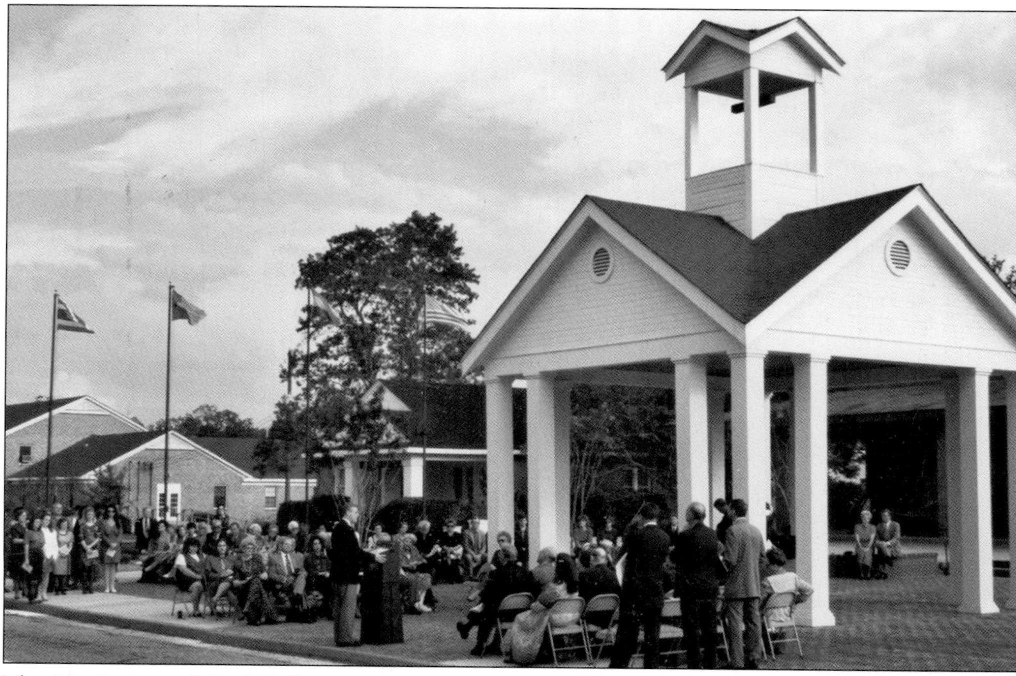

The Marjorie and Earl Kelly Missions Plaza and the Estelle Willis Tower were dedicated in 1994 to honor foreign missionaries. The president of the International Mission Board, Dr. Jerry Rankin, was the keynote speaker. At the center of the missions plaza is a sculpture titled *Genesis*, by Dr. Arthur Williams. Bricks in the plaza honor faculty, staff, and student missionaries. Pictured below are art faculty Dr. Arthur Williams (left) and Ted Rose.

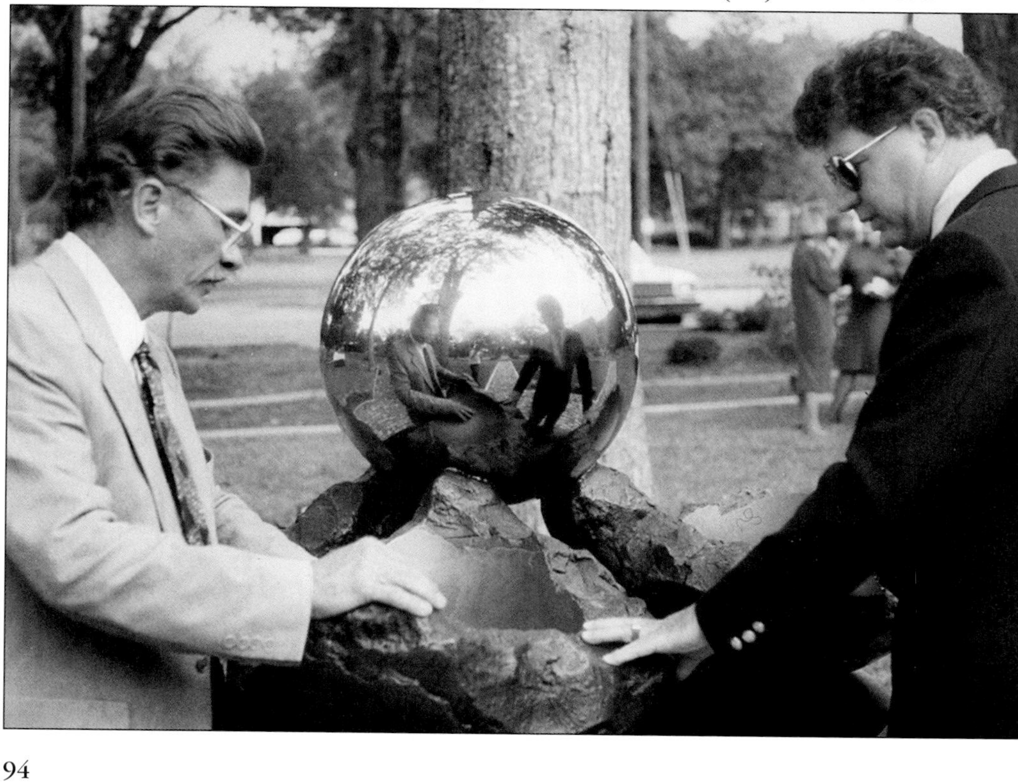

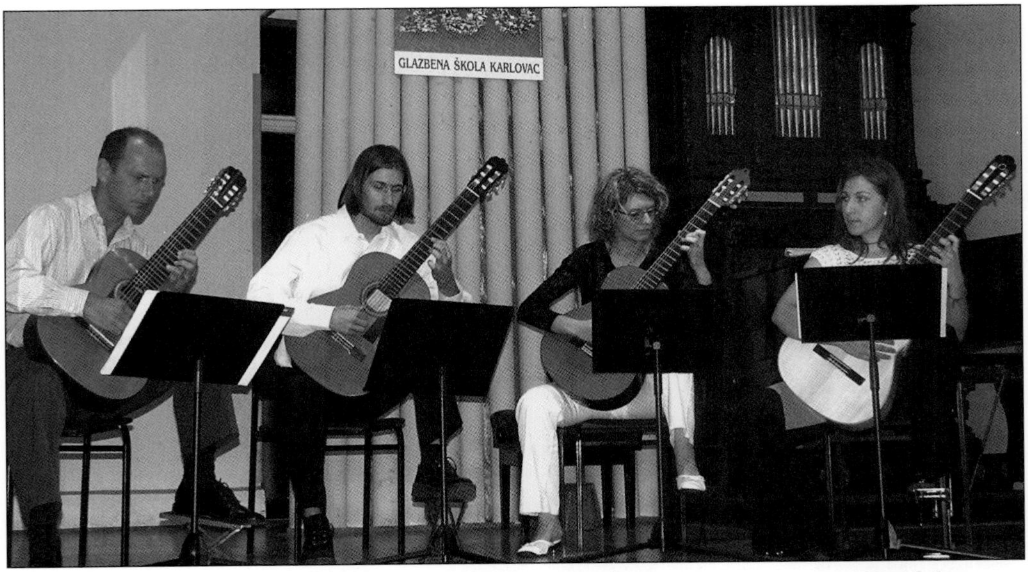


The guitar program, under the direction of Dr. Miroslav Loncar, attracts some of the most talented American and international students. The program focuses on both traditional and modern performance techniques. William Carey guitar students have been repeat winners at local and regional competitions. A concert series brings many internationally known guitarists to the campus for master classes and performances.

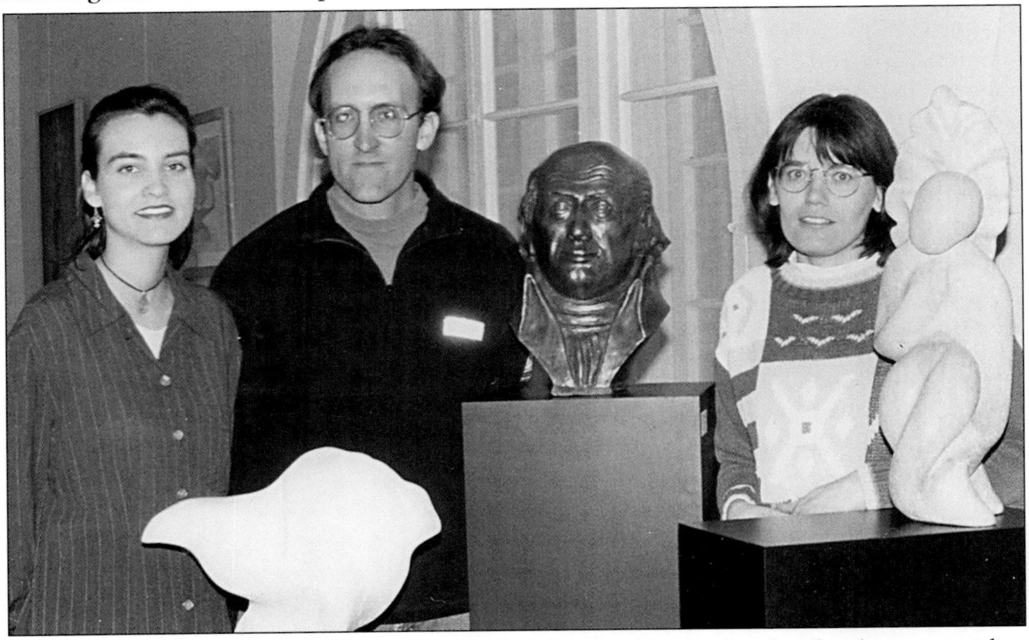

The art program is fast becoming the premier of its kind in the South. The department has a waiting list of students who want to be in the "select 60" chosen to study in the program. The Carey on the Coast students and faculty consistently have been winners in state, regional, and national competitions in sculpture, painting, and graphic design. In 2005, art students had the highest acceptance rate of any college or university in Mississippi that submitted entries into the Mississippi Gulf Coast Advertising Competition. Art students pictured here from left to right are Geinene Haynes, Don Smith, and Sheila Robnett.

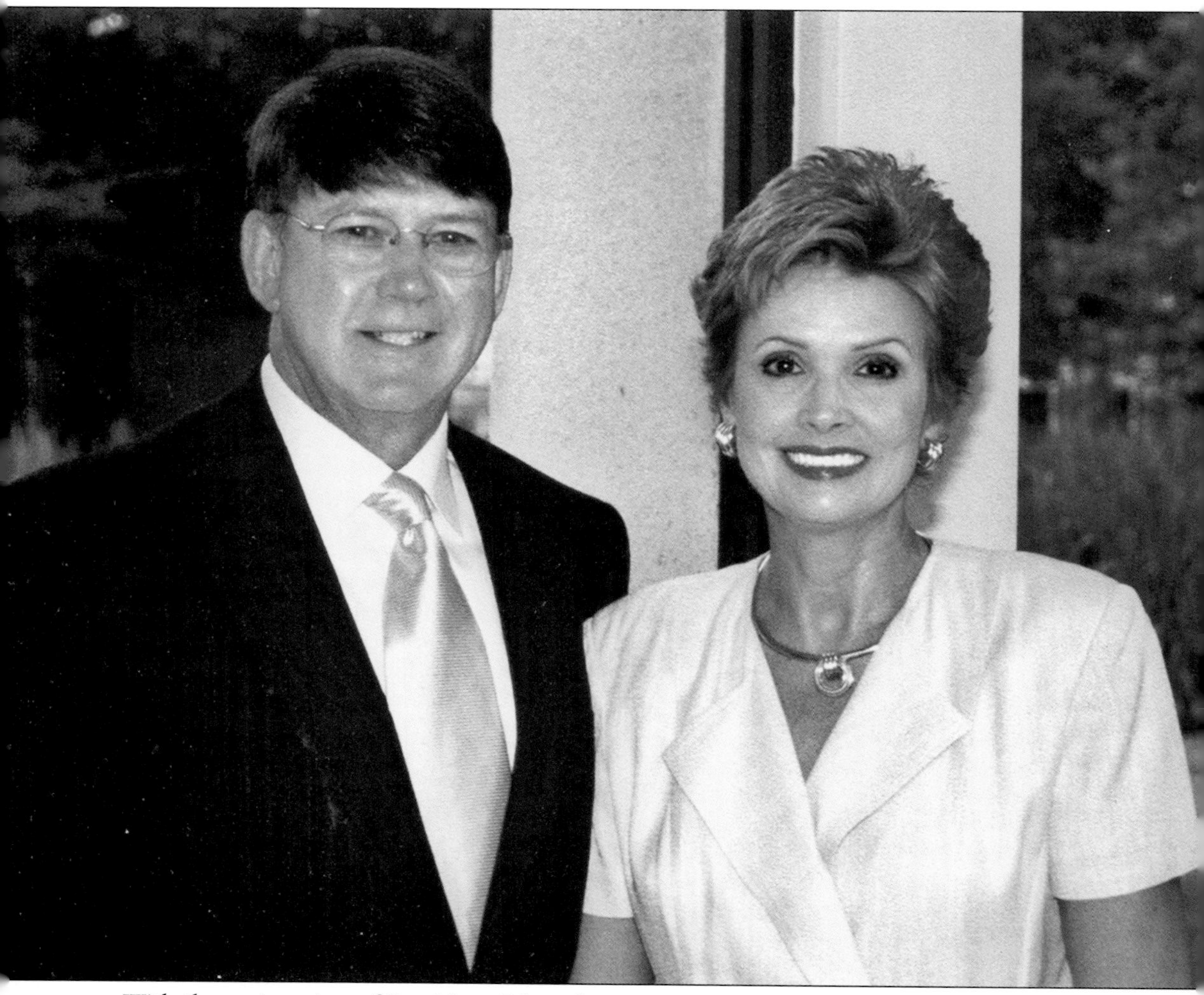

With the resignation of President Edwards in 1997, Dr. Larry Wells Kennedy, vice president for church relations and dean of the Cooper School of Missions and Biblical Studies, became interim president and in 1998 was elected the eighth president. Under his leadership, major renovations of physical facilities at all three campuses occurred, new buildings were constructed, and accreditation was reaffirmed by Southern Association of Colleges and Schools. Pictured with Dr. Kennedy is his wife, Sarah.

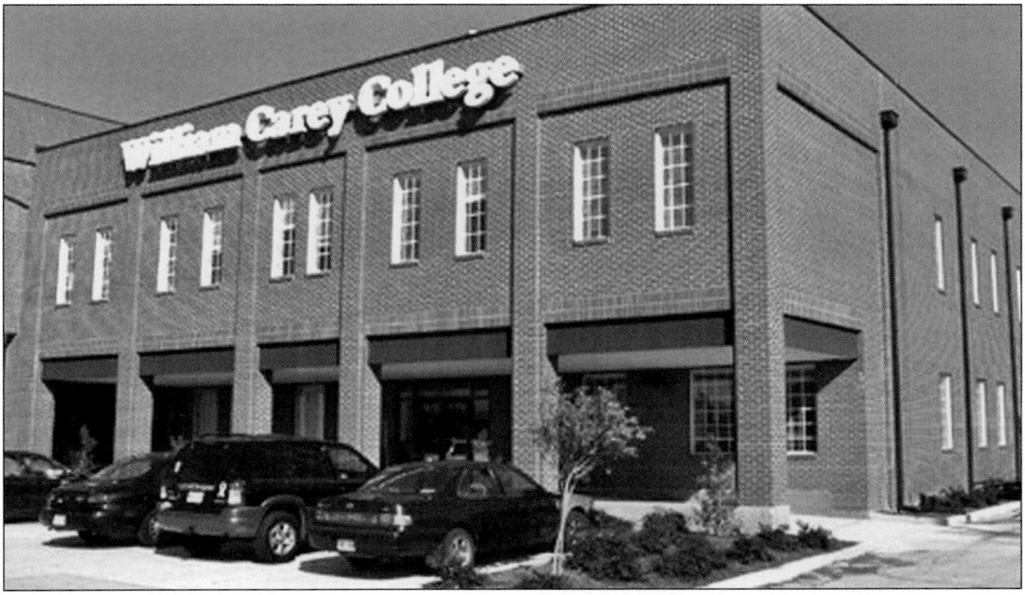


In 1998, after a long association with Southern Baptist Hospital in New Orleans, the nursing school was moved to the campus of New Orleans Baptist Theological Seminary (NOBTS). In 2004, a new building was constructed to house the expanding program. Although major damage to NOBTS occurred from Hurricane Katrina, the nursing building received only minor damage, and the program reopened in March 2006.

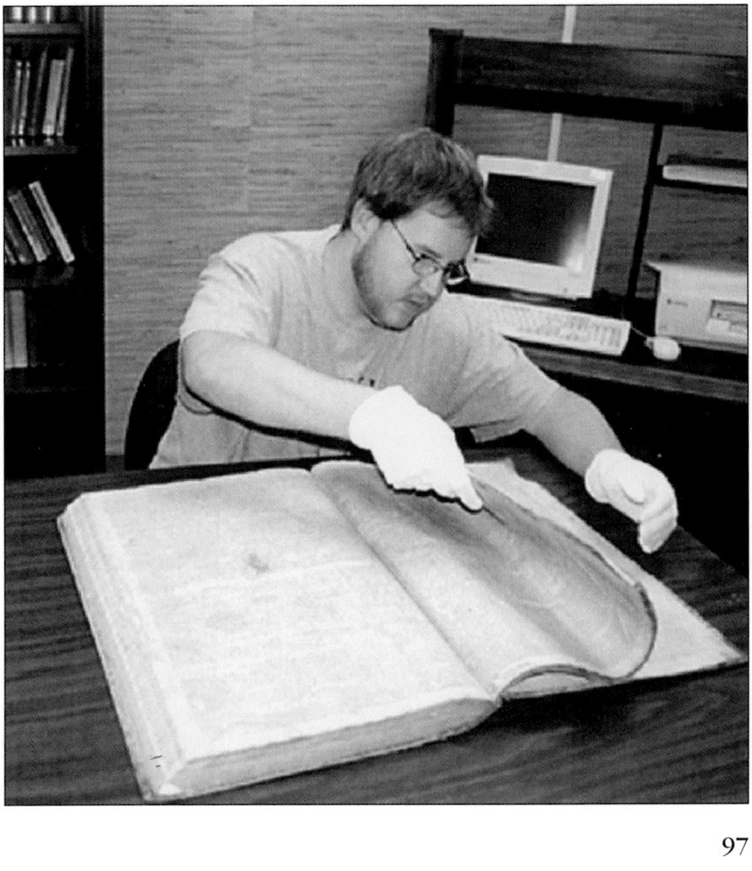

Initiated in the summer of 2000, the Center for Study of the Life and Work of William Carey promotes an understanding of the accomplishments of William Carey, DD (1761–1834), and enhances appreciation of the religious, cultural, scientific, and historical contexts in which Carey worked in Britain and India. The center's Web site has received local, national, and international acclaim.

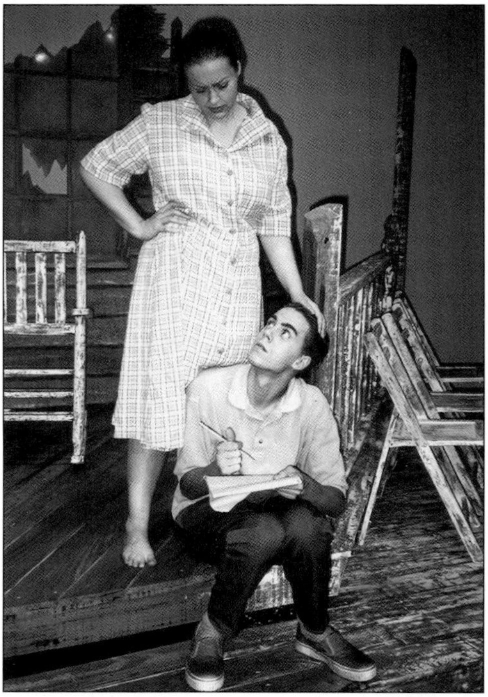

In 2001, an original play, *And David Danced,* written by theater alumnus Jonathan Pope Evans, was selected by the American College Theater Festival as a national finalist to be performed at the Kennedy Center in Washington, D.C. Evans received the national prize in the Jean Kennedy Smith Playwriting Competition. One month later, the WCC cast and crew participated in the Fourth Annual English Language Theatre Festival held in Bratislava, Slovakia, the first American theater group ever to be invited to the festival. This scene from *And David Danced* features students Beth Winter and Joseph Brack.

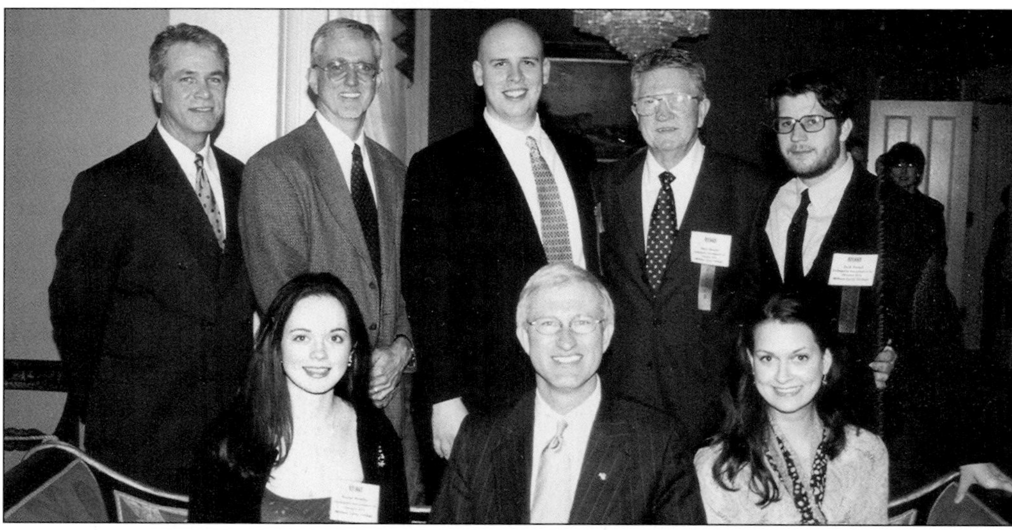

Obra Quave retired in 2002 after a 42-year career as chair of the drama and theater department. In 2005, he was presented a lifetime achievement award, the Gold Medallion of Excellence, by the John F. Kennedy Center for the Performing Arts. Mississippi governor Ronnie Musgrove in 2002 honored the department with the Governor's Award for Excellence in the Arts. Since his retirement, Quave has continued his association with the theater department. In a nine-year period, five productions that he directed were selected for presentation at the regional American College Theater Festival. From left to right are (first row) Karen Bowlby, theater major; Gov. Ronnie Musgrove; and Kristina Lucka, theater major; (second row) alumnus David Bush; Howard Keever, professor of music; Tim Matheny, alumnus and theater instructor; Obra Quave, director of theater; and Josh Penot, theater major.

The Fail-Asbury School of Nursing building was constructed on the Hattiesburg campus in 2002, the first new building since 1977. Named in honor of benefactors Joseph and Nancy Fail and the Asbury Foundation, the building gave the growing nursing program a central location for offices and classroom space. From left to right are Berdie Polk, Andrea Price, Lee Miles, Renae Soley, and Tabitha Edwards.

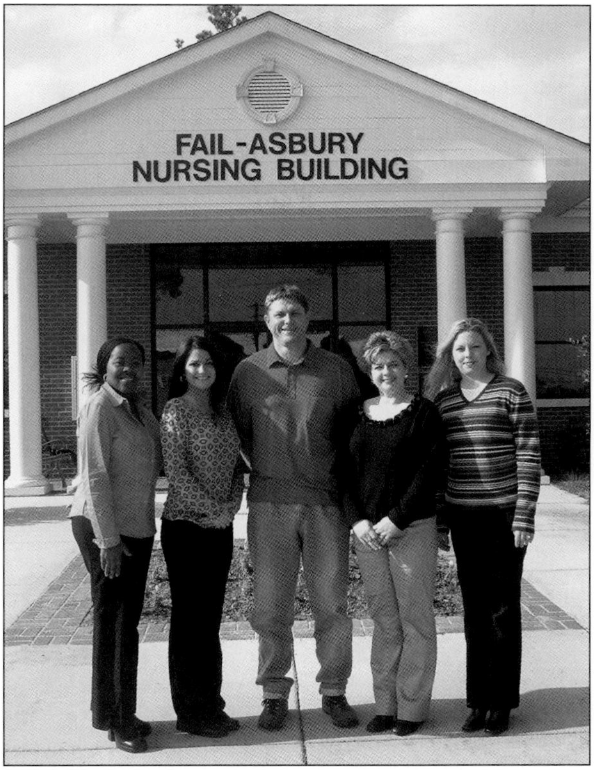


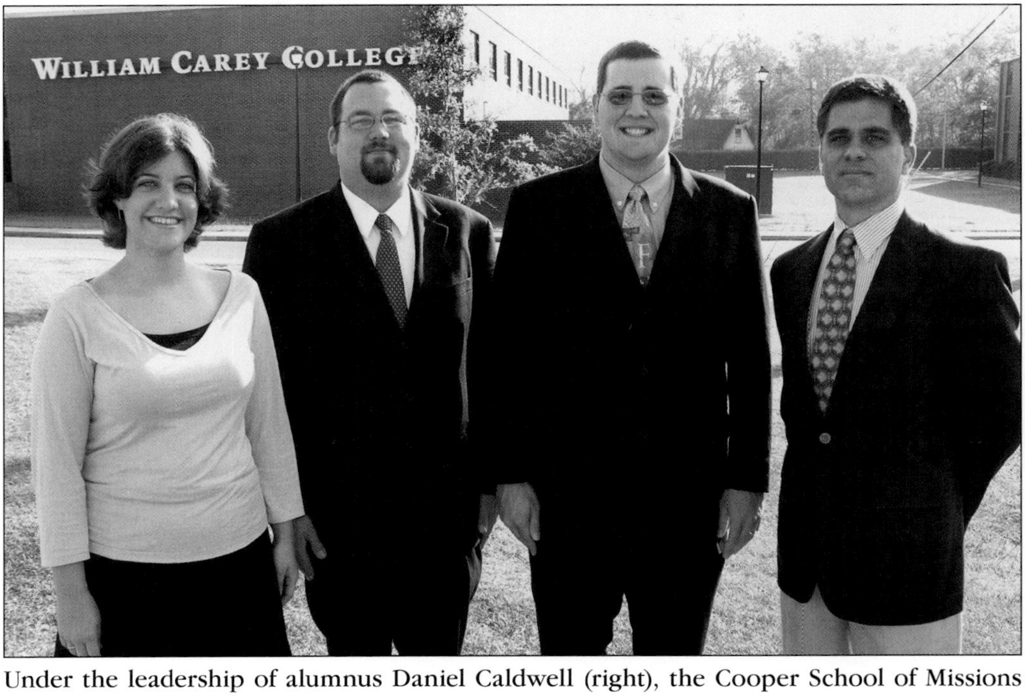


Under the leadership of alumnus Daniel Caldwell (right), the Cooper School of Missions and Biblical Studies continued to grow, with enrollment of church-related vocation students reaching an all-time high of 247 in 2002. From left to right, Corrie Covington, John Blackmon, and Joe Marsh received church-related vocation scholarships.

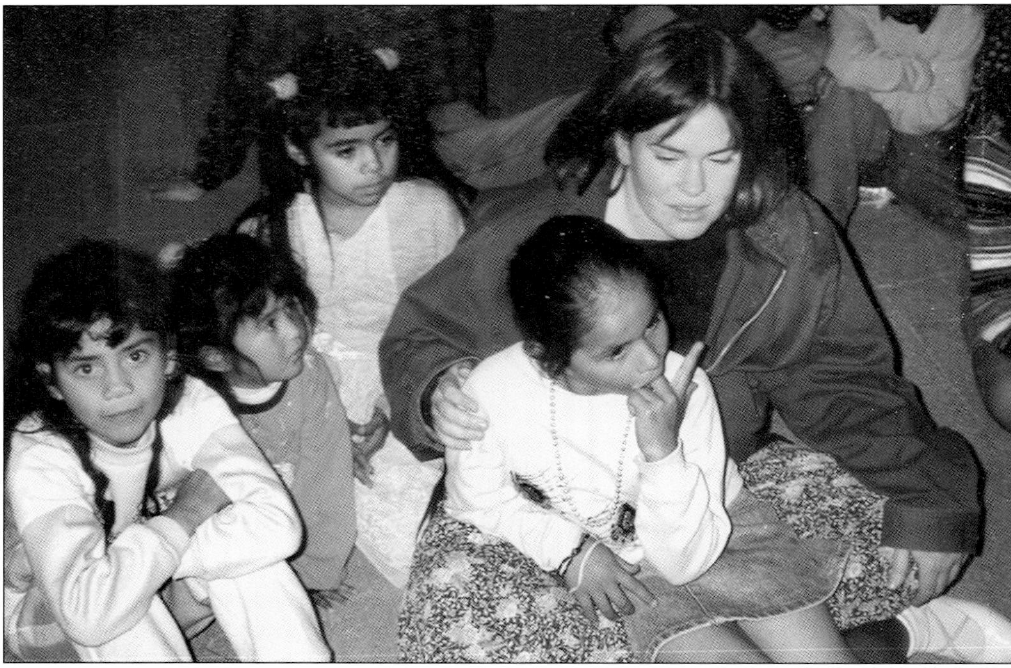

Students and faculty participate annually in mission trips across the United States and abroad. In the last several years, students have participated in 40 mission efforts, among them several to China, Russia, Chile, India, and Brazil. The mission emphasis took on even more of a key role with the employment of a full-time missions coordinator in 2004 and a gift of $100,000 in 2005 as an endowment to support the mission endeavors. Callie Carruth plays with children in South America.

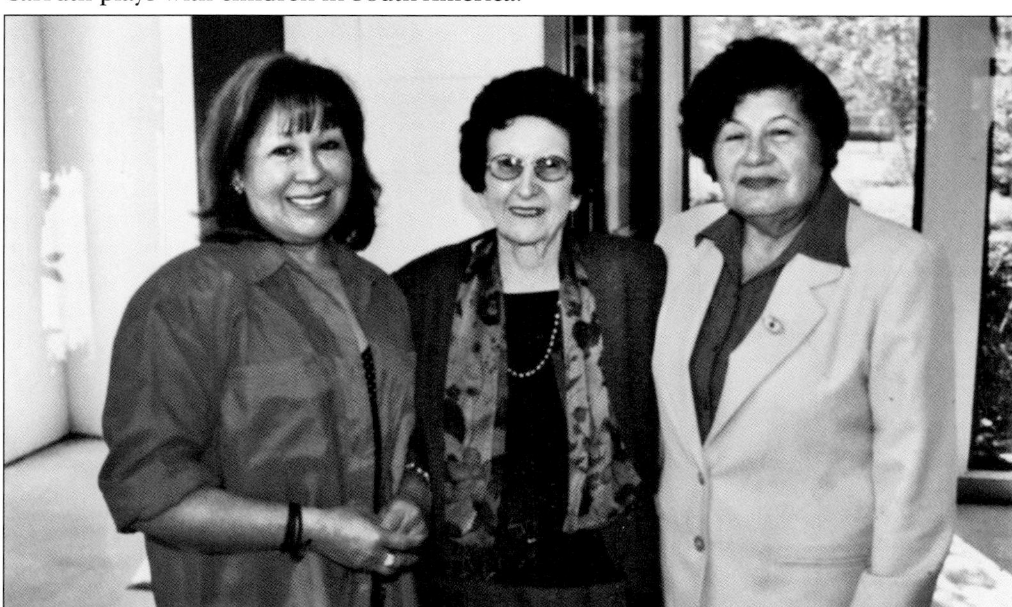

Alumna Betty Hart, a retired missionary, brought two of her friends from Chile to Carey for a visit in 2003. Beatriz Rubio, left, is from Santiago, and Belia Perez, right, is from Antofagasta.

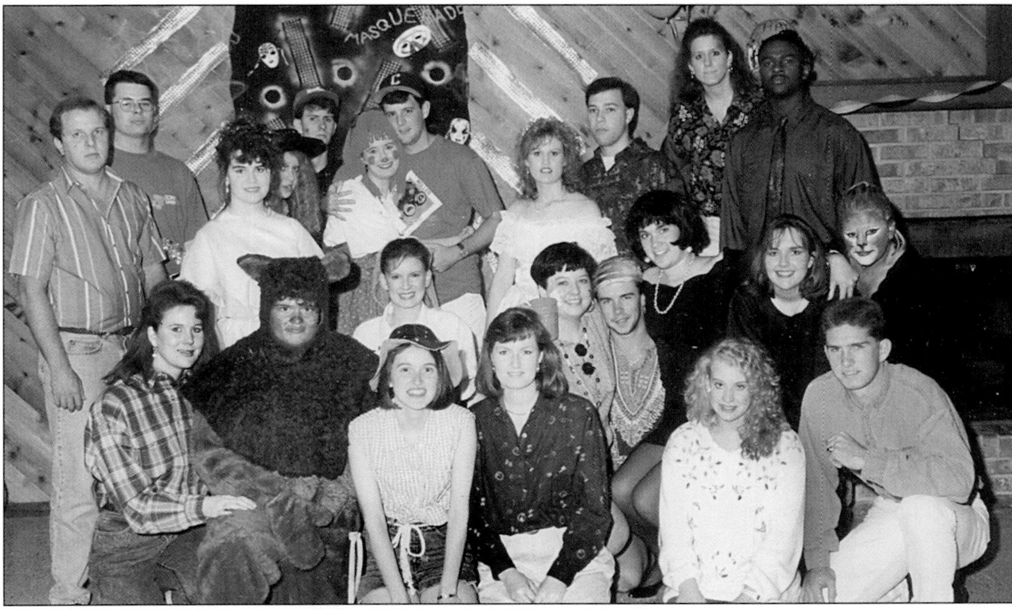

Three popular social clubs among women students were the Thalians, Litaeans, and Delphinians. In 1954, three men's clubs were formed, the Tuccinomians, Nikeans, and Herculeans. Currently Gamma Chi and Pi Omega provide social interaction for women, and Sigma Psi Nu is an active men's club. Gamma Chi held a 1992 Masquerade Bash.

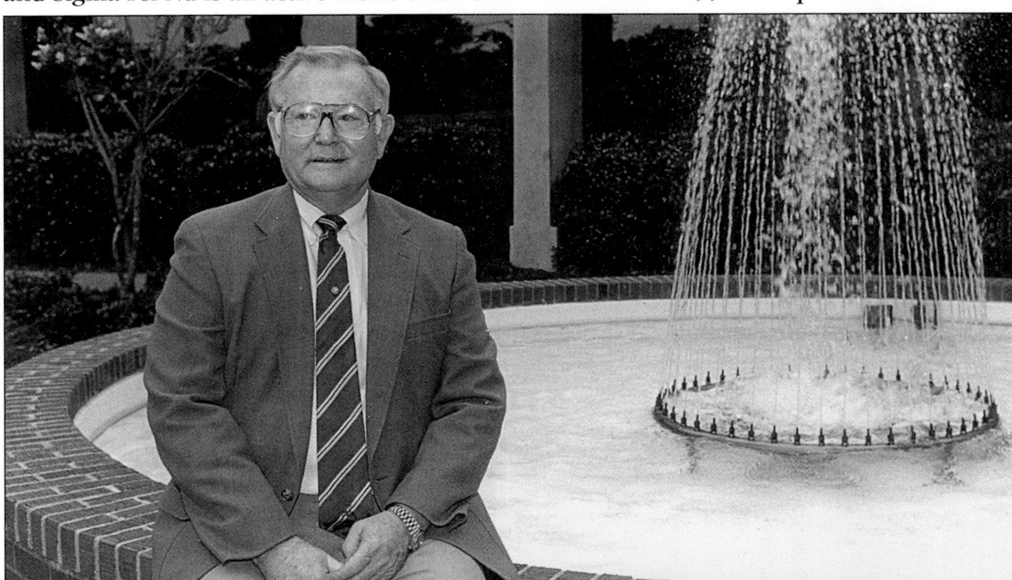

Built and dedicated in 1992, the Chain Garden received substantial damage during Hurricane Katrina. At printing time, Bobby Chain, local Hattiesburg businessman and former mayor, is restoring and improving the beauty spot of the Hattiesburg campus. Philo Fountain, thought to be constructed in the late 1920s, was originally in front of Tatum Court and was relocated to the front of Thomas Hall in 1966. In this 1991 photograph, Chain is seated on the edge of Philo Fountain, renovated in memory of his mother, Grace Sellers Chain.

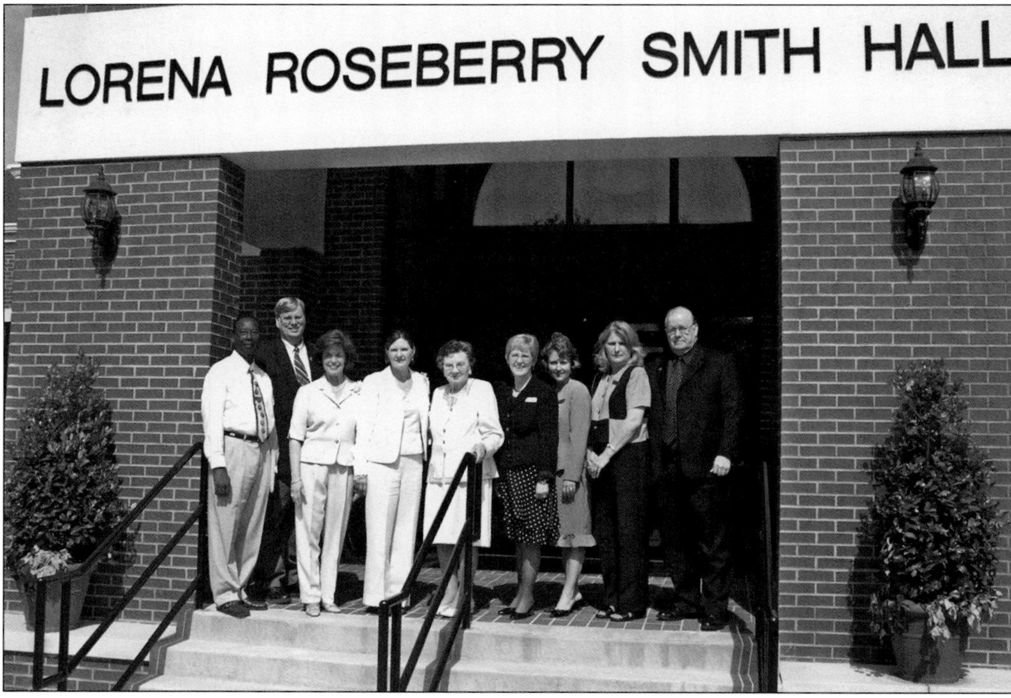


In 2005, the Lorena Roseberry Smith Hall was dedicated, offering the latest in technology and classroom space for the growing School of Education. Dumas and Lorena Smith, two longtime Carey benefactors, were first honored by the college in 1985 with the naming of the Thomas Hall auditorium as the Dumas L. Smith Auditorium. The couple made possible the remodeling of the 18-year-old 1,200-seat facility. The Smiths continued their generosity to the college, and in 2003, the renovated library was renamed Dumas L. Smith–I.E. Rouse Library. Smith (center, with hand on rail) is pictured with the education faculty.

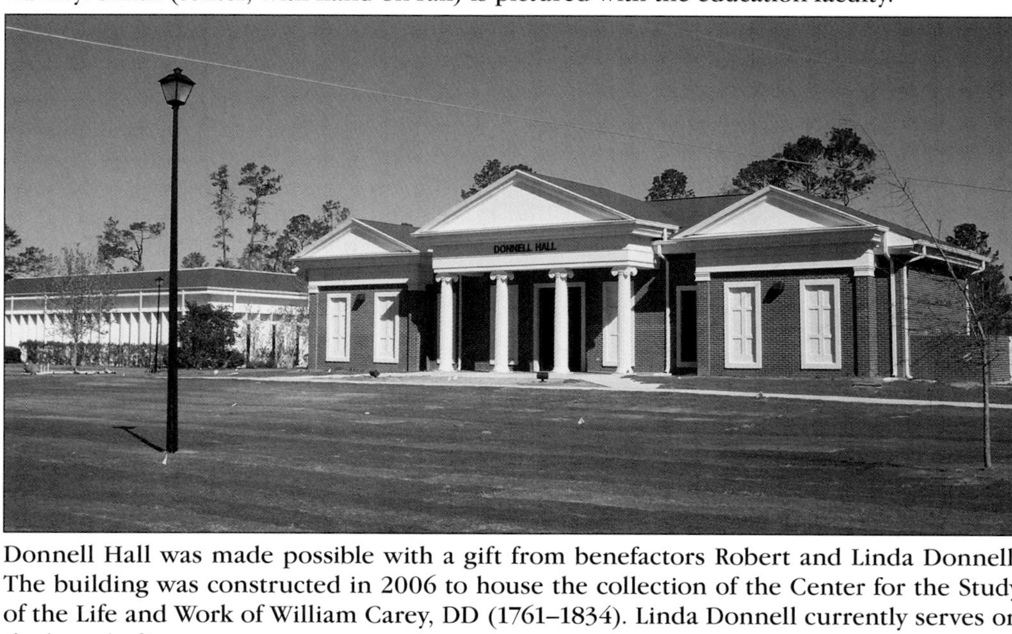


Donnell Hall was made possible with a gift from benefactors Robert and Linda Donnell. The building was constructed in 2006 to house the collection of the Center for the Study of the Life and Work of William Carey, DD (1761–1834). Linda Donnell currently serves on the board of trustees.

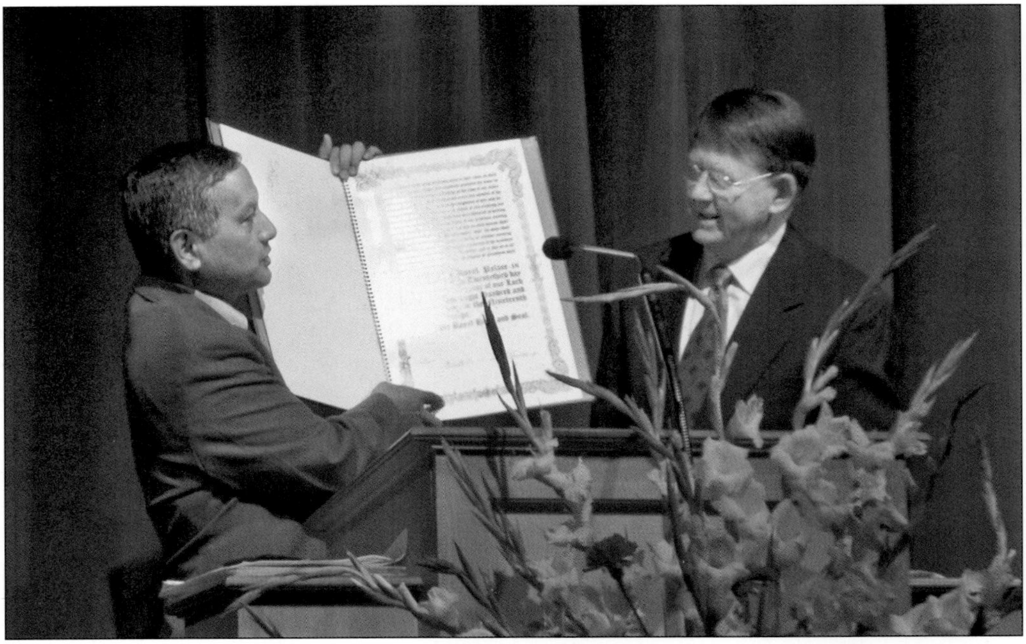

Dr. Lalchungnunga, principal of Serampore College, addressed faculty, students and guests in a special 2004 chapel service commemorating the changing of the college name to William Carey College 50 years earlier. He presented the college with a leather-bound folder containing a translation of the original charter of Serampore College, a college in India founded by William Carey. Pictured are Dr. Lalchungnunga (left) and President Kennedy.

In late August 2005, Hurricane Katrina brought destruction to all three campuses, delaying classes, causing structural damage to buildings, and uprooting trees in its path, especially the beautiful trees on the Hattiesburg campus planted by President Johnson in the 1920s. Four buildings at Carey on the Coast were destroyed, with severe damage to all others. The School of Nursing building in New Orleans received only minor damage and reopened in the spring of 2006. Repairs are mostly complete at the Hattiesburg campus, and at printing time, classes are being held in various locations on the Gulf Coast as a new site for that campus is sought. The damage to the Coast library is shown in this photograph.

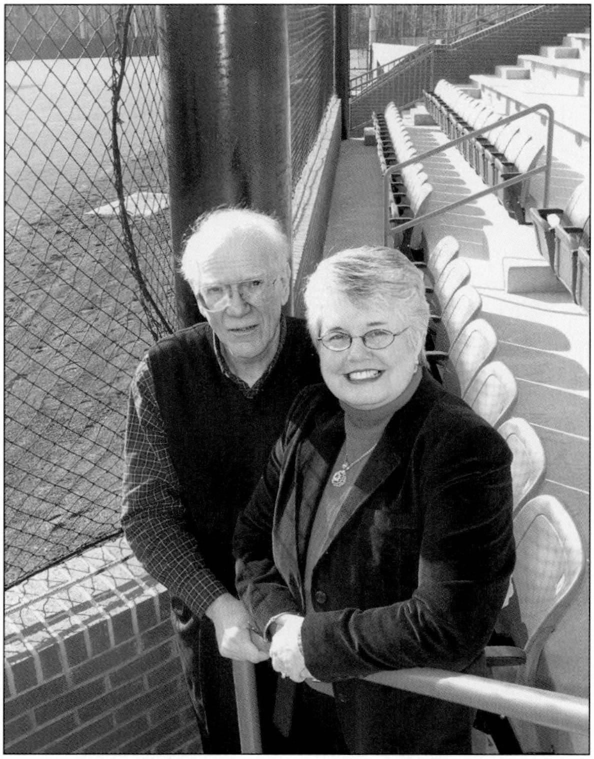

Milton Wheeler Field, a new baseball complex, was dedicated in 2006 in honor of Dr. Milton Wheeler, professor of history and Crusader baseball fan since 1957. The president's home, constructed in 1962, was renamed the Donna Duck Wheeler Alumni House in honor of Wheeler, who served since 1965 in various capacities, most recently as alumni director for 17 years. The Wheelers are both Carey alumni and have named William Carey College as the benefactor of their estate, estimated to be worth more than $2.3 million, the largest single gift in the history of the college.

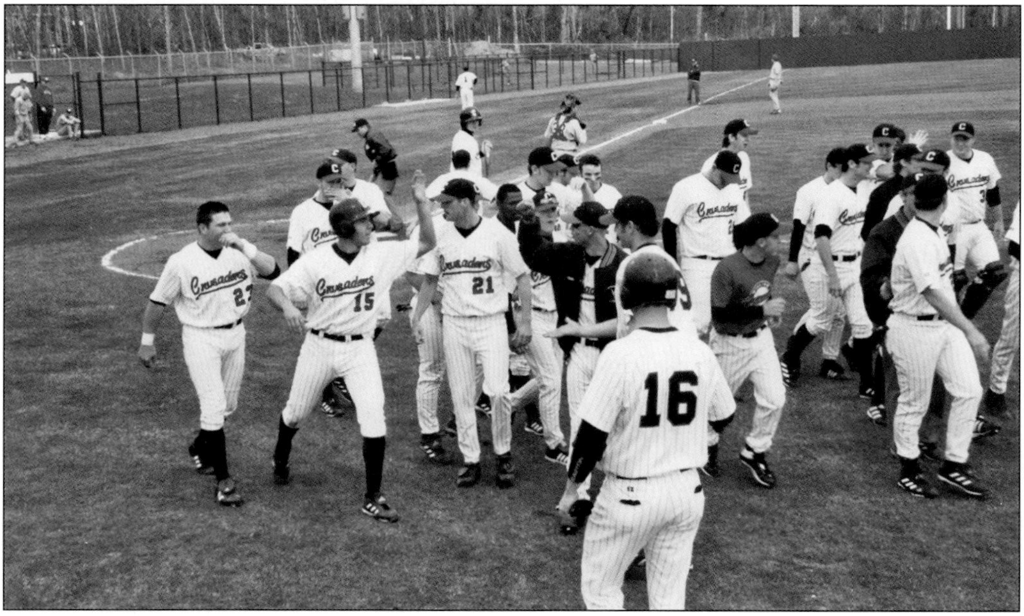


Baseball teams are perennial winners in district and conference championships. Under the leadership of coach Bobby Halford since 1986, the teams have won 14 Gulf Coast Conference championships and six District 30 regional titles, and they have participated in 16 NAIA regional tournaments. The 2006 team is pictured here as they congratulate Pat Burch for hitting the first home run in the first game played in the new Milton Wheeler field.

# *Five*

# Crusaders in Action

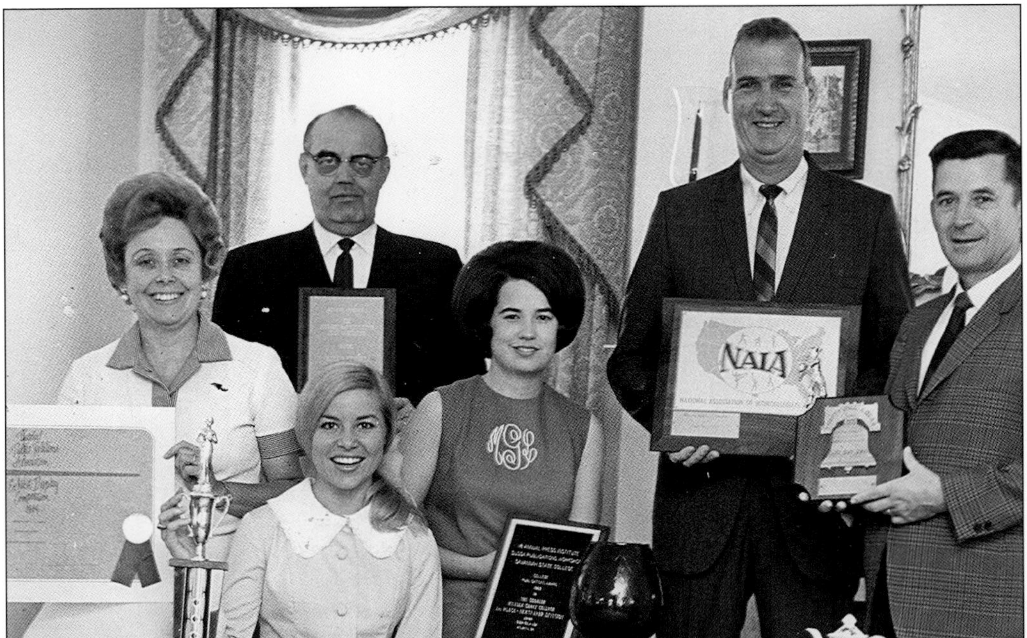

Many awards and honors came to the college in 1969. From left to right, Marjorie Rowden holds a certificate for the best display at the Southern Baptist Convention; Linda Waldon shows off her trophy for placing second in the Miss Mississippi Pageant; Dr. Donald Winters holds the certificate granting approval for offering master's degrees; Martha Gillon poses with the plaque given for Carey's student newspaper winning first place for the second year in the Southern Universities Student Government Association's Publications Workshop; John O'Keefe holds the Carey Crusaders NAIA baseball championship plaque; and President Noonkester holds his Liberty Bell Award. It was a very good year!

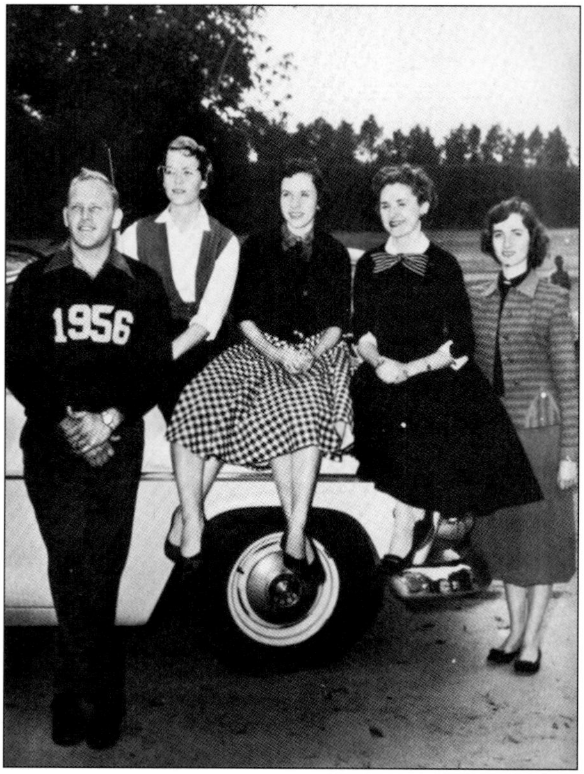


Billy Crosby played football and baseball, led as student coach of the baseball team, and served as class president in 1955–1956, as shown in this photograph. He is surrounded by fellow class officers, from left to right, Mary Lou Smith, Olga Hagler, Gloria Nell Smith, and Lona Pearl Cochran.

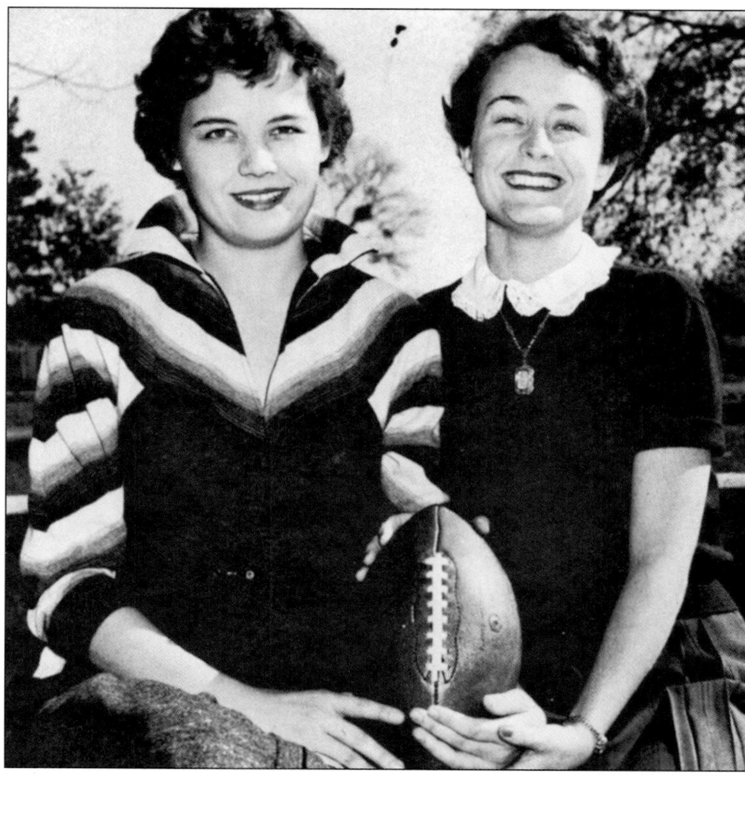

Two lovely coeds were chosen as football sweethearts in 1955. In future years, a homecoming queen was selected by the student body. The football sweethearts are Joyce Reid (left) and Pat Pinson.

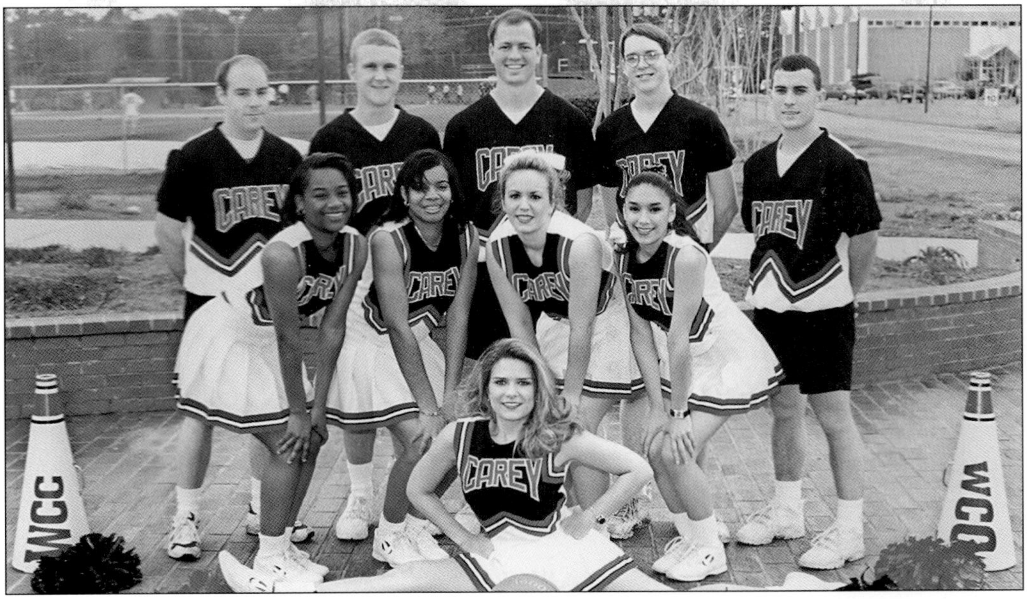


When Carey's athletic program began in 1954, cheerleaders were selected to urge their team to victories at football and basketball games. Cheerleaders in later years are just as energetic in cheering their teams to victories. The 1997 cheerleaders are, from left to right, (center, seated) Ginger Martin; (first row) Michelle Bowser, Tera Benjamin, Yariela Rodriquez, and Lacy McIntosh; (second row) Bobby Jo Panai, Shane Overstreet, Scott Alexander, Jason Padgett, and Brian Parker.

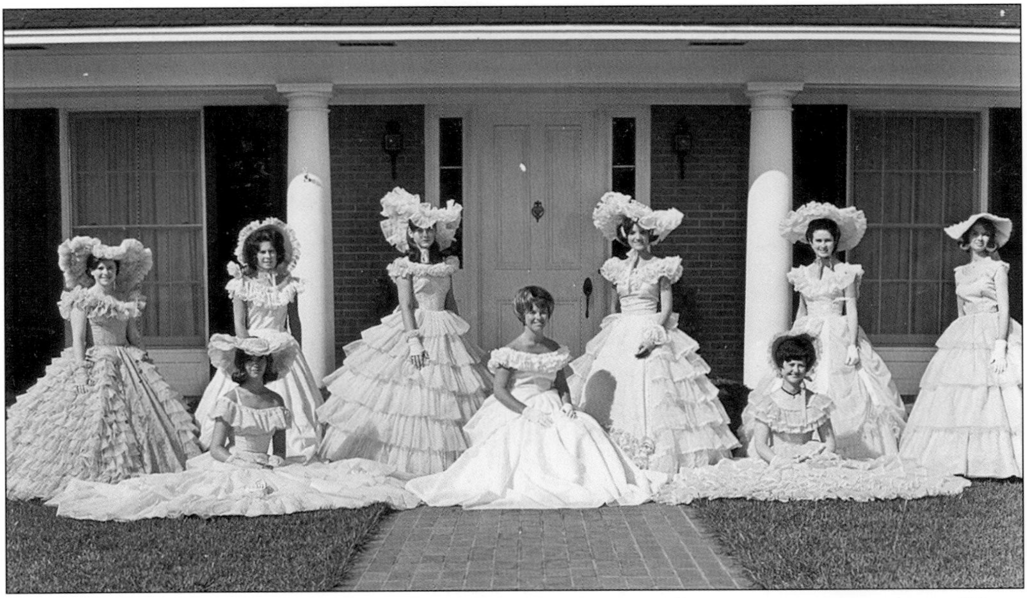

The May Day festival, a tradition of Mississippi Woman's College, was continued at William Carey College until the mid-1970s. The music, pageantry, and crowning of a May Day queen brought to the campus guests from all around South Mississippi. Captured in this 1969 photograph, the May Queen is surrounded by her court. Standing from left to right are Janice Rushing, Evelyn Anderson, Nancy Lindley, Deborah Balzi, Betty Cochran, and Anna Smith. Seated are Patti Brownlee, Queen Dolores Pfaffendorf, and Joyce Barnett.

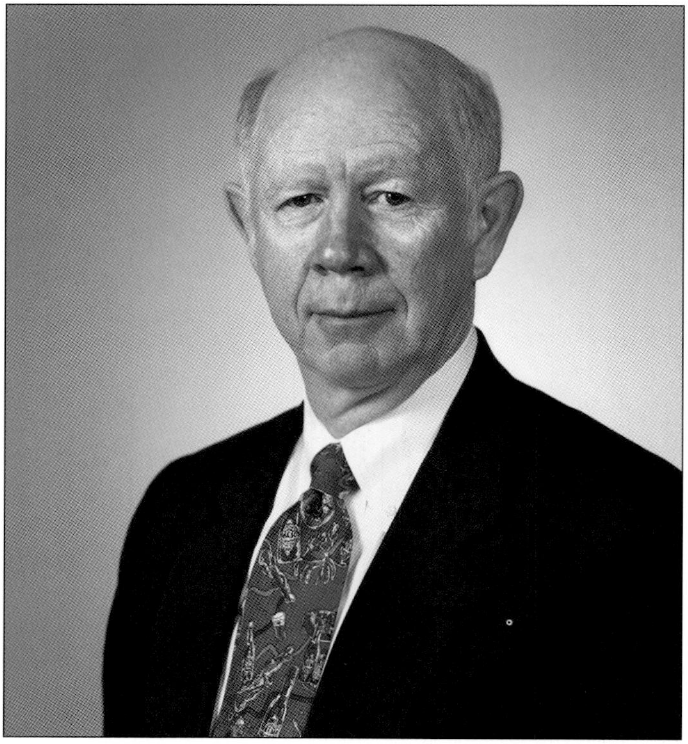

Elvin "Buddy" Smith, class of 1960, was the first William Carey College alumnus since 1954 to earn a PhD, graduating with a degree in physiology and biochemistry from the University of Mississippi Medical Center. He recently retired as the executive vice president of the Texas A&M University System Health Science Center in College Station, Texas.

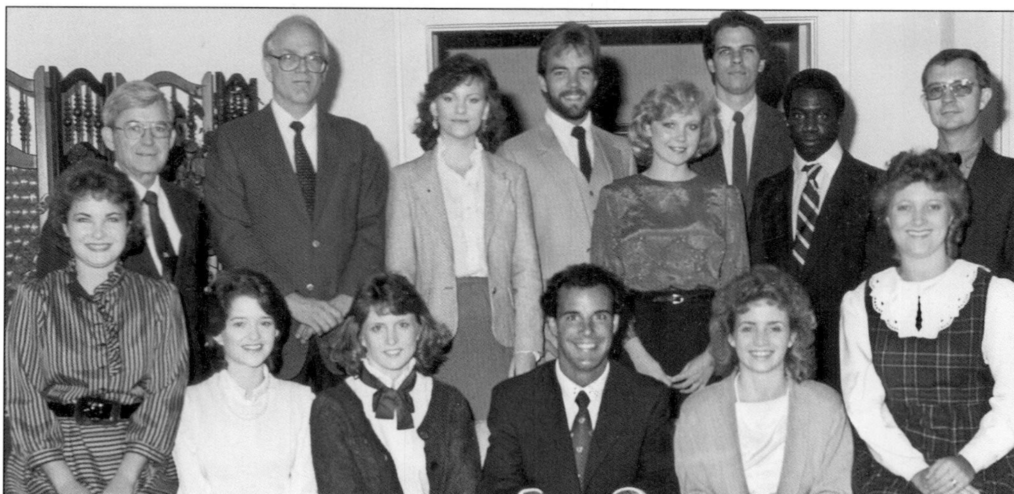

The Alpha Zeta chapter of Chi Beta Phi society, chartered in 1955, recognizes outstanding students in the field of science. Delta Omicron, international honorary music fraternity, established a chapter at William Carey College in 1964. Since the 1970s other honor societies formed chapters at the college, including Pi Gamma Mu, Alpha Chi, Omicron Delta Kappa (the first in the nation to admit women), Alpha Psi Omega, Kappa Mu Epsilon, Kappa Pi, Phi Beta Lambda, Pi Kappa Delta, and Sigma Tau Delta. Pictured at an Omicron Delta Kappa initiation in 1986 are, from left to right, (first row) Cindy Cash, Laura Broughton, Suzanne O'Quinn, Matt Jones, Linda Mabius, and Lisa Fowler; (second row) President Noonkester, Dr. Milton Wheeler, Judy Beth McLendon, Scott Martin, Terri Esterline, Alan Fowler, Dwayne Coleman, and Dr. Dorman Laird.

One of the characteristics advantageous to students was the smallness of classes. The current student-to-faculty ratio is 17 to 1 and was even smaller in the 1960s. On sunny days, professors would often move classes outside, as professor of history John McGraw did in 1967.

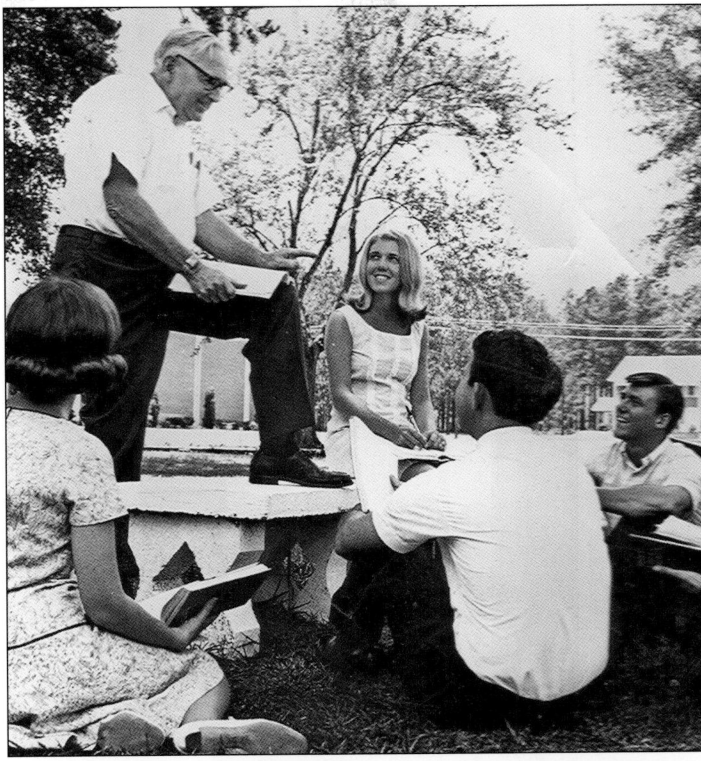

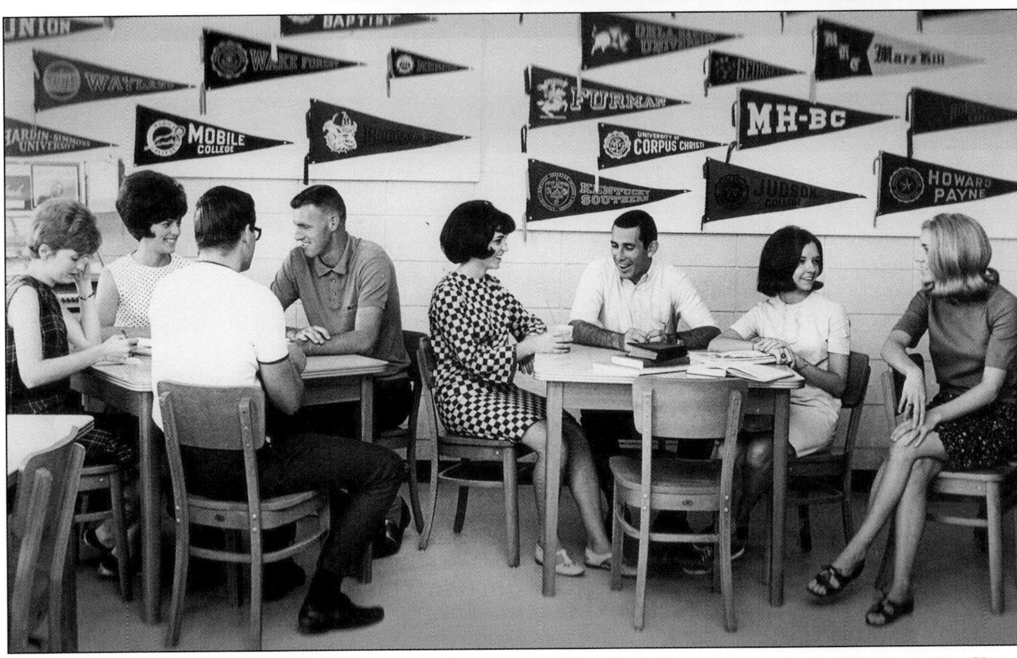


McMillan Student Center housed the campus grill, a bookstore, a post office, and offices for the Student Government Association when it opened in the mid-1960s. "Ultra modern and functional is the new grill which comfortably seats 100," was the description given of the new facilities in the alumni magazine. Taking a break from classes and study are students in the late 1960s.

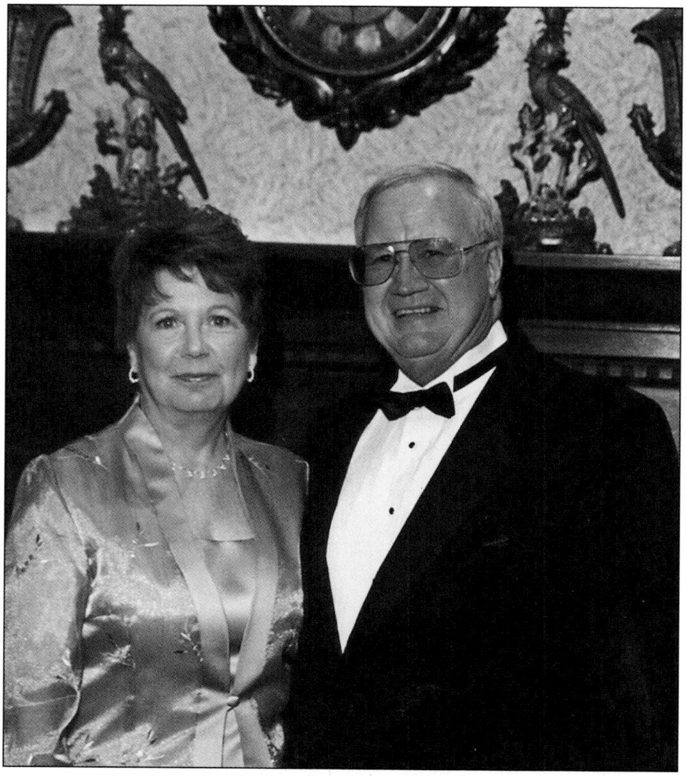

Alumnus Jerry Boone, class of 1964, retired in 2004 after serving for 15 years as president of Ferrum College in Ferrum, Virginia. His wife, Shirley Glover, also class of 1964, enjoyed her duties as Ferrum's first lady and her educational service as language arts coordinator in the Roanoke County Schools.

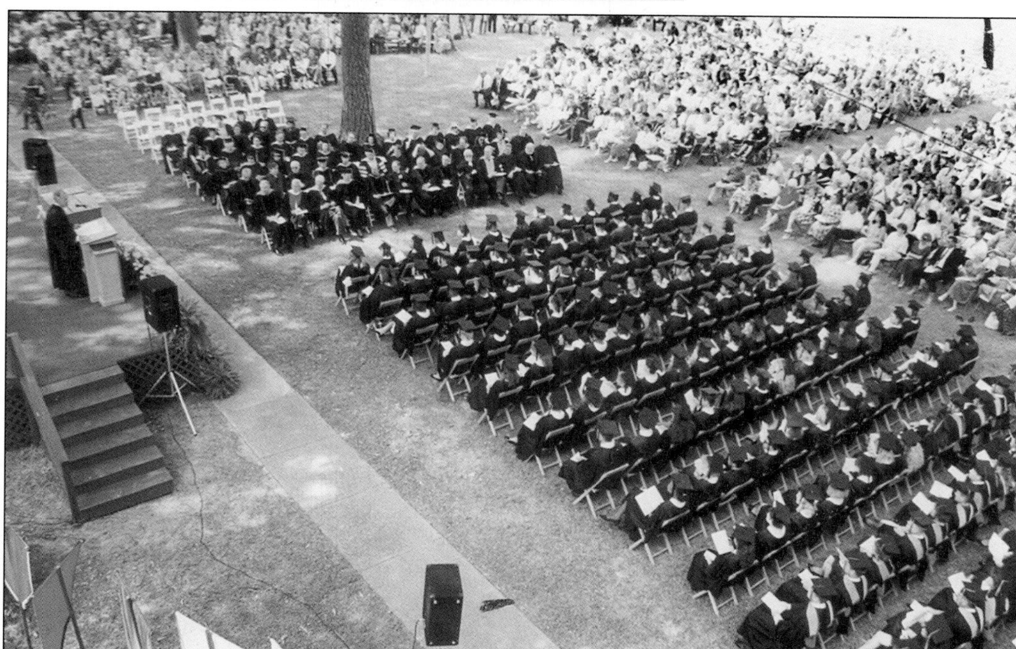

Commencement exercises grew too large for the 1,200-seat auditorium in Thomas Hall in the early 1990s. Ceremonies were held outdoors for several years, as seen in this 1995 photograph. Since then, graduations have been held on all three campuses. There were 512 graduates in 1995.

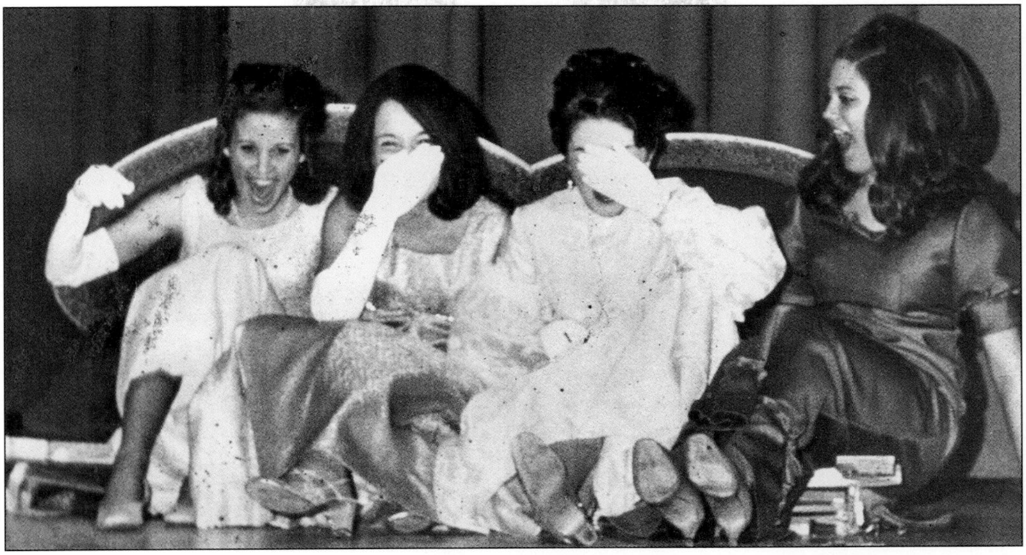

When William Carey College made the front page of the Sunday Chicago paper, it was news. When it also made the front page in Dallas, Denver, Los Angeles, Tulsa, and Sacramento, it was even bigger news. The college even found itself in three European papers as well as the *Army Times.* The occasion was a charming 1971 "unposed" photograph of four finalists in the Miss Carey Pageant who tumbled to the floor when an ornamental bench collapsed. No one was hurt so the capacity audience enjoyed the unsophisticated moment along with the victims. "All winners in the good-nature category," read one of the nation's newspapers. From left to right are Becky Ware, Kathie Benge, Miriam Moss, and Elaine Ross.

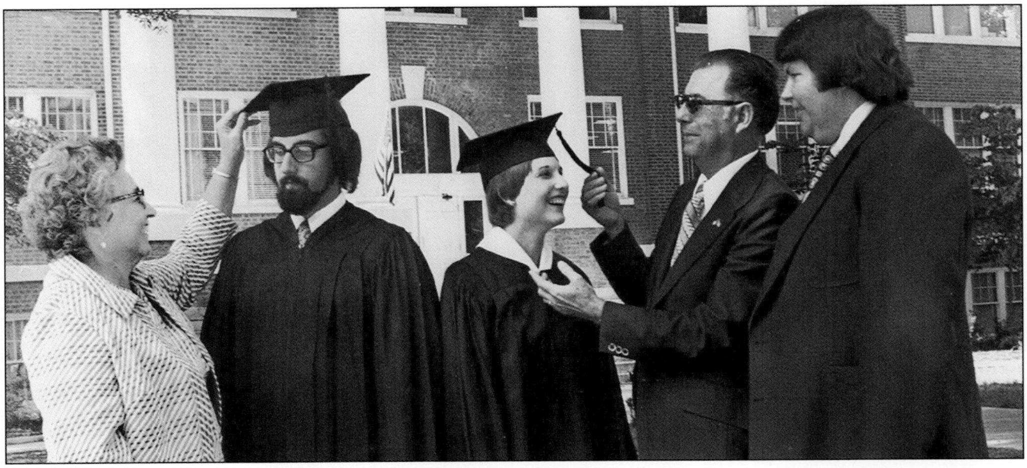

David Davis, class of 1976, won two Fulbright Fellowships to conduct archaeological research in Ghana, West Africa, and Indonesia. David won the national Pi Gamma Mu Fellowship at his graduation and earned a Ph.D. in African and Middle Eastern history at Northwestern University. He is currently associate professor of history and associate dean of arts and letters at Millsaps College in Jackson. David grew up in Ghana, the son of alumni missionaries Ralph and Cora Joyce Davis. The Davis family is shown in this 1976 graduation photograph, when both David and his sister Nan received degrees. From left to right are Cora Joyce Davis, David Davis, Nan Davis, Ralph Davis, and Richard Davis, Nan's husband, also a Carey alumnus.

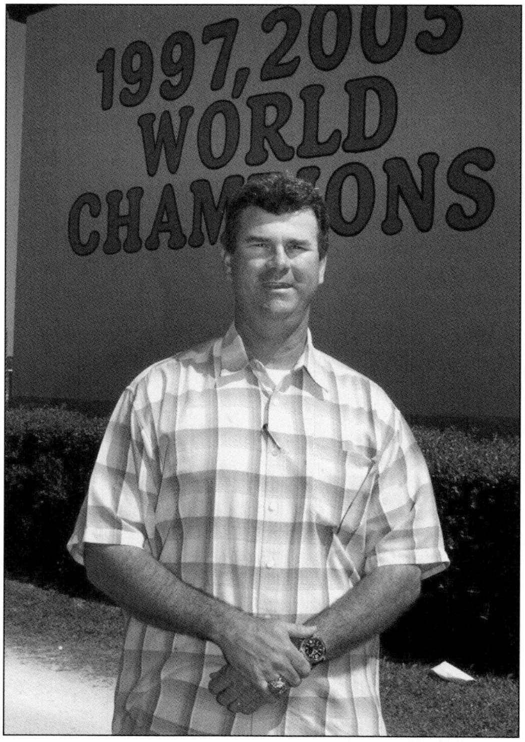


Dan Jennings, class of 1984, experienced the World Series up close and personal when the Florida Marlins beat the New York Yankees in 2003 to win the series. Dan is vice president for player personnel for the Marlins. He was a baseball pitcher during his Carey years.

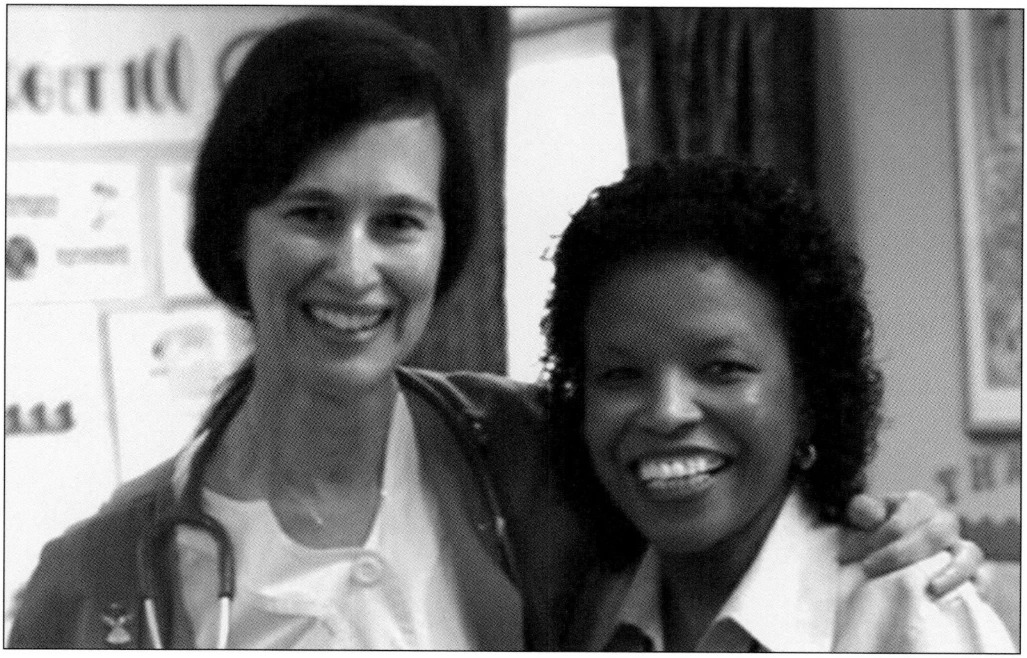

Carey school of nursing alumna Diana Willis Carter received the Tenet Healthcare Corporation's 2003 Chairman Award, which recognizes four outstanding health caregivers from among the 116,500 Tenet employees nationwide. Diana is the founder and director of the Diabetes Management Clinic at Memorial Hospital in New Orleans. Diana (right) is shown in this photograph with her 1976 classmate and associate Jennifer Doiron.

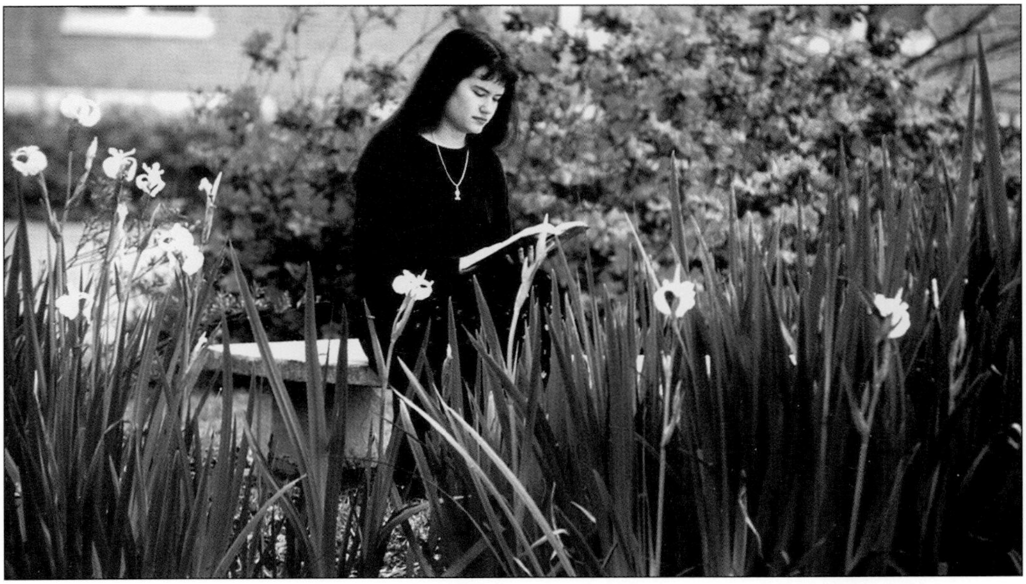

It is not known when the pond on the front of the campus was constructed, but it is seen in yearbook photographs as far back as the 1920s. Long a popular place to study and relax, hold picnics, steal a kiss, and even propose marriage, the pond was enlarged and improved in 1990 and rededicated at homecoming 1994 as the Gertrude B. Smith–Pearl McKinnon Pond. The pond was destroyed by Hurricane Katrina in 2005, and plans for its rebuilding are incomplete. Emily Jones enjoys a quiet moment near the pond.

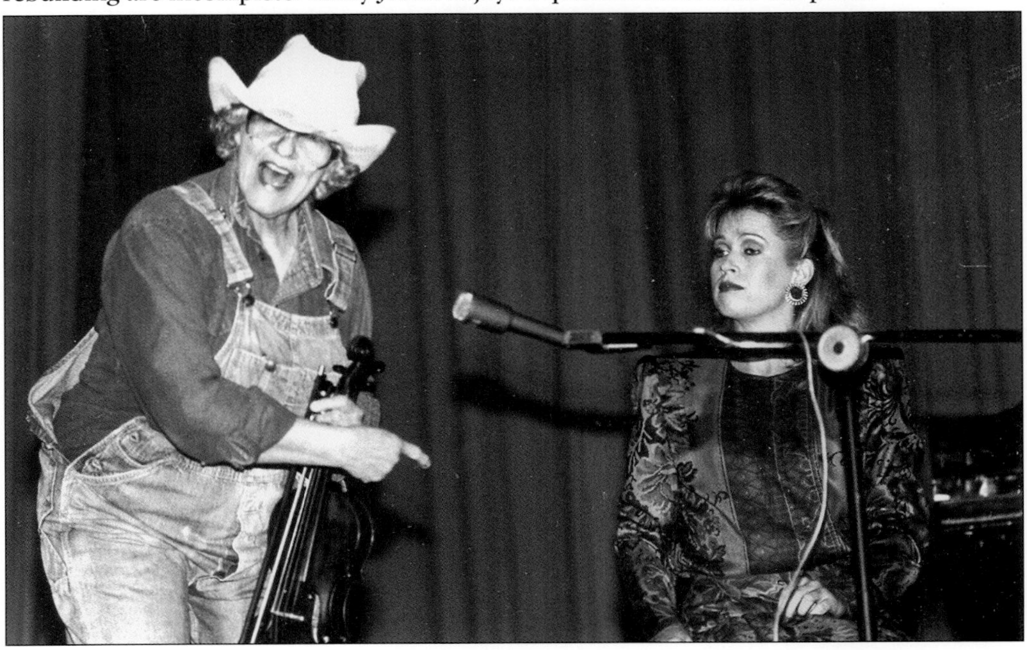

Alumni fondly refer to the "Carey family" when remembering their experiences as students. Faculty often participated in friendly competitions with the students and provided entertainment for campus events. Instructor of violin and piano Jennie Lou Breland lets everyone know that she is not only a violinist, but that she is a fiddler as well! Alumna Diane Dobson looks on.

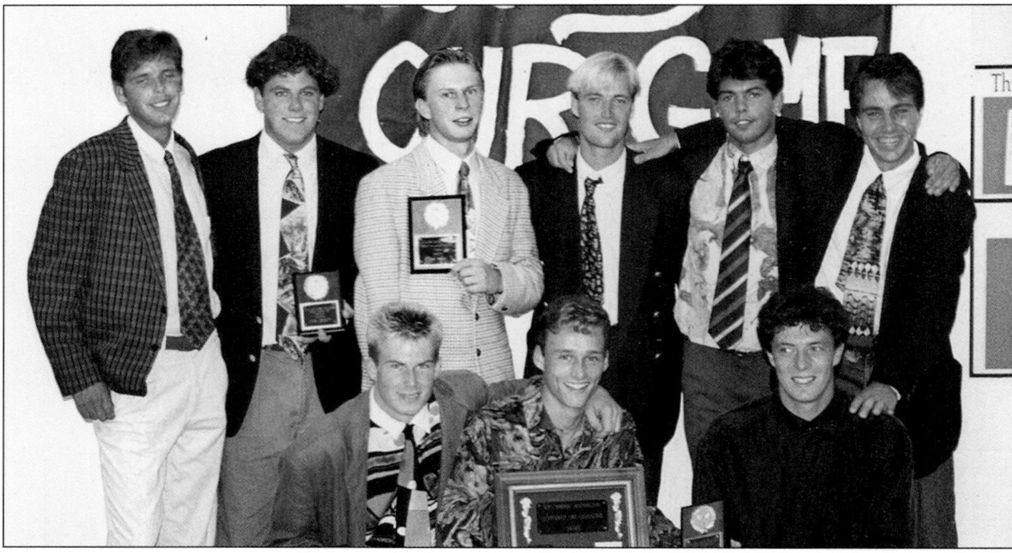

At the NAIA national championships in Kansas City in 1991, the tennis team's No. 1 doubles combination of Eddie Brown and Marco Zannoni earned first-team NAIA All-American status, the first in William Carey College history. In 1993, the program produced seven All-Americans, six Academic All-Americans, and the winner of the 1993 Arthur Ashe award. The team, coached by Jack Jones, also won the 1993 Rolex Gulf States doubles competition and was second in the national competition. Jack Jones was named the Mississippi Tennis Association Coach of the Year. This photograph was taken at the awards banquet in 1994. From left to right are (first row) Peter T. Schudin, Marco Bruggner, and Marco Zannoni; (second row) Mark Nagels, Tyler Leverette, Jiri Novak, Sascha Wullchleger, Marco Keller, and Alessio Albisetti.

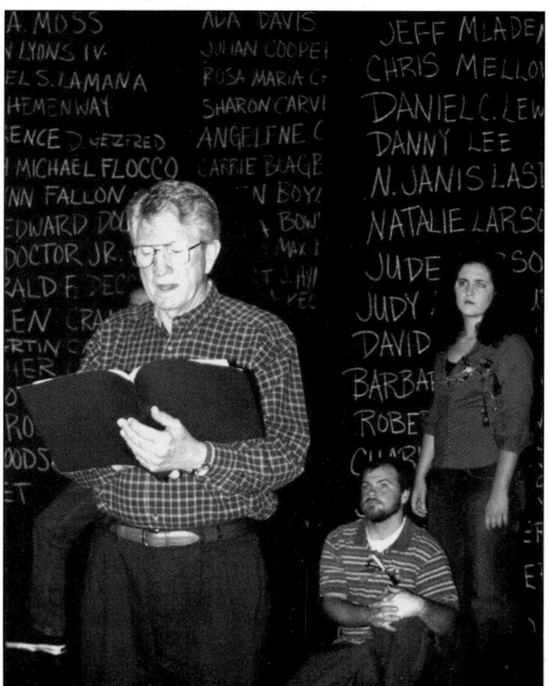


As the nation mourned, so did the Carey campus after the tragedy of September 11, 2001. By noon of that eventful day, students were gathering in small groups all over the campus to pray. They wore yellow ribbons and draped red, white, and blue banners on buildings. Blood drives and a program presented by the theater department, *September 11: In Remembrance*, benefited the American Red Cross.

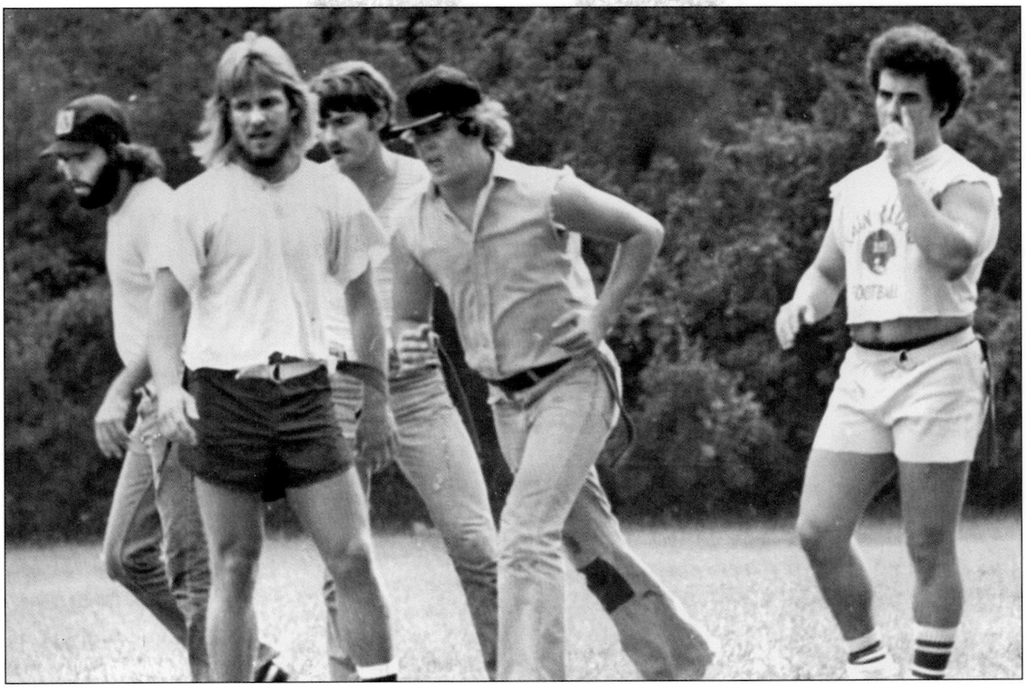

Through the years, students enjoyed the leisure of intramural sports. Whether flag football, basketball, soccer, or ultimate Frisbee, students enjoy a tough contest. With names like "Mamas Boyz," "Heartbreakers," and "Lionhearts," students know how to have fun and play hard. Most of the intramural games were played anywhere there was an open grassy area, but in 2003, a new state-of-the-art lighted intramural field was constructed.

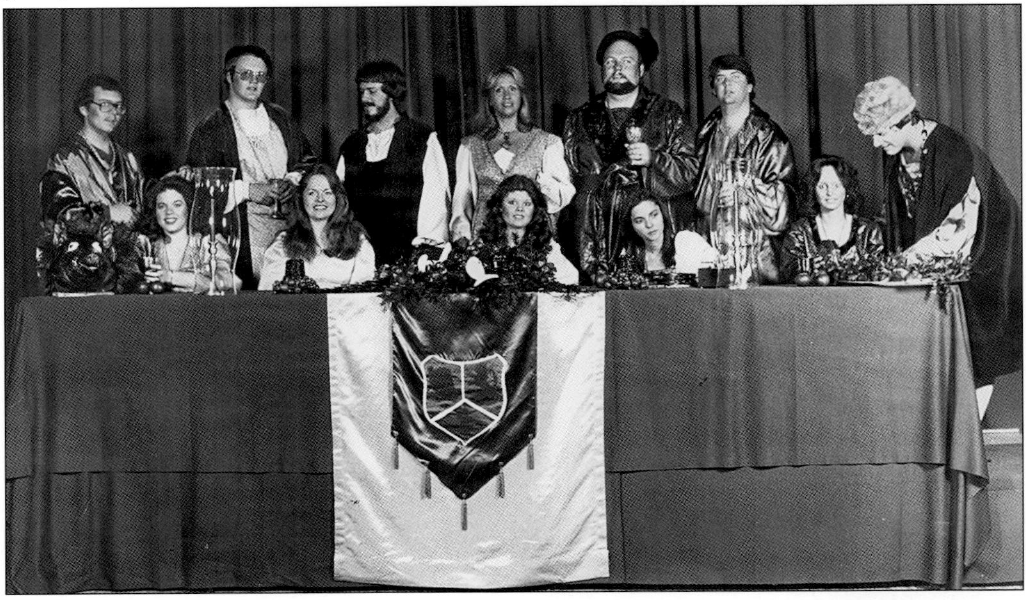

Christmas madrigal dinners were much-anticipated events by students and the Hattiesburg community during the 1970s and 1980s. Alumna Josephine D'Arpa, who is in her 41st year of teaching at Carey, directed the performances for 17 years. The program was reinstated in 2005 under the direction of music and theater faculty.

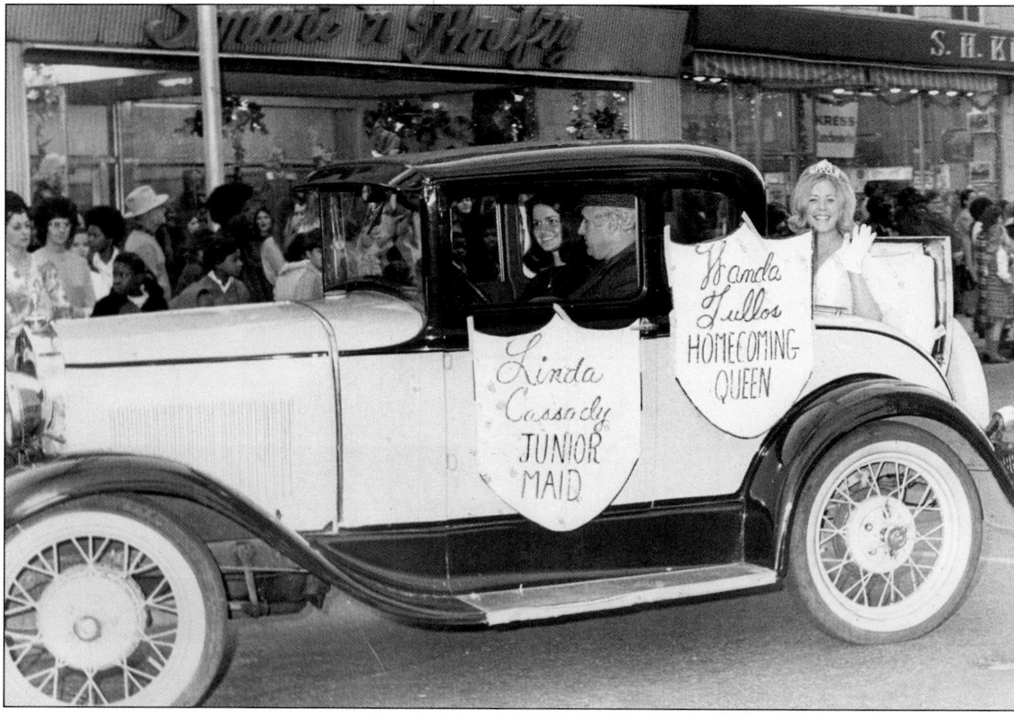


Wanda Tullos, homecoming queen, smiles to the downtown Hattiesburg crowd in the 1972 homecoming parade. Though not as classy as the vintage car, the Volkswagen beetle below did its part in the parade to boost the Crusader basketball team. Standing in the car from left to right are Sandra Thomas, Judy Duck, Patty Jo Smith, unidentified, and Pam Ethridge.

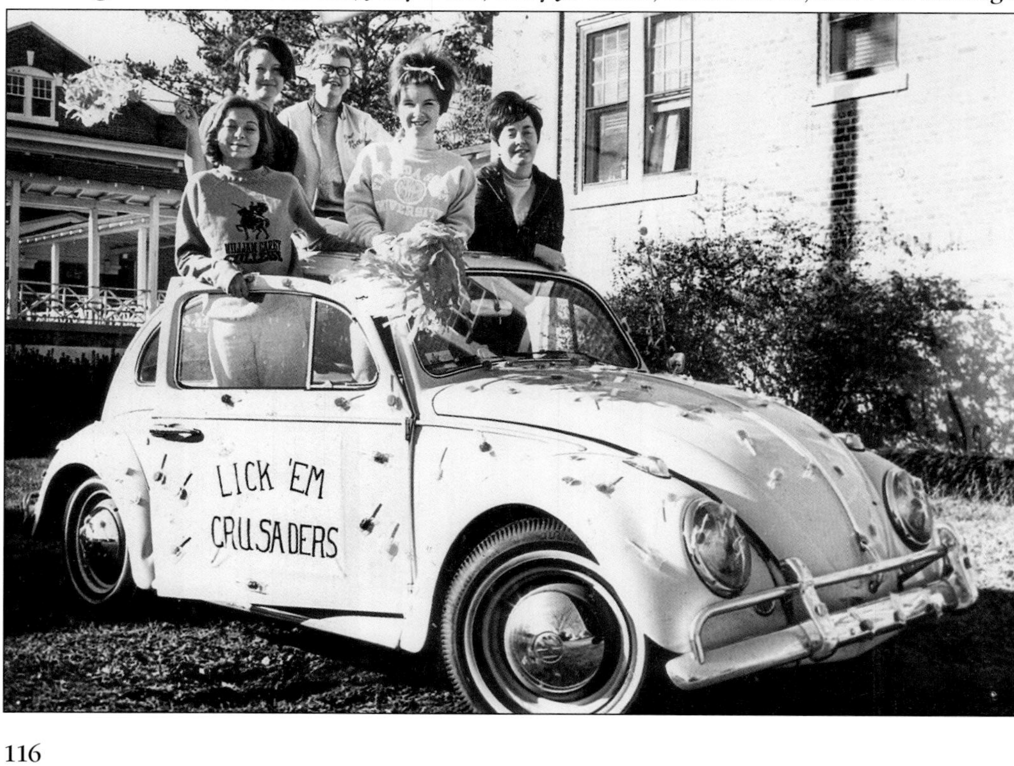

Happy White, public relations director in 1954, holds the student newspaper that announces the arrival of men on campus.

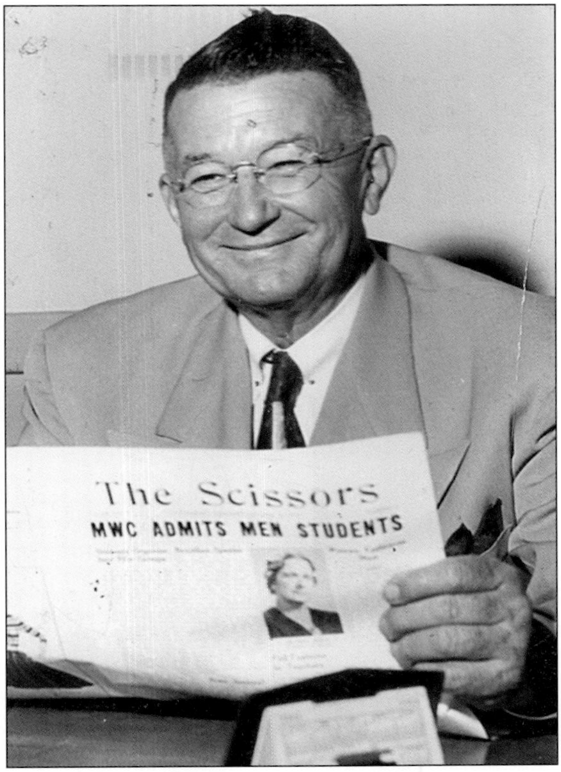


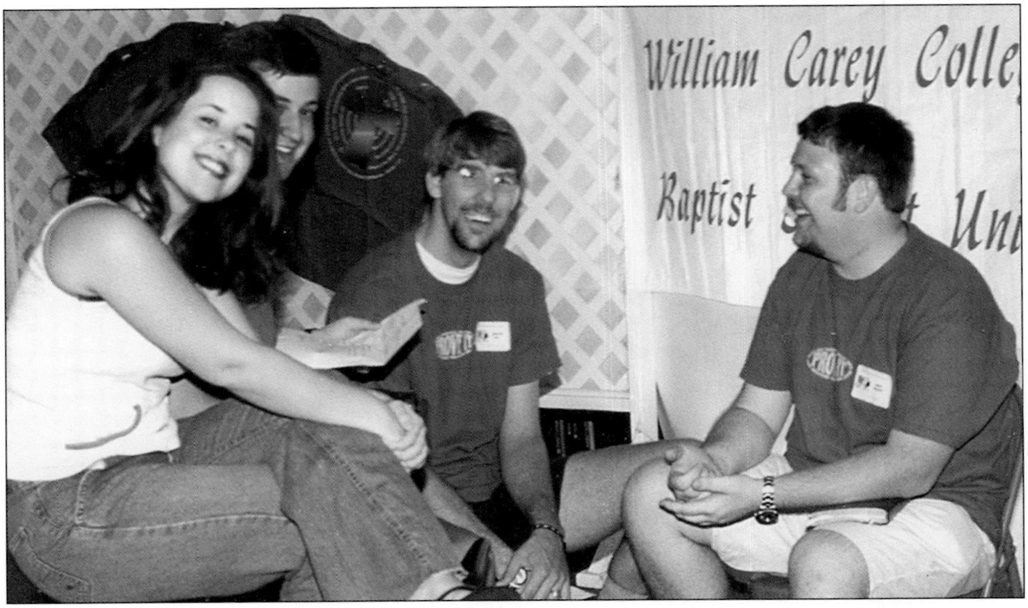


The Baptist Student Union (BSU) has the largest student participation of any organization on campus. Each fall, the BSU sponsors Survival Weekend for new students and Spiritual Emphasis Week for the entire campus. Throughout the year, the BSU provides evening worship events, biweekly "homework clubs" at nearby apartment complexes, mission trips during term breaks, and Priority Lunch, a ministry for commuter students that offers a free meal and devotion for students on the go.

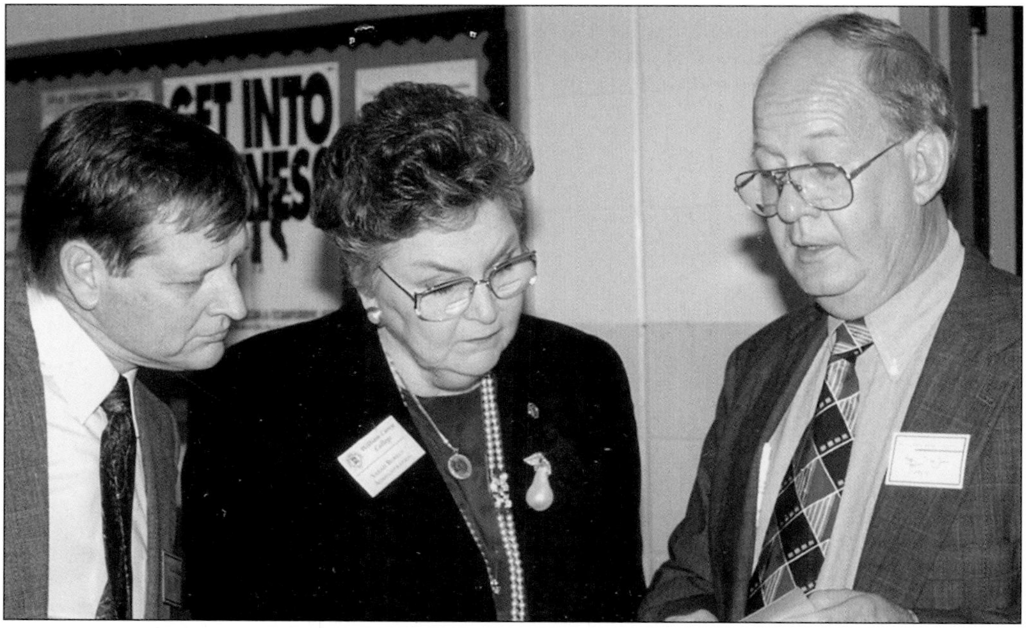

For 38 years (1959–1997), alumna Sarah Gray Burrus served as the college registrar. She estimates that she approved almost 11,000 applications for degrees in that time period. Students observed her caring attitude, noting that she was both friend and counselor. Burrus visits with alumni Rex Dubose, left, and Andy Schottgen, right, at Homecoming 1993.

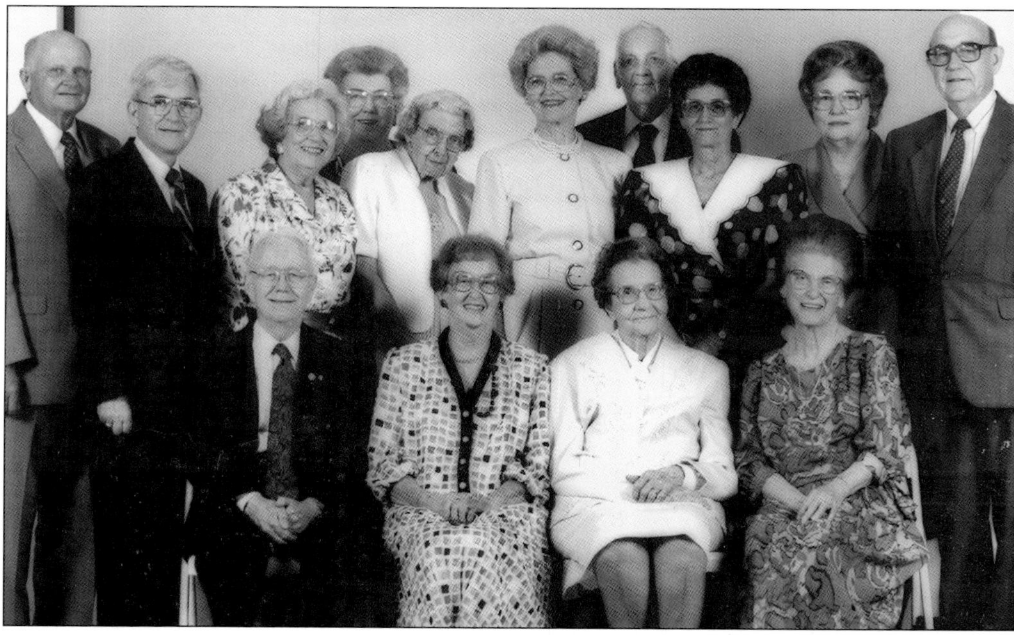

This 1992 photograph of retired faculty and staff includes many who were teachers and administrators in the 1970s. From left to right are (seated) Joseph Ernest, Grace Smith, Julia Loper, and Elise Curtis; (standing) Walter Butler, President Noonkester, Elma McWilliams Cameron, Georgiann Holliman, Frances Winters, Helen McWhorter, Roy Hood, Carmen Simmons, Evelyn McClure, and William Clawson.

President Noonkester visits with Dr. Clyde Bryan (right), pastor of First Baptist Church in Hattiesburg, who, in 1959, was the first recipient of an honorary doctoral degree given by the college.

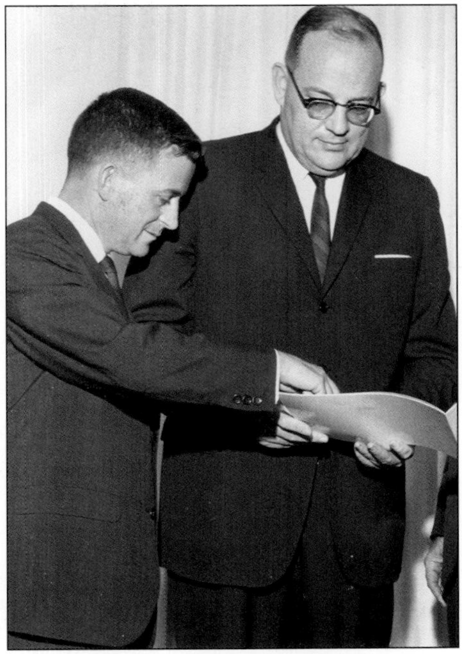

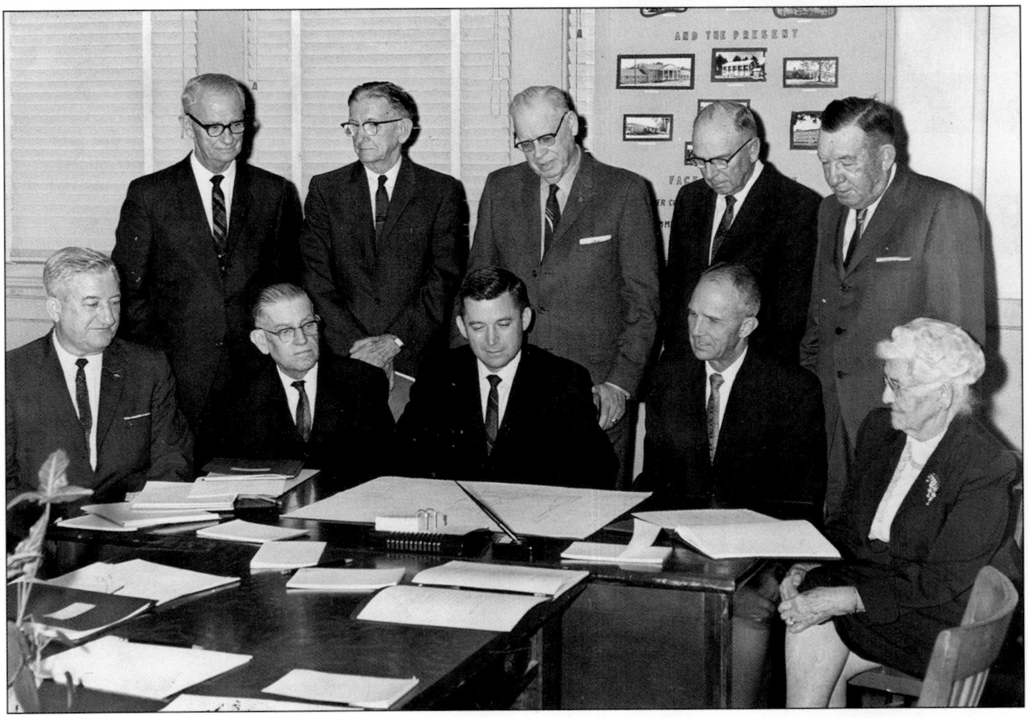

Ada Crawford, wife of. W.W. Crawford, was one of the earliest women to serve as a Carey trustee. She had a special interest in the students and helped numbers of them find financial aid. Ada is shown here with her fellow trustee members in the early 1960s. From left to right are (seated) B.J. Martin, Dr. T.E. Ross, President Noonkester, Purser Hewitt, and Ada; (standing) Crawford Lipsey, R.B. Thomas, Wheeler Bryant, M.F. Rayburn, and Walter Clinton. In 1976, the renovated home economics building was named for Crawford.

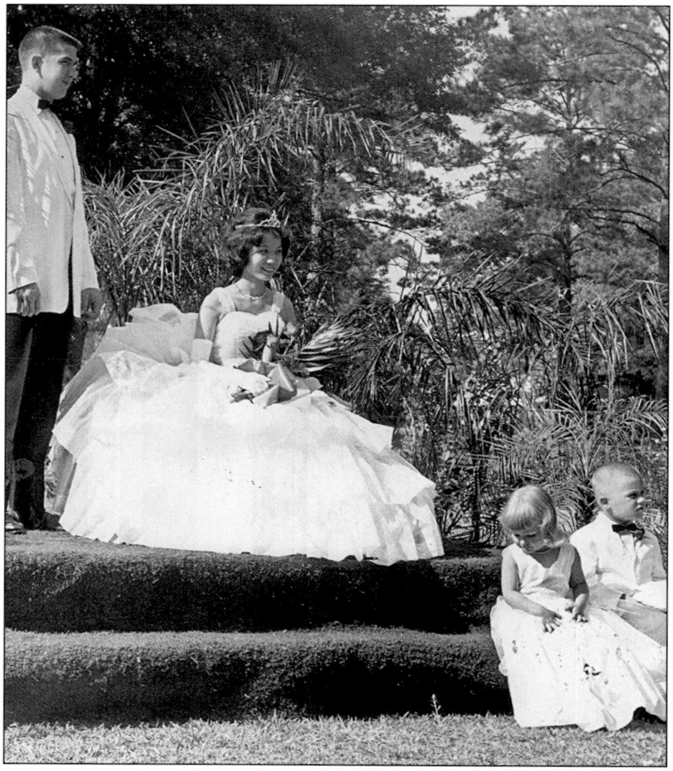

Through the years, international students have added a special flavor to Carey's student body. The 1963 May Day queen, Cecilia Koh, was an international student from Malaysia. At homecoming 2006, Naul Bodden of the Cayman Islands was honored as the distinguished alumnus of the year. Naul was the first indigenous Caymanian to become a CPA, and has established himself as a leading financial consultant. His sister, Martha, is a Carey alumna and space scientist at NASA, while another sister, Carol Sue, also a Carey alumna, has had a distinguished career in nursing. Bodden is pictured below with his wife Thora, his son Landon, and President Kennedy.

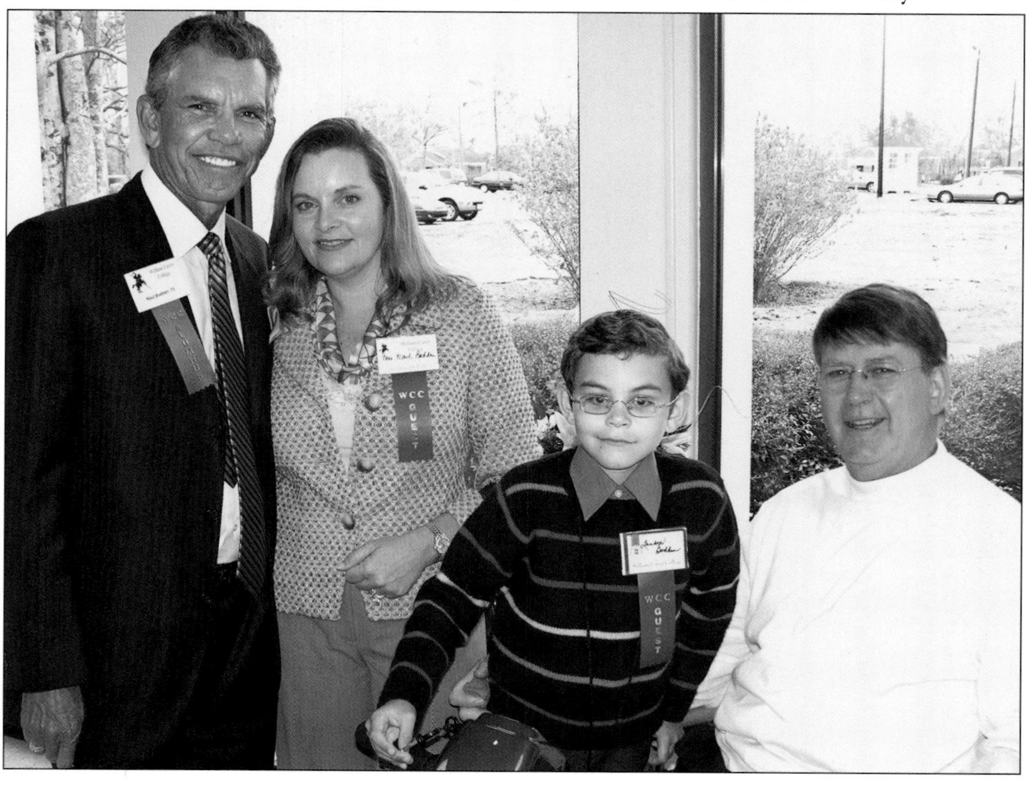

Alumna Jacque Rogers, an English teacher in Collins, Mississippi, was selected by Walt Disney Company as one of five English teachers in the United States to be included in *The Disney Channel Salutes the American Teacher*, a weekly series of video profiles aired nationally in 1992. She was also Mississippi's first Christa McAuliffe Fellow, Mississippi Power Company's Teacher of Excellence, and the winner of a Milken Award. Jacque earned both the master's and education specialist degrees at Carey. Her mother, Anna Mae Edwards Williams, is a 1935 Mississippi Woman's College alumna.

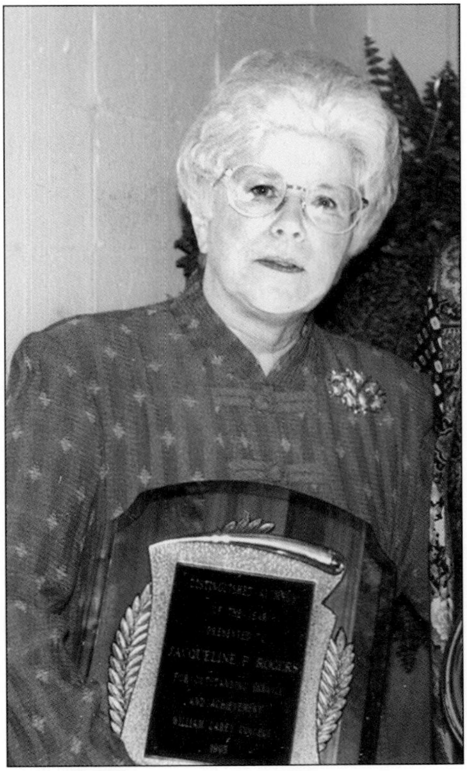

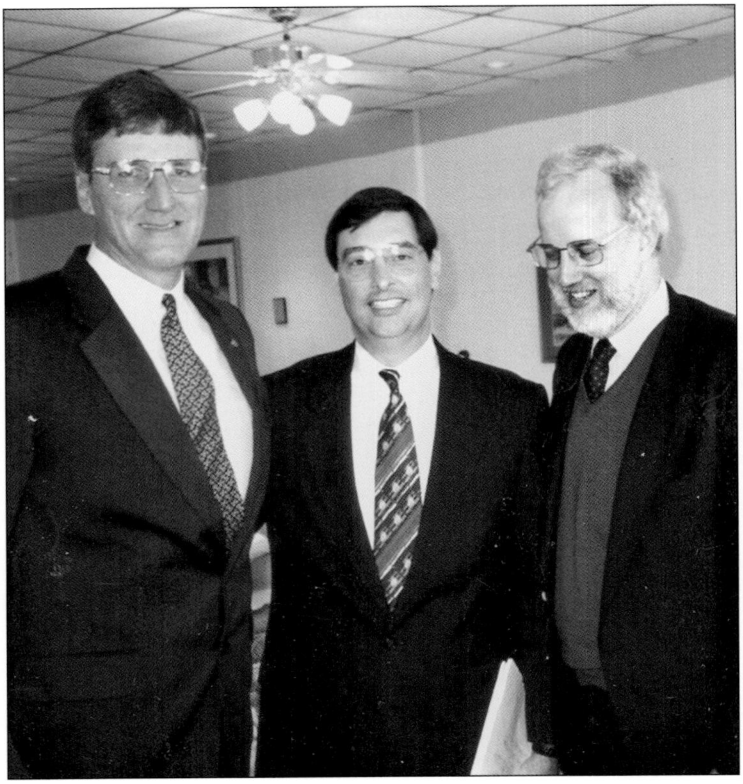

The Honorable Louis Guirola, US district judge for the Southern District of Mississippi, was recognized at Homecoming 2004 as the Distinguished Alumnus of the Year. He is a member of the graduating class of 1973 and is a former Crusader baseball player. Guirola (center) is pictured with classmates Jim Smith (left), senior vice president of Grand Bank, Hattiesburg, and Dr. Douglas Inglis (right), director of the Texas Tech University Center in Seville, Spain.

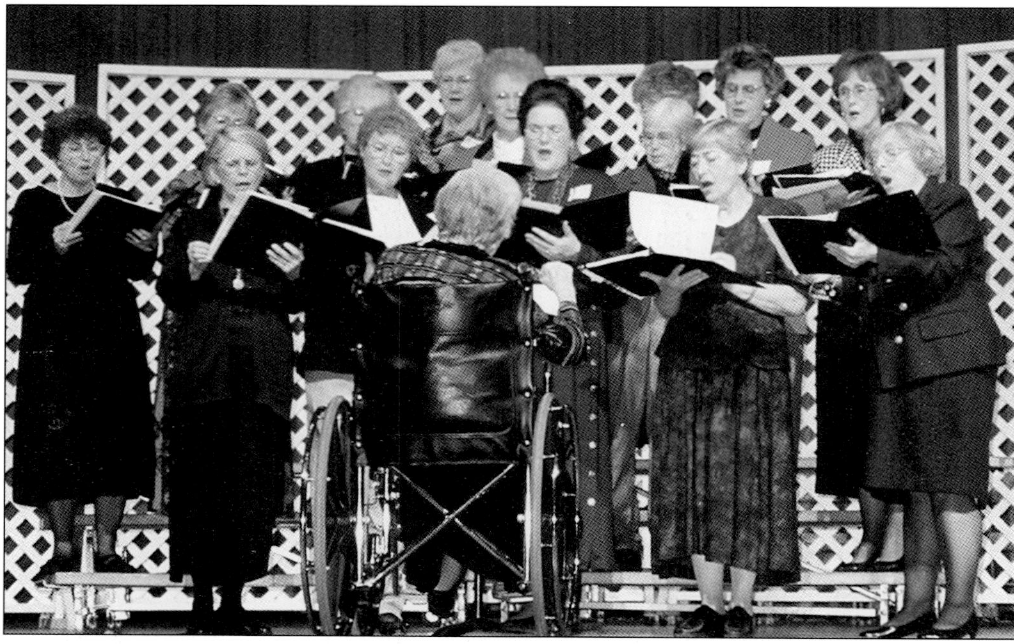

The William Carey College alumni association serves as a link between the present and the past. It counts more than 15,000 living alumni. Many alumni return annually to the campus for homecoming events and class reunions. Mississippi Woman's College alumnae (1946–1954) gathered in 1997 to reunite with their choral director, Julia Guess.

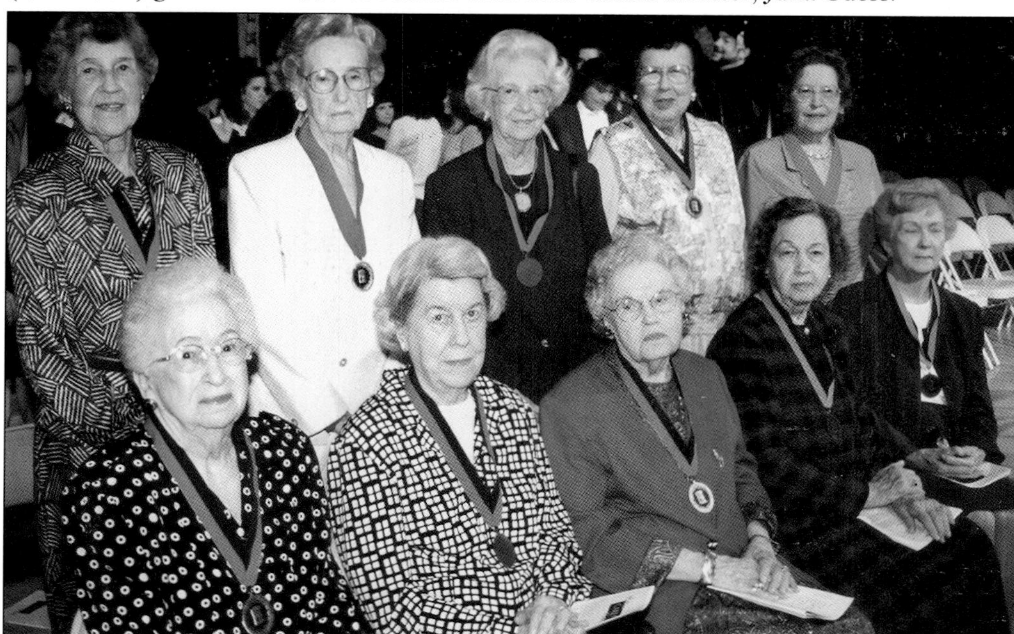

At Honors Day 2000, members of the Mississippi Woman's College Golden Heritage Society were recognized. They are, from left to right, (seated) Sara Batson Riggs, Nancy Hemeter O'Shanick, Helen Cameron Young, Bess Hurst Mason, and Ruby Parker Fortenberry; (standing) Margaret Lou Hemeter Gillespie, Nina Clinton Clearman, Fern Morris Lyter, Mildred Breland Leake, and Mary Webb Perlman.

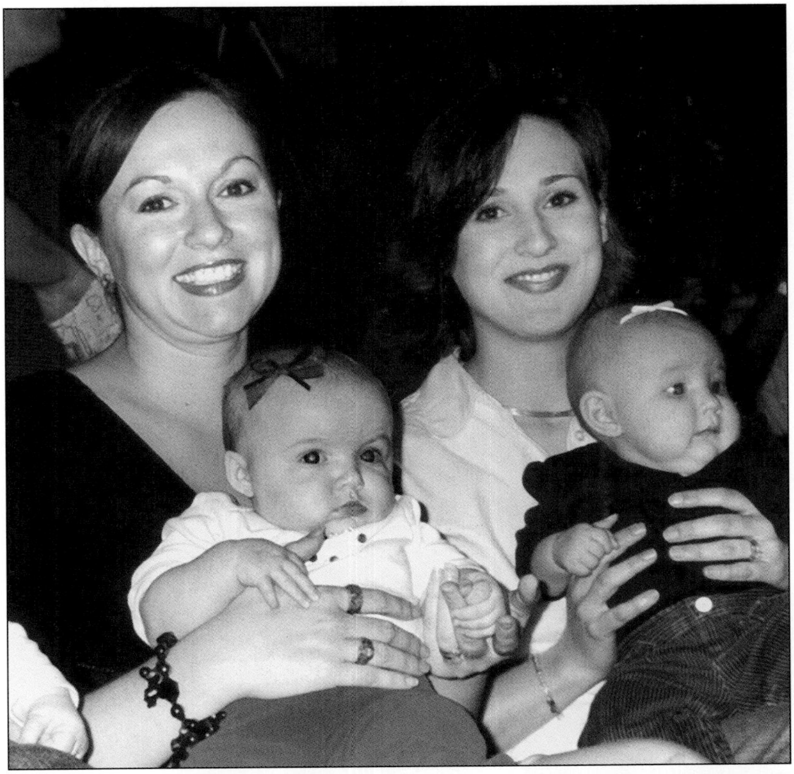

Future Crusaders enjoy the basketball games at Homecoming 2005. Pictured are alumnae Serita Watkins with Aspen Grace (left) and Amy Meaux with Ella Grace (right).

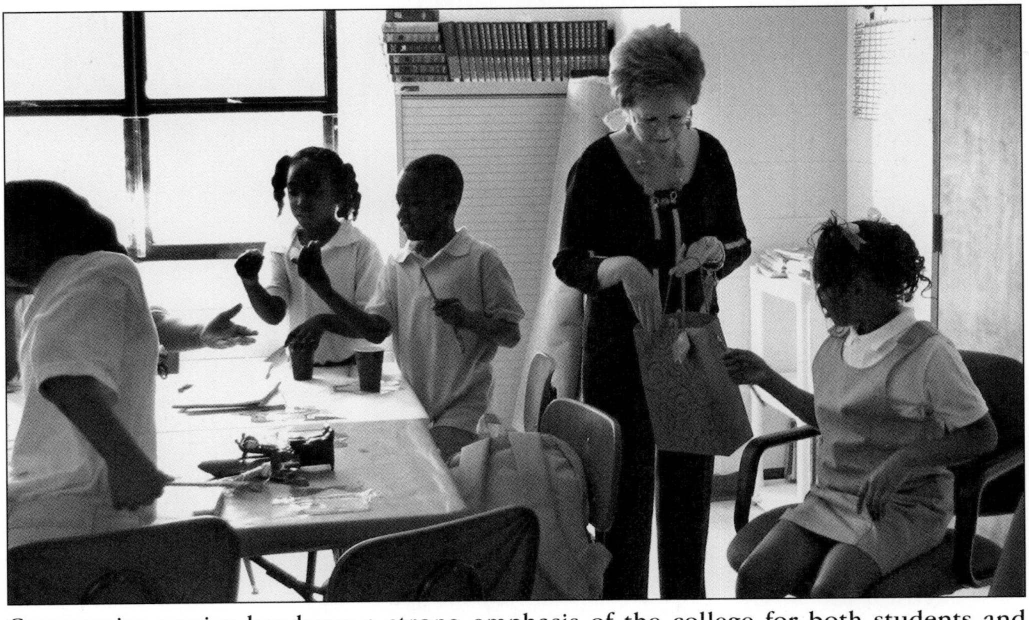

Community service has been a strong emphasis of the college for both students and faculty. Habitat for Humanity, Christian Service Center, and the Boys and Girls Club are just some of the avenues of service. Education students conduct tutoring programs, offering children the opportunity to experience real college classrooms with a myriad of supplies and the latest computer technology to help with lessons. Dr. Patty Ward works with children in a learning laboratory in 2005.

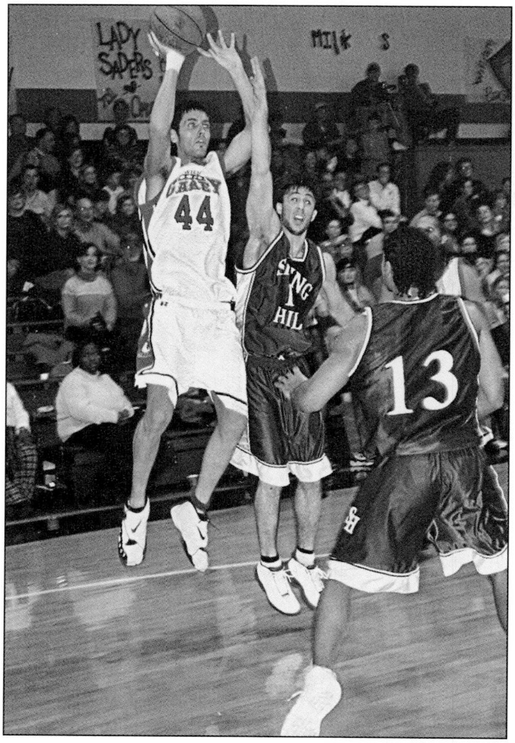


Anticipation was great and stands were packed at basketball games during the 2003–2005 seasons, when Jaeson Maravich, the son of basketball legend Pistol Pete Maravich, played for the Carey team. Jaeson has been busy since then preparing to join the NBA Developmental League team of the Seattle Sonics.

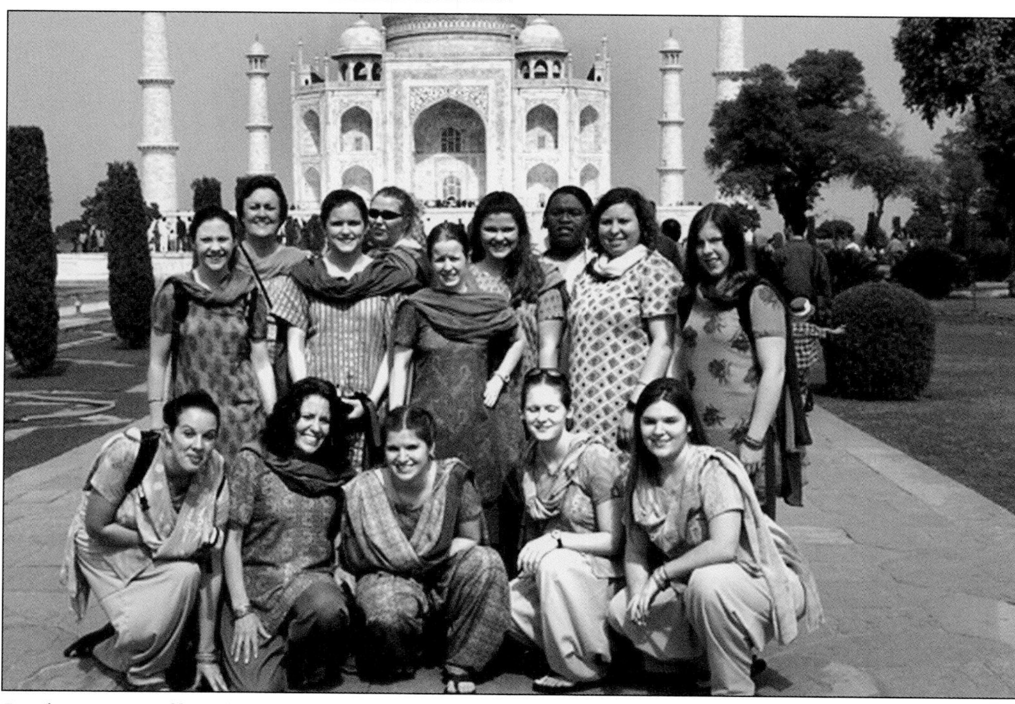

Students are offered numerous opportunities for mission-related travel at Carey. Missions coordinator Dr. Sharon Thompson (second from left, first row) organized this trip to India in 2004. The all-female contingent is pictured in front of the world-famous Taj Mahal. In 2005, Thompson returned to India with members of the William Carey College Chorale.

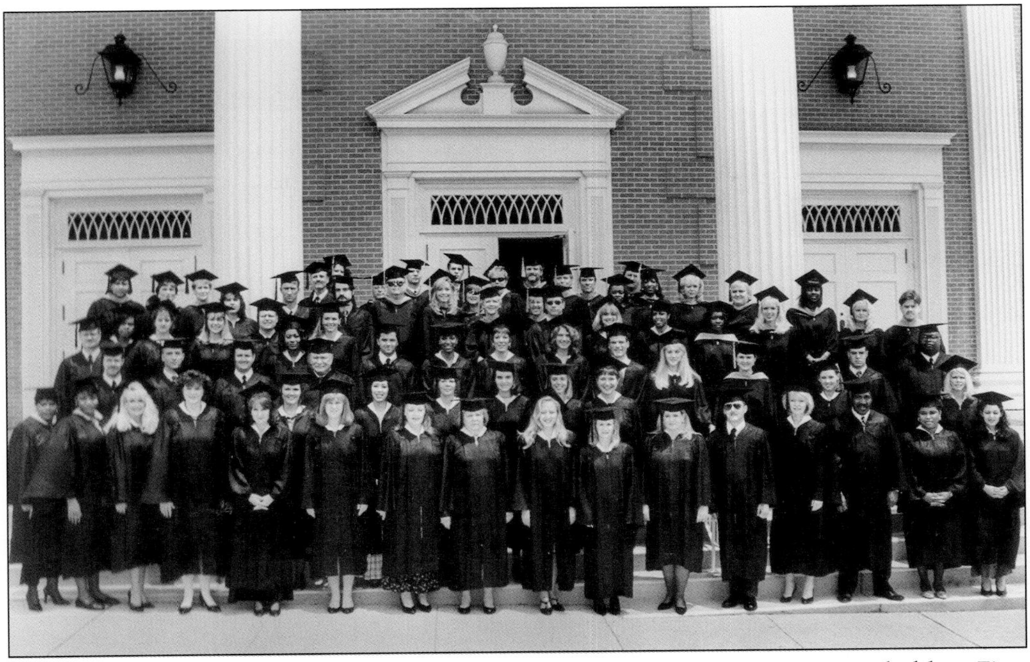

For several years, commencement exercises for Carey on the Coast were held at First Baptist Church, Gulfport, as shown in this early-21st-century photograph. The church building was destroyed by Hurricane Katrina.

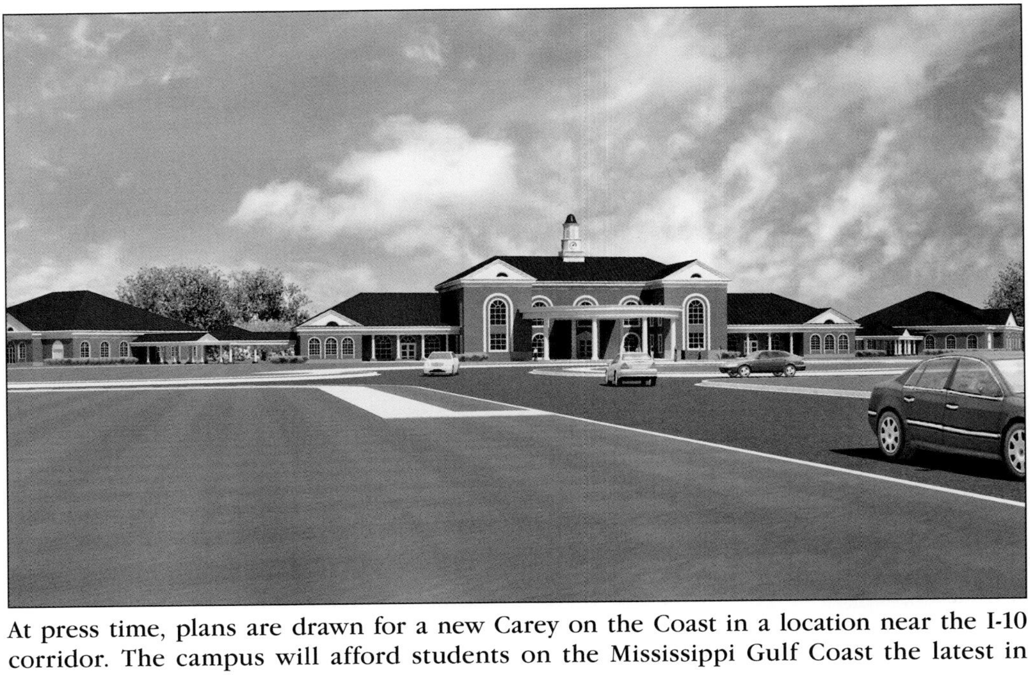

At press time, plans are drawn for a new Carey on the Coast in a location near the I-10 corridor. The campus will afford students on the Mississippi Gulf Coast the latest in facilities and technology.

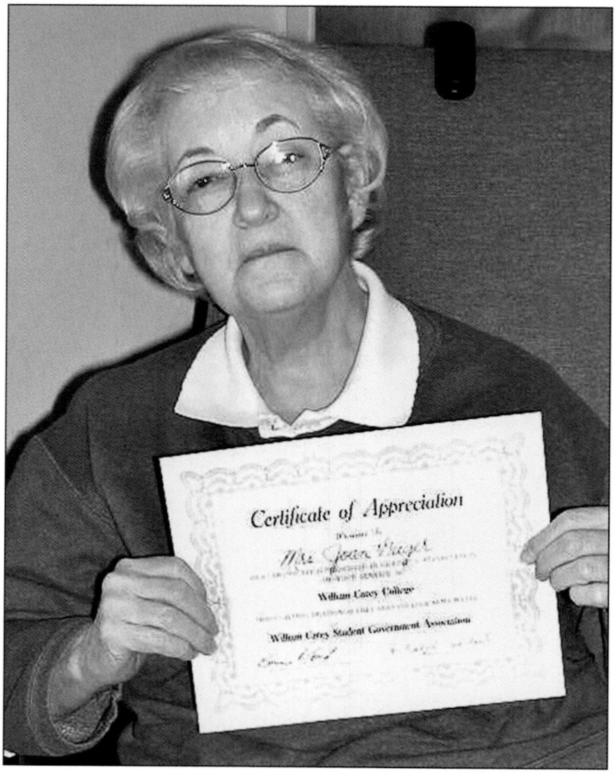


Student Joan Geiger composed the words to the William Carey College alma mater, and it was adopted by acclamation of the student body in chapel on May 25, 1961. Dr. Robert Gauldin, professor of theory, composed the music. The college thanked Geiger at William Carey College's 50th anniversary.

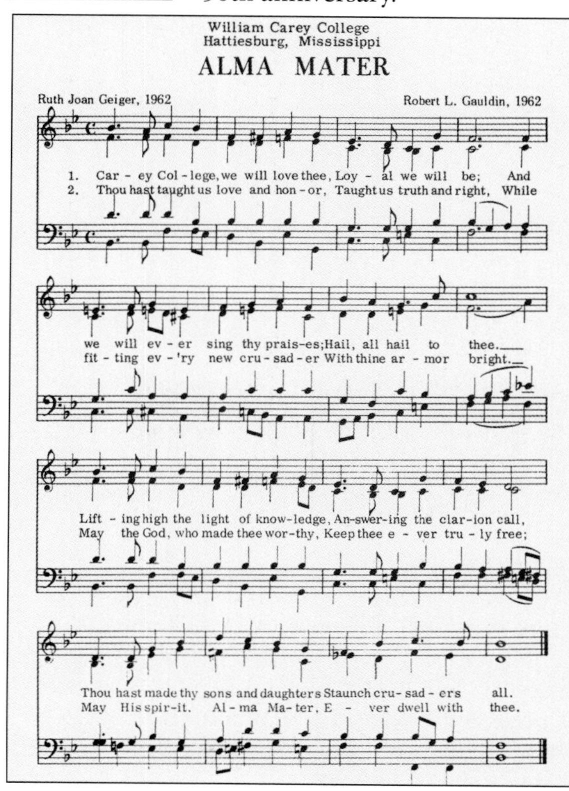

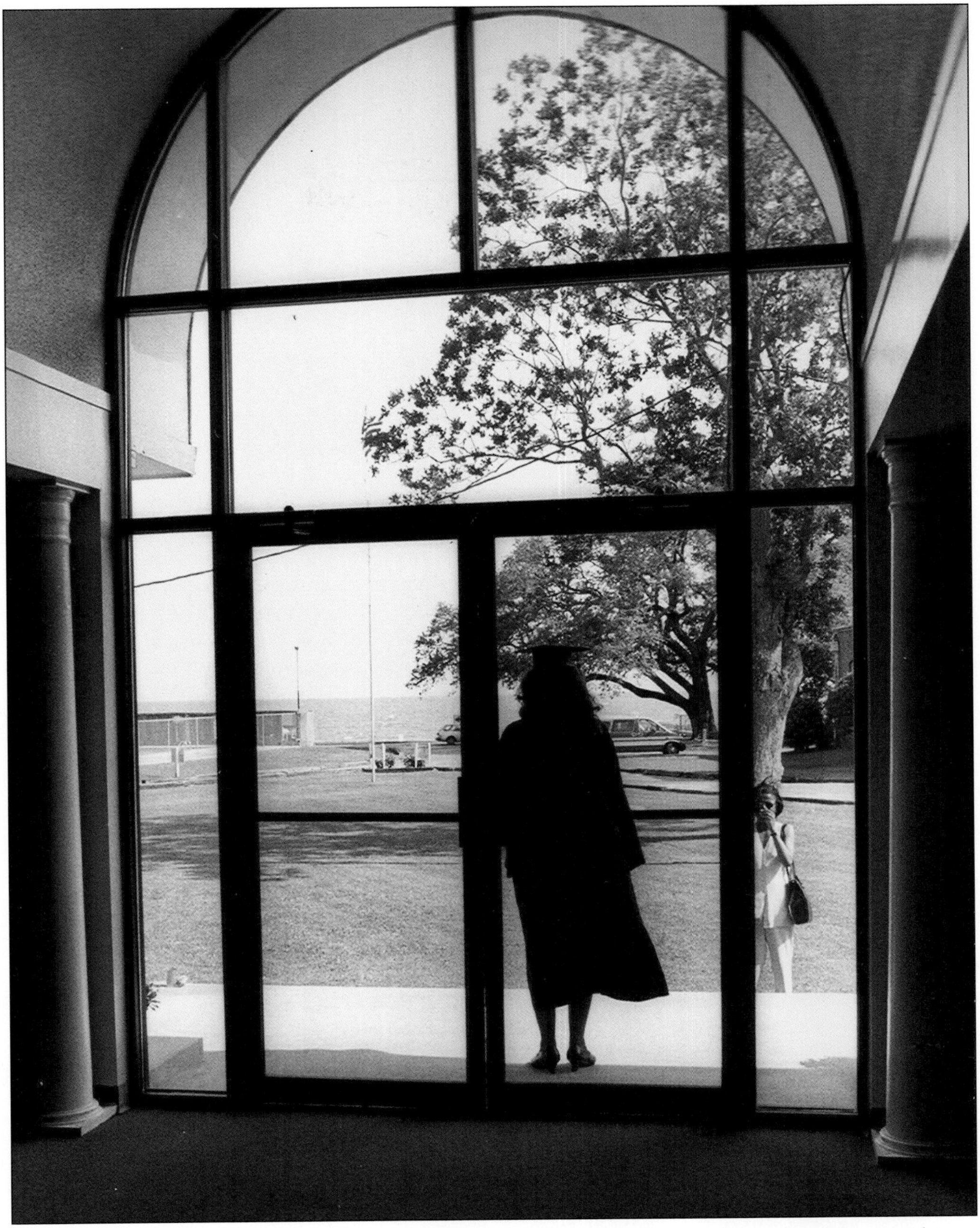

William Carey College in its first 100 years has provided a quality education within a Christian environment to more than 18,000 graduates who are serving across the nation and abroad in many professions. Just prior to Hurricane Katrina, 3,026 students from 19 states and 14 countries were enrolled, majoring in 25 areas of concentration. Enrollment dropped after many students on the Mississippi Gulf Coast and in New Orleans were displaced by the storm. The enrollment is steadily rebuilding. The college motto, taken from a sermon given by William Carey, will guide our next 100 years as we "Expect great things from God; attempt great things for God." William Carey College celebrates its past and embraces its future.

# About This Edition

In 2006, William Carey College celebrated what was believed to be the institution's centennial year. It was a year of celebration capped with a major announcement: a name change to William Carey University in recognition of the institution's continued growth. University administrators and the board of trustees believed the new name would further enhance the growth of the university while also increasing its potential in an increasingly global environment. The name change, the fifth in the university's history, was made effective during a special convocation at the Hattiesburg campus on August 14, 2006.

The name change came at a difficult time for the university. Hurricane Katrina, which struck land roughly a year prior to the convocation, had affected all three campuses but had totally destroyed the picturesque Mississippi Gulf Coast campus, located along Beach Boulevard on 20 acres in Gulfport. All buildings, including the newly renovated administration building, saw significant damage. Enrollment dropped from a pre-Katrina high of 605 students to 462 students one year later as officials searched for a new home along the Gulf Coast. The New Orleans campus, located on the grounds of the New Orleans Baptist Theological Seminary, escaped the crippling flooding that devastated much of the city but also suffered from a staggering enrollment drop.

A bright spot was found in the growth of the Hattiesburg campus, which avoided most of the catastrophic damage delivered to its sister campuses by Hurricane Katrina. The campus had reached a record enrollment of 1,240 students, including 42 international students, and officials were preparing to add two new 190-bed residence halls to accommodate residential student growth. New athletic fields had been added to accommodate a growing roster of sports teams, including the soccer program that was previously located at the Gulf Coast campus. Donnell Hall, home of an impressive collection of research materials and artifacts related to university namesake William Carey, opened in May 2006.

At the helm of Carey's growth and rebuilding from Hurricane Katrina was Dr. Larry Kennedy, the institution's leader since 1997. A former professor of religion, dean of the Cooper School of Missions and Biblical Studies and vice president of church relations, Kennedy was named Carey's interim president in October 1997 before being installed as the eighth president in August 1998. During his tenure, enrollment increased by more than 1,000 students as new degrees and programs were added. Kennedy supervised numerous construction and renovating projects totaling more than $22 million while also leading the university to debt-free status at the time of the name change.

Kennedy was diagnosed with amyotrophic lateral sclerosis (ALS), also known as Lou Gehrig's disease, in July 2005. He bravely fought the disease, which has no known cure and usually no known cause, for more than a year—while also continuing his work as president—before passing away at the age of 64 on September 21, 2006. The Larry W. Kennedy Sports Complex was dedicated to his memory the following year.

Kennedy, beloved by his colleagues, his students, and Mississippi Baptists, was succeeded by a familiar face to all of those groups. Dr. Tommy King, the executive vice president under Kennedy and an integral part of the day-to-day operations of the university during Kennedy's illness, was named acting president. He was confirmed as Carey's ninth president on February 8, 2007. The first alumnus to hold the position, King was the "unanimous and enthusiastic choice of the Board of Trustees," said Stan Burton, then-chairman. "Dr. King's extensive background in education, his strong role in Baptist life, his dedication to the mission of Carey, and his sound management skills make him the right choice for continuous growth and accomplishments at the university."

A former counselor, pastor, principal, and teacher, King joined the Carey faculty in 1999 as a professor of psychology. He was promoted to dean of psychology and counseling and later served as vice president of graduate and off-campus programs before becoming executive vice president under Kennedy. A 1964 graduate who also met his wife, Sandra, during their student days, King's goals as president were found in the university's motto, a famous quote first uttered by the university's namesake during a 1792 sermon: "Expect great things from God; attempt great things for God."

King would prove to be a stable and effective leader for Carey, especially following the frenetic years of 2005 and 2006. My addition to this book will follow King's presidency through early 2017 and will also go back in time to 1892 in Poplarville, Mississippi, where a boarding school will become significant to our story. The revised book will conclude with the sad events of early 2017, which saw the Hattiesburg campus devastated by an EF3 tornado. Although the campus has seen major devastation, this volume—both Donna Wheeler's original words and my addition—show the resolve of the Carey community and our belief in "expecting and attempting."

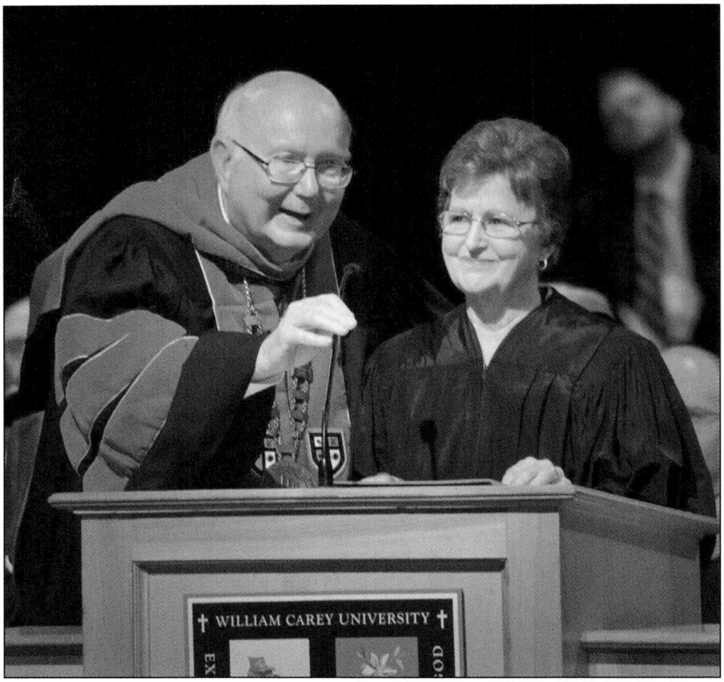


Dr. Tommy King, pictured with his wife, Sandra, succeeded Dr. Larry Kennedy as president in 2007. Dr. King is the first alumnus to hold the position. His steady leadership has prompted an enrollment growth to nearly 4,500 students, the construction of a new Gulf Coast campus, the addition of the College of Osteopathic Medicine and a School of Pharmacy, other building projects, and numerous new degree offerings.

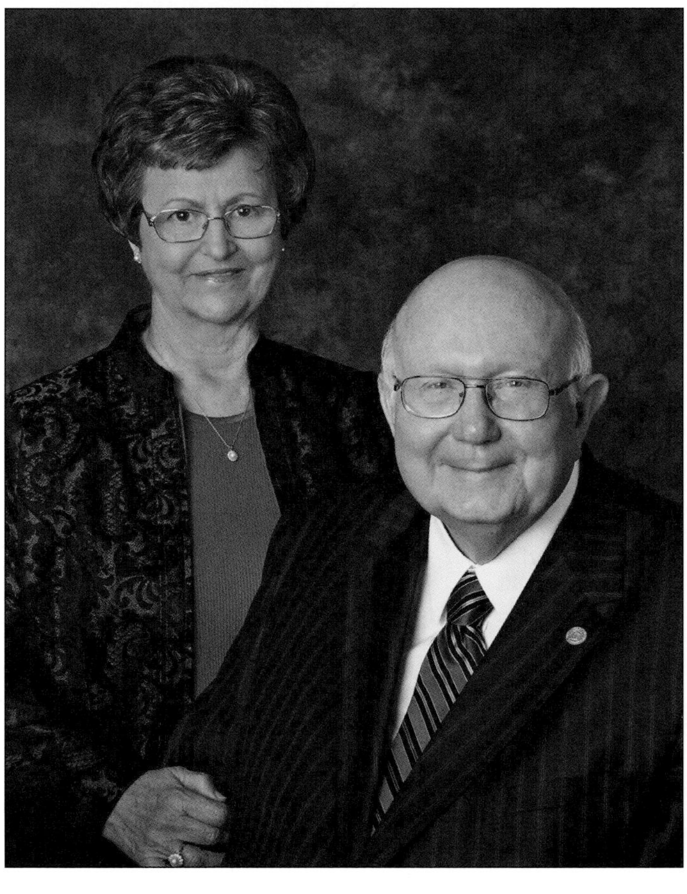

Dr. Tommy King is the third-longest-serving president in Carey's history. During his time in office, the university has finished rebuilding from Hurricane Katrina and is recovering ahead of schedule from a devastating tornado in January 2017. King has positioned the university as a modern, forward-thinking institution with a strong focus on equipping graduates to meet the various needs of communities throughout the Southeast and around the world. His wife, Sandra, is an active first lady and has been instrumental in the growth of the university during King's tenure.

# *Six*

# William Carey University 2006–2012

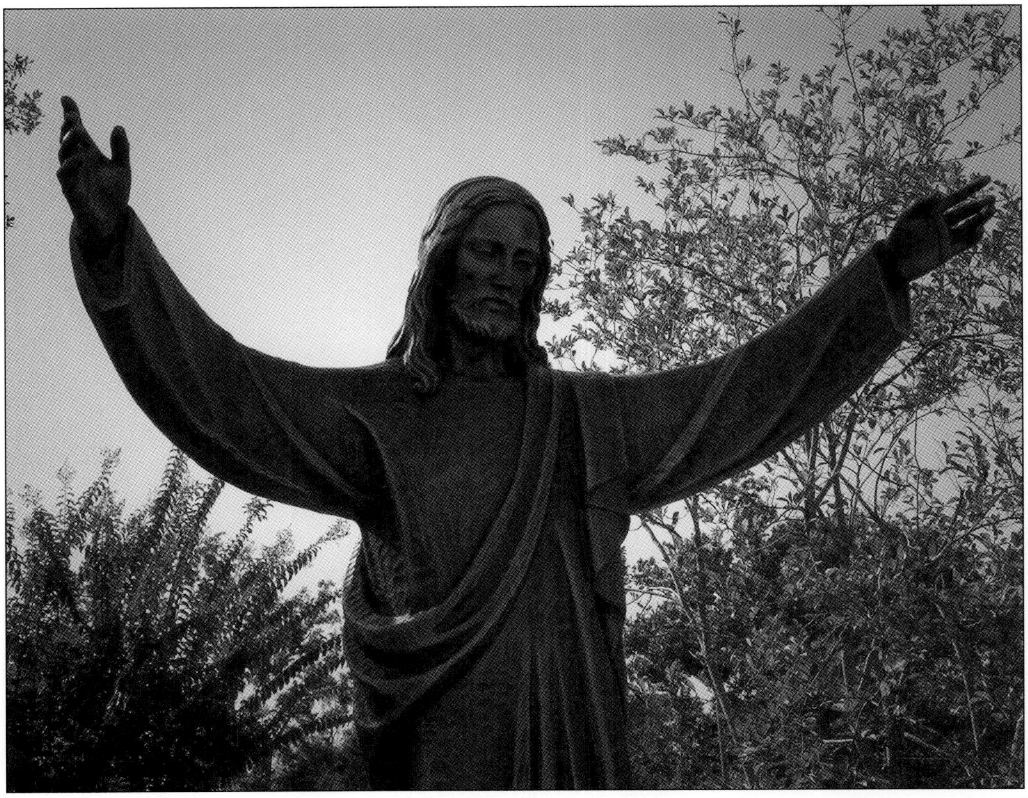

*The Risen Christ* statue, created in Italy, was added to Chain Garden in 2006. The sculpted bronze, which stands six feet tall, features biblical scripture surrounding the base and a memorial plaque honoring the late president, Dr. Larry Kennedy. The garden, which was heavily damaged by Hurricane Katrina, was renovated by the Chain family during the same year.

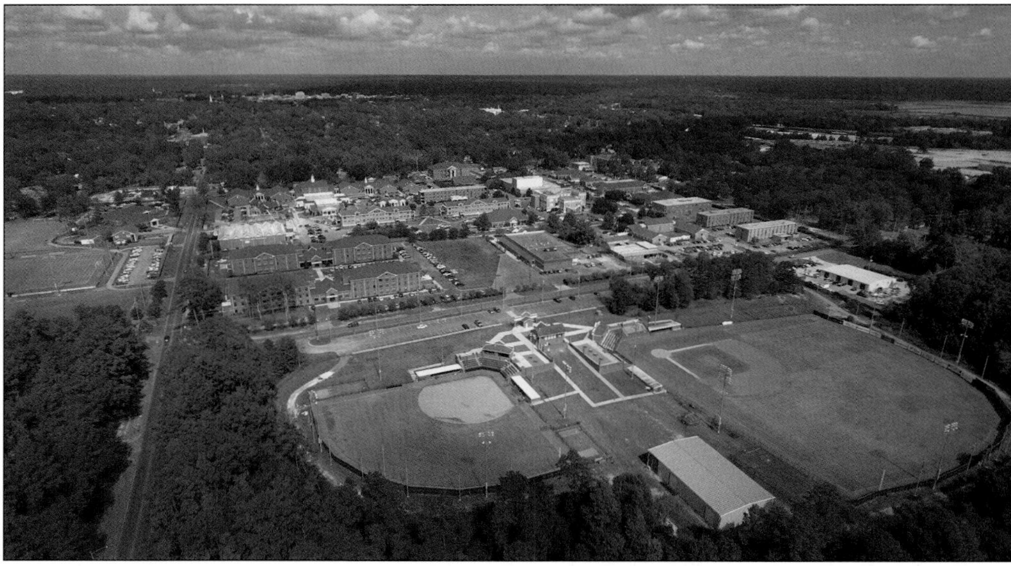

The Larry W. Kennedy Sports Complex was dedicated in 2007 and includes the Milton Wheeler Baseball Field, the Joseph and Nancy Fail Softball Field, soccer fields, an intramural field, a jogging track, concession and ticket booths, and athletic offices. The complex was expanded with a new tennis complex and the Jack Jones Field House for soccer and tennis players in 2011.

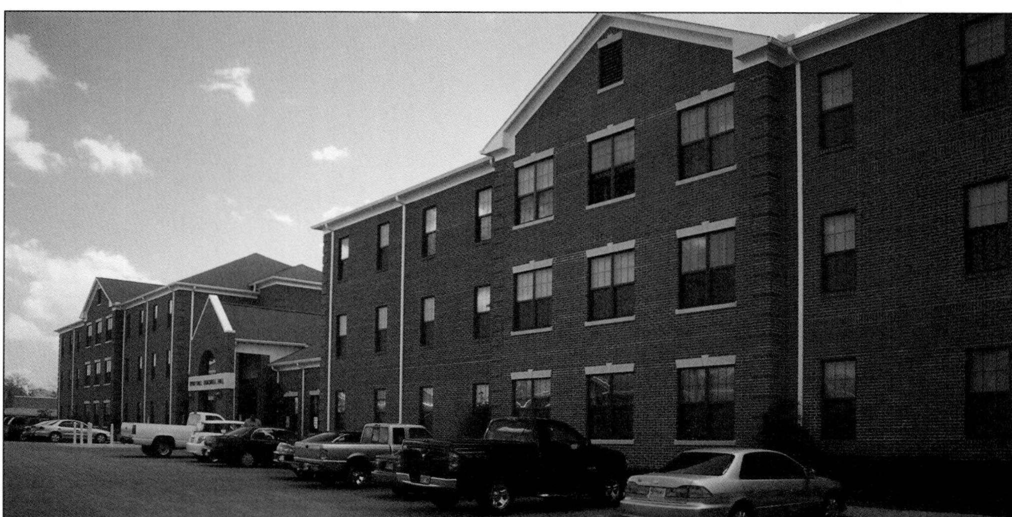

Byrd and Braswell Halls, twin residence halls, were dedicated in 2007 to accommodate an increasing residential population. Each three-story hall has 89 resident rooms in suite arrangements, with two rooms sharing a bathroom, and an apartment for a resident director. Byrd Hall, which houses female students, and Braswell Hall, which houses male students, share a common lobby with lounging areas.

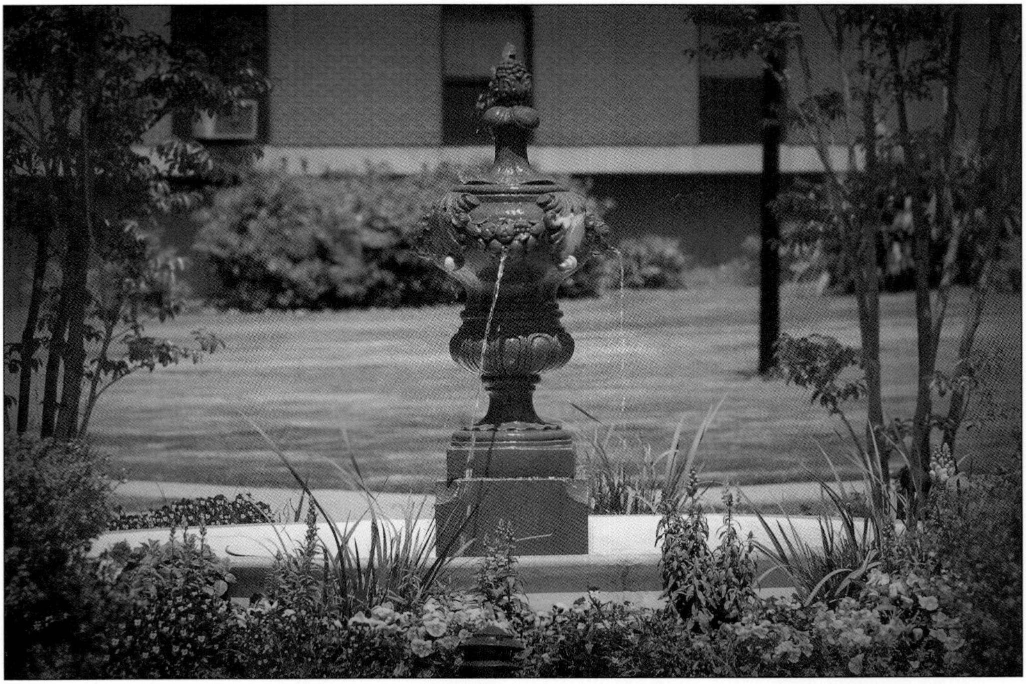

Mississippi Woman's College Heritage Plaza was dedicated in 2008 in memory of Margaret Lou Hemeter Gillespie, a 1931 alumna of Woman's College. The plaza includes benches for meditation, garden plantings, and a memorial fountain. Funds for the plaza were donated by Woman's College alumnae and by Gillespie's husband of 70 years, Robert. Woman's College, a predecessor of William Carey University, operated from 1911 to 1954.

Students, in keeping with Carey's mission of challenging the individual student to excel in scholarship, leadership, and service, served in growing numbers on both the domestic and foreign mission fields in 2007–2008, including (pictured) local tutoring ministries in areas near the Hattiesburg campus. Students also volunteered for summer mission projects and traveled to areas including California, Hawaii, Canada, Kenya, and Peru.

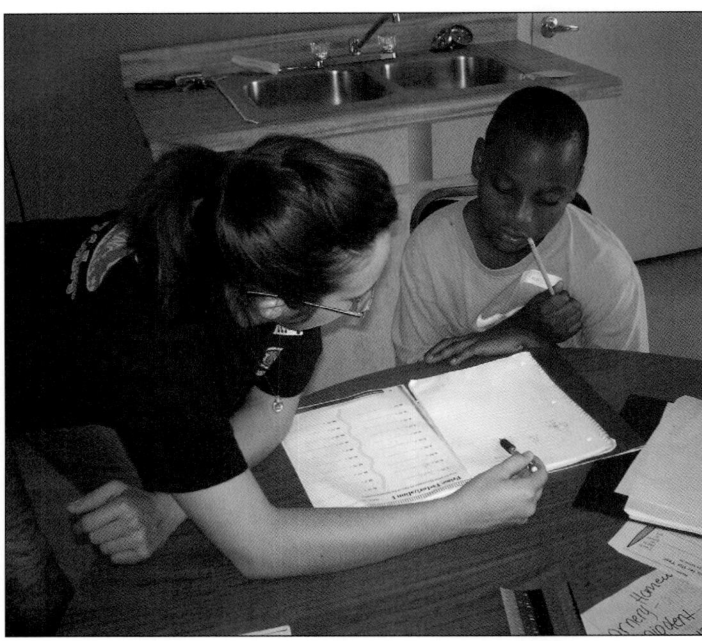

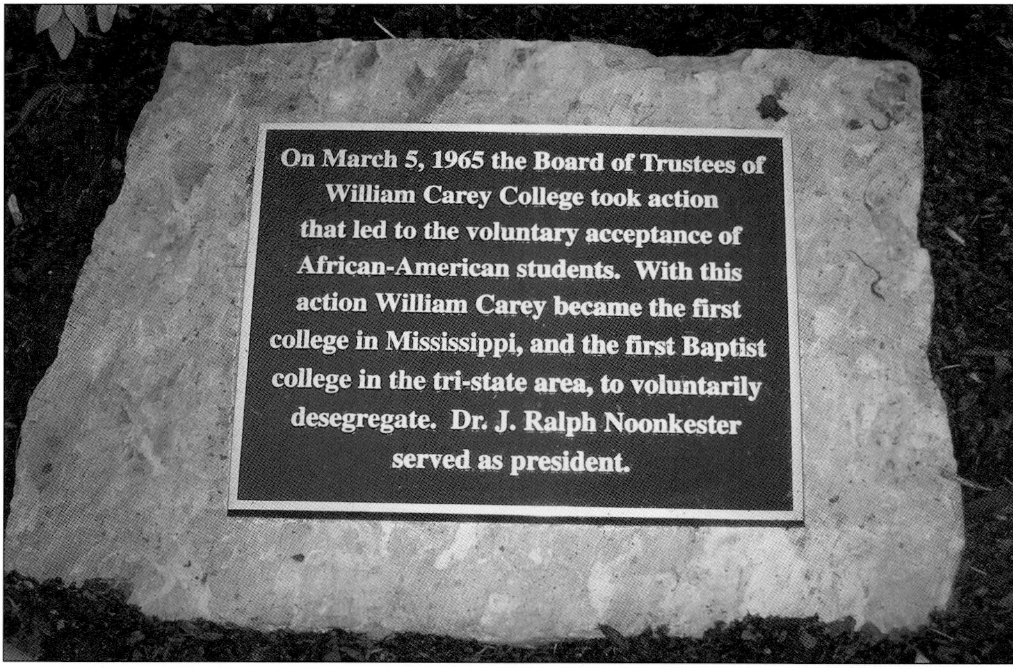


This plaque, placed in 2008 near Tatum Court, commemorates the peaceful desegregation of Carey in 1965. The board of trustees, acting unanimously upon a recommendation from then-president J. Ralph Noonkester, voluntarily admitted the first two African American students, Vermester Jackson Bester and Linda Williams Cross. Carey was the first college in Mississippi and the first Baptist college in the Deep South to voluntarily integrate.

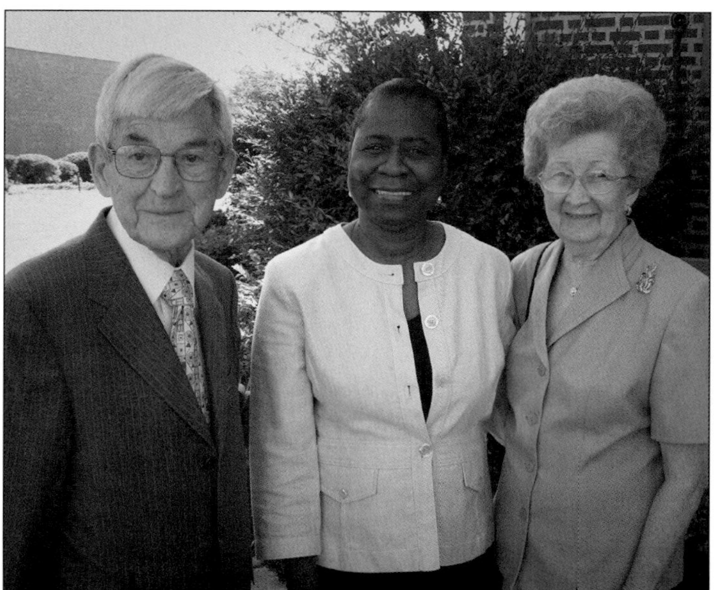

President emeritus Dr. J. Ralph Noonkester and his wife, Naomi, are pictured with Vermester Jackson Bester, one of the first two African American students admitted to Carey, during a 2008 plaque dedication honoring Carey's voluntary desegregation under Noonkester in 1965. Bester graduated from Carey with a bachelor's degree in mathematics in 1989 and started a 40-year-career with the Hattiesburg Public School District.

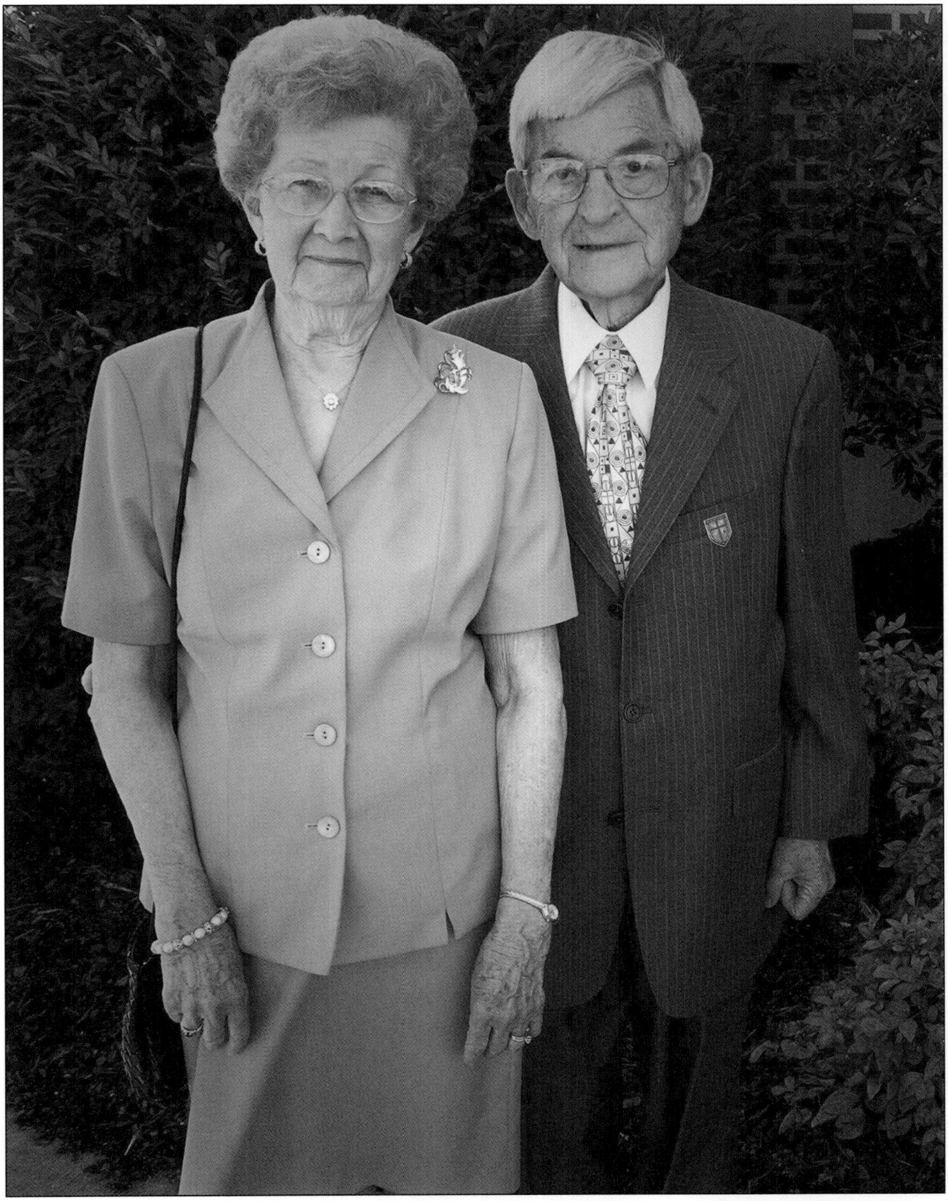

In 2008, the School of Arts, Humanities, and Sciences was renamed the Ralph and Naomi Noonkester School of Arts and Letters in honor of the couple's service to Carey. A portrait of the couple was unveiled and hung on the third floor of Tatum Court near the dean's office. Dr. J. Ralph Noonkester served as president from 1956 to 1989 with his wife, Naomi, serving as an active and supportive first lady. His tenure was marked with the voluntary integration of the college, building additions, new academic programs, athletic excellence on a national scale, the opening of the Gulf Coast campus, a rise in student mission efforts, and a high percentage of acceptances to medical school. Following his presidency, he served as an active president emeritus, attending graduations, special events, and continuing to teach classes in biblical studies. Ralph Noonkester died in September 2012 and Naomi Noonkester died in February 2013. The couple was married for 65 years. Their son, Myron, currently serves as dean of the Noonkester School.

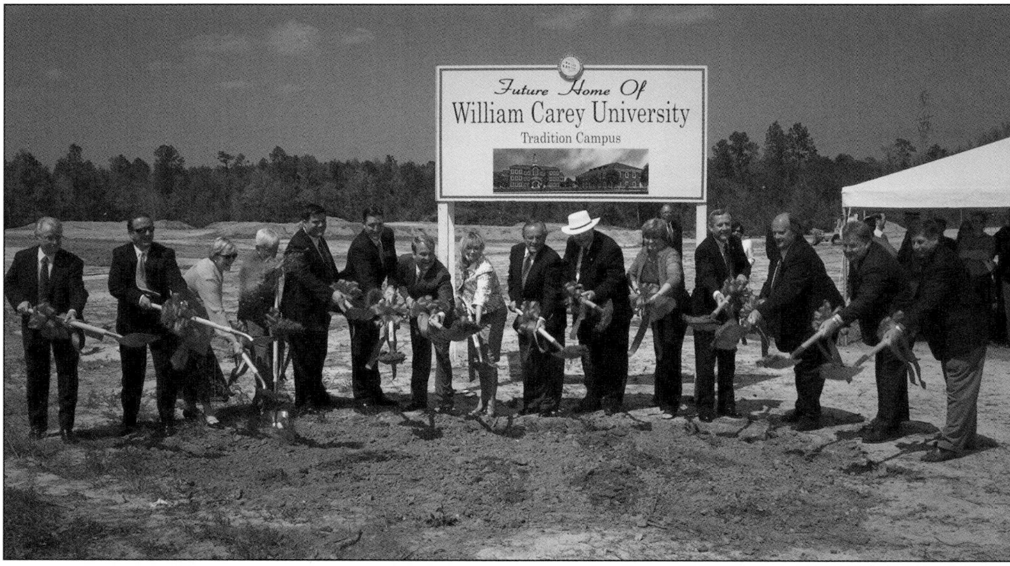


University officials broke ground on a new Mississippi Gulf Coast campus, located on Highway 67 in central Harrison County, in April 2008. The $14 million Tradition campus, as it would later be named, is a part of the 4,800-acre Tradition Planned Community, the largest master-planned community under development in the state. The campus replaced the beachfront Gulfport campus, which was lost during Hurricane Katrina in 2005.

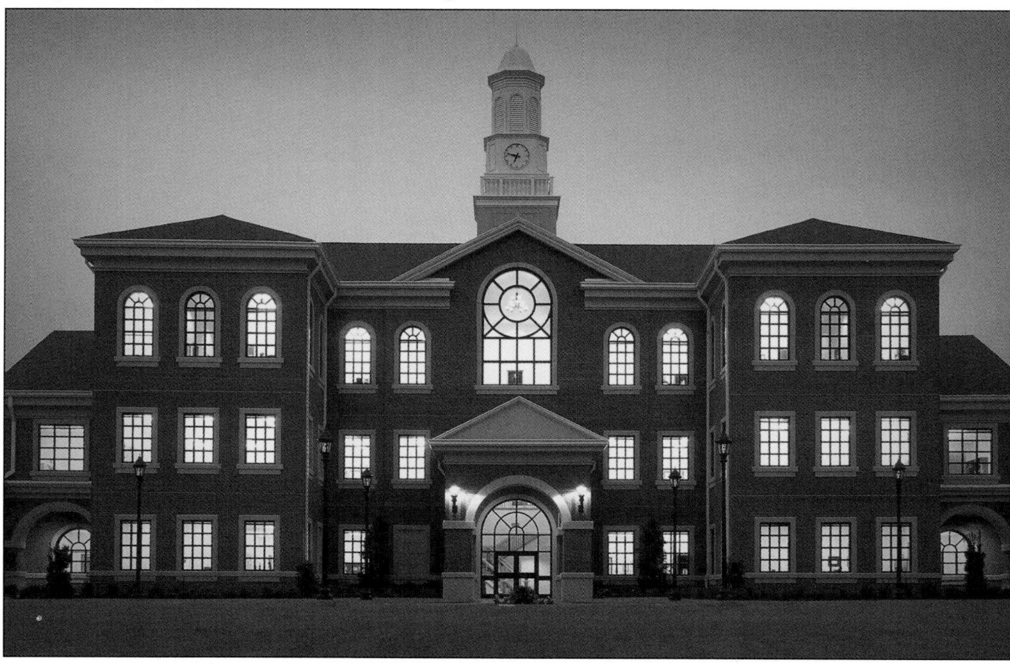

The first phase of the Tradition campus opened in August 2009 with 710 students in undergraduate and graduate programs. Four buildings, including two three-story buildings and buildings for maintenance and security, encompass a total of 58,559 square feet. There are 30 general classrooms on the campus along with labs, student lounges, offices, and an expansive library. Additional phases of the campus are planned and could accommodate up to 3,000 students.

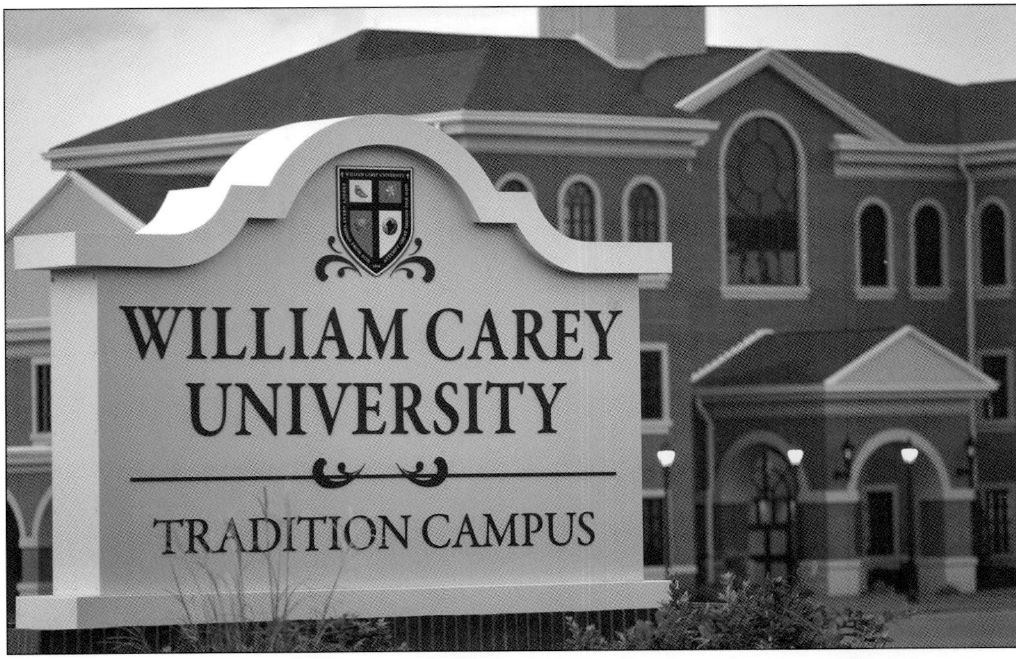


Tradition provided a welcome new home for Gulf Coast campus faculty, staff, and students, who had been largely displaced since the 2005 hurricane. Classes were held in temporary facilities along the Gulf Coast and mobile facilities on the former Gulfport campus, which is now for sale. University officials made the decision to move away from the beachfront property due to high insurance premiums and the risk of another hurricane.

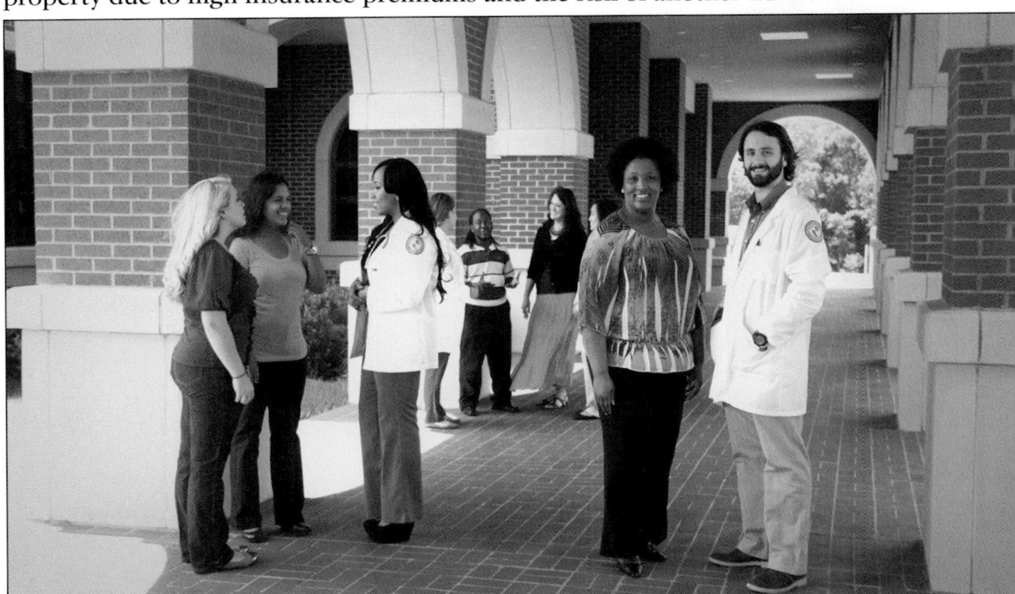

Since opening in 2009, Tradition has seen steady enrollment growth and the addition of new programs, including bachelor's and master's degrees in criminal justice. Nursing, education, business, and biology programs are popular on the campus, which boasted a record enrollment of nearly 1,200 students in 2015. The campus will soon be expanded to include facilities for a pharmacy school, which is set to open in the fall of 2018.

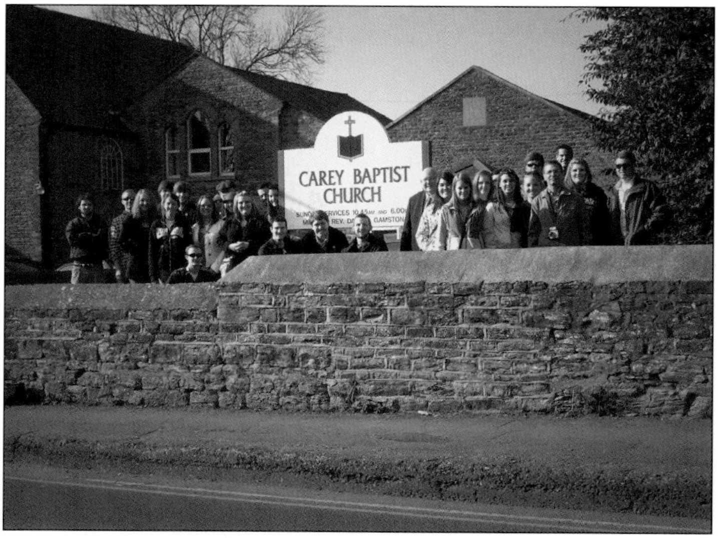


The Carey Scholars, a group of students earning more than 29 on the ACT, made their first trip to England in 2008. The group is pictured in front of Carey Baptist Church in Moulton, where William Carey was once minister. The trip to "Carey Country"—where Carey grew up, worked, and later ministered—is now a tradition for the scholars during their freshmen or sophomore years.

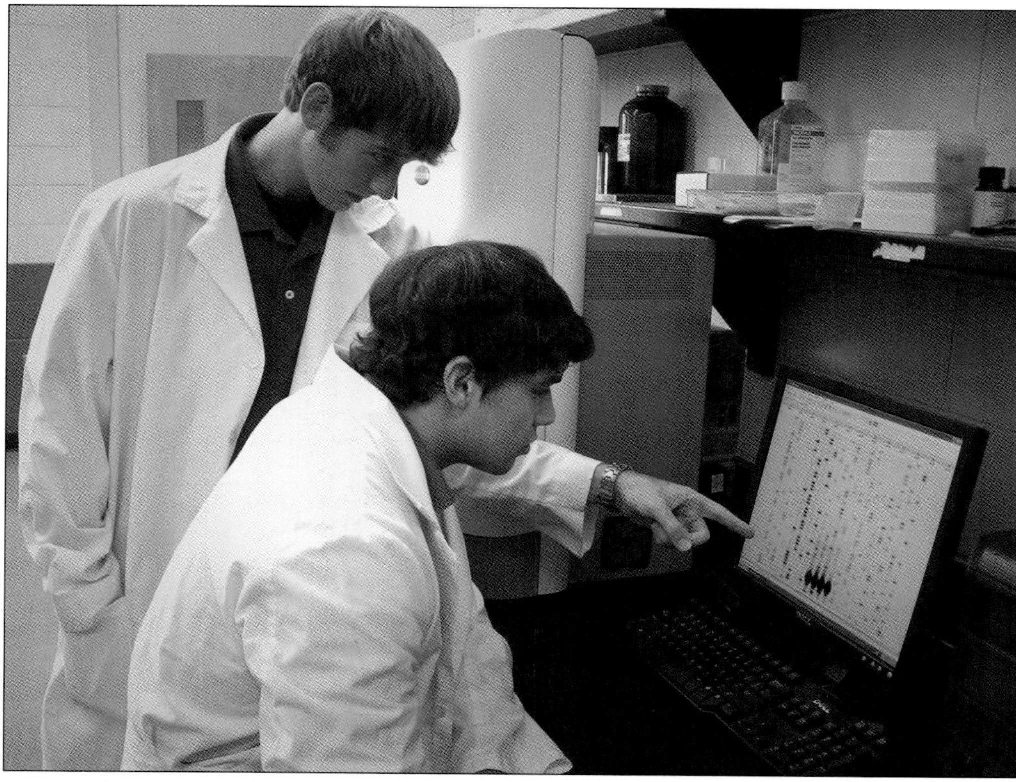

Tremendous growth in the biological sciences program started during the 2007–2008 school year with the news of the establishment of an osteopathic medical school. Advanced equipment, such as the pictured DNA sequencer, was purchased to facilitate student and faculty research. A master's degree in biology was added in fall 2009. The acceptance rate for Carey students to medical schools across the country was 75 percent in 2009.

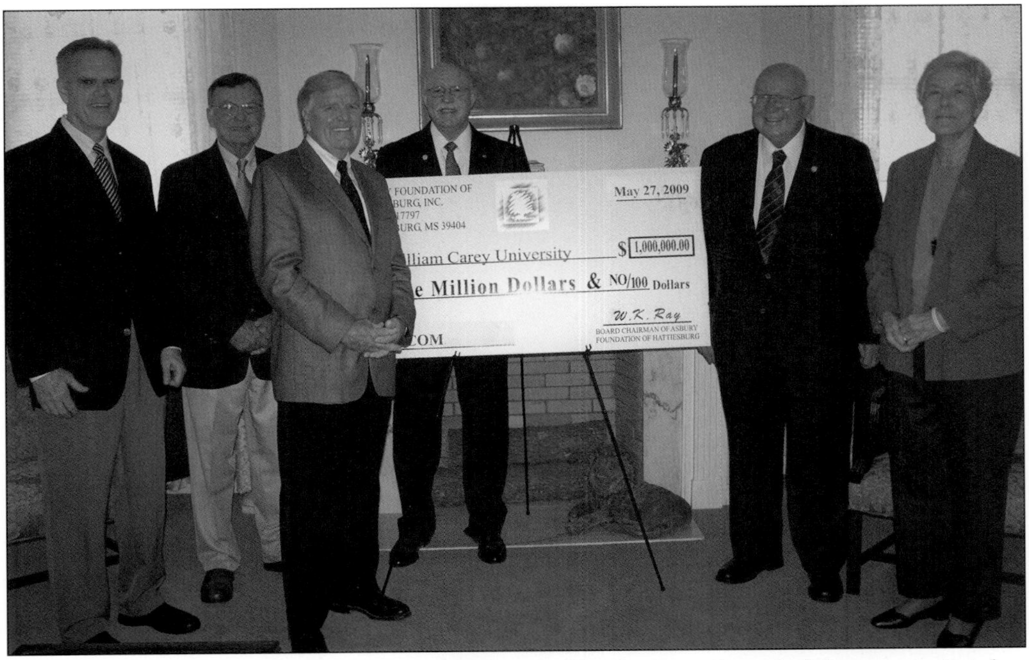


The College of Osteopathic Medicine was authorized by the Carey Board of Trustees in October 2007 with the goal of educating physicians to work in underserved areas in Mississippi and the Southeast. A founding dean was hired in January 2008. Construction on the medical college complex started in May 2009 with a lead gift of $1 million from the Asbury Foundation of Hattiesburg.

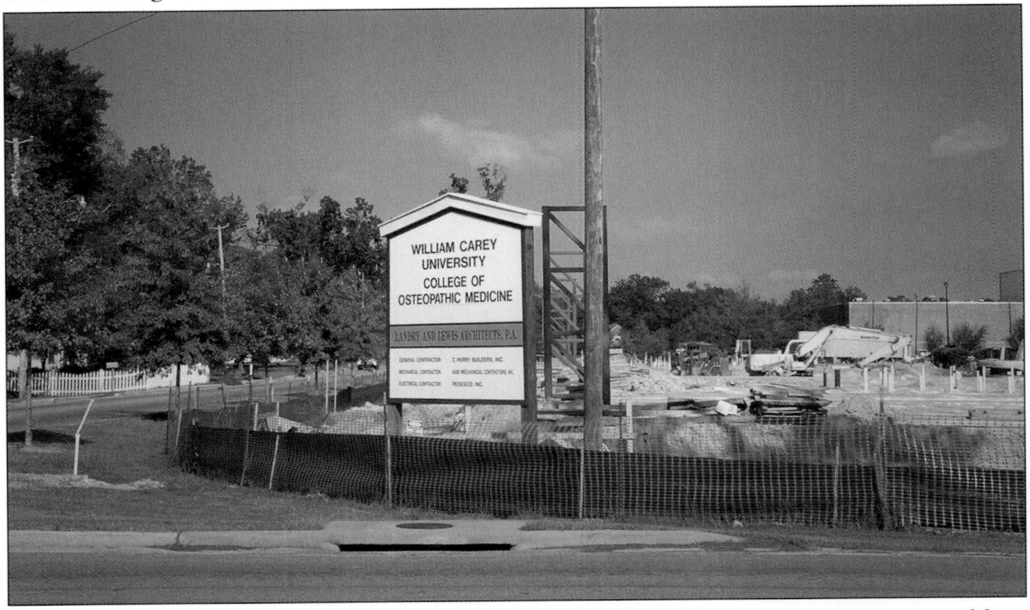


The medical college was an ambitious project for Carey, involving the construction of four new buildings; a national search for faculty, staff, and students of the inaugural class; the creation of new curriculums; and the building of a support network, including area doctors, to assist students in their training. The college is Mississippi's second medical school and first osteopathic medical school.

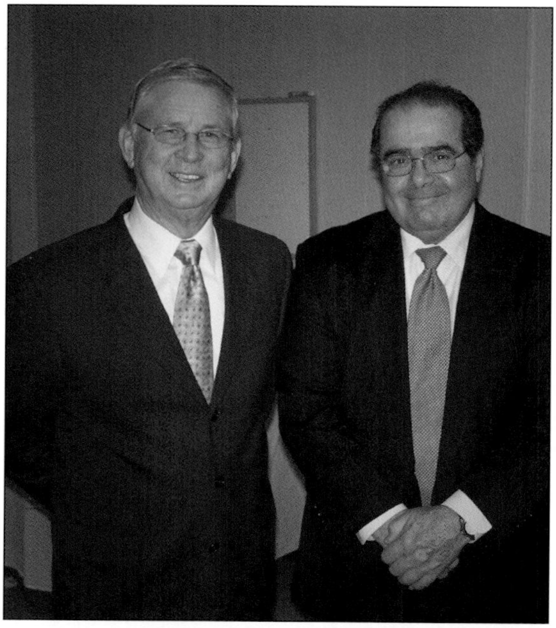

US Supreme Court justice Antonin Scalia (right), pictured with retired federal judge and Carey trustee Charles W. Pickering Sr., visited Carey in April 2009 for an hour-long address in Smith Auditorium. Scalia discussed his love for the US Constitution, referring to it as a "brilliant document," and said it should be cherished by all Americans. The justice previously spoke at Carey in 2004.

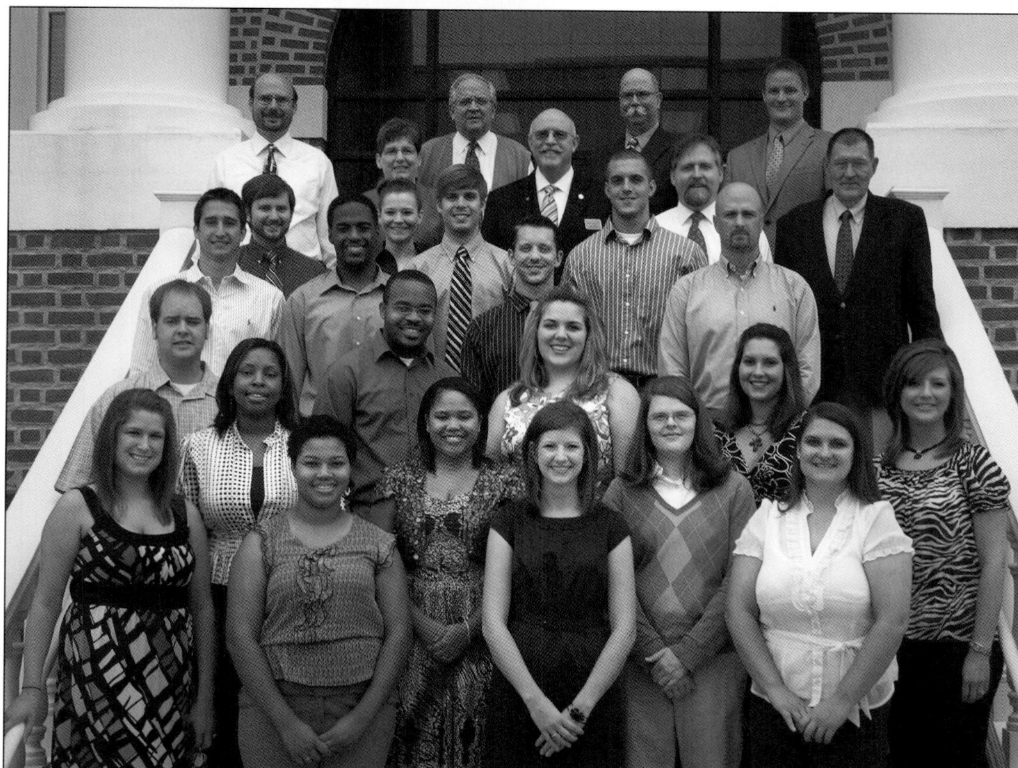

The inaugural class of the Master of Biomedical Science program was admitted in August 2009. Part of the College of Osteopathic Medicine, the program's mission is to help students become stronger applicants to professional schools, such as medical, dental, and pharmacy schools. The program offers pre-medical/dental, pre-pharmacy, and general pre-health professional tracks.

The Sarah Ellen Gillespie Museum of Art was dedicated in 2009 and houses the Gillespie Collection, which contains over 600 pieces of art and is considered to be the most comprehensive collection of art executed by Mississippians in the 20th century. The collection was relocated to the Hattiesburg campus from the Gulfport campus following Hurricane Katrina in 2005. The museum is an annex of Smith/Rouse Library.

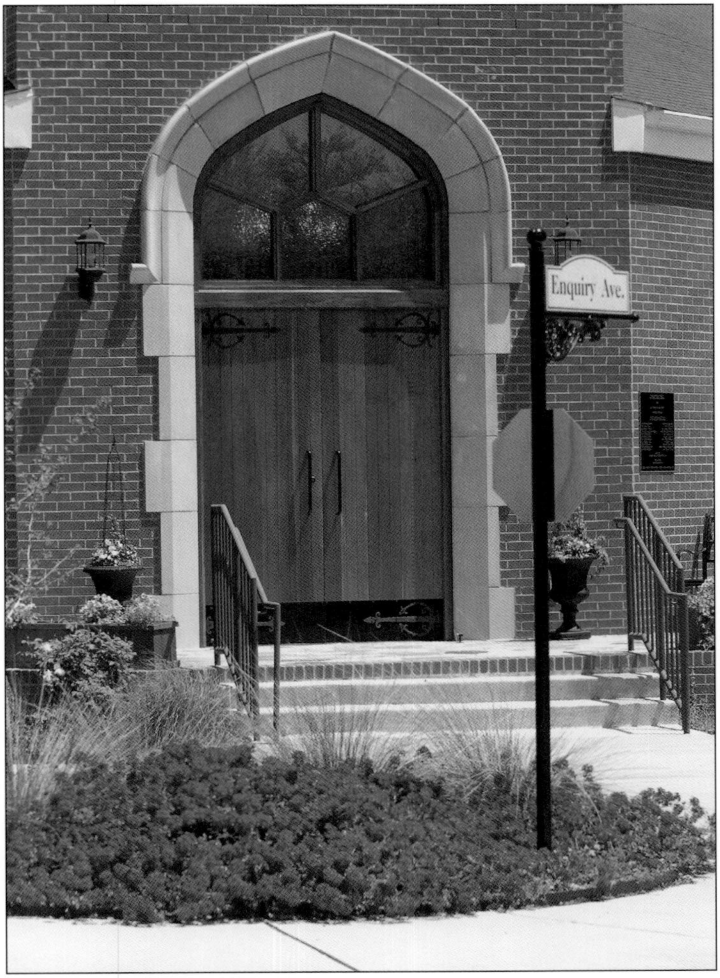


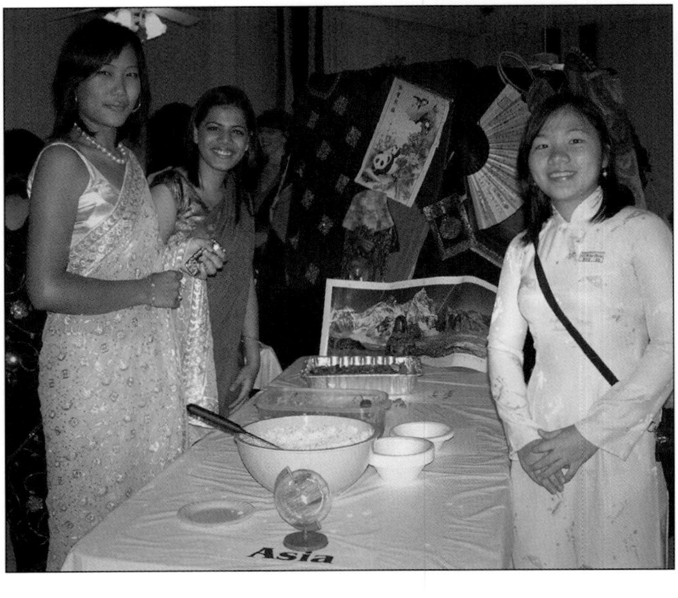


The International Food Fair was first held in February 2009 as a way for Carey's international student population to teach their classmates and Carey personnel about the cuisines and cultures of their home countries. The food fair is now a popular annual event for students, faculty, and staff. The international student population has steadily increased since the establishment of a dedicated international admissions office and an English Language Center.

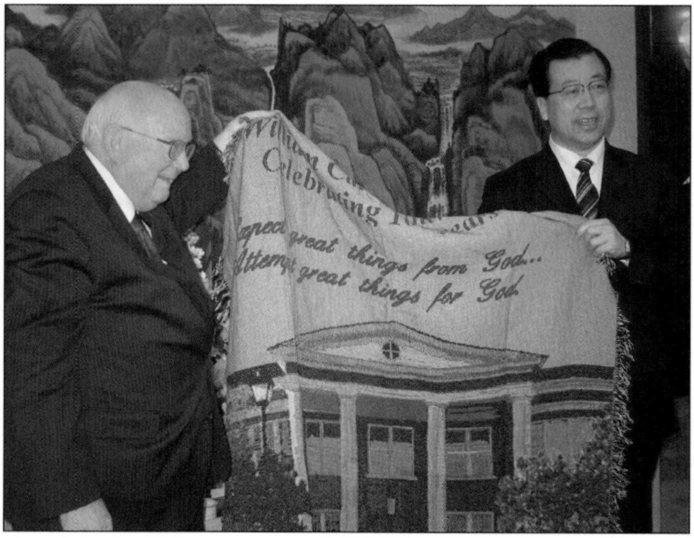

In March 2010, Carey officials, along with Hattiesburg mayor Johnny DuPree, visited Linyi University in Linyi, China, to sign a faculty-and-student and library exchange agreement between the two universities. During the trip, DuPree also signed an agreement making Linyi and Hattiesburg sister cities. Pictured is Dr. Tommy King (left) accepting a gift from Chinese officials following the signing ceremony.

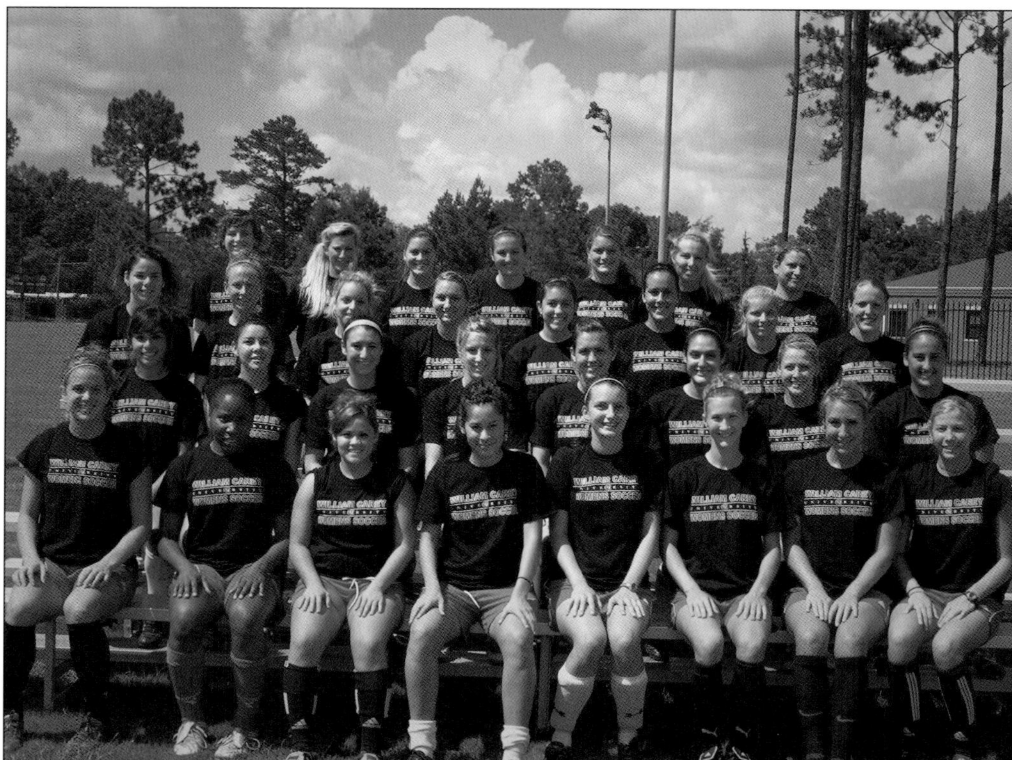

After 29 years of membership and 44 conference championships, Carey left the Gulf Coast Athletic Conference (GCAC) to join the Southern States Athletic Conference in 2010. The move allowed Carey to increase its number of athletic offerings while also offering better opportunities to compete for conference championships. During the last year of GCAC competition in 2010, the women's soccer team, coached by Danny Owens, won their third consecutive conference championship.

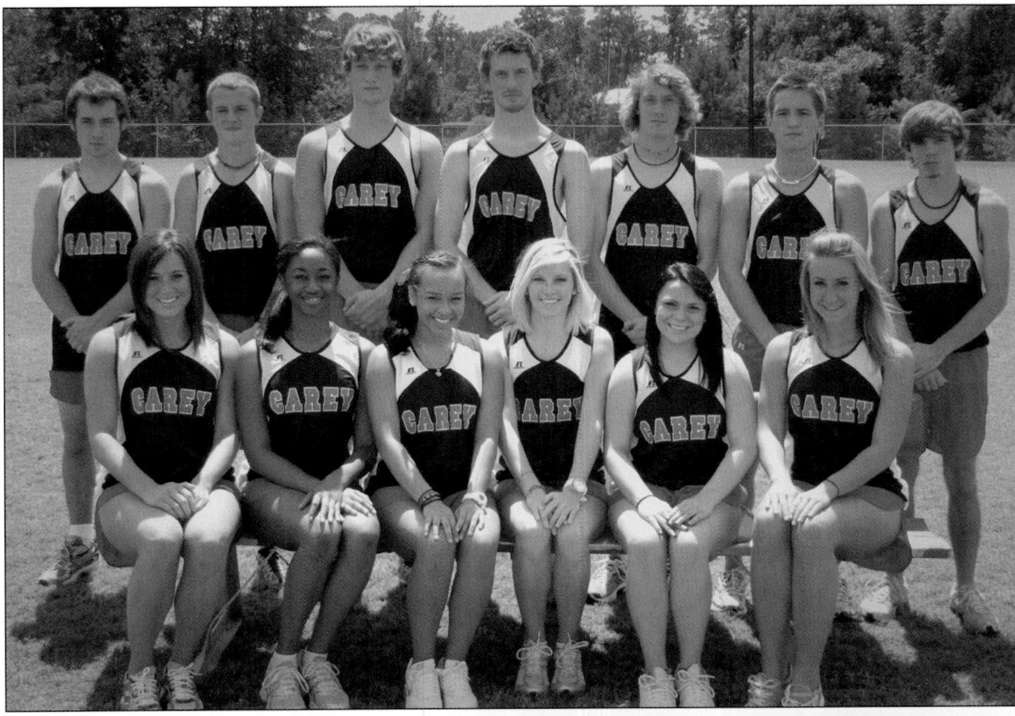


In 2009, the Crusaders competed in nine sports, including baseball, softball, men's and women's basketball, men's golf, men's and women's soccer, and men's and women's tennis. The 2010 move to the Southern States Athletic Conference, which fields a total of 15 sports, allowed the university to add three new sports, including men's and women's cross-country (pictured) and women's golf.

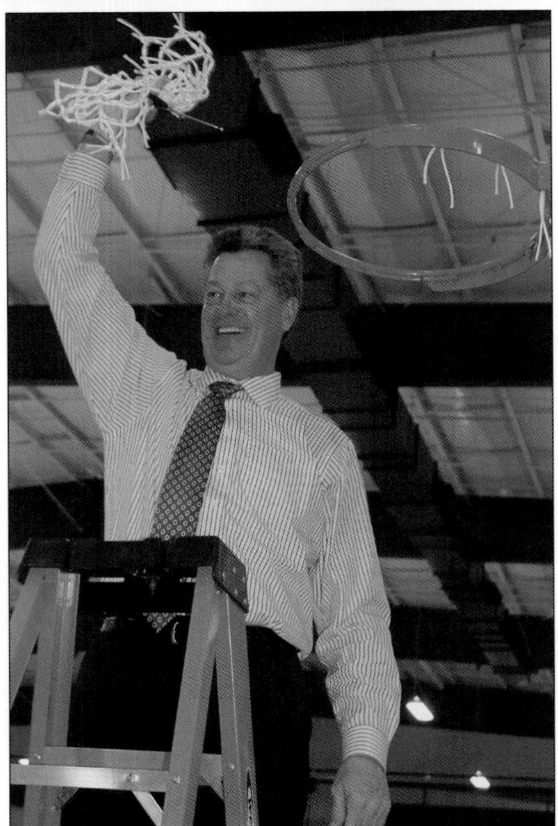

The 2009–2010 season marked a special occasion for Steve Knight, head coach of men's basketball and athletic director since 1987. He achieved 500 career wins on February 4, 2010, and would finish the season with 506 wins, just four shy of being Mississippi's all-time winningest coach at the same four-year university. Knight shattered the record in November 2010 and continues to hold the title today.

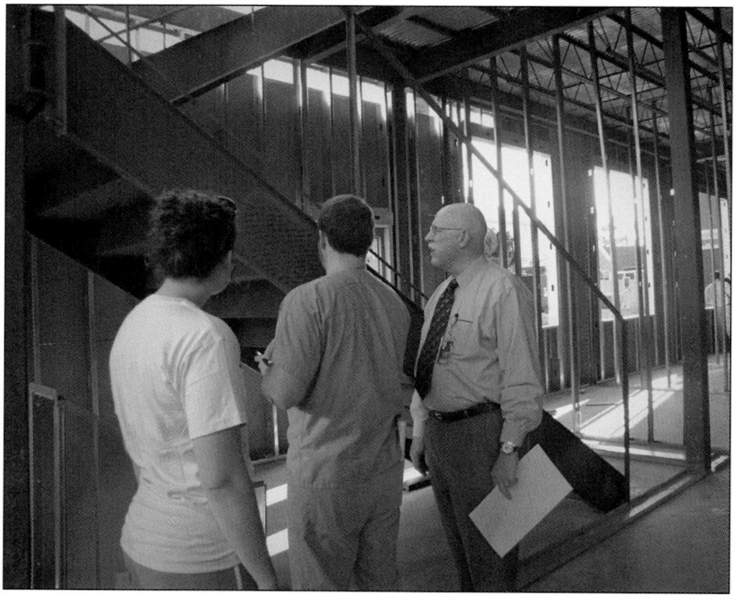

In this September 2010 photograph, Jason DeFatta, president of the 2010 inaugural class of the College of Osteopathic Medicine, inscribes the 23rd Psalm on a rafter in the medical college complex while Dr. Michael Murphy, founding dean, looks on. The inaugural class of 110 students started their four years of study in August 2010 following a rigorous selection process from a pool of more than 1,000 applicants.

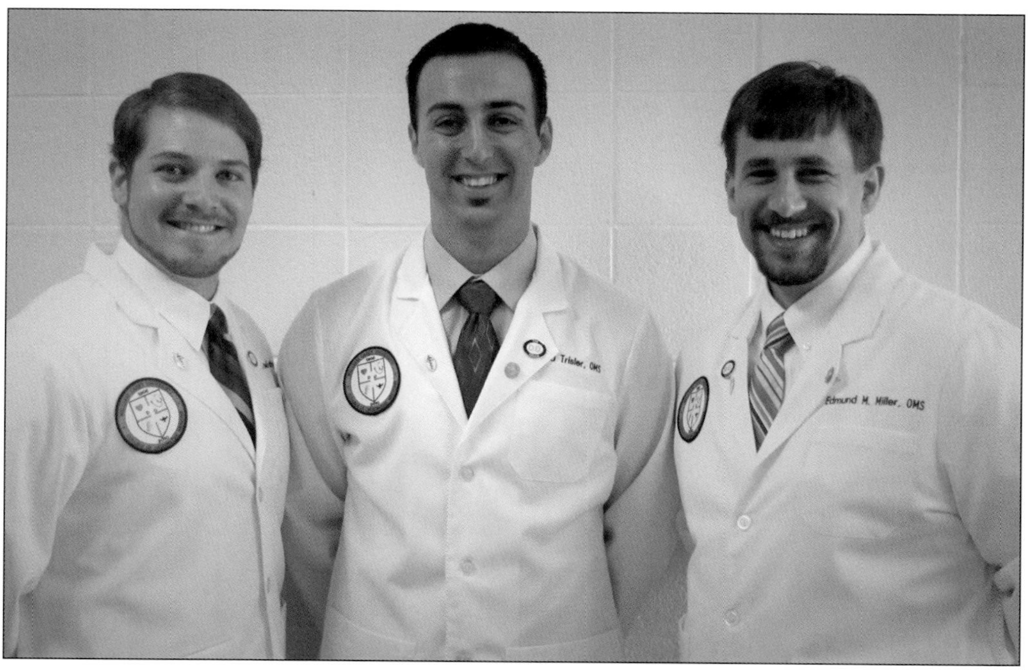


The inaugural White Coat Ceremony for the College of Osteopathic Medicine was held on August 21, 2010. During the ceremony, each student was ceremonially cloaked with a white medical coat, which signifies the excellence and caring nature demanded of those entering the medical profession, in front of university administration, faculty, and family members. Pictured from left to right are Jason DeFatta, David Trisler, and Edmund Miller.

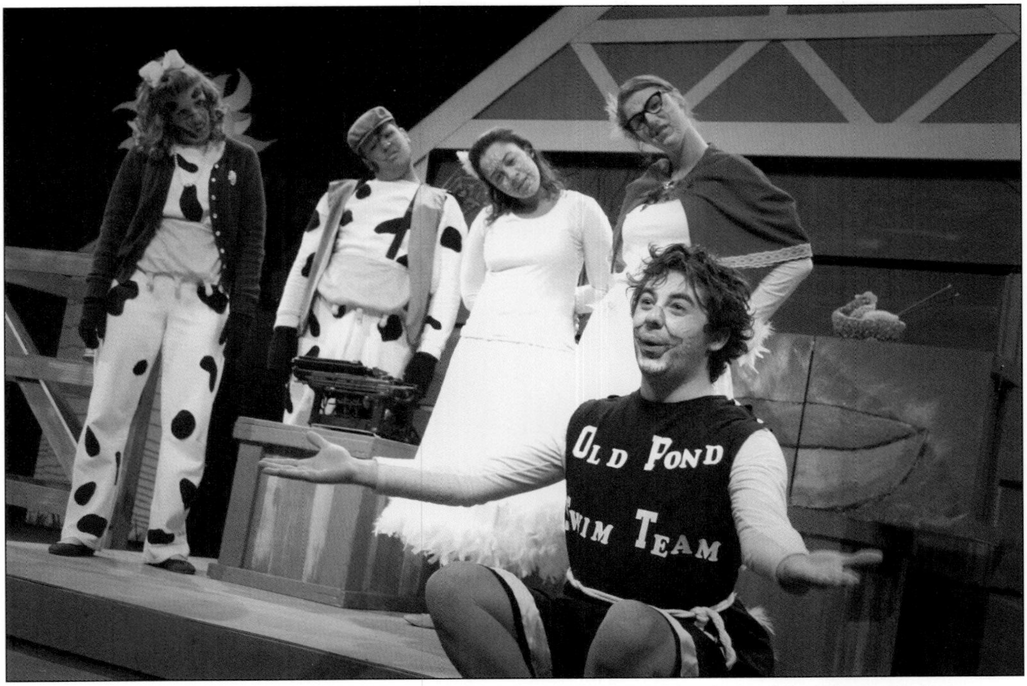

The Joe and Virginia Tatum Theatre, a $1.4 million facility with a large black box performance area, box office, dinner theater serving area, and catwalks for lighting and sound crews, opened in 2010. *Click, Clack, Moo: Cows That Type*, a children's musical (pictured), was one of the first productions by theatre students in the facility. The theater is also the site of the popular Carey Dinner Theatre each summer.

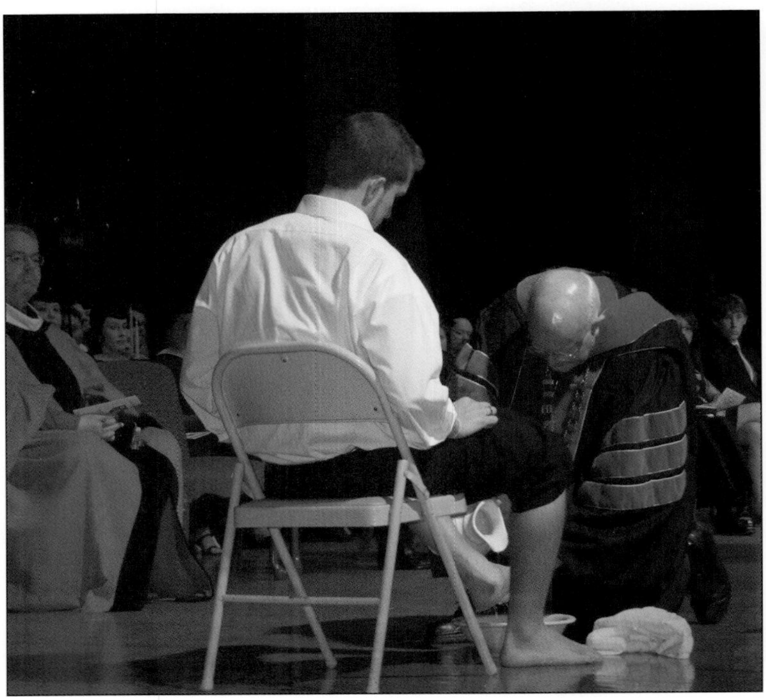

Carey adopted the theme verse of "Not to be served, but to serve" (Matthew 20:28) for the 2010–2011 school year. The theme supported Carey's emphasis on campus and community service and was emphasized by Dr. Tommy King washing a student's feet during fall convocation. The adoption of a yearly theme is now a tradition designed to provide a focus and a sense of unity for students, faculty, and staff.

The speech and debate team, led by Jennifer Talbert, won second place overall at the Pi Kappa Delta National Tournament at Mt. Hood Community College in Portland, Oregon, in March 2011. Second place was the highest ranking Carey has ever achieved at the national tournament. The team competed against 83 colleges and universities, including Ohio University, Oregon State University, and Texas A&M University.

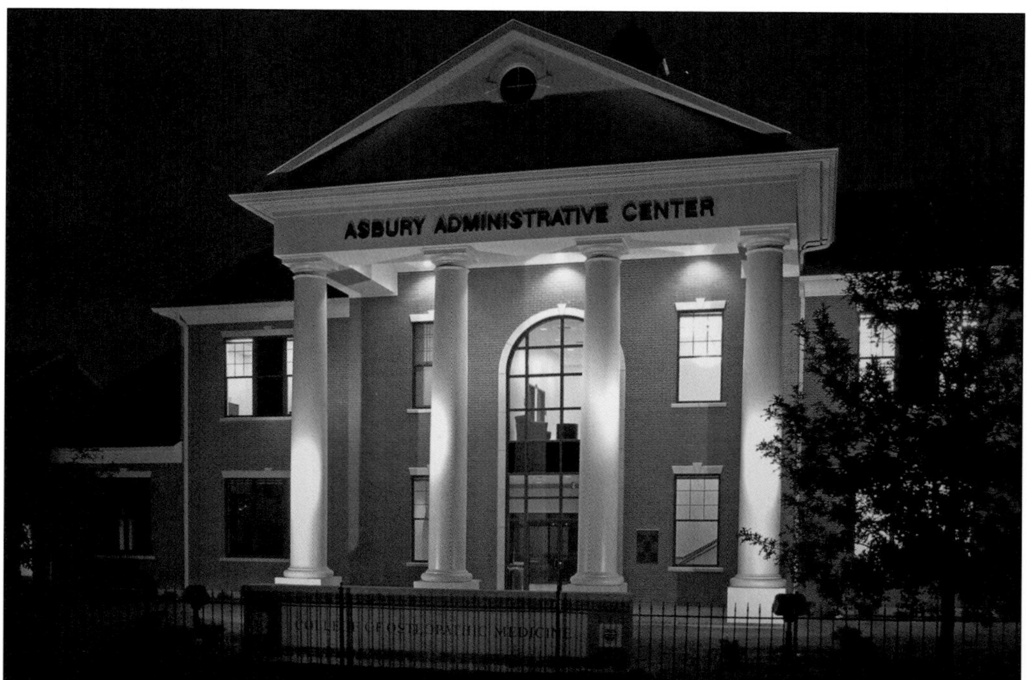


Asbury Administrative Center, the third building in the medical college complex, was completed in the spring of 2011 and connected the Academic Building and the Medical Arts Building, both completed in 2010. The three buildings would be joined by the Ross Anatomy Wing, the final building in the complex, in 2014. The complex includes lecture halls, study rooms, labs, treatment and diagnostic rooms, conference areas, student lounges, and offices.

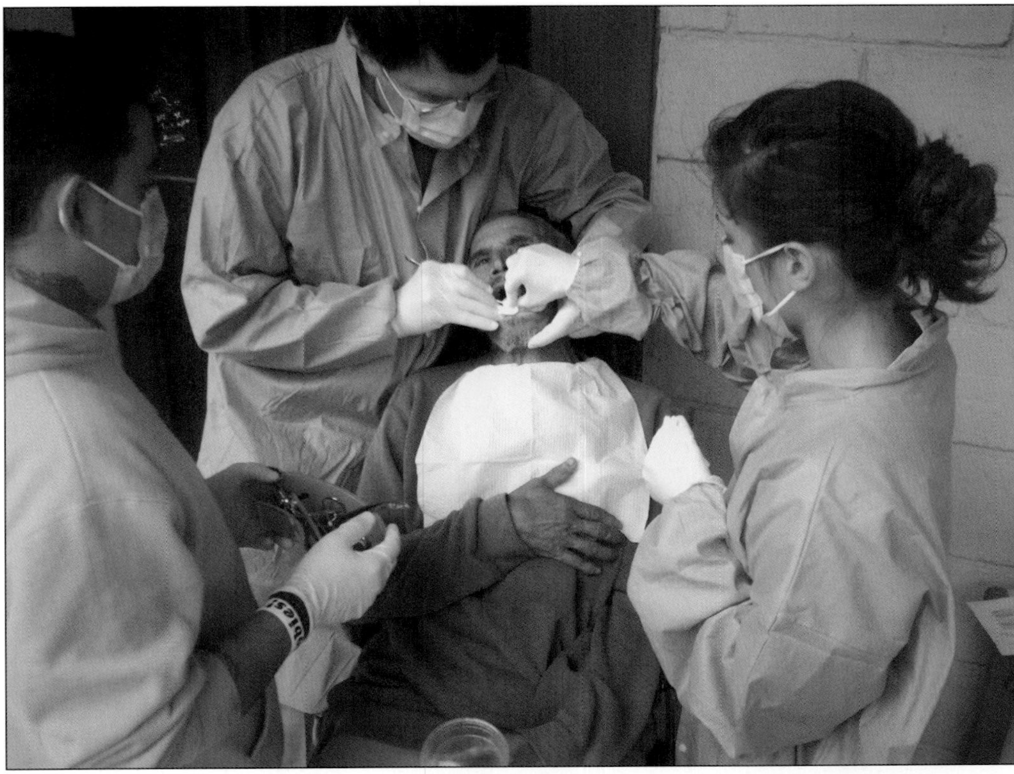

Carey nursing students traveled with Baptist Medical and Dental Mission International to Honduras in March 2011 to minister to the local population and provide health care services. The academic year's theme verse of "Not to be served, but to serve" was exemplified in students serving in tutoring ministries near the Carey community, in summer mission projects across the country, and in international missions in countries like Peru and China.

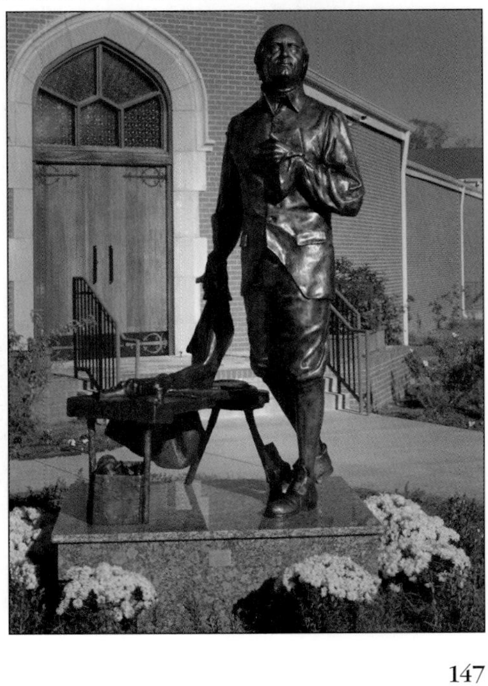

During 2011, students, faculty, staff, and alumni celebrated the 250th birthday of William Carey, known as the "father of modern missions." The culmination of the celebration was the November dedication of *Carey Turns to the World*, a seven-foot, 600-pound statue created by sculptor Ben Watts of Columbia, Mississippi. Dr. Thomas Elliff, president of the International Mission Board of the Southern Baptist Convention, was the guest speaker at the dedication.

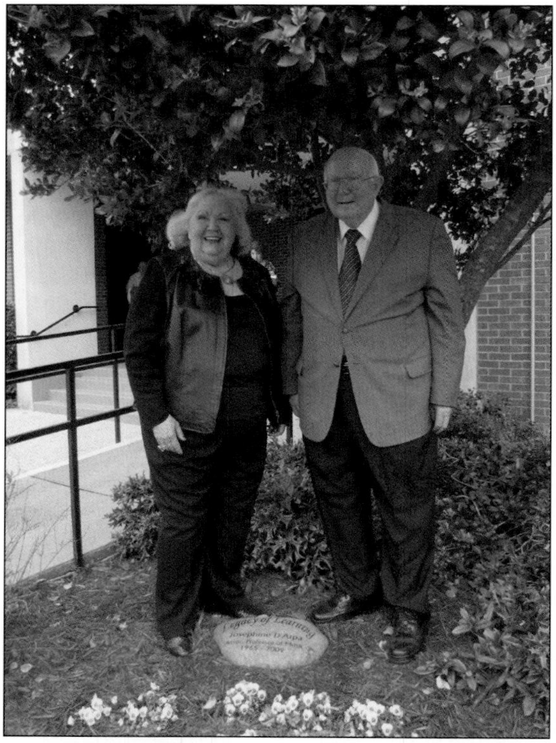

Josephine D'Arpa, pictured with Dr. Tommy King, was presented with the first Legacy of Learning stone in 2011. D'Arpa taught in the Winters School of Music for 44 years before retiring 2009. Her legacy stone was installed in front of the music building, Thomas Fine Arts Center. The legacy stones, now placed throughout campus, honor faculty who have left a legacy of learning and staff who have left a legacy of leadership.

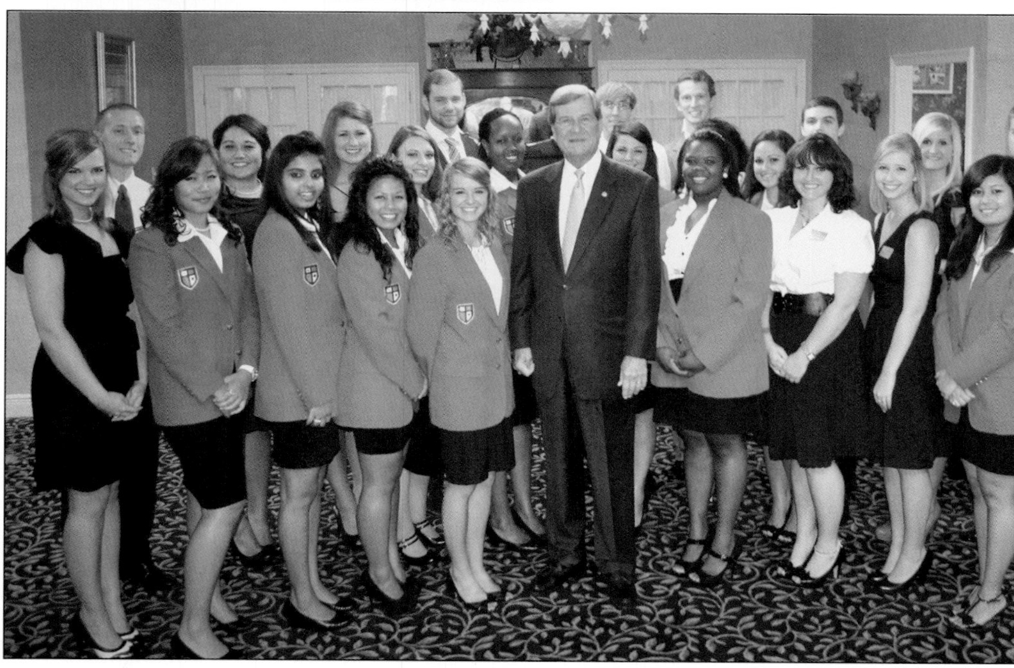

Carey hosted a scholarship dinner featuring Trent Lott, former US senator from Mississippi, in September 2011. During the dinner, Lott performed "A Tribute to the Singing Senators," a reference to the barbershop quartet consisting of Lott and three Senate colleagues, with students from the Winters School of Music. He also spoke about the quality of Carey's programs. The dinner, now an annual event, raised more than $350,000 for scholarships.

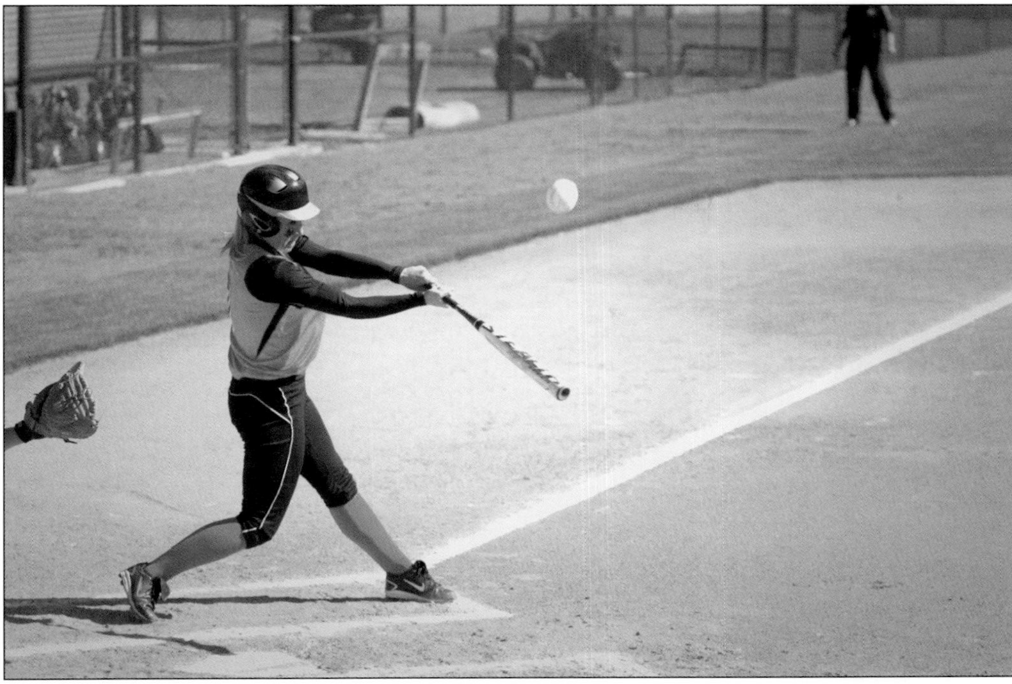

The Carey softball team, under the direction of Wendy Hogue and Craig Fletcher, enjoyed an incredible 2012 season. The Lady Crusaders went 20-4 in conference play before capturing the 2012 Southern States Athletic Conference championship in a shutout against Auburn University at Montgomery. The win entitled the team to a spot, their fifth consecutive one, in the national tournament hosted by the National Association of Intercollegiate Athletics.

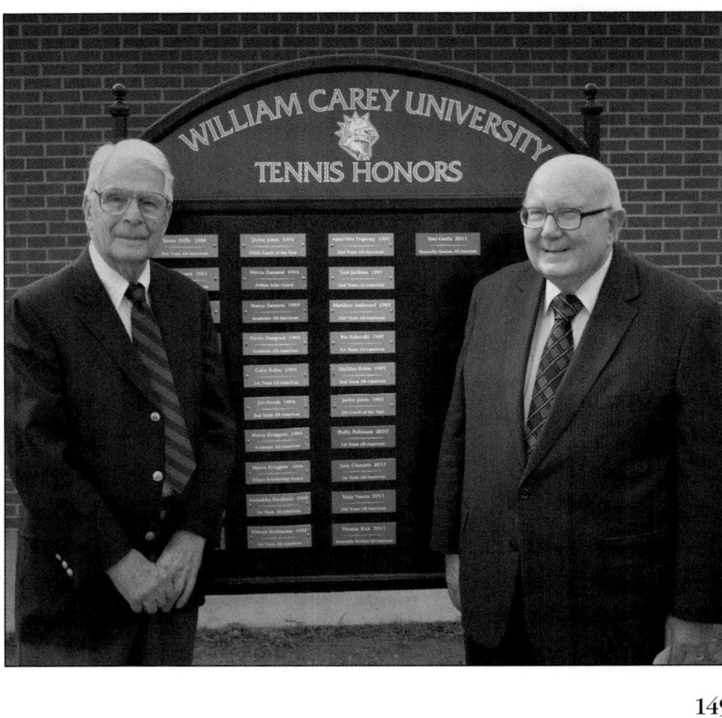


The Jack Jones Field House was completed in 2011 and features concession areas and locker rooms for the soccer and tennis teams. Jones served as tennis coach from 1988 through the late 1990s and was responsible for the establishment of the women's tennis program. Jones played tennis for Carey in the mid-1980s and, at age 55, was the oldest college player in Mississippi. Jones (left) is pictured with Dr. Tommy King.

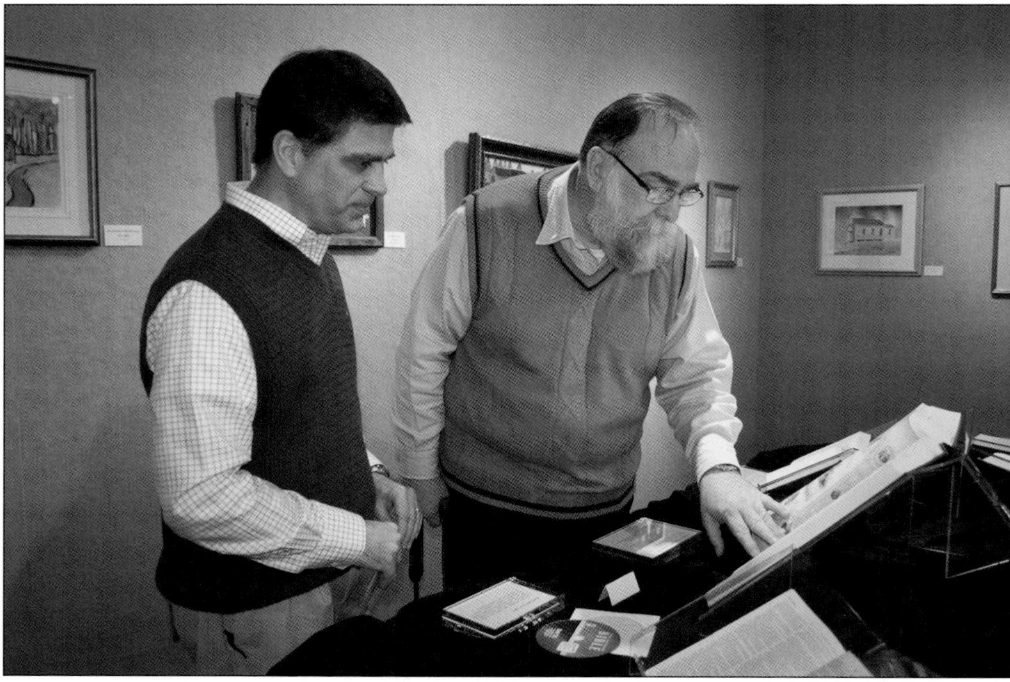

Carey hosted the exhibit "Manifold Greatness: The Creation and Afterlife of the King James Bible" in the Sarah Gillespie Museum of Art from January 18 through February 17, 2012. The exhibit, which celebrated the 400th anniversary of the first printing of the King James Bible, drew hundreds of visitors. The Carey library also hosted scholarly lectures, workshops, and panel discussions about the Bible and its effect on the world.

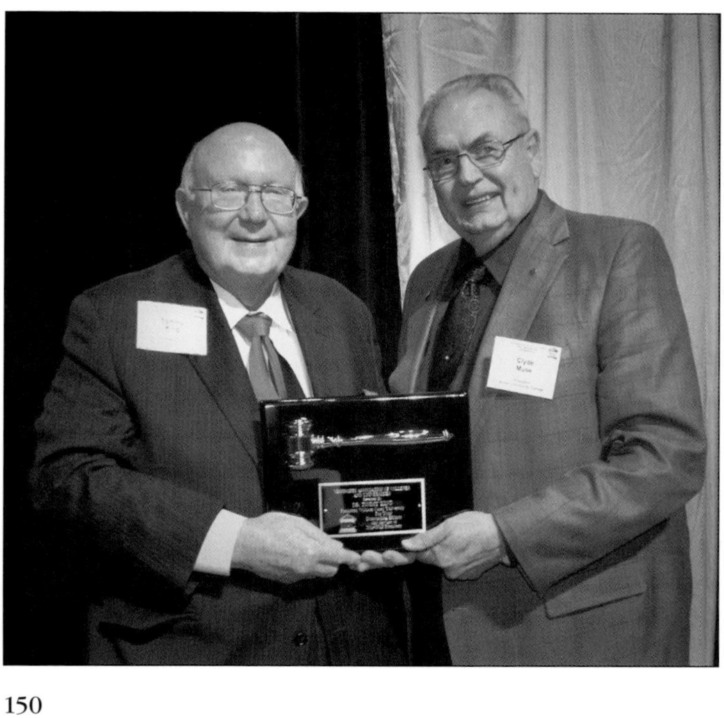

In 2012, Dr. Tommy King was elected president of the Mississippi Association of Colleges and Universities. The association's annual two-day conference, with the theme of "Leadership to Lift Mississippi," was hosted on the Carey campus and welcomed dignitaries from across the state. Pictured is King (left) receiving the association president's gavel from past president Dr. Clyde Muse, president of Hinds Community College.

# *Seven*

# William Carey University 2012–2017

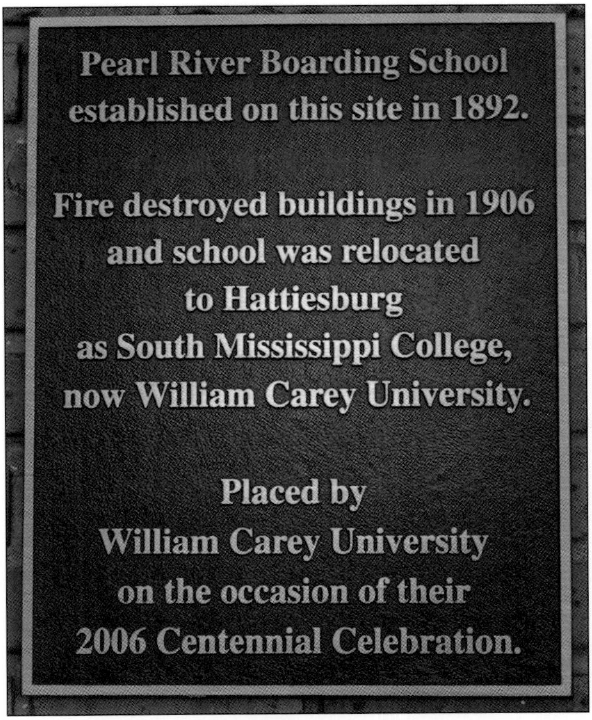


A plaque marks the former location of Pearl River Boarding School in Poplarville, Mississippi. Founded in 1892 by W.I. Thames, the school—the largest institution of its kind in Mississippi—is the earliest ancestor of William Carey University and offered elementary, preparatory, and some college classes before its destruction by fire in 1905. Thames attempted to rebuild the school on the same site but failed to gain the needed financial support. He moved his endeavor to Hattiesburg, acquiring 10 acres of the current Carey campus and opening South Mississippi College in 1906. The boarding school's existence was discovered by university officials during research for the university's centennial celebration in 2006. During the rebranding and refreshing of the university's logos and marketing materials in 2012, the founding date was adjusted from 1906—the date Carey opened in Hattiesburg—to 1892, the date that Thames, recognized as the university's inaugural president, opened his boarding school in Poplarville. The plaque was placed on the site by the university in 2007.

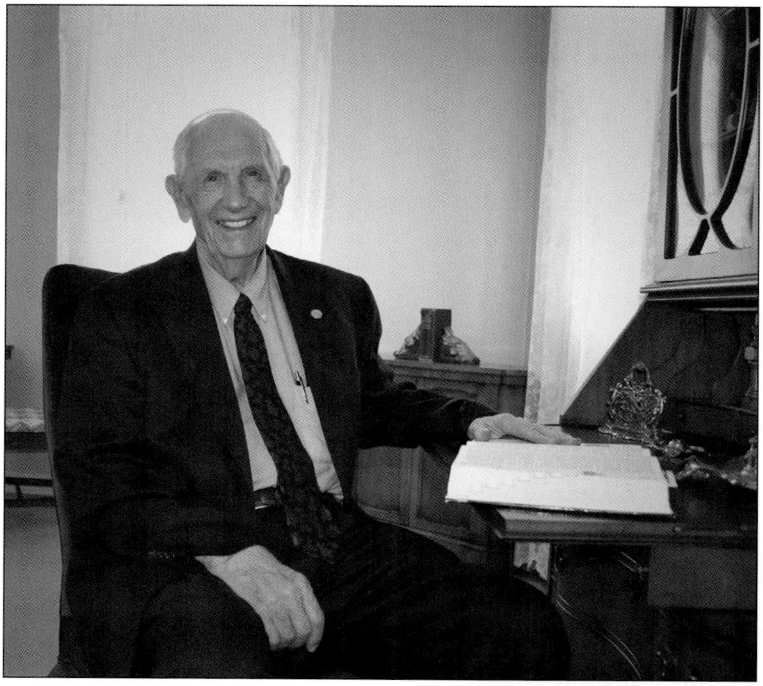

Dr. Benjamin Waddle, professor of health, physical education, and recreation, was honored for 45 years of service in August 2012. Waddle started his tenure in 1967 and served for many years as the department chair and as head of the intramurals program. From 1974 to 1982, he also served as athletic director. He offered this bit of advice on his longevity: "Eat fruits, veggies, and grains and lay off the red meat."

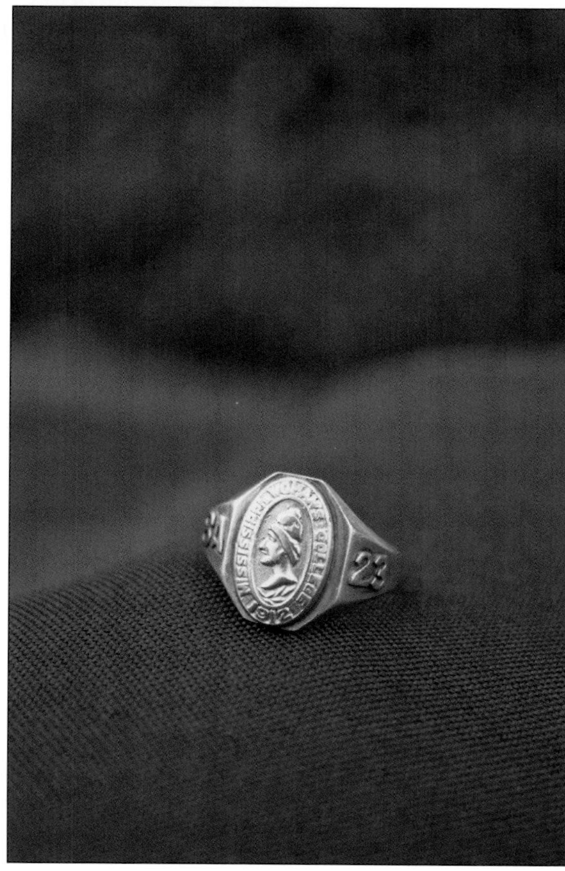

Reed Banjanin was scuba diving in Longwood, Florida, when he found this 1923 Mississippi Woman's College ring inscribed with the name Louise Hearst. After researching Hearst, he returned the ring to her grandson, John Entzminger. Entzminger decided to return the ring, which was lost for 83 years and is in near-perfect condition, to Carey in 2012. Both Banjanin and Entzminger visited the campus to tell the story.

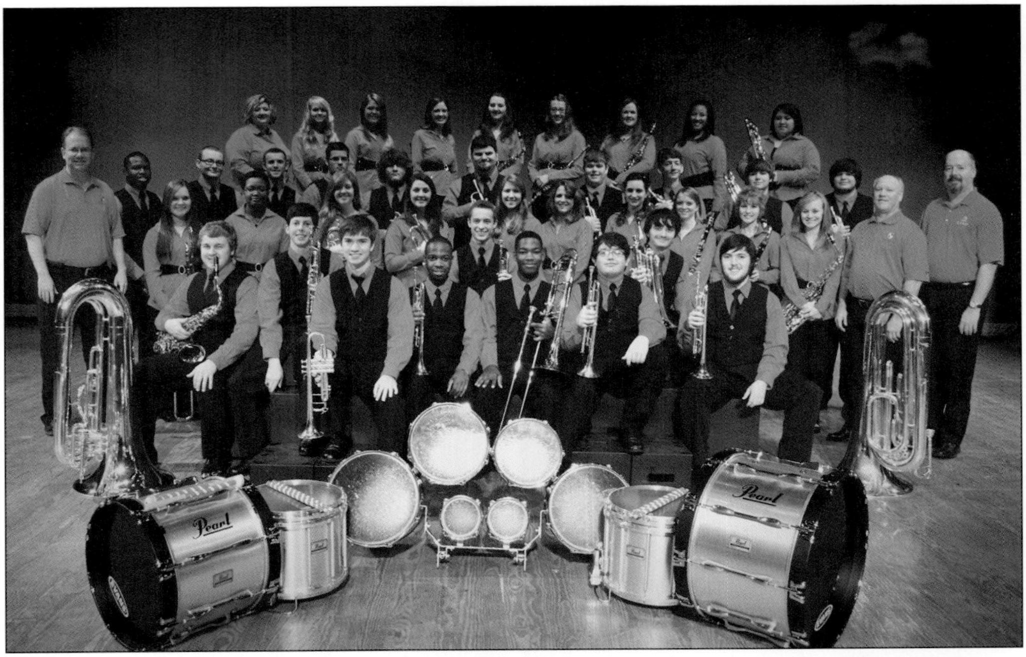

The Winters School of Music instrumental department experienced a rebirth in 2012 with the hiring of Wes Dykes as coordinator of instrumental activities and the establishment of the Spirit of Carey marching band, the Grace Notes woodwind ensemble, the Tuscan Reeds saxophone ensemble, and a revamped Jazz Band. The groups travel as university ambassadors. Enrollment in the school, led by Dean Don Odom, nearly doubled from the 2011–2012 year.

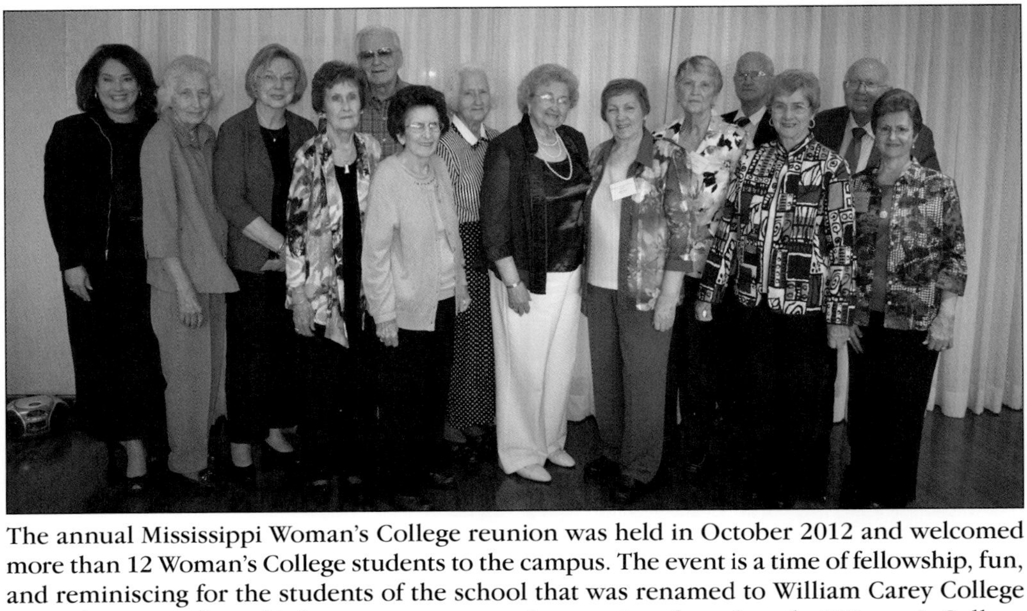

The annual Mississippi Woman's College reunion was held in October 2012 and welcomed more than 12 Woman's College students to the campus. The event is a time of fellowship, fun, and reminiscing for the students of the school that was renamed to William Carey College in 1954. Stories of mischief are more common than stories of good grades! Woman's College opened in 1911 and became coeducational in 1953.

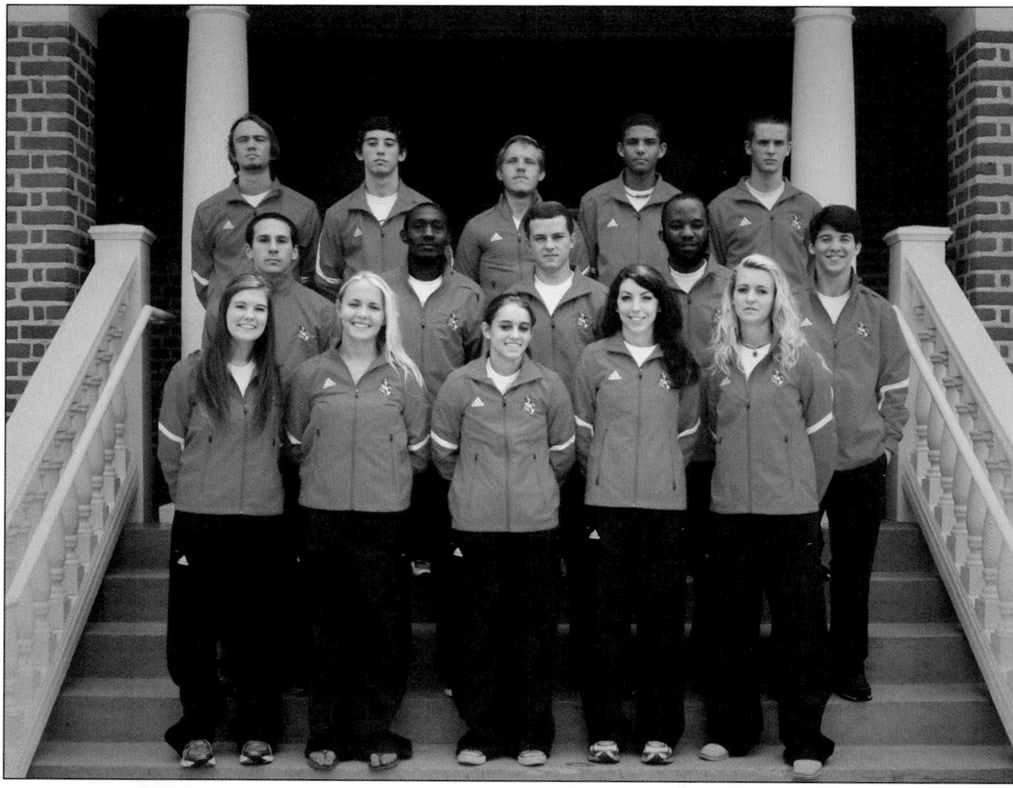

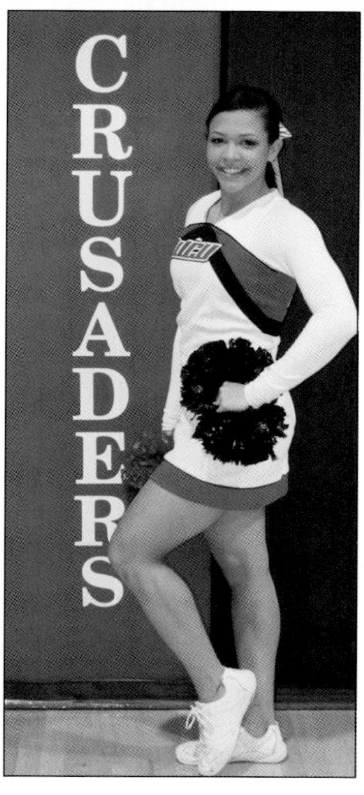


Another year, another set of new athletic programs could be the theme for Carey Athletics. Men's and women's track and field teams were added to the university's roster of sports beginning in the fall of 2012. "We feel this to be a natural progression of our athletic program as we continue to expand our offerings," said Steve Knight, athletic director. Carey grad Blake Hegstrom was named head coach.

Cheerleader and nursing student Ashlee Arnau made national and international headlines in February 2013 when she successfully completed a front-flip half-court shot during halftime at a home basketball game. A video of Arnau's trick was viewed more than three million times on YouTube and was featured on ESPN's SportsCenter. Arnau would later complete the trick again and appeared on several national news outlets, including NBC's *The Today Show*.

Dr. Scott Hummel, formerly the vice president for advancement and church relations, was named executive vice president and provost in 2013. Hummel, a 1987 Carey graduate, is also a professor of religion. As provost, Hummel assists Dr. Tommy King in the daily operations of the university. Hummel previously served as an associate professor of biblical studies and department chair at LeTourneau University in Longview, Texas.

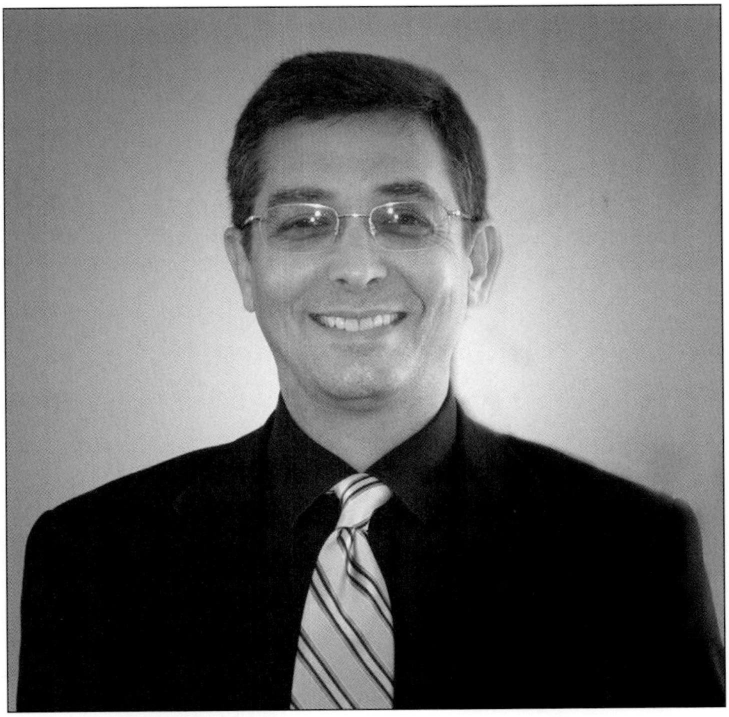

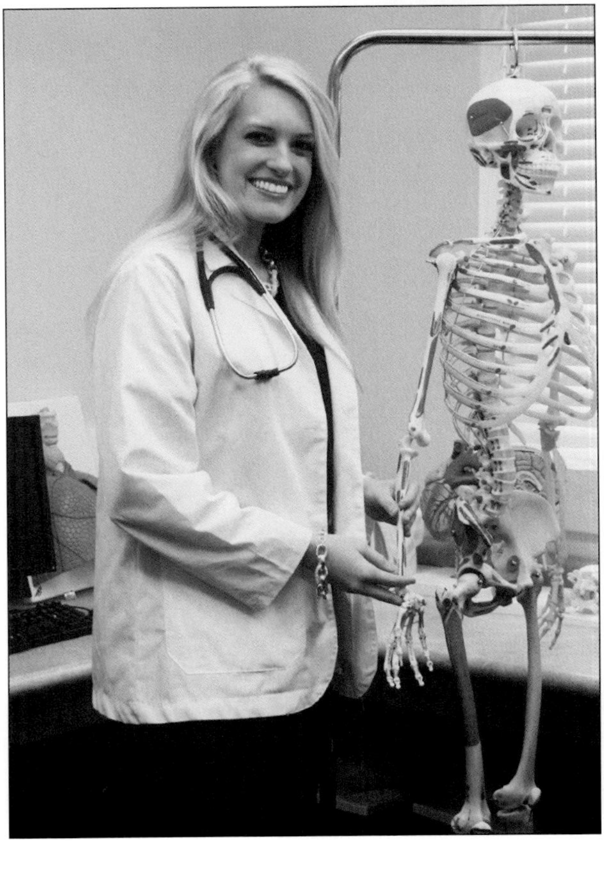

College of Osteopathic Medicine student Chelsea Rick was crowned Miss Mississippi in July 2013. Her platform, "Full Plates, Healthy States," focused on ending child hunger. She competed in the Miss America Pageant and finished in the top 15, winning a preliminary in health and fitness. Throughout her reign, Rick served as an ambassador for Carey and made numerous appearances while also positively impacting children's health efforts across the state.

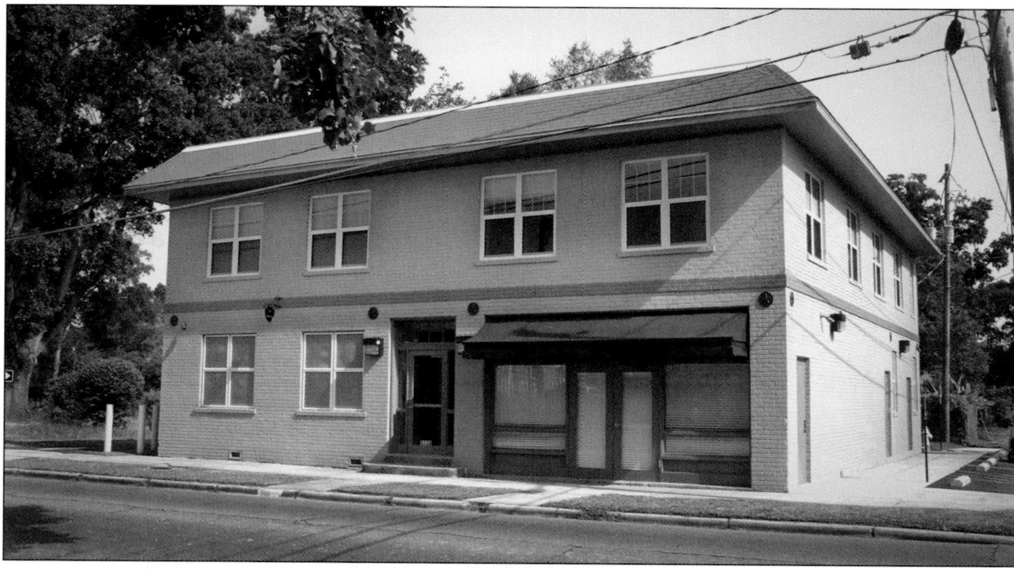

512 Tuscan Avenue, built in 1924 and used for many years as a neighborhood store and post office, was purchased by Carey and completely renovated. The building opened in 2013 with five apartments for students and as the new home of the Lucile Parker Gallery. The gallery, formerly located in Thomas Fine Arts Center, is named for a former art department chair and houses more than 500 paintings, drawings, stamps, and prints.

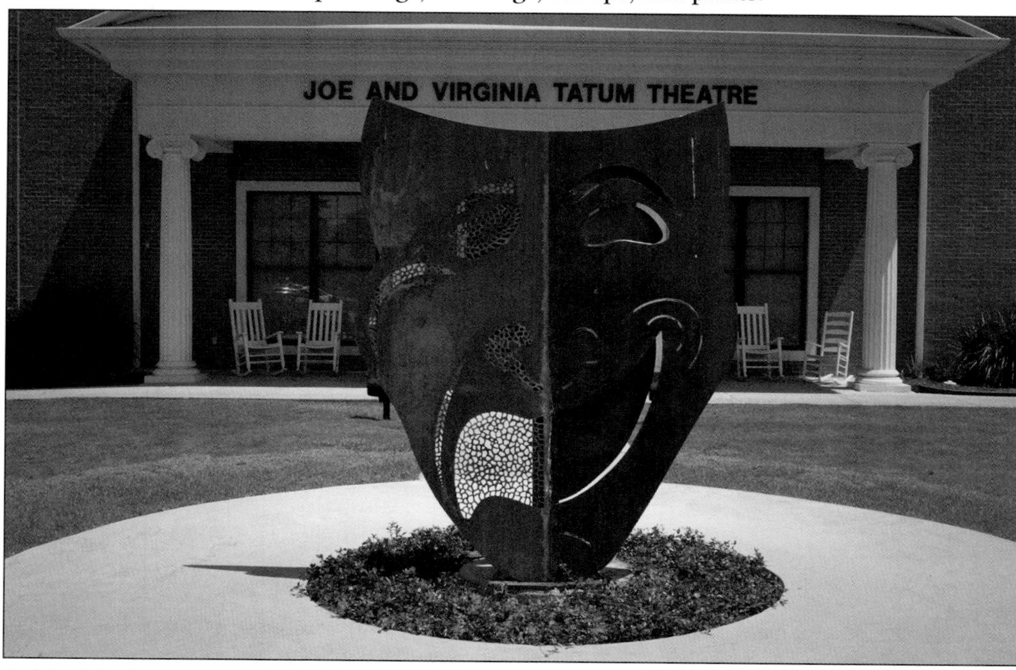


*Behind the Scenes*, a thespian mask sculpture by Jeremy Thomley of Mohawk Steel Company in Hattiesburg, was installed in front of the Joe and Virginia Tatum Theatre in June 2013. The design was inspired by traditional comedy and tragedy theater masks with a flair for the dramatic. The sculpture acknowledges the experience of actors, the amusement of the audience, and the work of those supporting the actors. The sculpture was dedicated to former president Ralph Noonkester.

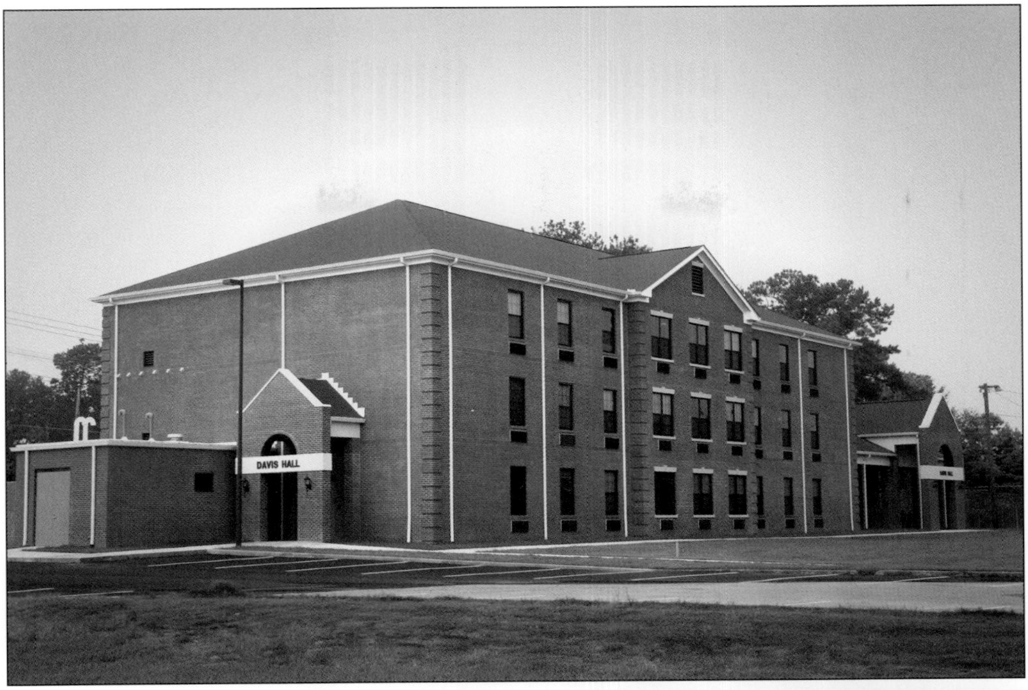


Davis Hall, a women's residence hall, opened in August 2013. The building is named for Ralph and Cora Joyce Davis, alumni of Mississippi Woman's College and the first missionary couple to represent the institution overseas. The Davises served as missionaries to Nigeria for 20 years and to Ghana for 15 years. While at Woman's College, Cora Joyce served as campus nurse in Mary Ross Infirmary and Ralph was night watchman. Ralph was the first male graduate of Mississippi Woman's College.

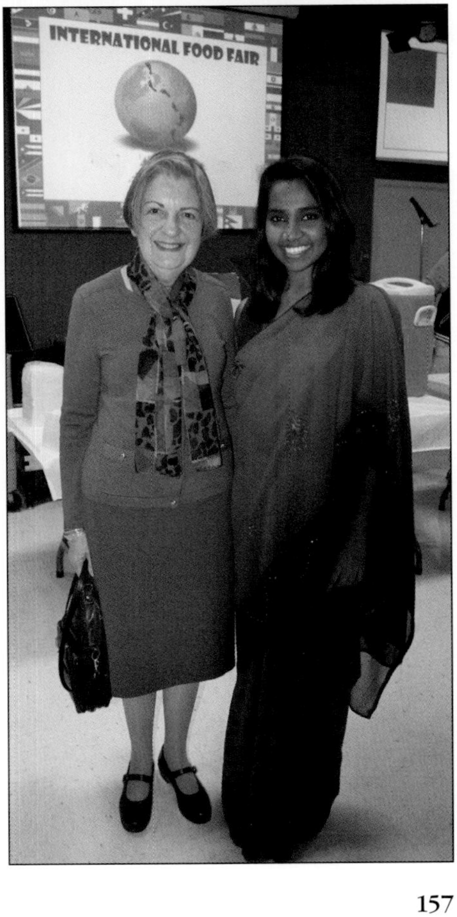


Dr. Rebekah Naylor, global health care consultant for Baptist Global Response and a former missionary to India, visited the campus in October 2013 as part of the Baptist Student Union's Global Opportunities (GO) Week. During her time as a missionary, Naylor led major expansions of facilities and services at Bangalore Baptist Hospital and established the Naylor School of Nursing. Naylor is pictured left with student Gracia Sircar of Serampore, India.

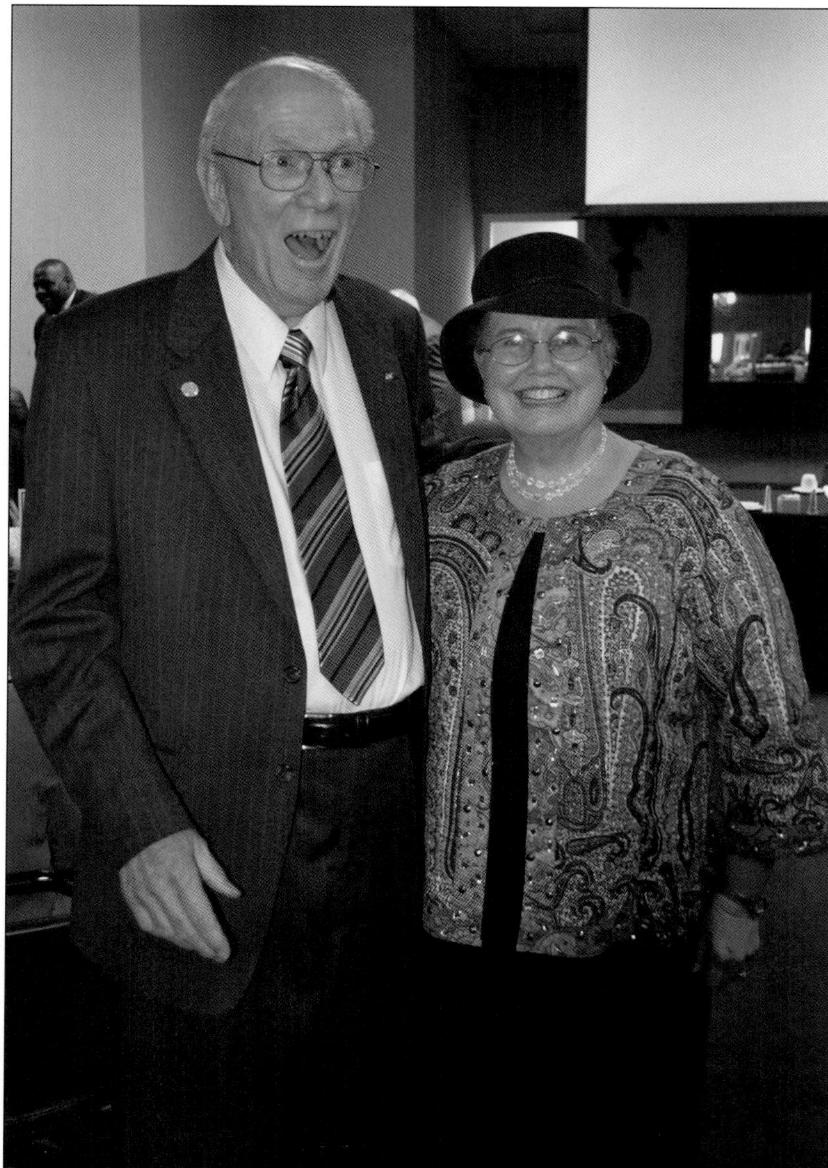

Donna Duck Wheeler, the author of the first edition of this book, died following a courageous battle with brain cancer on November 13, 2013. A 1965 alumna, Wheeler served her alma mater for 42 years, including 17 years as alumni director, before retiring in 2007. It was at Carey that Donna met the love of her life, a young professor and 1961 alumnus named Milton Wheeler. The couple's marriage lasted 48 years. Their "children" numbered in the thousands—all Carey students touched by the Christian love and attitude of service best exemplified by the Wheelers. Milton Wheeler served Carey for 51 years, holding numerous administrative appointments in addition to his role as a professor of history. He died following an extended illness on March 24, 2014, and rejoined his "Sweet Donna." In addition to the dedications of the Milton Wheeler Baseball Field and the Donna Duck Wheeler Alumni House in 2006, the university furthered honored the couple by awarding Donna an honorary doctorate in 2007 and inducting Milton into the Sports Hall of Fame in 2014.

Carey was recognized as the number-one "Best Value" in the South among regional universities in the 2014 college rankings released by *U.S. News & World Report*. In addition to academic quality, the rankings were determined using cost and financial assistance availability information. News of the ranking came after years of no tuition increases despite a national trend of rising college tuition and fees.

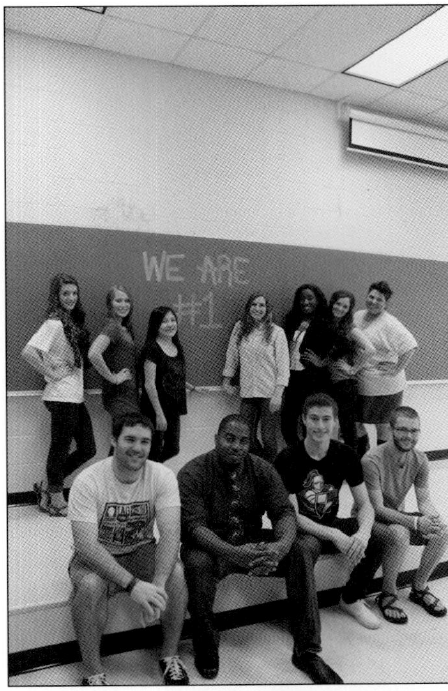


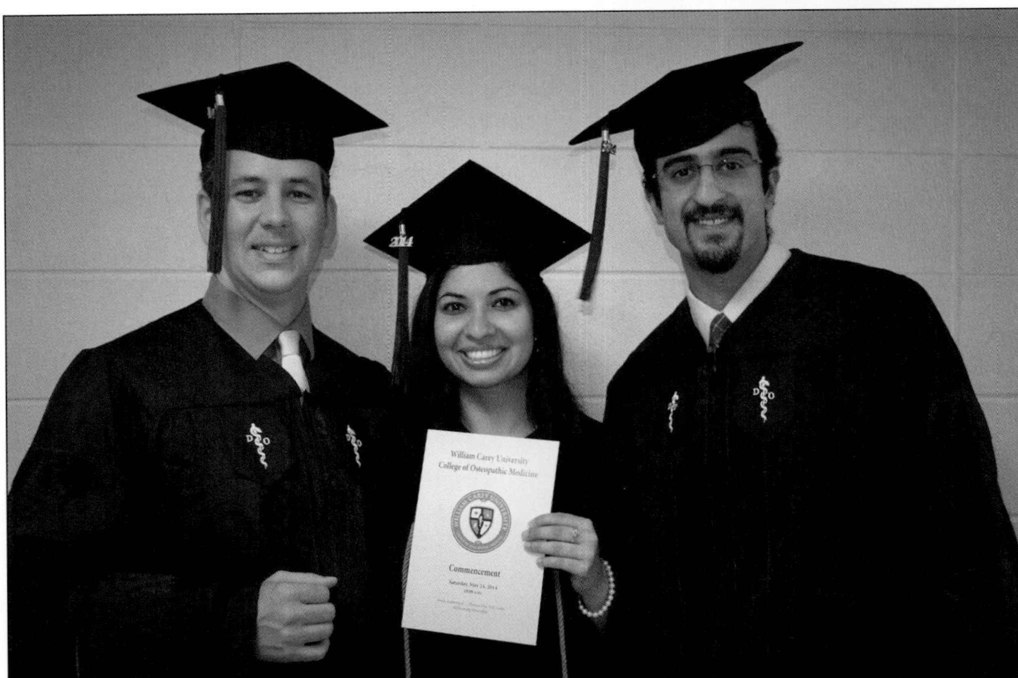


The inaugural class of the College of Osteopathic Medicine graduated on May 24, 2014. Following their graduation, the 94 new doctors of osteopathic medicine entered residency programs across the country to continue their training. The medical college officially obtained full accreditation from the American Osteopathic Association's Commission on Osteopathic College Accreditation after the graduation. Medical college personnel are currently working to make more postgraduate residency options available in Mississippi.

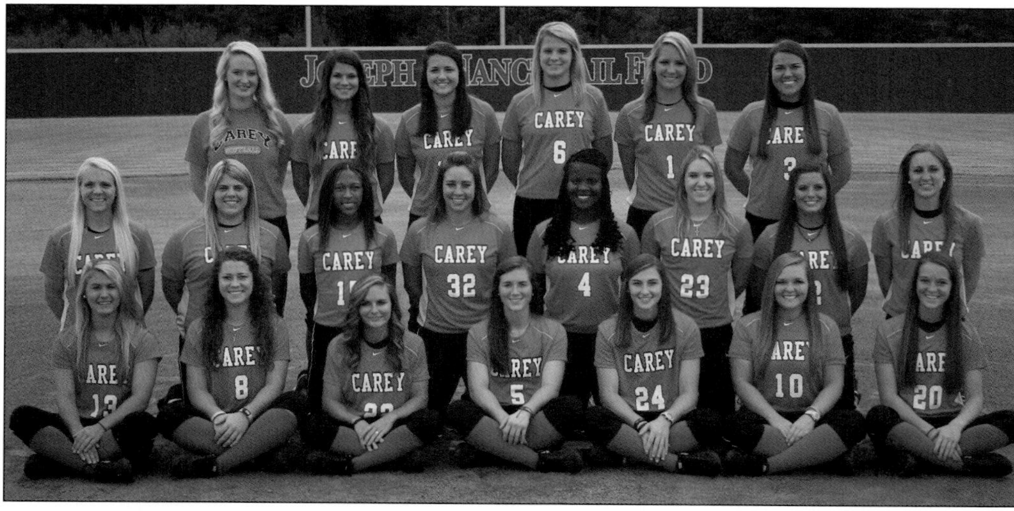

The Carey softball team finished the 2014 season with a 52-12 record and a five-victory run in the 34th annual National Association of Intercollegiate Athletics Softball World Series. The Lady Crusaders, coached by head coach Wendy Hogue and assistant head coach Craig Fletcher, ranked sixth in the nation at the conclusion of the season.

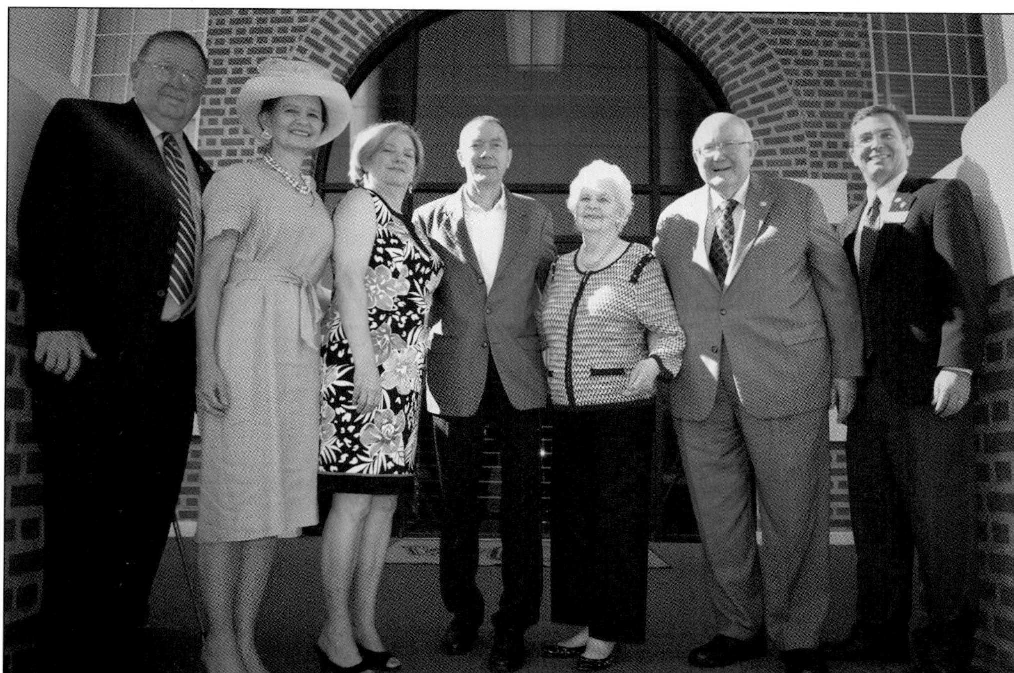

Carey hosted a centennial celebration for Tatum Court in August 2014. Construction of the Colonial-style administration building, which was completed in 1914 for more than $312,982.09, was made possible by W.S.F. Tatum, a wealthy local lumberman, and other local businessmen. Several of Tatum's descendants, including his oldest-surviving great-grandson, Bill, attended the celebration. Pictured from left to right are Bill Tatum, Dr. Virginia Angelico Tatum, Dee Tatum, Toddy Tatum, Mary Margaret Tatum, Dr. Tommy King, and Dr. Scott Hummel.

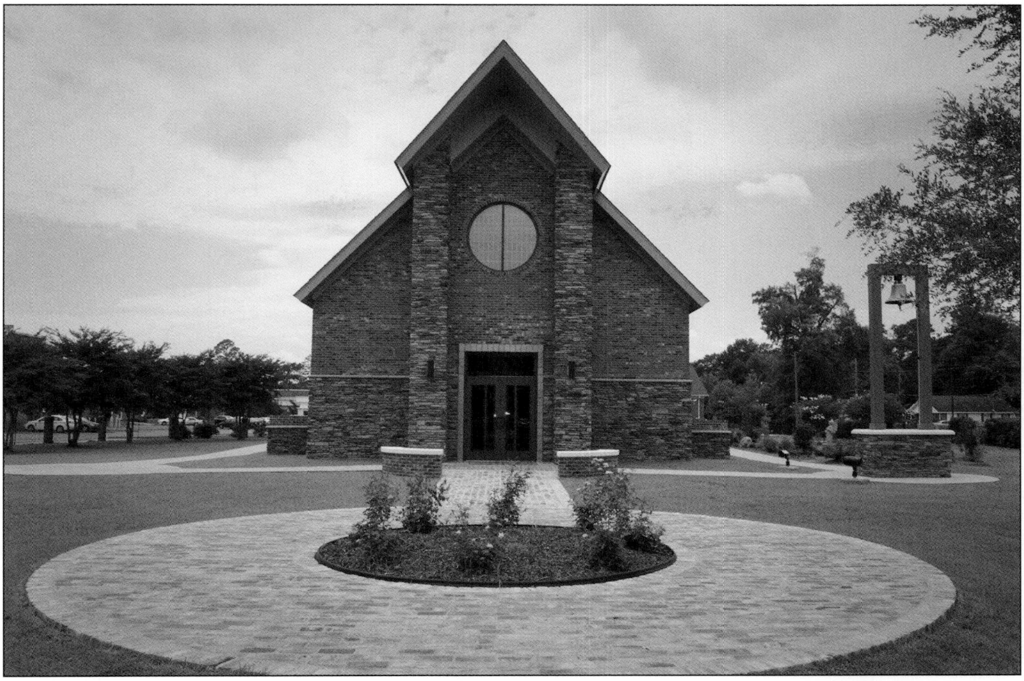

The Caroline and Ray Bass Memorial Chapel was dedicated in August 2014. The building, located directly behind Chain Garden, features the life of Christ illustrated through stained glass. Other stained-glass windows, including a life-sized depiction at the back of the building, feature university namesake William Carey and events of his life.

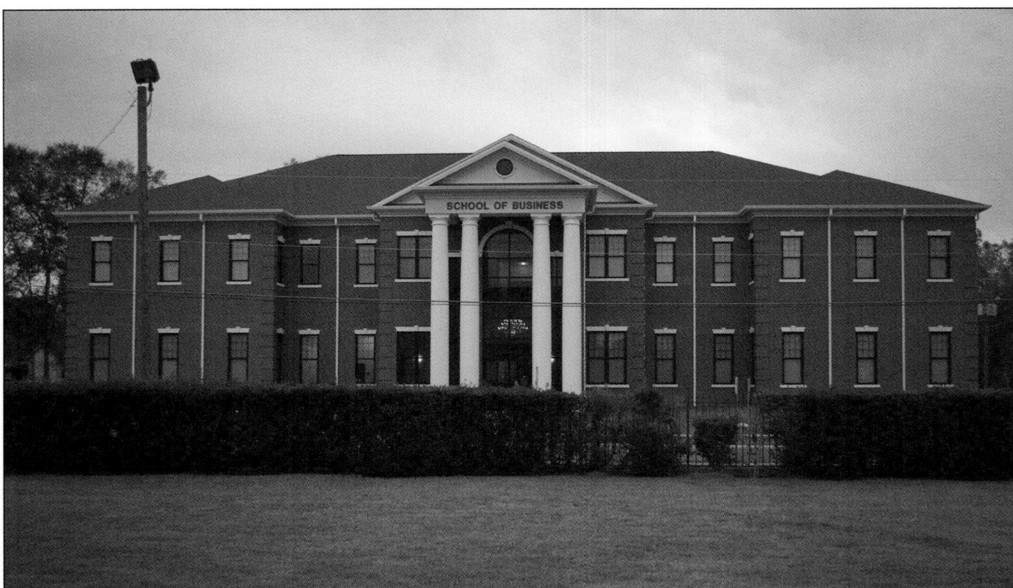


A new state-of-the-art home for the School of Business was dedicated in August 2014. The facility includes two lecture halls on the ground floor, classrooms and a computer lab on the second floor, faculty and staff offices, study areas, a lounge, and a conference room. Other features of the building include an expansive lobby with a grand staircase and an eight-foot European crystal chandelier donated to the university.

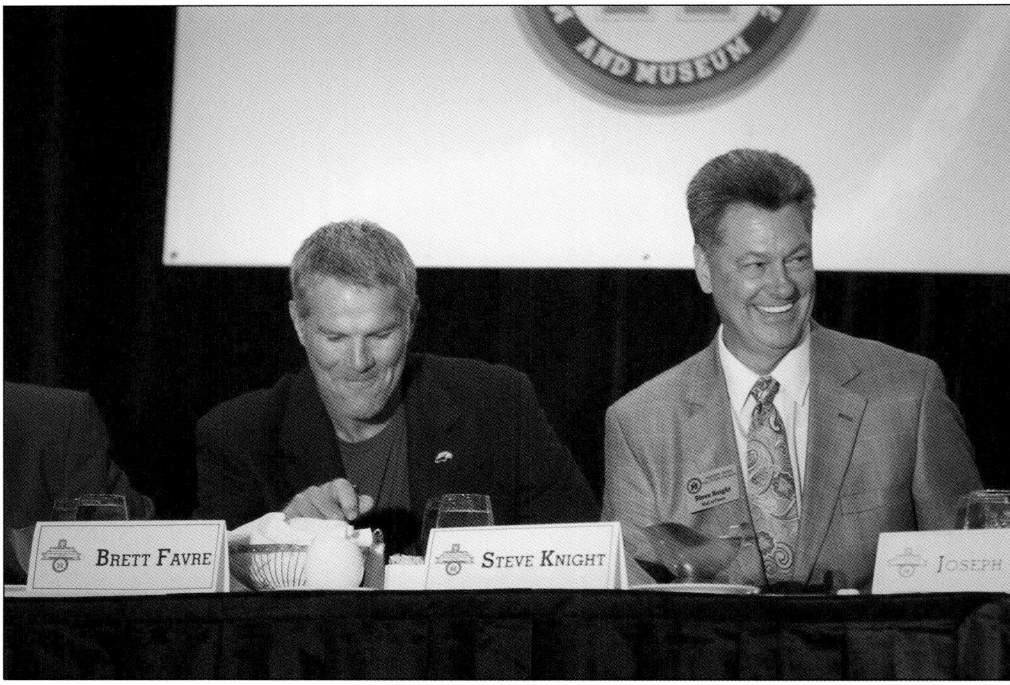


Steve Knight, men's basketball head coach and athletic director, was selected for the Mississippi Sports Hall of Fame 2015 class. A reception honoring Knight was hosted at Carey in October 2014. Knight, fresh from a 2014 conference championship win, was also named 2014 Men's Basketball National Coach of the Year by the National Association of Intercollegiate Athletics. Knight is pictured at right with fellow inductee and retired NFL quarterback Brett Favre.

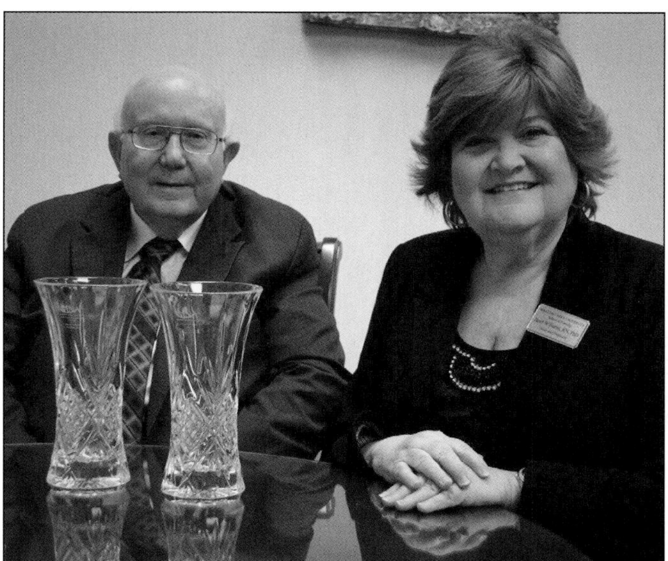

Dr. Janet Williams (pictured with Dr. Tommy King), dean of the Fail School of Nursing, was named School of Nursing Administrator of the Year in 2015 by the Mississippi Nurses' Association and the Mississippi Nurses' Foundation. The Fail School of Nursing was also named School of Nursing of the Year. The nursing school was recognized for adding new programs, including a PhD in nursing education and administration and a health information management undergraduate program.

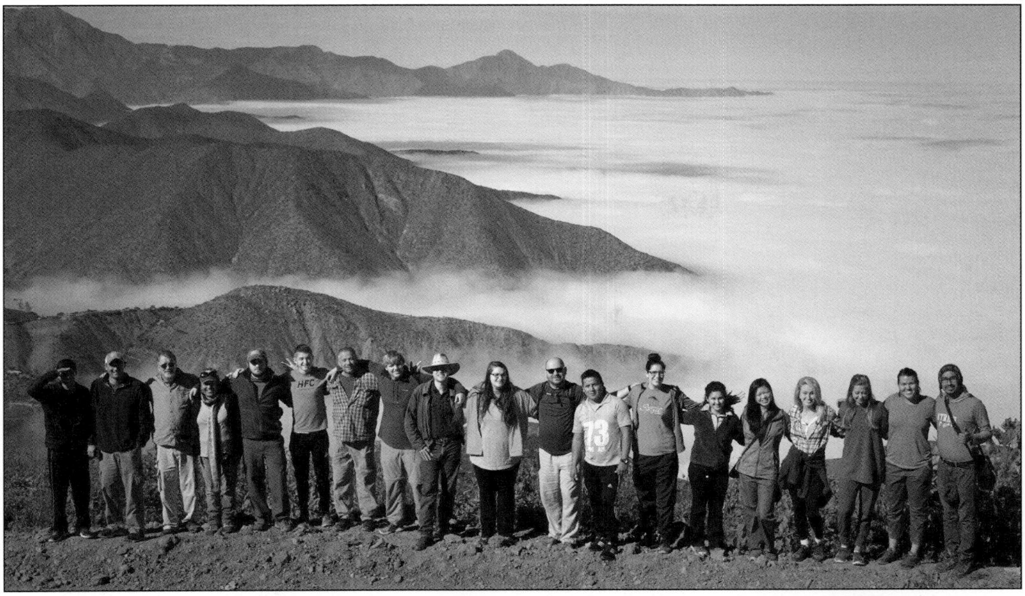

Students in the intercultural studies program traveled to Peru on a mission trip working with the Quechua Indians in the Andes Mountains in 2015. The program helps students prepare for careers in evangelism and missions while also requiring a second major in another field, such as business, to create a well-rounded professional. It is part of the new Department of Christian Ministries and the expanded Winters School of Music and Ministry Studies.

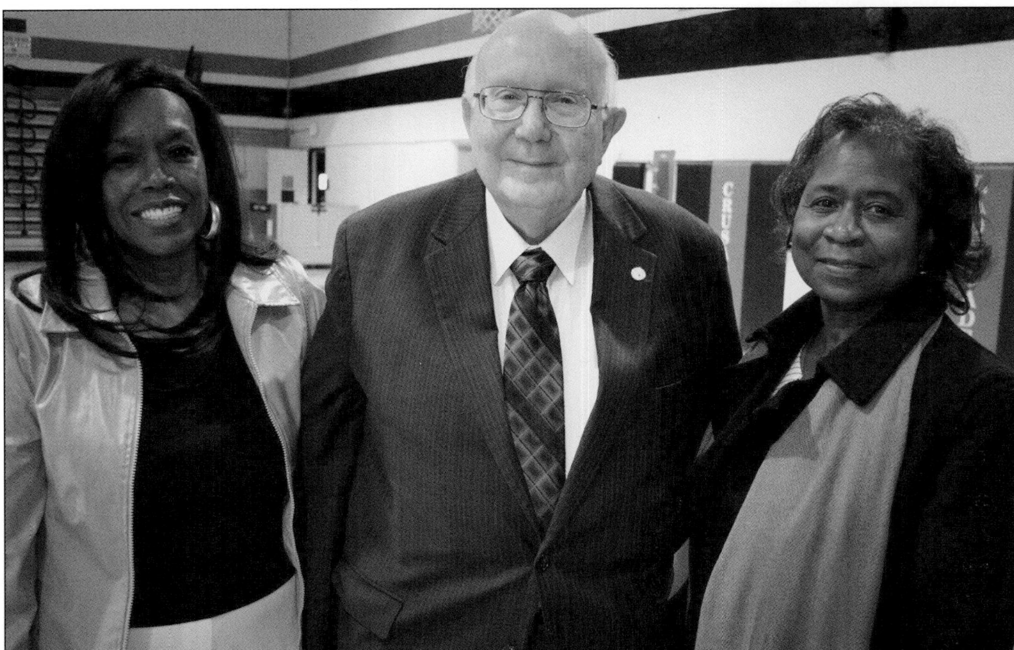

To celebrate the 50th year of its integration, Carey dedicated the Jackson-Williams Garden in March 2015 in honor of the university's first African-American students. Linda Williams Cross and Vermester Jackson Bester enrolled at Carey in August 1965 after the institution voluntarily integrated, becoming the first Mississippi college and the first Baptist college in the Deep South to do so. Pictured from left to right are Cross, Dr. Tommy King, and Bester.

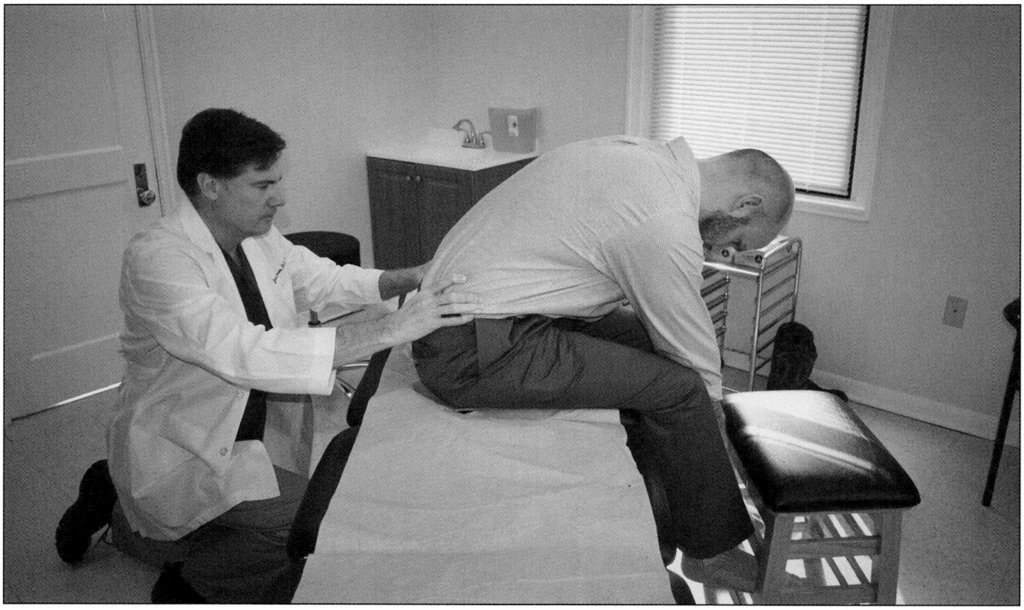

An osteopathic manipulative treatment (OMT) clinic, located in Mary Ross Hall, opened in January 2015. The clinic uses OMT procedures, including the movement of muscles and joints using stretching and gentle pressure, to diagnose, treat and prevent illness or injury. It is operated by faculty members from the College of Osteopathic Medicine and is open to students and employees. Pictured is Dr. John Jones (left) using OMT procedures on a patient.

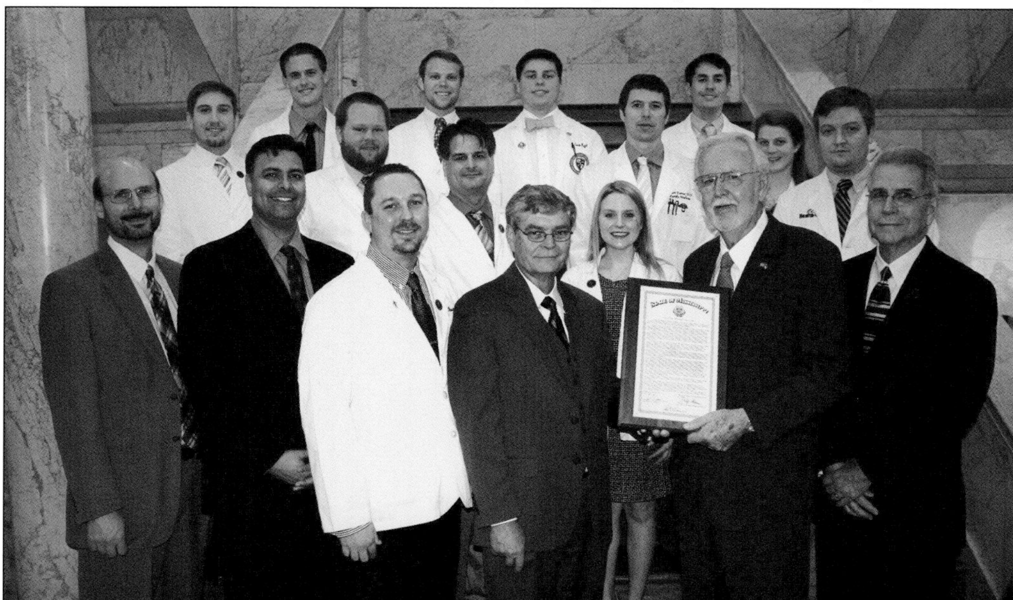

The Mississippi Legislature, in a concurrent resolution approved on March 9, 2015, recognized the College of Osteopathic Medicine and named the week of April 19–25 as National Osteopathic Medicine Week in Mississippi. The resolution, sponsored by state senators John Polk and Billy Hudson, honored the medical college and its work in educating future osteopathic physicians while also providing volunteer services, such as free health care in the impoverished Mississippi Delta.

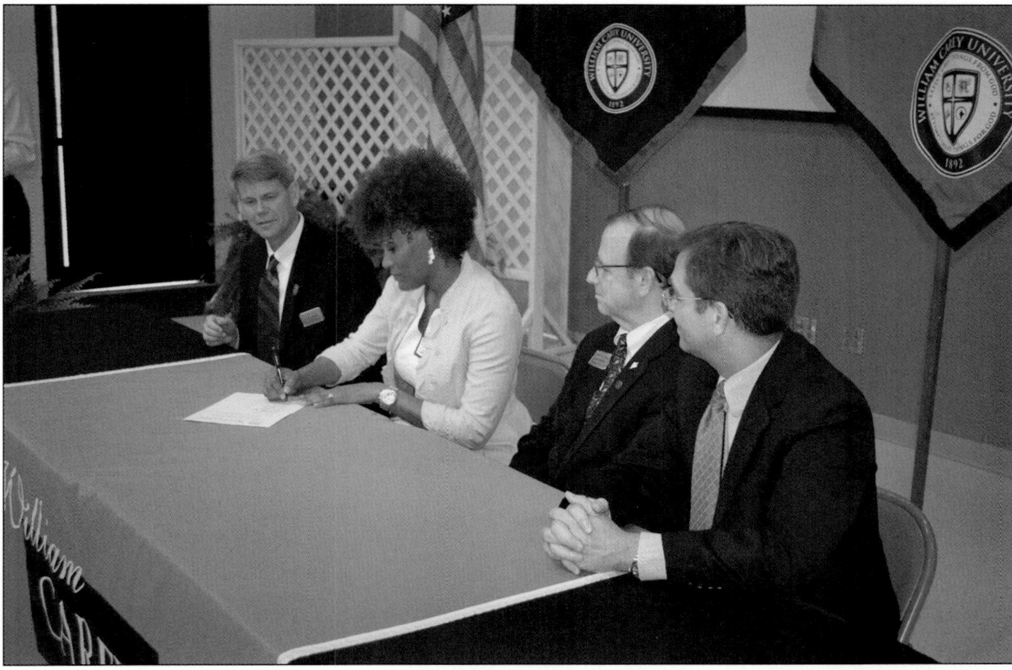


The first Education Signing Day, an event to honor teacher candidates and student teachers, was held in April 2015. Benita Lang signs up as a teacher candidate as, from left to right, School of Education dean Dr. Ben Burnett, vice president for Academic Affairs Dr. Garry Breland, and provost Dr. Scott Hummel look on. Enrollment in the education school hit a record 1,270 students in August 2015 due to new programs and enhanced online offerings.

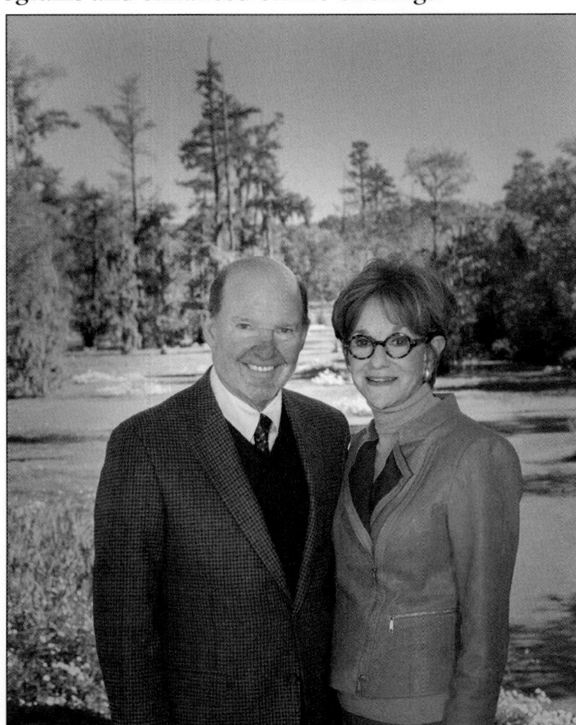

Joe F. Sanderson Jr., CEO of Sanderson Farms, and his wife, Kathy, donated $1.1 million, the largest gift from an individual in the university's history, to Carey in early 2015. The bulk of the gift will be used for startup costs at the pharmacy school on the Tradition campus, while $100,000 will go to the new physical therapy program. Both programs are only the second of their kind in Mississippi.

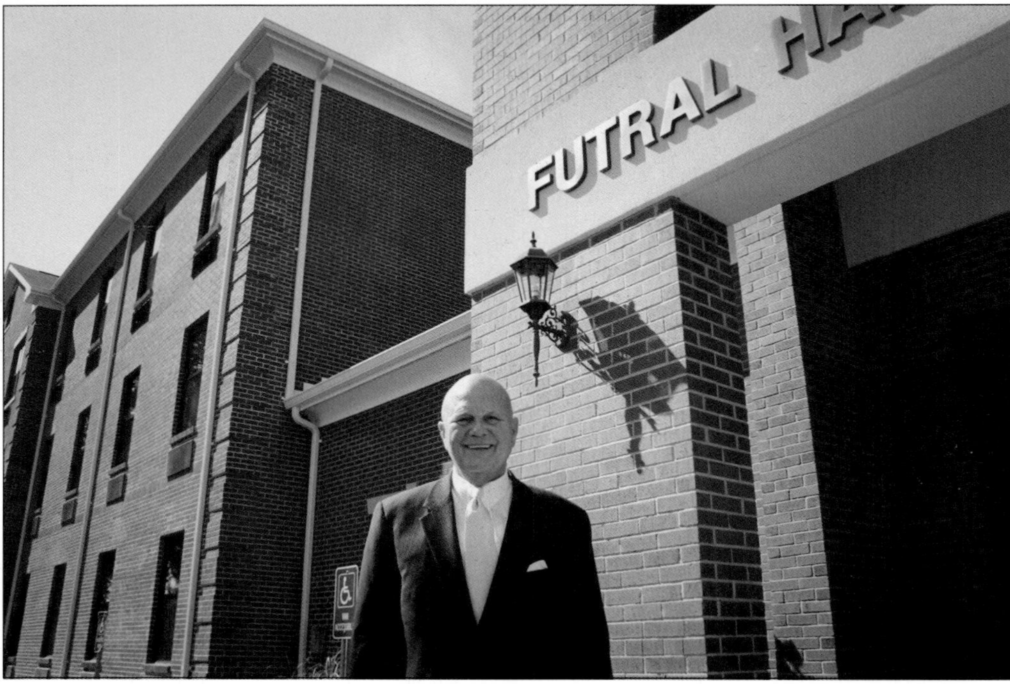


Futral Hall, named for Mississippi Baptist Convention executive director-treasurer and great friend to Carey Dr. Jim Futral, opened in August 2015 and completed a quadrangle of new residence halls constructed on the south end of the campus since 2007. The building houses 96 male students in rooms with private baths. It is connected to Davis Hall, which was completed in 2013 and is named for missionaries Ralph and Cora Joyce Davis.

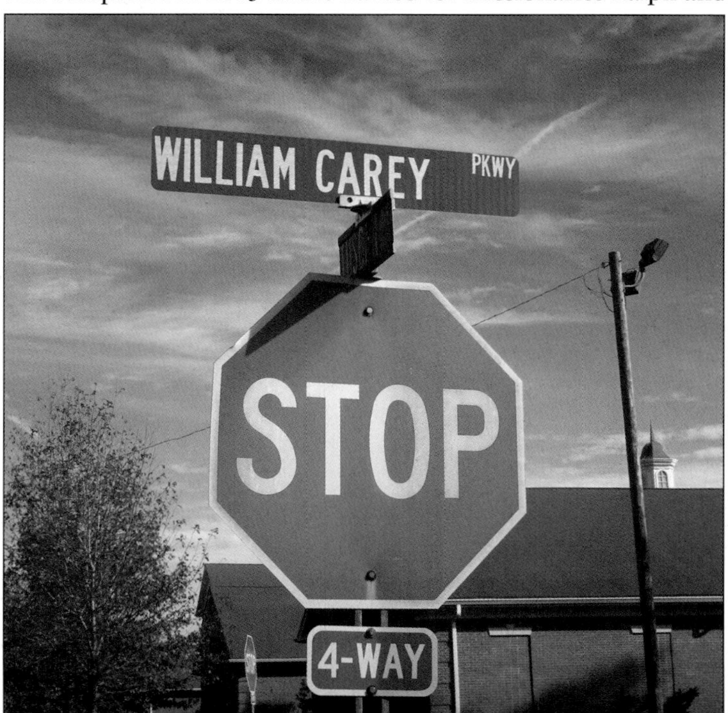


The Hattiesburg City Council unanimously approved renaming Helveston Road and one block of Penton Street to William Carey Parkway in December 2015 in recognition of the university's growth. The campus has now expanded to more than 170 acres. The parkway connects the campus to Highway 49. Prior to requesting the name change, university officials held informational meetings with neighborhood associations and residents, finding great support for the change.

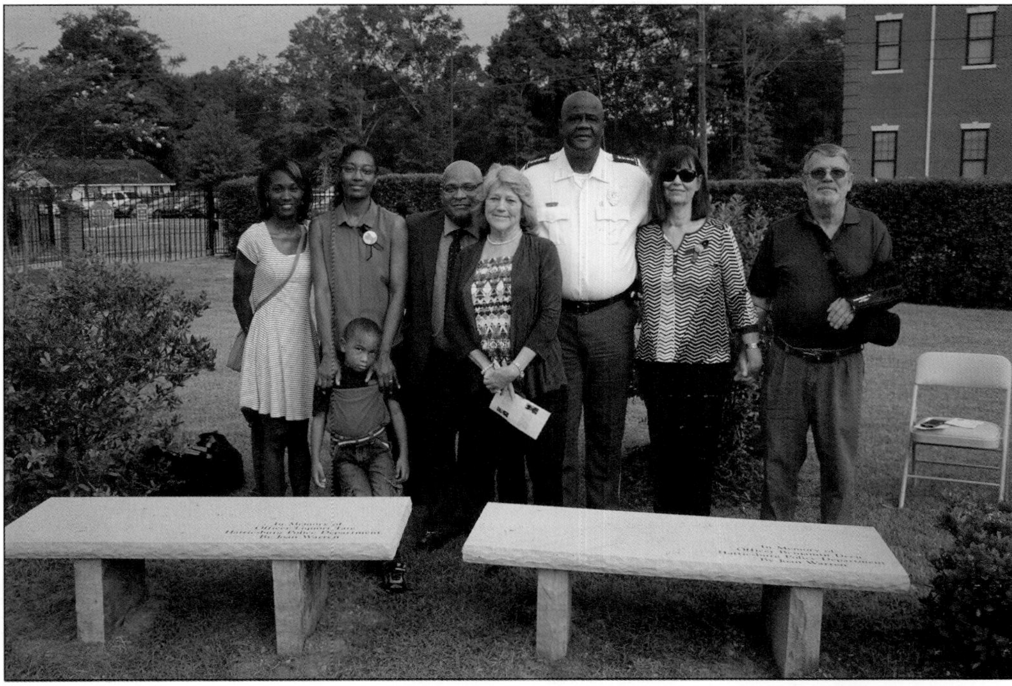

Two benches were dedicated in the Warren Prayer Garden in September 2015 in memory of fallen Hattiesburg police officers Benjamin Deen and Liquori Tate, who were killed in the line of duty on May 9, 2015. The benches were purchased with a special gift from Joan Warren of Hattiesburg, a Carey trustee. Warren (center) is pictured with police chief Anthony Parker and the Tate (left) and Dean (right) families.

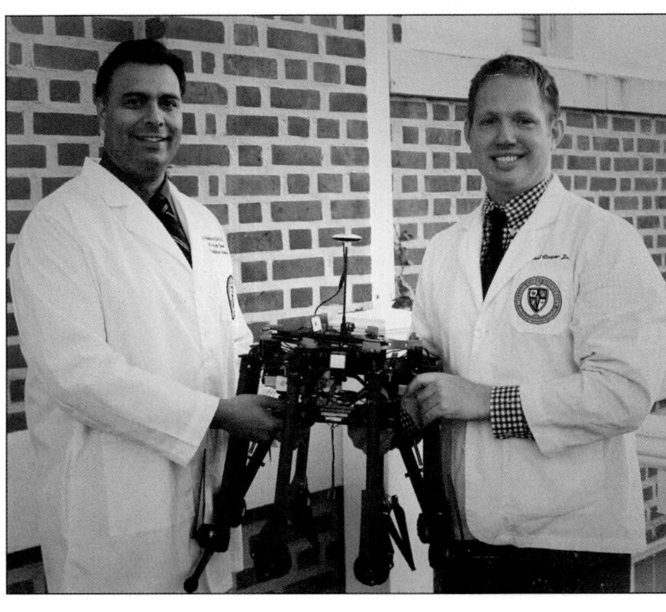

The first multirotor drone with telemedicine capability was developed in 2015 by Dr. Italo Subbarao, associate dean at medical college, and Paul Cooper Jr., a medical student from Wheaton, Illinois. The drone, called Healthcare Integrated Rescue (HiRO), can carry an advanced, 20-pound telemedical kit and deliver it to someone in need of medical attention in areas emergency personnel may not be able to quickly reach. The drone received national and international attention.

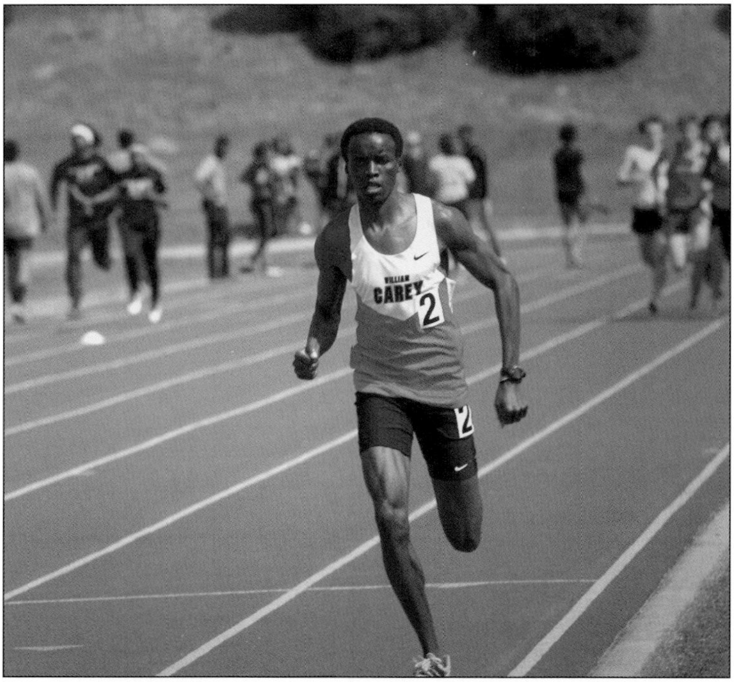


Geoffrey Kipchumba, a native of Eldoret, Kenya, won his second consecutive National Association of Intercollegiate Athletics (NAIA) national title in the men's 10,000-meter final in May 2016. Kipchumba, a two-time Southern States Athletic Conference Runner of the Year, has also claimed two NAIA national championship titles in cross-country. His ultimate goal is to finish his education and qualify for the 2020 Tokyo Olympics as a representative of the United States.

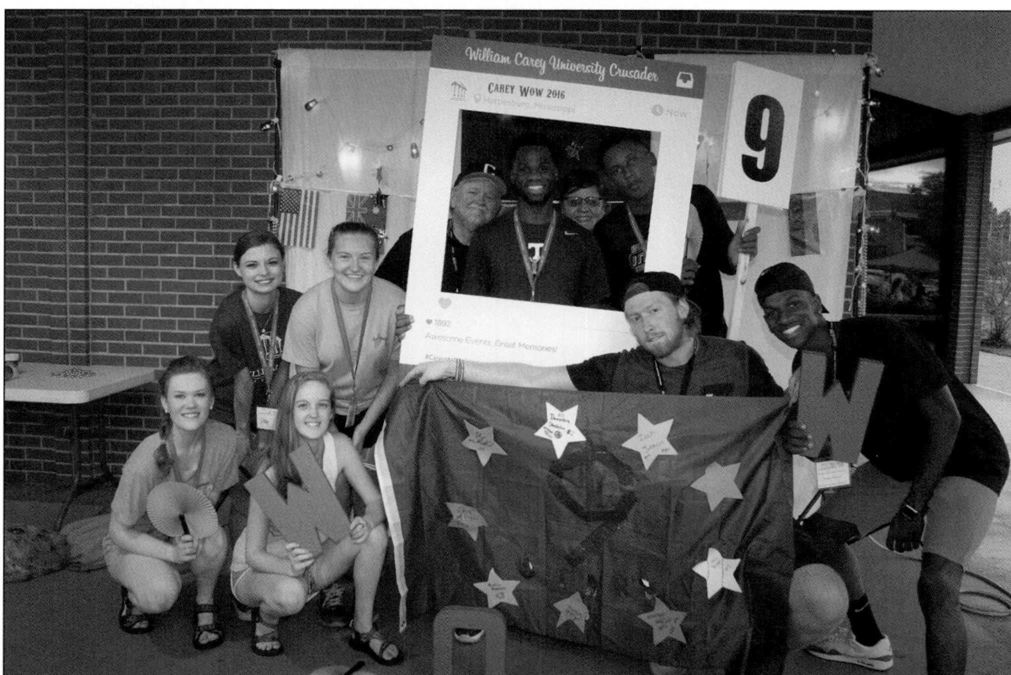


Carey hosted the third annual CareyWOW (Welcome and Orientation Weekend) in August 2016. The weekend of activities includes welcoming ceremonies, special dinners, devotional times, recreational activities, nature walks, and orientation sessions. New students also participate in HubSERVE, a Carey tradition of reaching out and helping others in the community. Students are divided into teams, led by student and faculty mentors, to encourage relationship building and friendly competition with fellow teams.

# *Eight*

# WILLIAM CAREY UNIVERSITY

## 2017 AND THE FUTURE

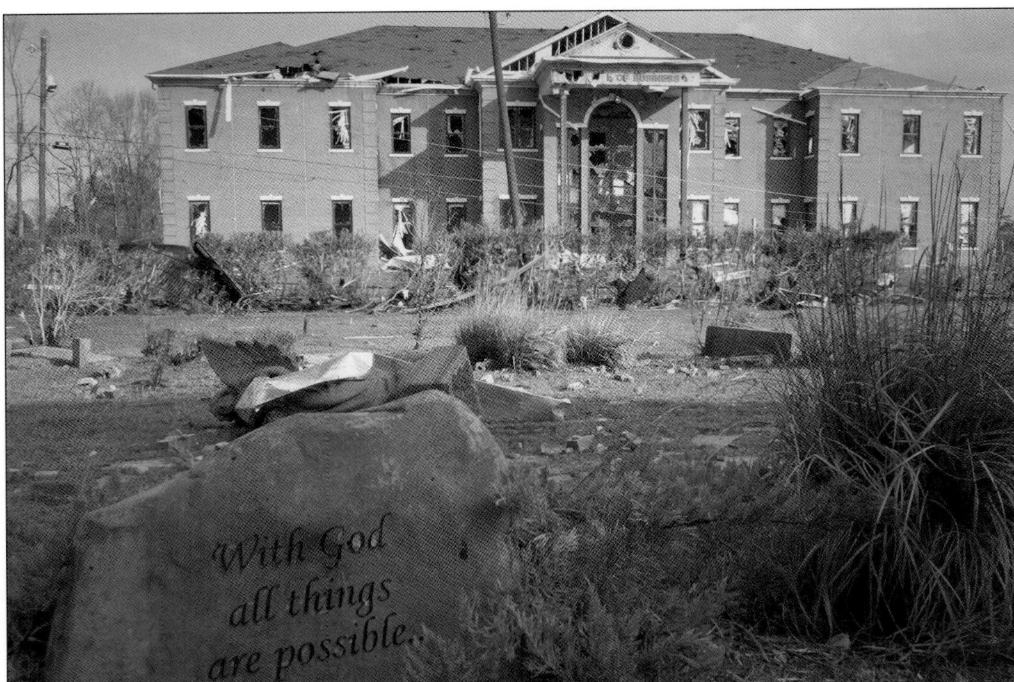


In the early morning hours of January 21, 2017, an EF3 tornado with wind speeds up to 165 mph struck William Carey University during its 31.3-mile trek across the area. The tornado, which left all buildings with significant damage, caused several injuries but no fatalities on the campus. When its path ended, four were dead and twenty more injured in Forrest County with more than 1,100 homes damaged or destroyed.

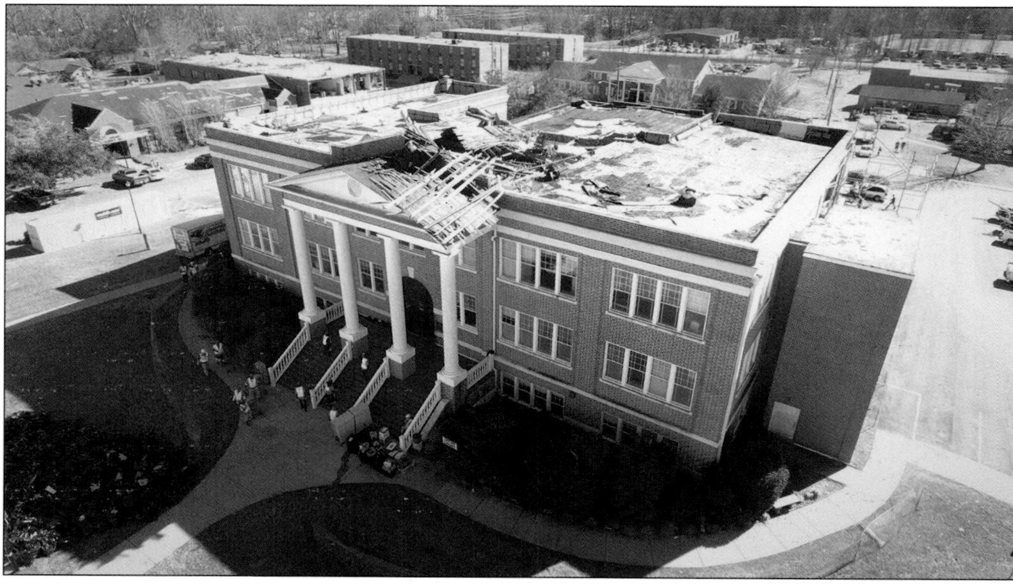

Tatum Court, the oldest building on the campus and the most iconic, was a casualty of the tornado. The historic building, which was completed in 1914, sustained severe roof damage (pictured) and structural damage, including the loss and weakening of exterior walls. The building, which housed the university administration and support offices, the theater and communication department, the O.L. Quave Theatre, the Noonkester School of Arts and Letters, and classrooms, was demolished and cleared from the campus. Bricks and other artifacts from the original building will be used in the construction of a new Tatum Court, which will be located where Ross and Johnson Halls were before the tornado.

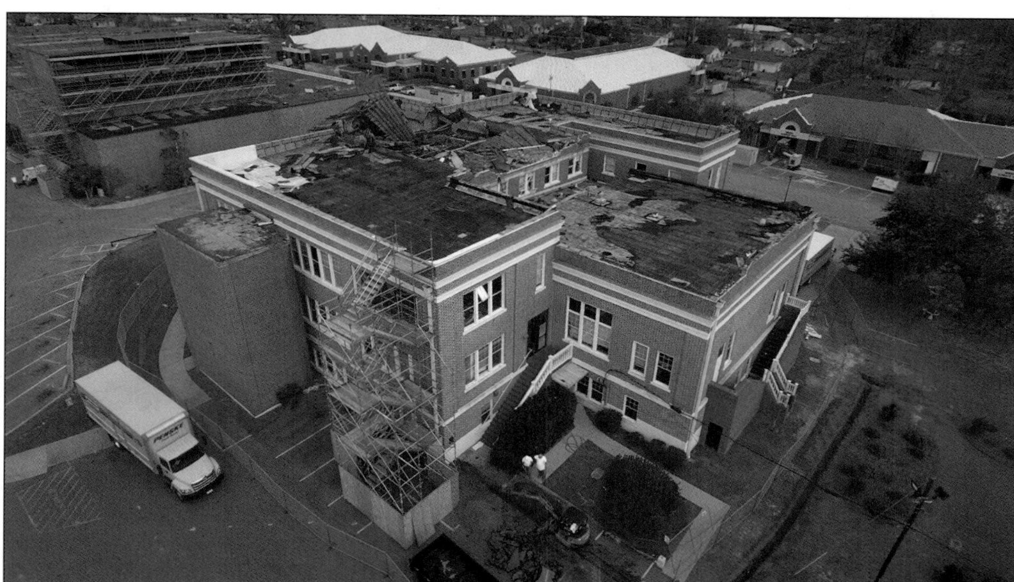

Gov. Phil Bryant (at podium), Rep. Steven Palazzo (left), and Hattiesburg mayor Johnny DuPree held a press conference at the College of Osteopathic Medicine Complex in the hours following the tornado. All three officials pledged their support and commitment to the university's strong recovery. Bryant and DuPree also declared states of emergency for the affected areas.

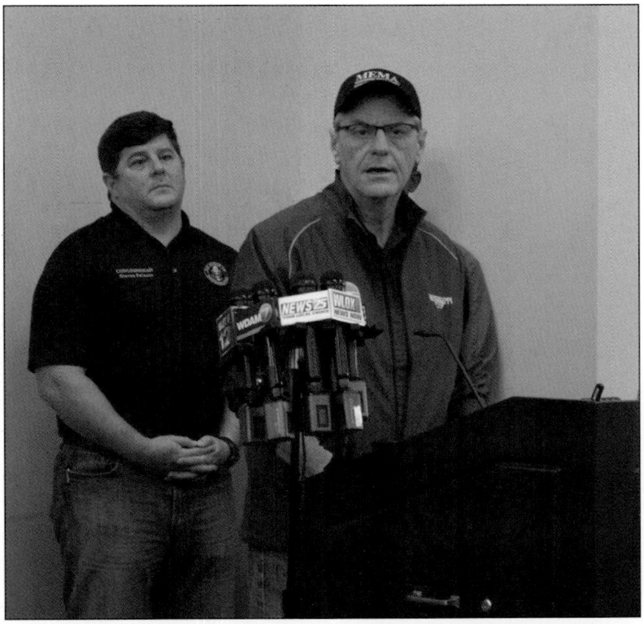


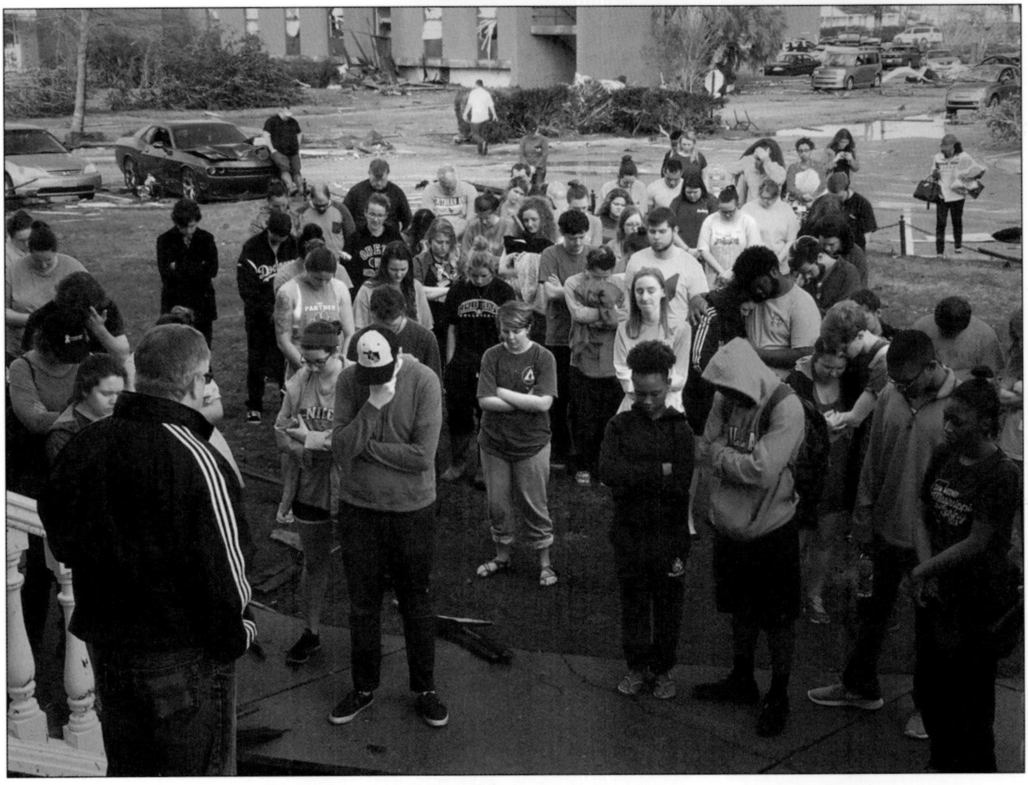

Dr. Tim Glaze, director of the Baptist Student Union, leads a group of students in prayer on the steps of Tatum Court on January 21. Although there were no fatalities on the campus, there were several injuries as walls collapsed and windows shattered. Students prayed for their classmates and for the future of their university. The phrases of "Carey Strong" and "Sader Strong" became common rallying cries.

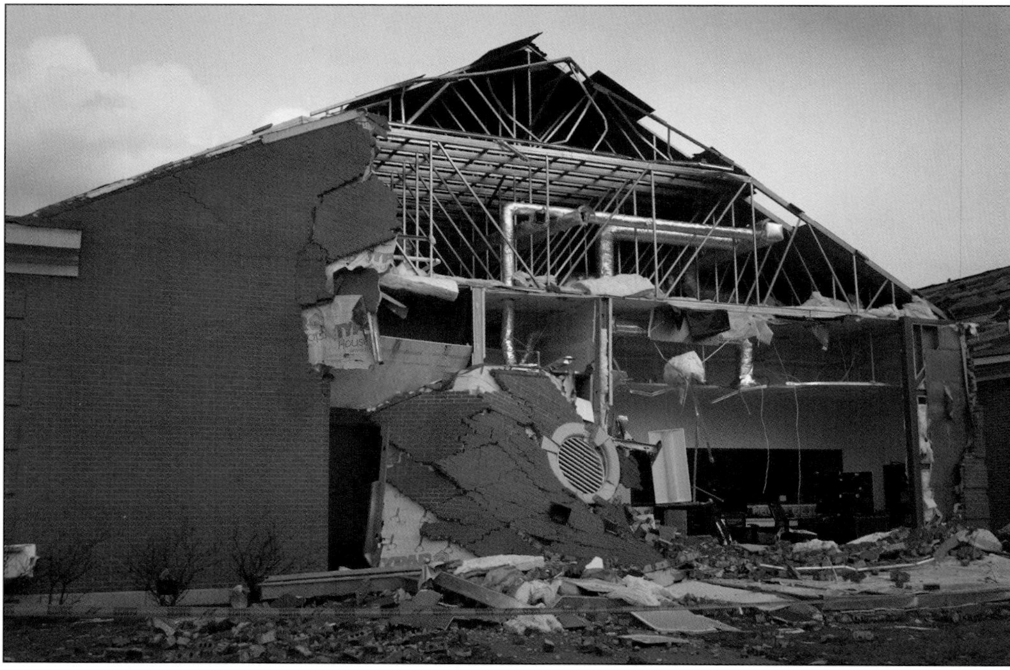

The four buildings of the College of Osteopathic Medicine—the Academic Building, Asbury Administrative Center, the Medical Arts Building, and Ross Anatomy Wing—sustained heavy exterior and roof damage during the tornado. Ross Anatomy Wing, which opened in 2014, was totaled and has been demolished. The three surviving buildings are being repaired. The medical college's faculty, staff, and students temporarily relocated to space generously provided by the University of Southern Mississippi in its former nursing building. Medical college personnel and students returned to the Carey campus in July 2017.

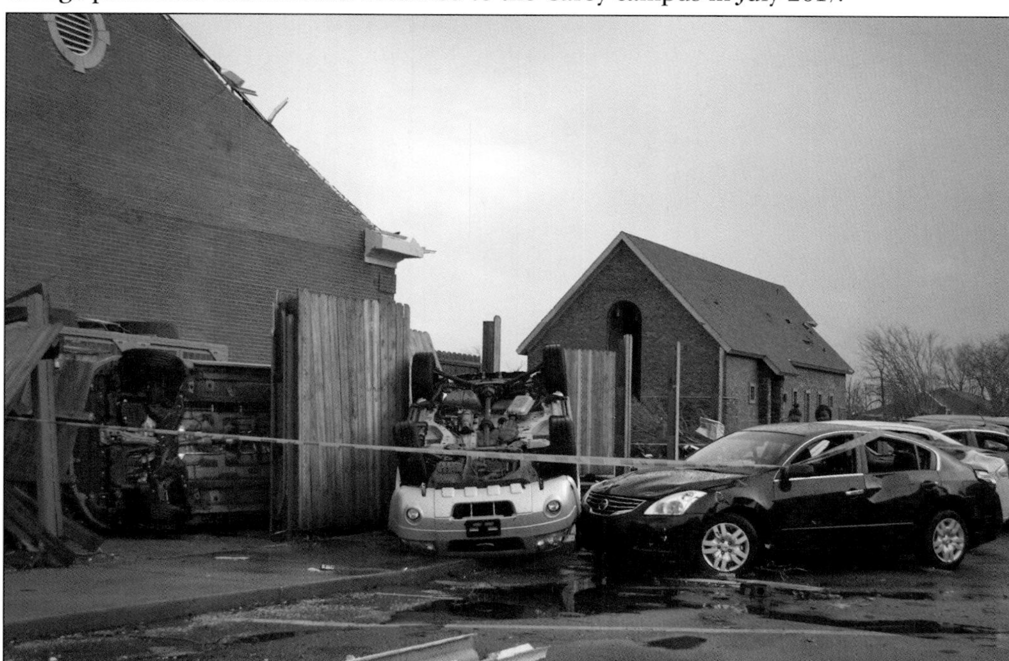

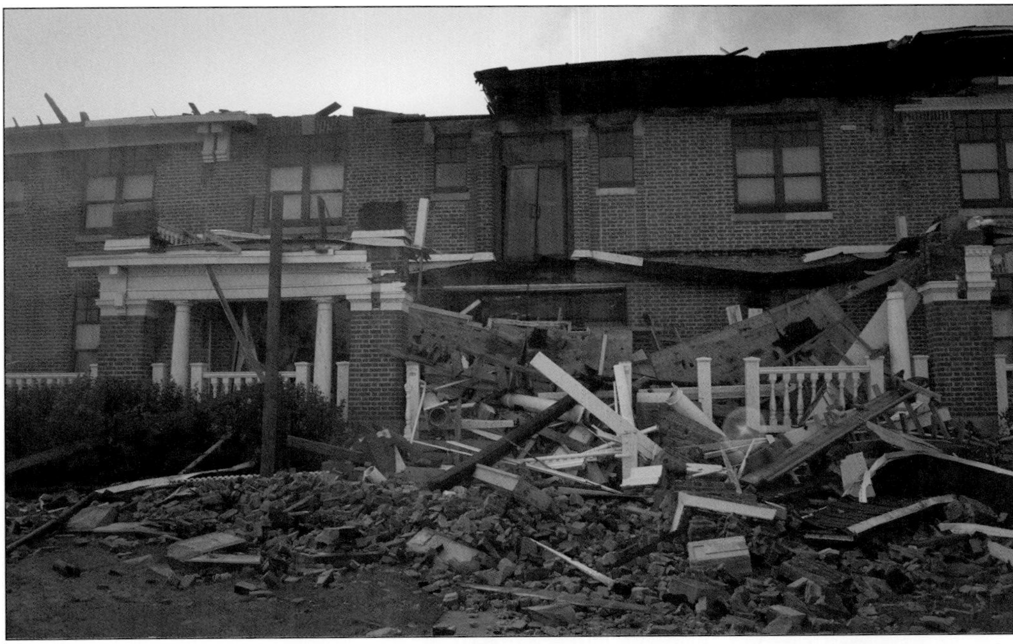

Ross and Johnson Halls, two of the oldest buildings on the campus, were destroyed by the tornado and have been demolished. The twin residence halls, which were constructed in 1919, accommodated approximately 100 female students in apartment-style living and also housed living space for guests. Ross-Johnson Lawn, a large green space used for special events in recent years, lost trees. The Mississippi Woman's College Heritage Plaza, located between the residence halls, was destroyed. The former site of Ross and Johnson Halls will be the home of the new Tatum Court and an academic building housing Lucile Parker Gallery, which are expected to be completed in 2019. Two residence halls will be constructed perpendicular to Byrd, Braswell, Futral, and Davis Halls and will be of the same design.

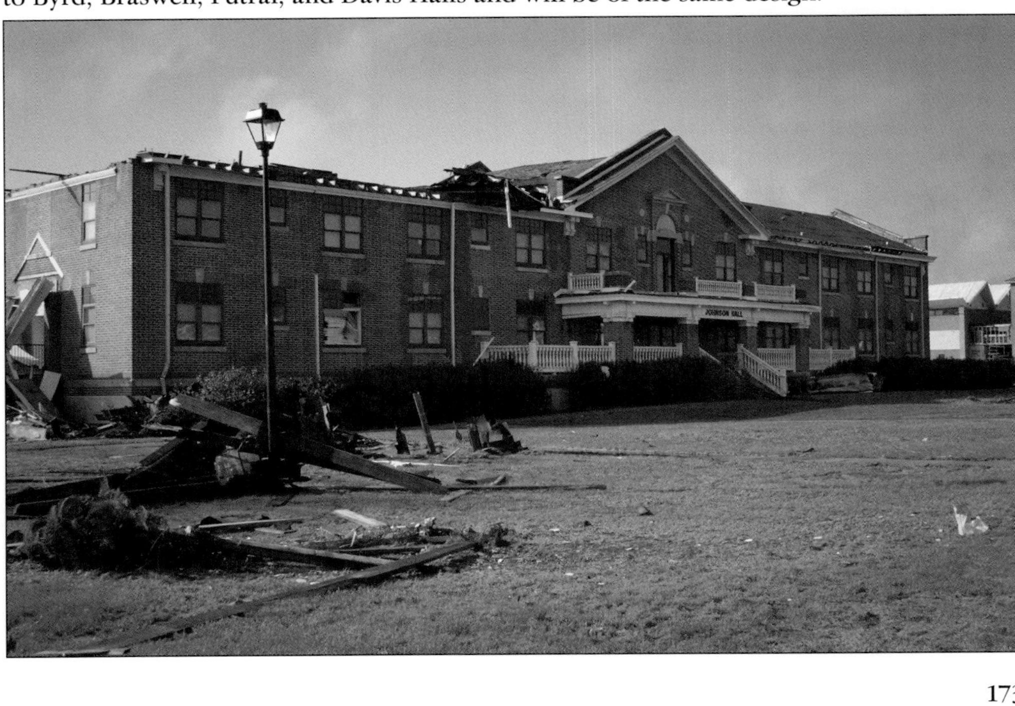

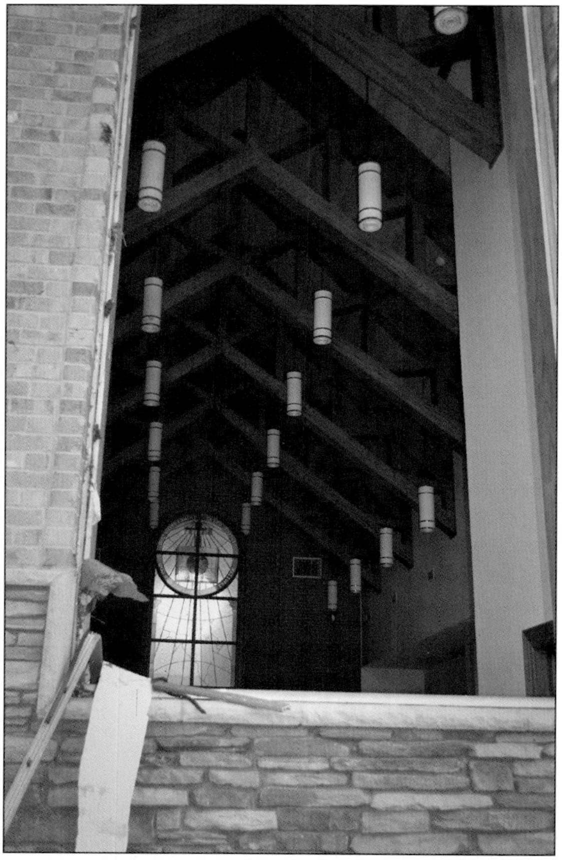

Bass Memorial Chapel, which opened in 2014, was damaged by the tornado with pieces of the exterior wall missing, roof damage, and the stained-glass windows, featuring scenes from the life of Jesus and scenes from university namesake William Carey's life, shattered. The chapel's back window, the largest piece of stained glass in the building, featured a depiction of William Carey and the scripture Isaiah 54:2 in four languages. The chapel is being repaired with the stained glass planned for replacement. The chapel Bible, which was on the pulpit inside, was found undamaged at Psalm 46, which begins with "God is our refuge and strength, a very present help in trouble." *The Risen Christ* statue, seen below, which sits in Chain Garden in front of the chapel, survived the tornado unscathed.

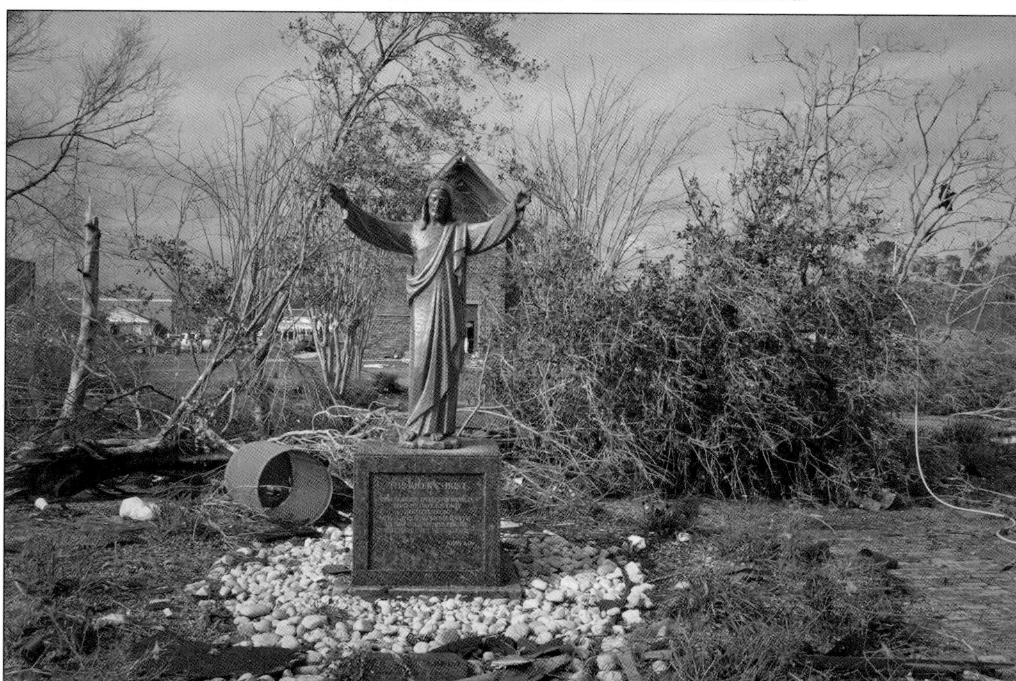

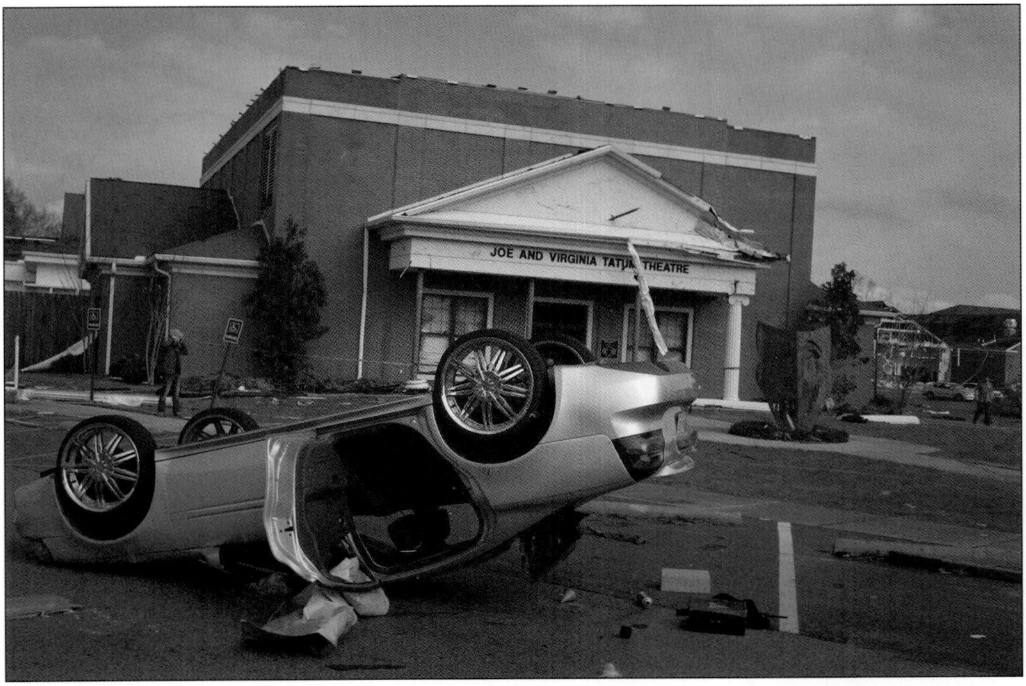


The Joe and Virginia Tatum Theatre, home of several productions a year from theater students and the site of Carey Dinner Theatre, suffered exterior and roof damage. The theater was repaired and hosted the dinner theater in the summer of 2017. The O.L. Quave Theatre, on the ground floor of Tatum Court, was lost with the building along with theater offices and storage areas.

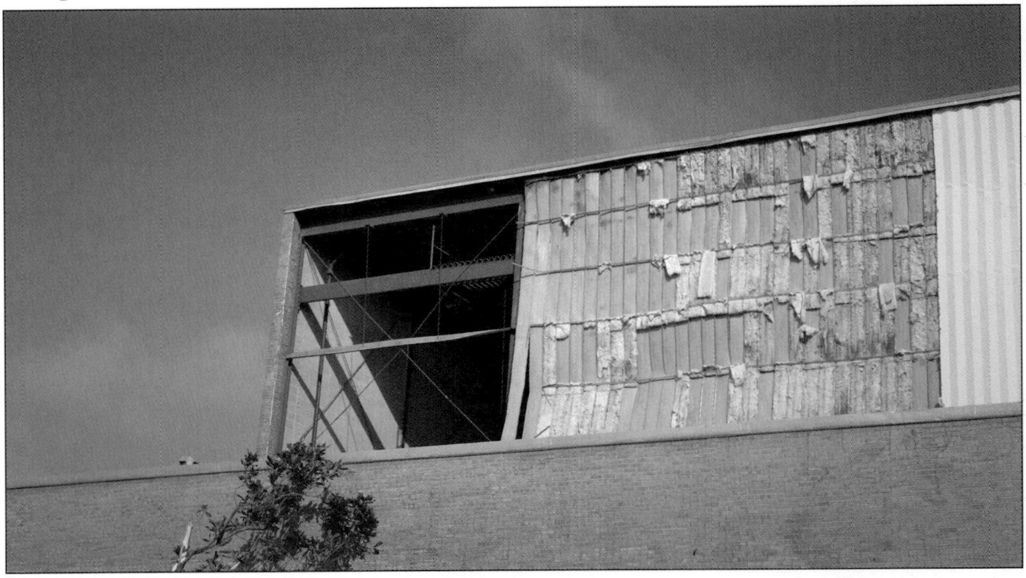

Thomas Fine Arts Center, home of the music department and Smith Auditorium, lost an exterior wall and is being repaired. Classes were temporarily moved to Hardy Street Baptist Church. Neighboring buildings, including Fairchild Hall, Smith Hall, Smith/Rouse Library, and Green Science Hall are also being repaired. Art from the Sarah Gillespie Museum of Art, attached to the library, was rescued and has been temporarily relocated to off-site storage.

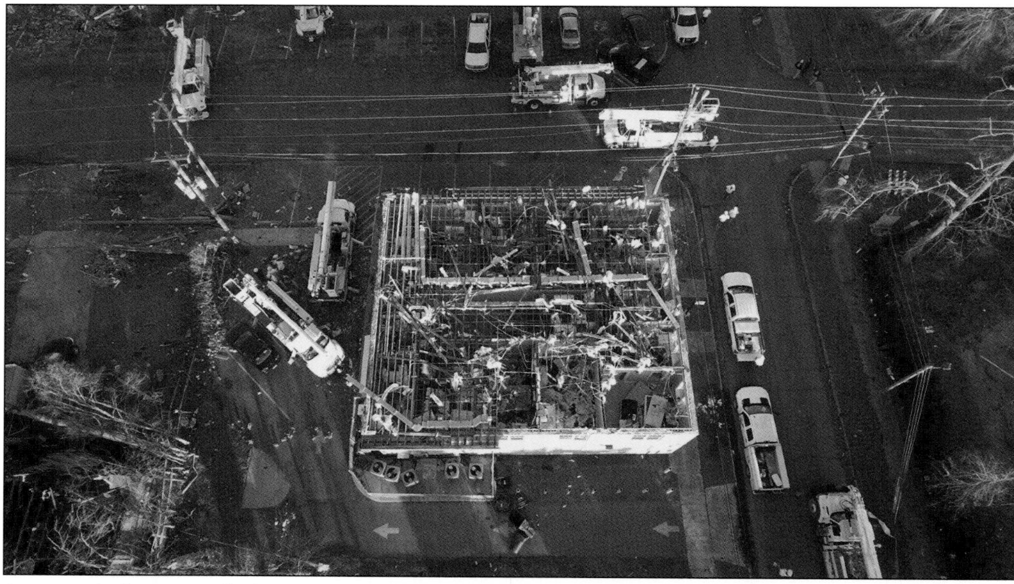

An aerial photograph shows the significant roof, interior, and exterior damage to 512 Tuscan Avenue, home of the Lucile Parker Gallery and five apartments for students. The historic building, erected in 1924 as a neighborhood store and remodeled by the university in 2013, was demolished shortly after the tornado. Art from the Parker Gallery has been temporarily relocated to off-site storage.

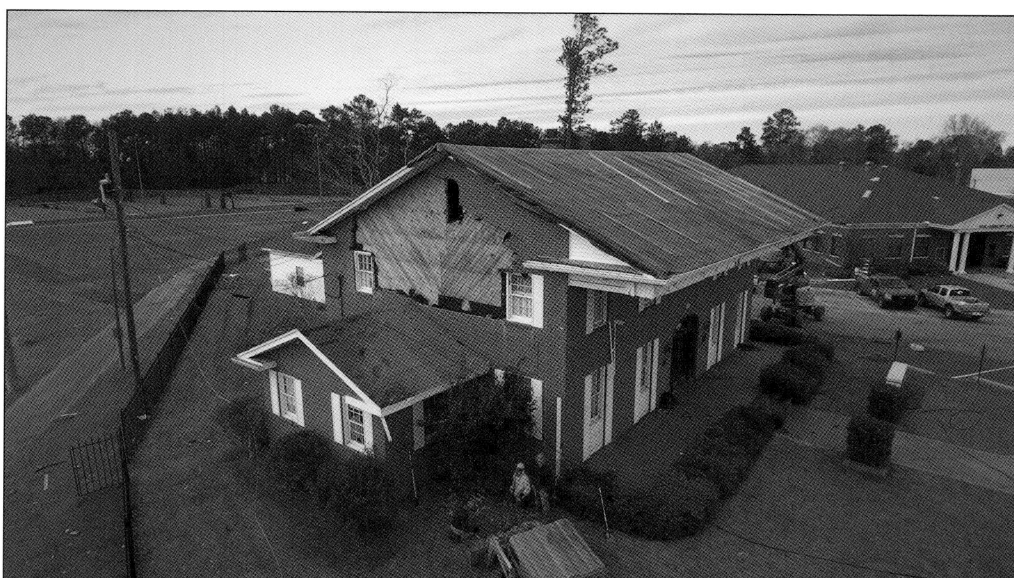

The Donna Duck Wheeler Alumni House, home of the alumni relations and admissions offices, lost all four of its front columns as well as a significant portion of its exterior walls. The building, the former president's home, is being repaired. The neighboring Fail-Asbury Hall, home of the College of Health Sciences and Fail School of Nursing, sustained minor damage but did not see an interruption in classes.

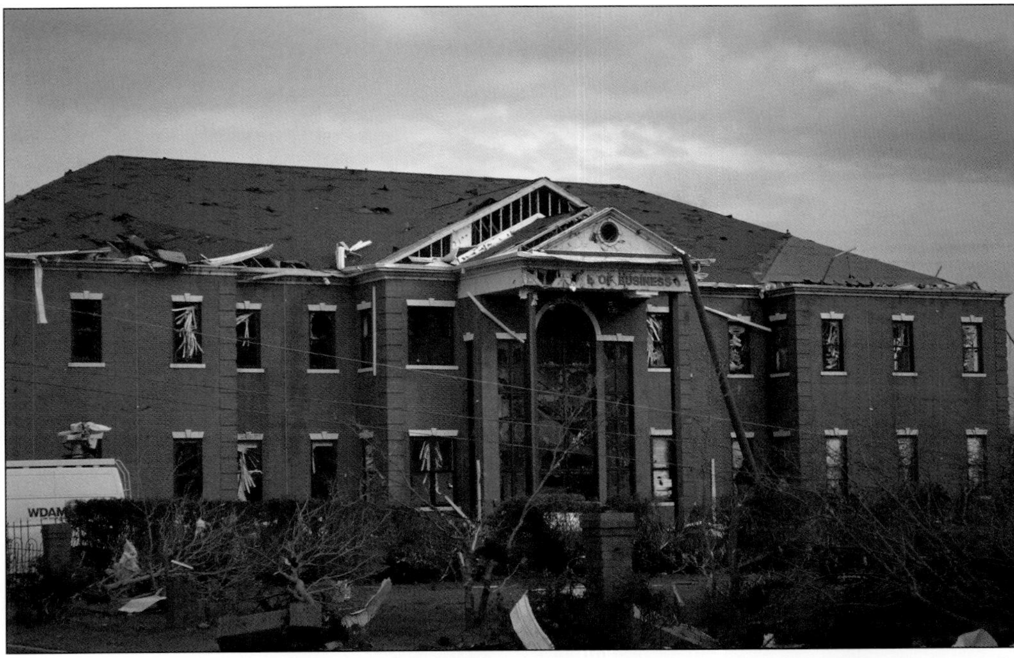

The School of Business building, dedicated in 2014, was in the direct path of the tornado and took a heavy hit. Originally considered a loss, the building is salvageable and is being repaired. Photos of its heavily damaged front were featured in local and national newscasts and also heavily on social media because of the easy access to the building, which is located outside of the main campus.

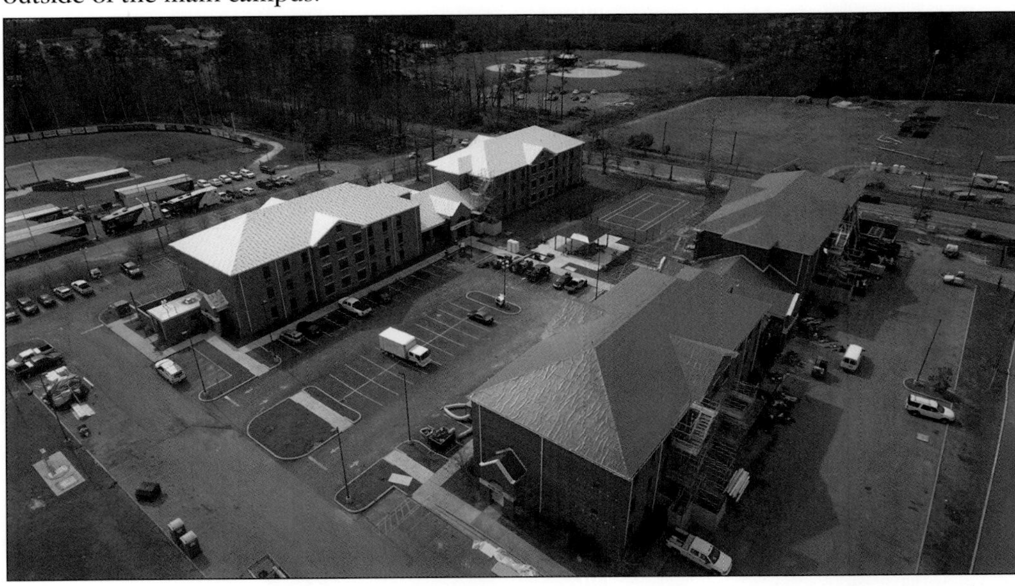

Carey's newest residence halls—Byrd and Braswell (completed 2007), Davis (completed 2013), and Futral (completed 2015)—suffered roof damage and broken windows but were structurally sound. They were quickly repaired and were ready for occupancy less than one month after the tornado. Students moved back into the four residence halls beginning on February 18. Students have also reoccupied Bass, Bryant, and Polk Halls and the Penton Street Apartments.

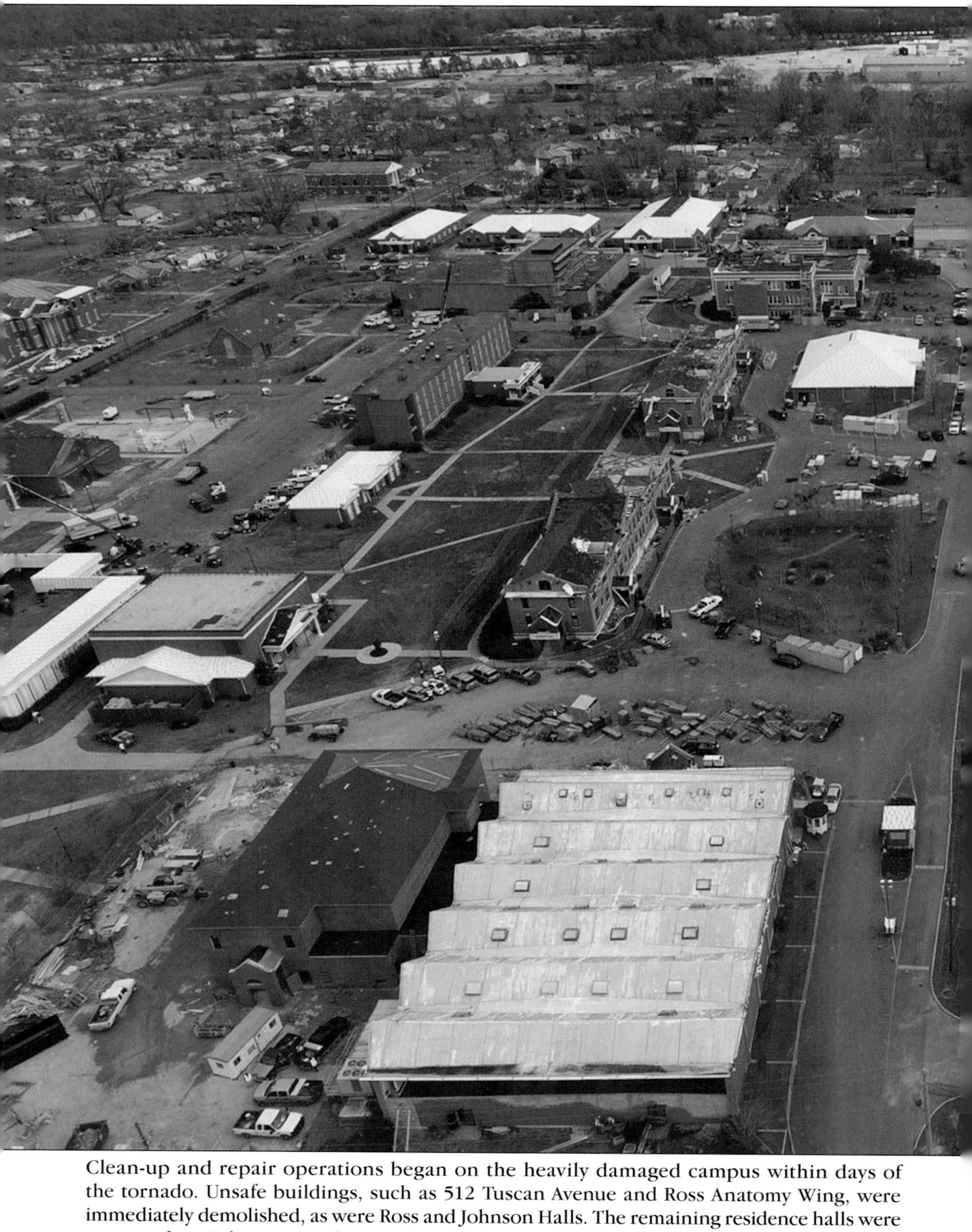

Clean-up and repair operations began on the heavily damaged campus within days of the tornado. Unsafe buildings, such as 512 Tuscan Avenue and Ross Anatomy Wing, were immediately demolished, as were Ross and Johnson Halls. The remaining residence halls were reopened on February 18 along with several classroom buildings, including Fairchild and

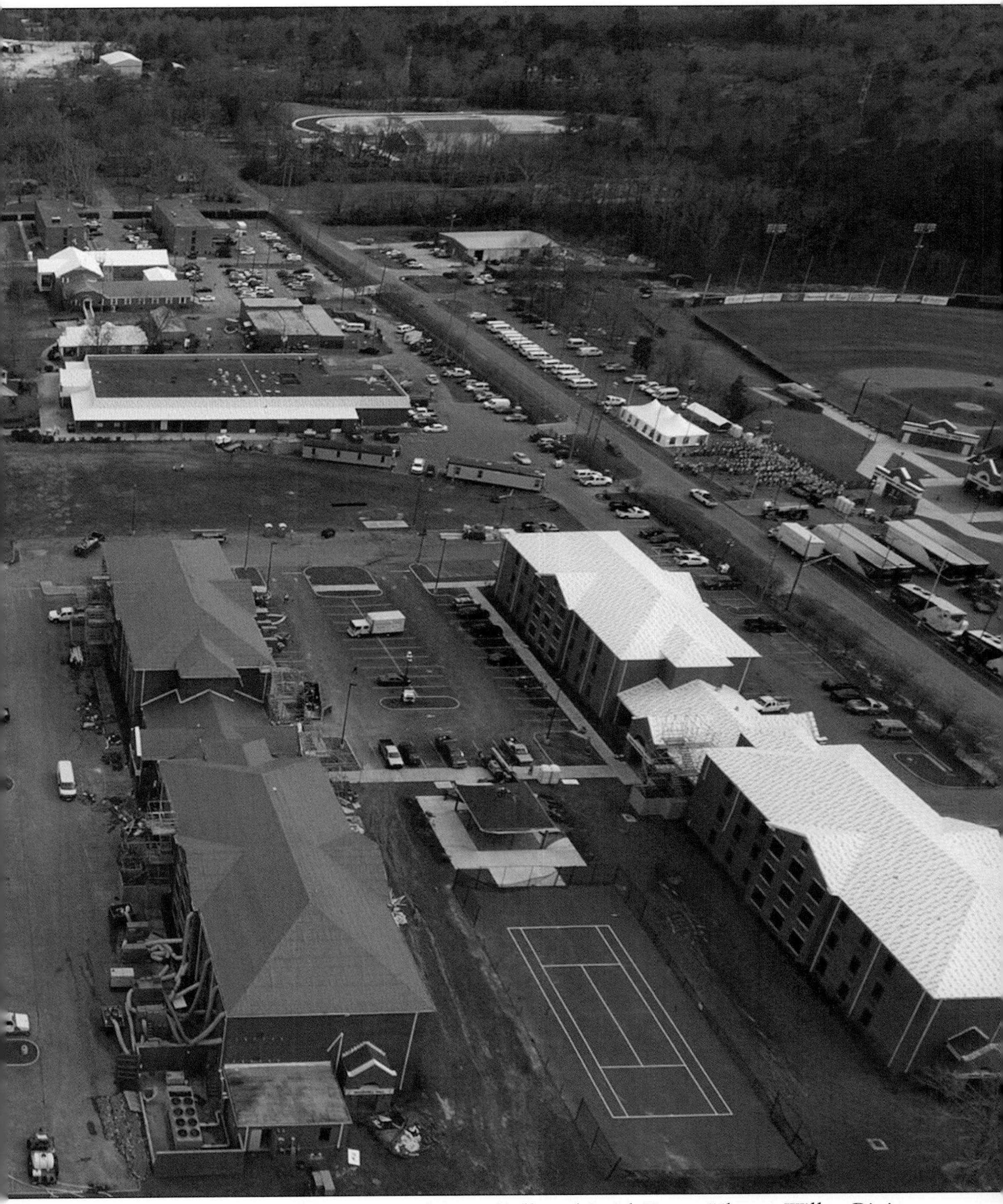

Smith Halls, Thomas Building, Green Science Hall, and Smith/Rouse Library. Wilkes Dining Hall, the Student Center, and the Common Grounds Coffee House were also reopened after sustaining roof damage. Tatum Court, the administration building and the oldest building on campus, was demolished.

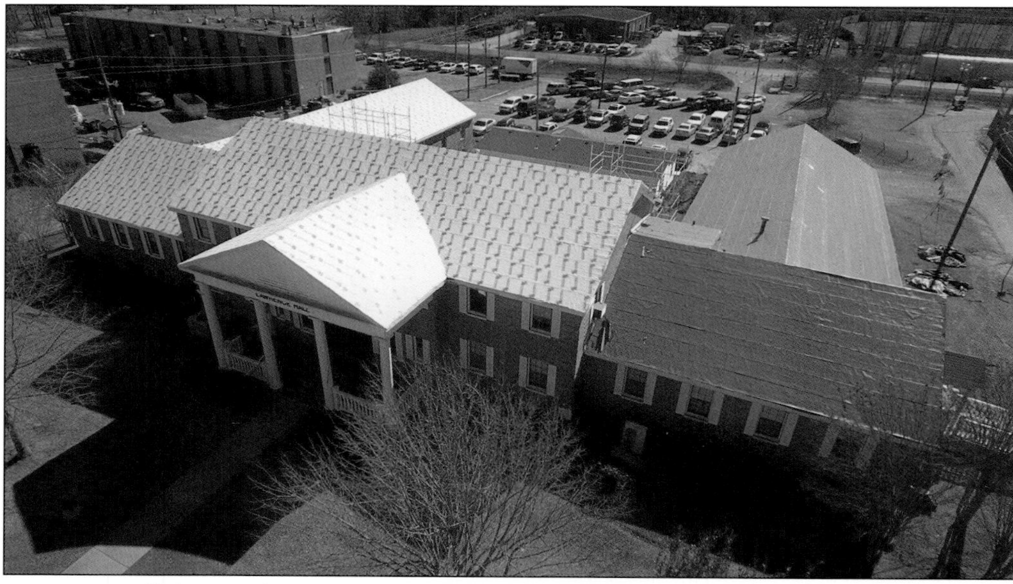

Lawrence Hall, home of student support, housing, institutional effectiveness, religion faculty offices, and classrooms, received roof damage but was repaired and now serves as the temporary administrative headquarters for the university. The building houses the university administration and support, including the business office, financial aid, registrar, and faculty offices. Built in 1954 as a men's dormitory, Lawrence Hall will remain the administration building until the construction of the new Tatum Court.

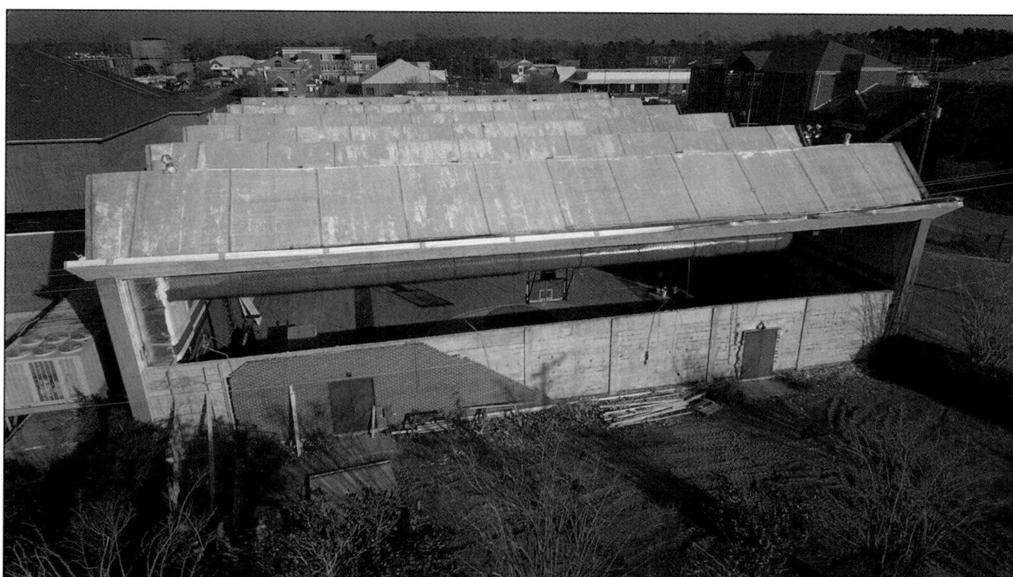

Clinton Gymnasium lost much of an exterior wall in the tornado's assault on the campus. The gym's prominent "William Carey Crusaders" sign, which has greeted campus visitors for decades, remained affixed to the building but was heavily damaged. The gym will be repaired. A nearly completed addition suffered little damage. The Crusaders went on to win the regular season Southern States Athletic Conference title despite being displaced.

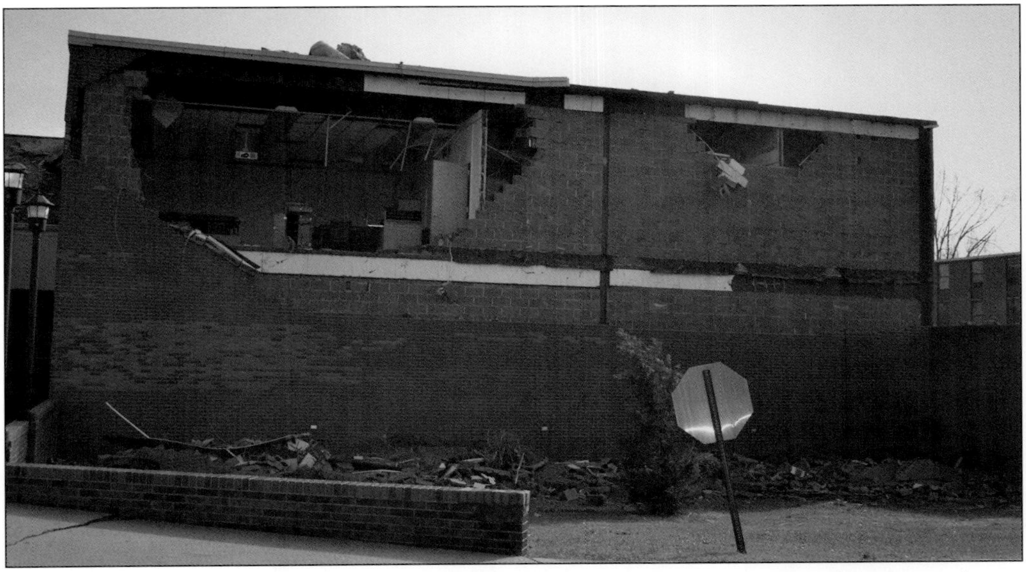

Green Science Hall, which houses the School of Natural and Behavioral Sciences, lost a significant portion of an exterior wall and suffered roof damage during the tornado but can be repaired. Partial areas of the building reopened for classes beginning the week of February 20. A new biology lab, completed in 2017, received minimal damage and has been occupied.

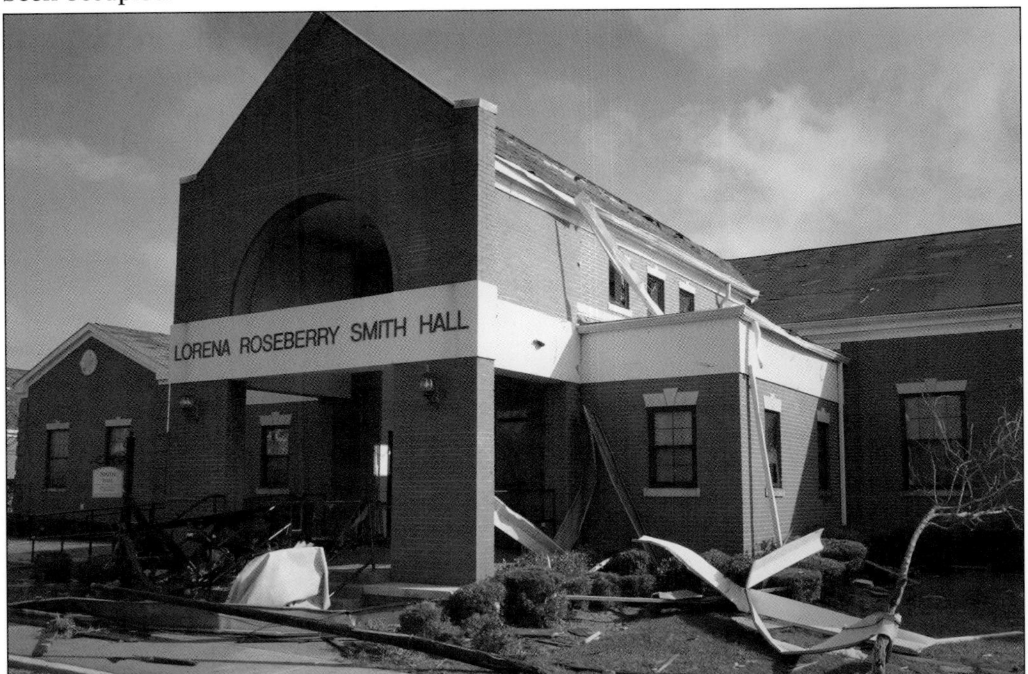


Smith Hall and Fairchild Hall, home of the School of Education, received roof damage and broken windows during the storm but were reopened for classes beginning the week of February 20. During the campus closure, faculty turned to the Canvas online learning system to deliver information and course content. The School of Education, which offers many online degree options, was able to easily transition into the temporary course delivery method.

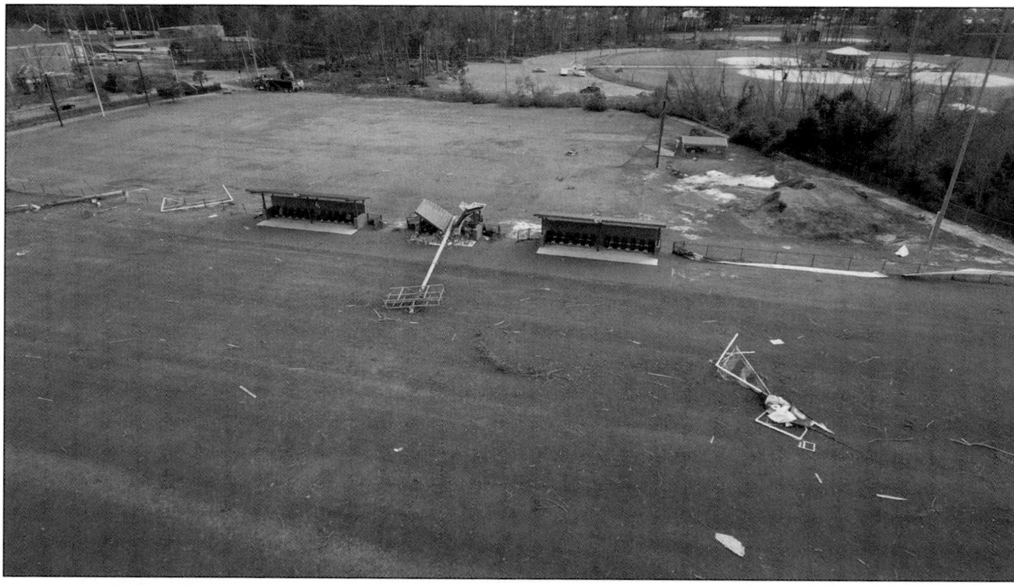

Carey's athletic facilities were damaged in the tornado, with the loss of scoreboards, major damage to Clinton Gymnasium, and some damage to other physical facilities. Athletic fields were covered with debris, including broken glass, and have been carefully combed over by recovery teams. The basketball team played home games at The University of Southern Mississippi's Reed Green Coliseum and at other area schools. Baseball and softball returned to their fields on campus in early March.

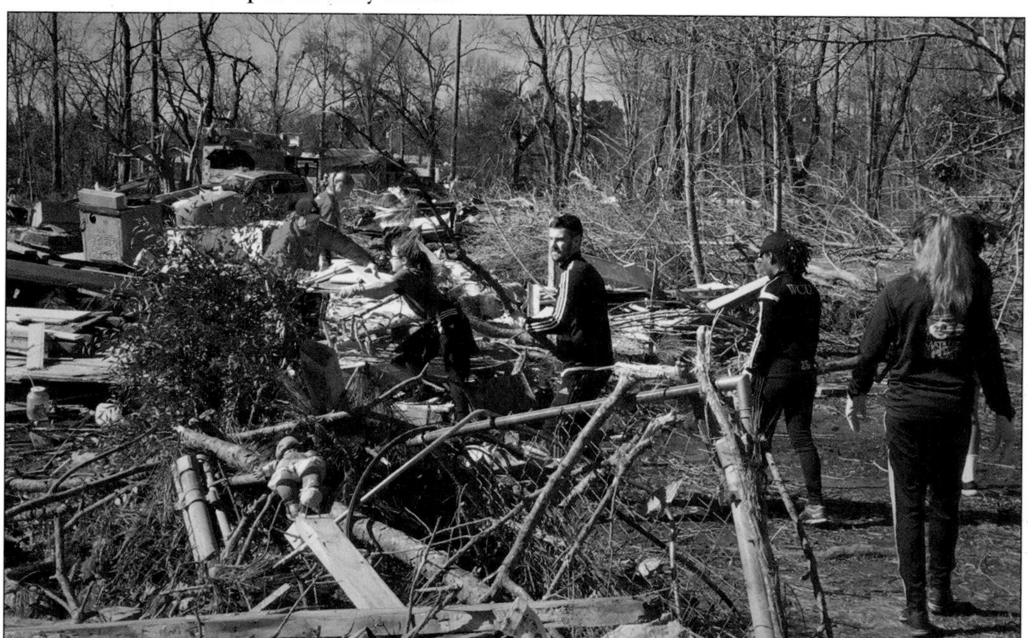

Despite the devastation at home, students, faculty, and staff members assisted with clean-up efforts for Carey's neighbors. The storm destroyed or severely damaged many homes, churches, and a fire station near the campus and also caused fatalities in a nearby mobile home park. The tornado traveled directly down William Carey Parkway from Highway 49 before traveling to nearby Petal, Mississippi.

Bass Hall, one of the women's residence halls on campus, was heavily damaged by the tornado (right), with both roof and exterior damage as well as broken windows on all floors. The building was quickly repaired (below) and welcomed its residents home beginning on February 18. University administrators pushed for a speedy recovery for the residence halls in order to restore a sense of normalcy to Carey's students, who were displaced for nearly a month. Residential students were welcomed to the University of Southern Mississippi, which created a special resources center for Carey students and opened its classrooms, living spaces, gym, athletic facilities, and counseling center to them.

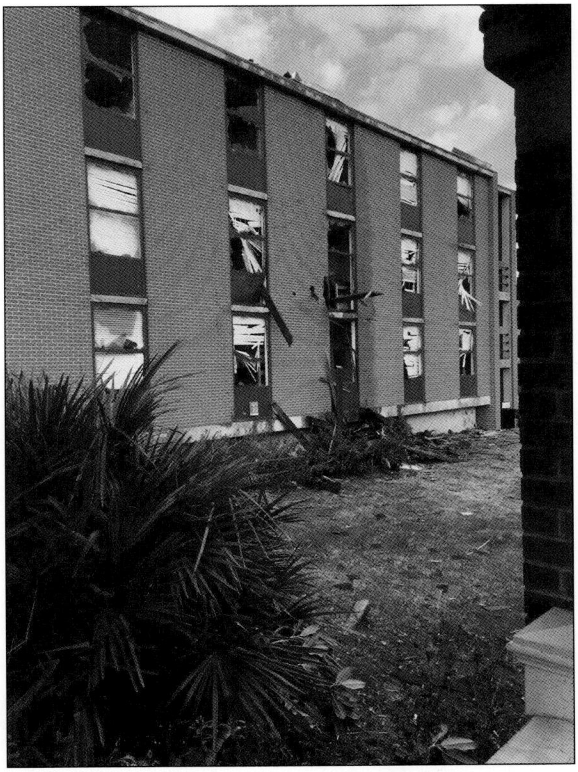

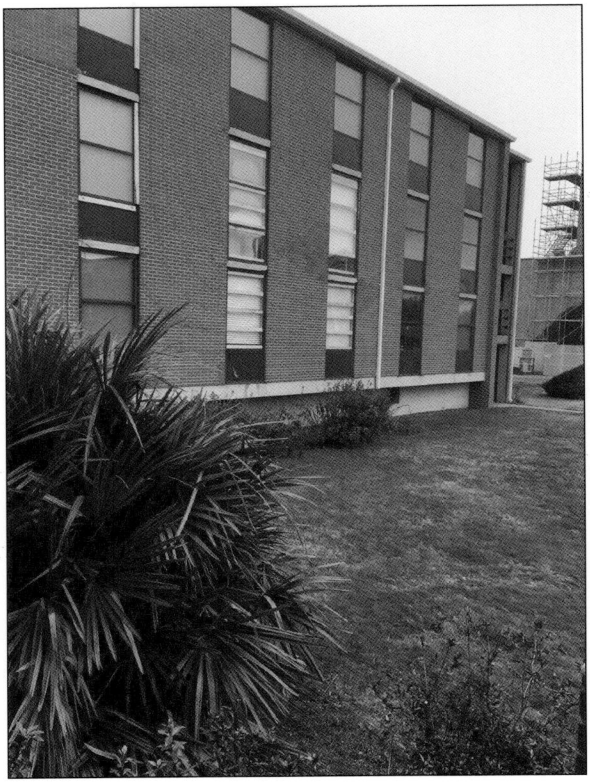

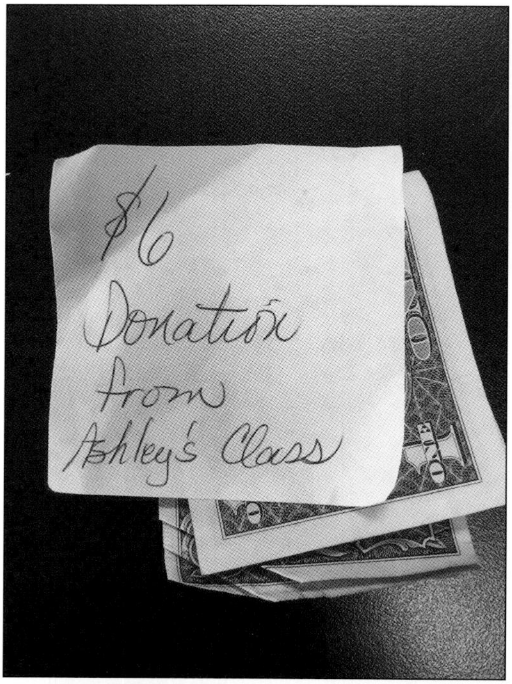


A third-grade student from North Florida Christian School in Tallahassee, Florida, sent her $6 allowance to help with the tornado recovery efforts at Carey. Almost immediately after the storm, financial donations, as well as donations of clothing and other items for students, poured into the university. These funds will be used to help replace belongings lost by students and will also help fund the recovery process on campus.

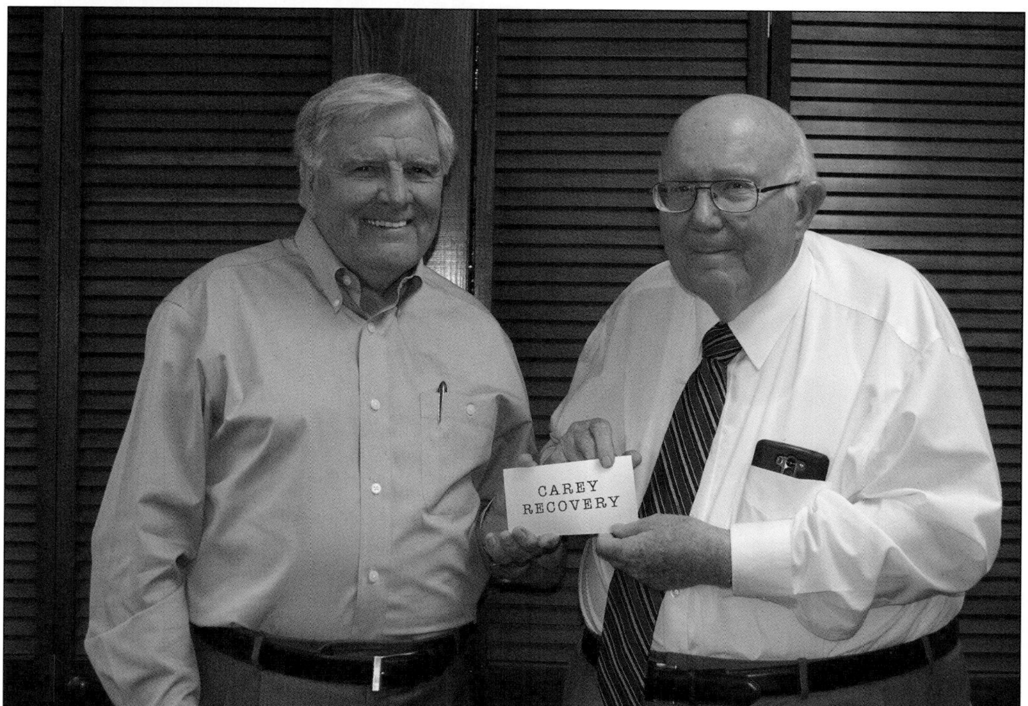


The Asbury Foundation of Hattiesburg pledged $2 million to Carey to assist with recovery. The funding will be used to cover any shortfall between the cost of rebuilding and the insurance coverage. Pictured giving the gift to Dr. Tommy King is William K. "Bill" Ray (left), CEO of Asbury Foundation and a Carey trustee. Other major donations were made by local banks, car dealerships, the Mississippi Baptist Foundation, and individuals.

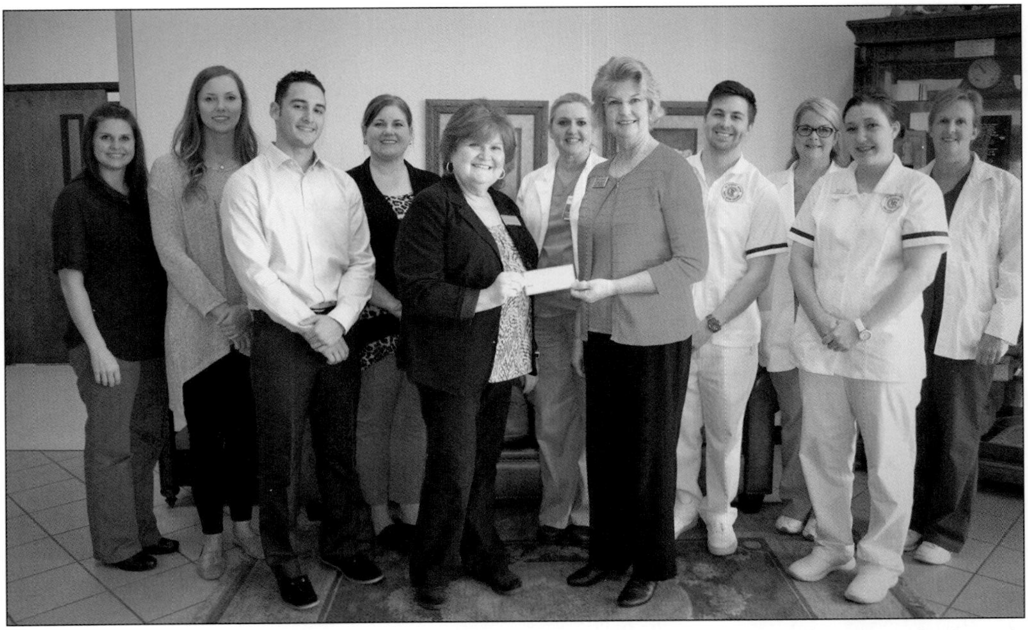

Student nurses at Pearl River Community College (PRCC) held a bake sale to benefit Carey's tornado recovery. Carey nursing students and Dr. Janet Williams, dean of the Fail School of Nursing, accepted the donation on behalf of Carey. PRCC employees also donated to the university's rebuilding efforts. Partnerships between Carey and its sister educational institutions in the Pine Belt provided invaluable resources in the days following the storm.

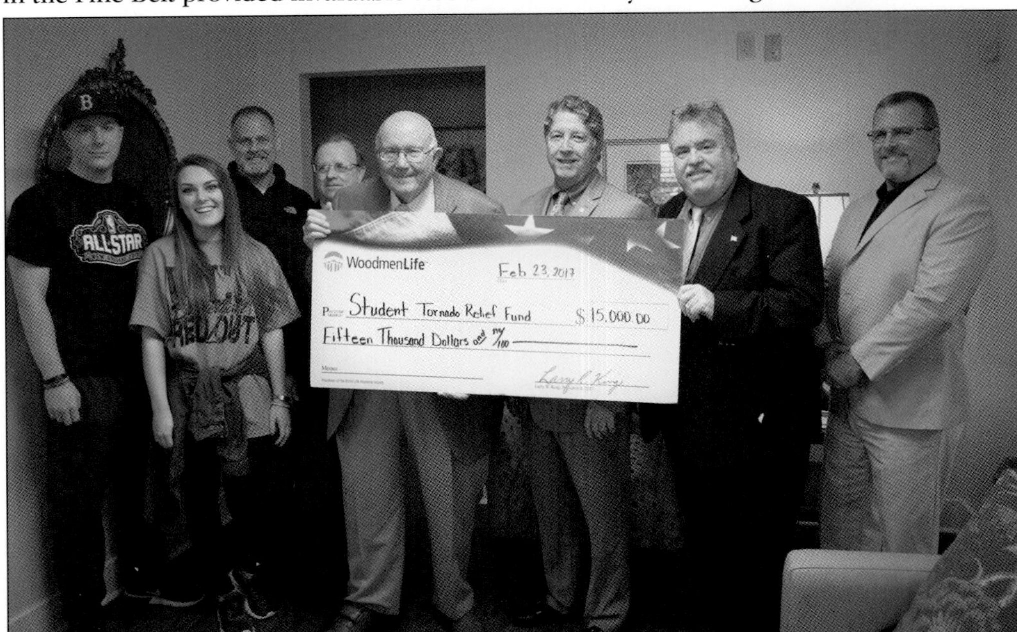


WoodmenLife donated $15,000 to rebuilding efforts. Between individual donors, the Asbury gift, and other corporate gifts, almost $3.5 million has been raised for recovery efforts and to help students replace lost belongings. Any funds not used for the rebuilding of the campus will be invested in future campus building projects and in continuing to grow the university.

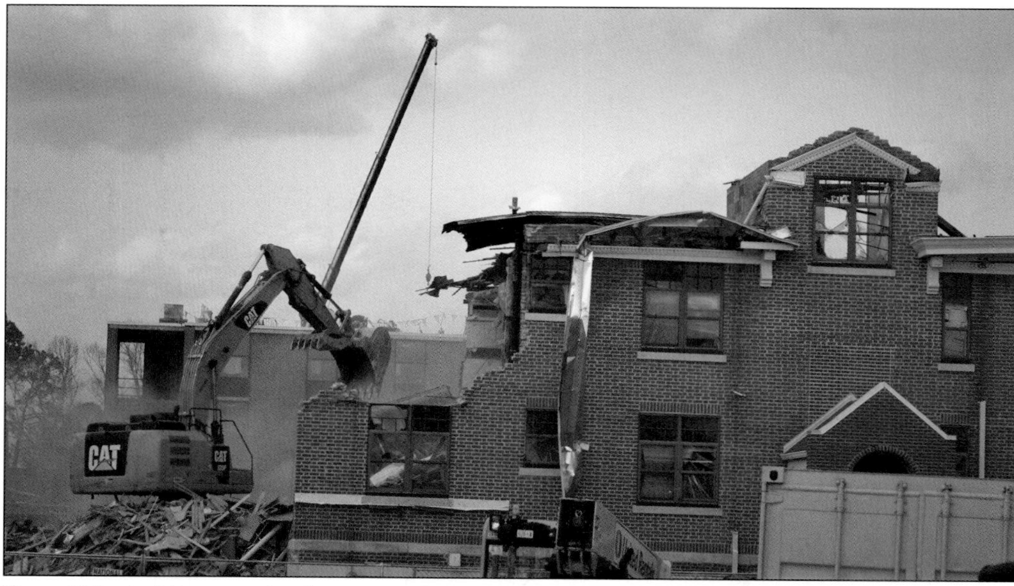


Demolition of Ross and Johnson Halls started in early February. Bobby Daniel, a former resident, shared, "I lived at the end of Johnson from 1992 to 1994. A lot of life and a lot of growing up was done there. Sitting at the kitchen table, I felt God leading me to apply as a summer missionary and then spend that next summer in Zimbabwe. A piece of my heart is in that rubble."

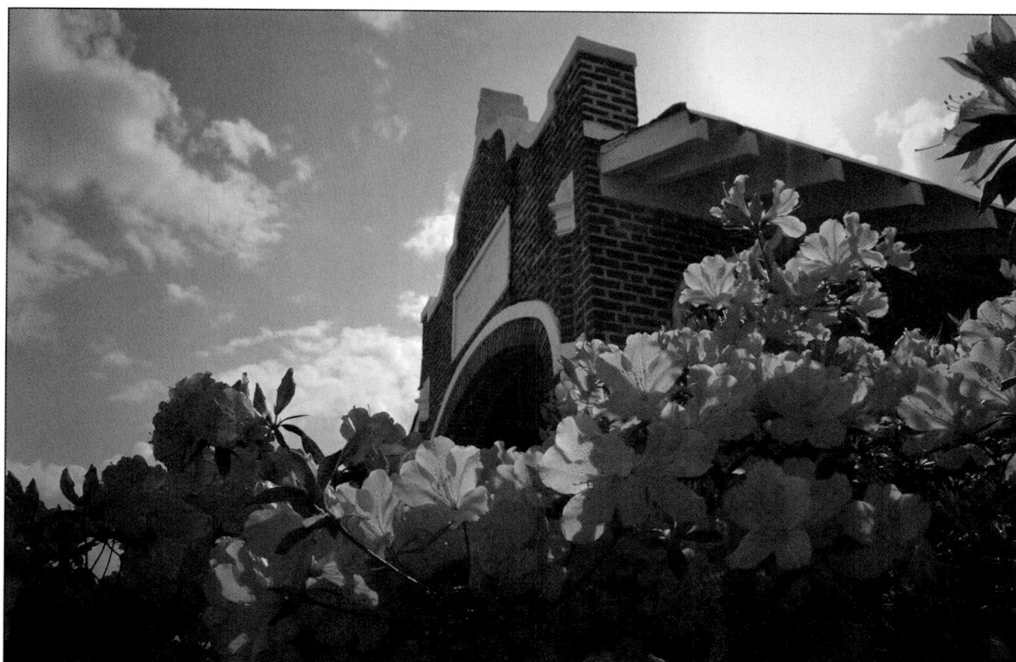

Despite the loss of much of the campus landscaping, azaleas were in full bloom in February near the Mary Ross Building. The historic building, constructed in 1920 as the campus infirmary, will be repaired after receiving minor damage in the storm. The neighboring Thomas Building, which serves as the home of the physical therapy program, was quickly repaired and is already hosting classes.

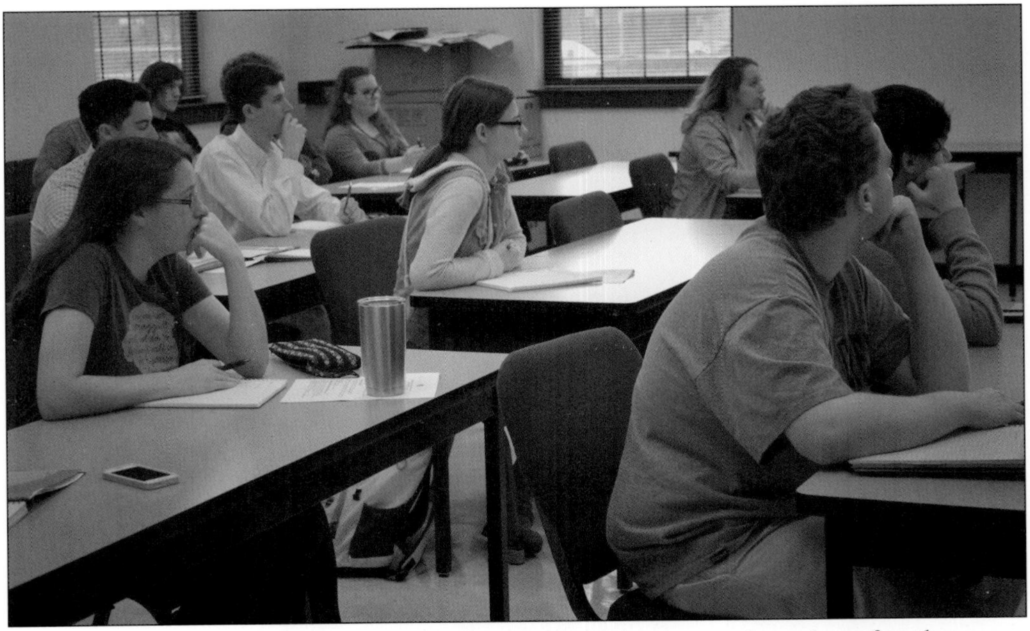

"Carey is looking a lot better already," said Dr. Tommy King a mere three days after the storm. A little over three weeks later, the campus was looking even better as students returned home to their residence halls and to academic buildings. Classes resumed on campus on February 20—a miraculous recovery for such significant damage. The full scope of repairs could take up to 18 months.

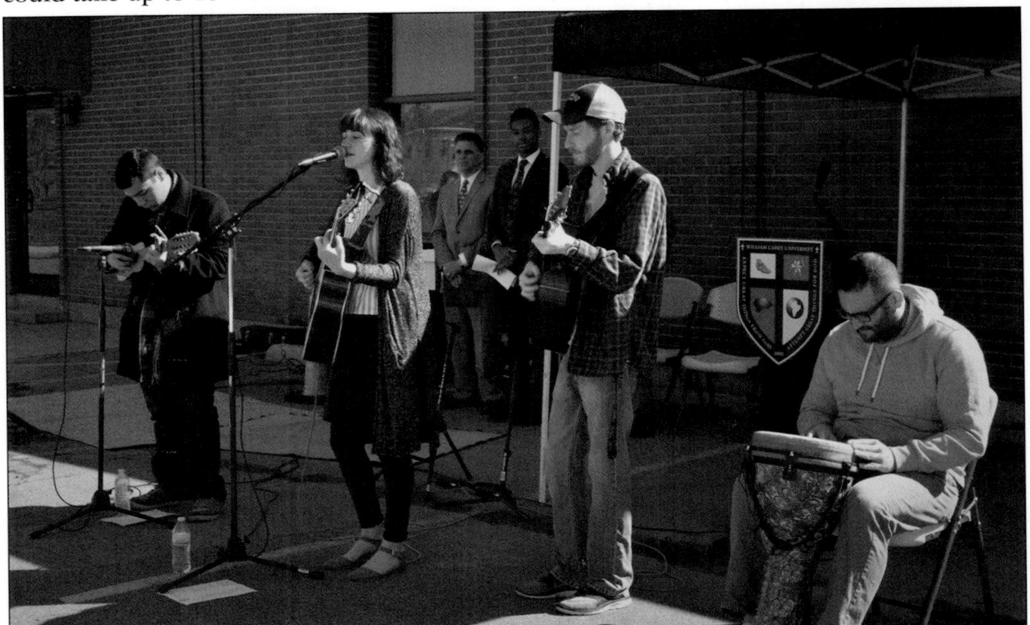

Students, faculty, and staff gathered for a chapel service—the first since the storm—on the grounds outside Wilkes Dining Hall on March 8. After worshipping together, Dr. Tommy King updated students on recovery plans, including the site of the new Tatum Court and replacement residence halls for Ross and Johnson Halls. He also mentioned that a new academic building would be built.

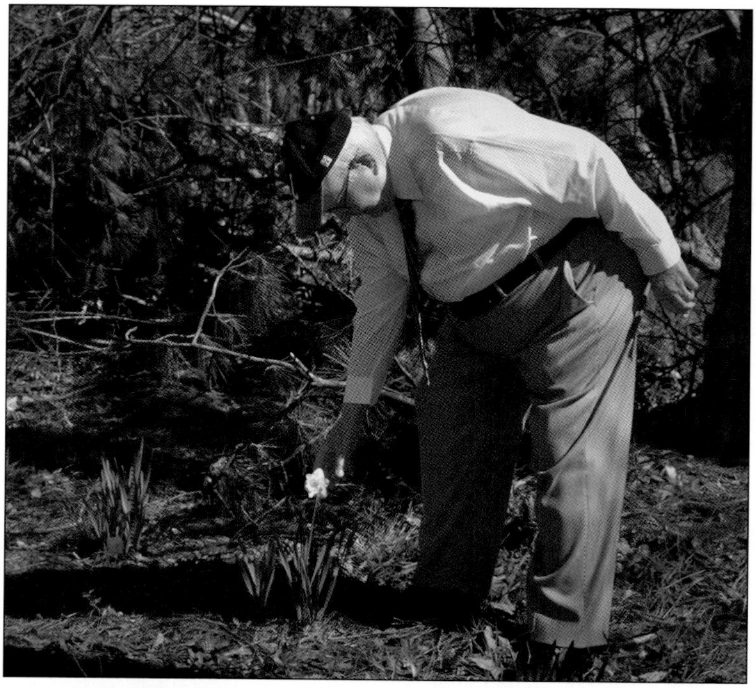

"Carey will pick up the pieces and move toward a brighter future, building on the strong foundation of the past 125 years," said Dr. Tommy King. There are many things to look forward to as the campus rebuilds, as new programs begin, and as students come and go, leaving their own unique contributions. As this book wraps for printing, spring flowers are in full bloom—a perfect symbol of Carey's future.

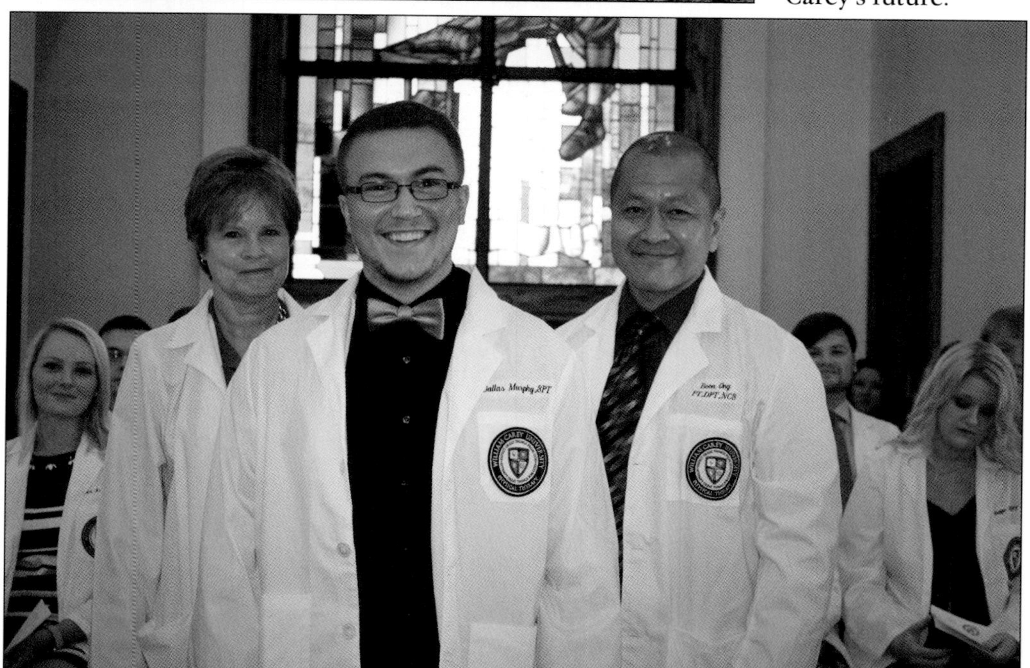

Dallas Murphy, a physical therapy student from Raleigh, Mississippi, smiles after receiving his white coat from physical therapy professors Judy Prehn and Boon Ong. The physical therapy program's 30-member inaugural class, consisting of students from Mississippi, Alabama, Tennessee, and Louisiana started their studies in August 2016. The program will help combat the shortage of physical therapists in Mississippi, which only had one physical therapy school prior to Carey's program.

Dr. Michael Malloy was hired in June 2016 as dean of the proposed pharmacy school, which will be located on the Tradition campus. The school is expected to open in 2018 with 60 to 70 students and 20 to 25 faculty and staff. It will anchor the Health Care Industry Zone, a five-mile radius around the campus established by the Mississippi Legislature in 2012 to promote the growth of health care along the Gulf Coast.

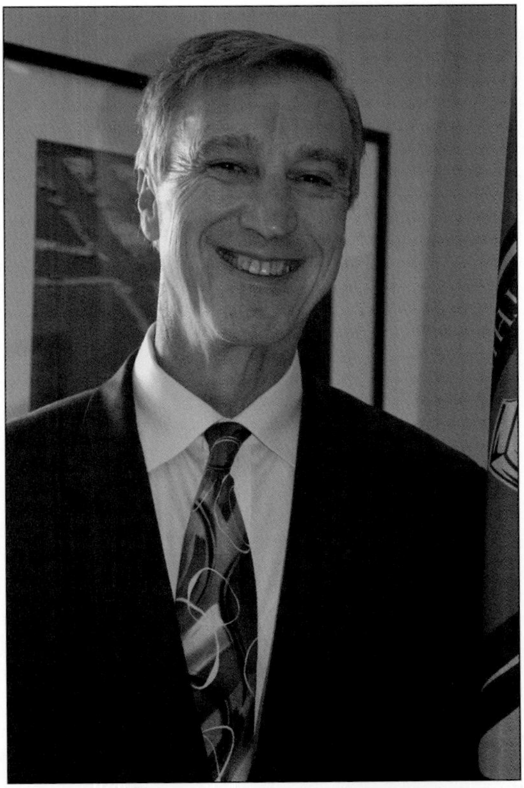

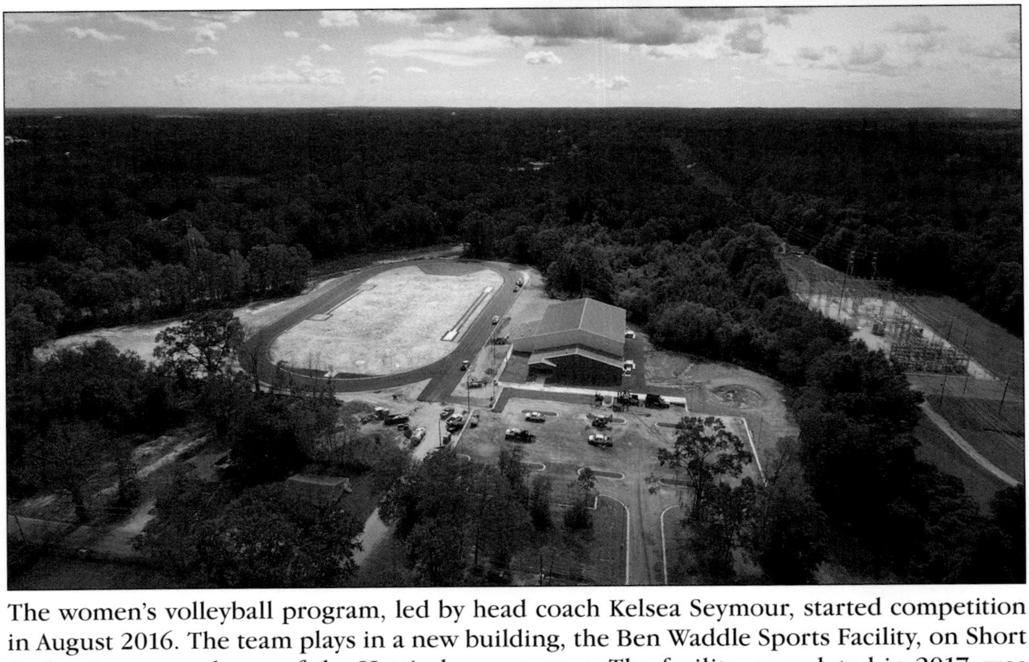

The women's volleyball program, led by head coach Kelsea Seymour, started competition in August 2016. The team plays in a new building, the Ben Waddle Sports Facility, on Short Cedar Street southeast of the Hattiesburg campus. The facility, completed in 2017, was undamaged by the tornado and will also be used by intramural sports and the Spirit of Carey marching band. A new competitive track and a classroom building were also built near the Waddle Facility.

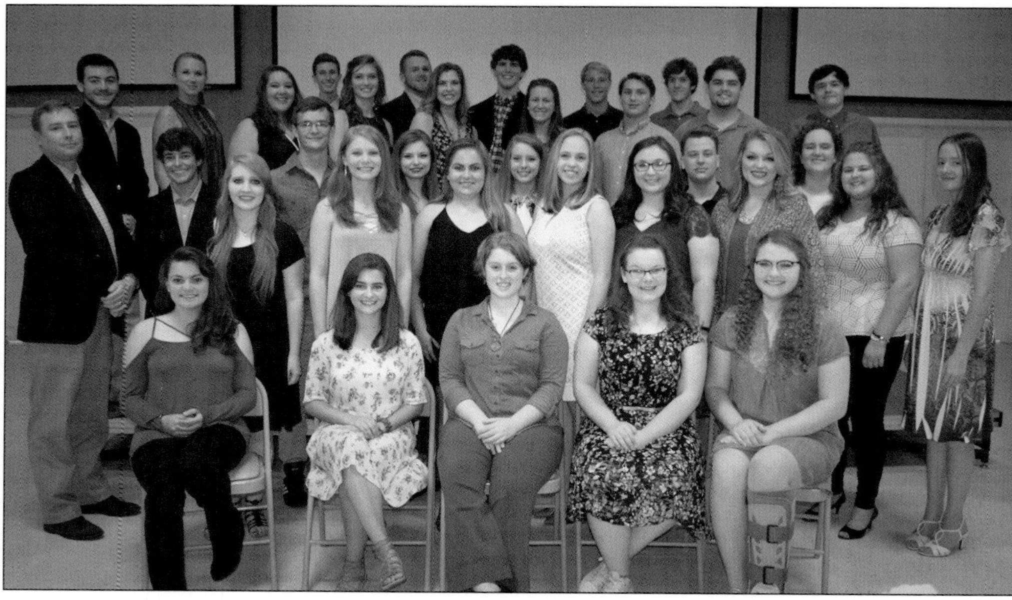

Carey recently welcomed the largest class of Carey Scholars in the institution's history. Thirty-six scholars, students who have earned a 29 or higher composite score on the ACT or a 1300 on the SAT, enrolled in 2016. University enrollment has continually increased for the past 11 years, with enrollment currently at nearly 4,500 students. The 2017 spring trimester saw a one-and-a-half percent increase over its 2016 equivalent, despite the tornado.

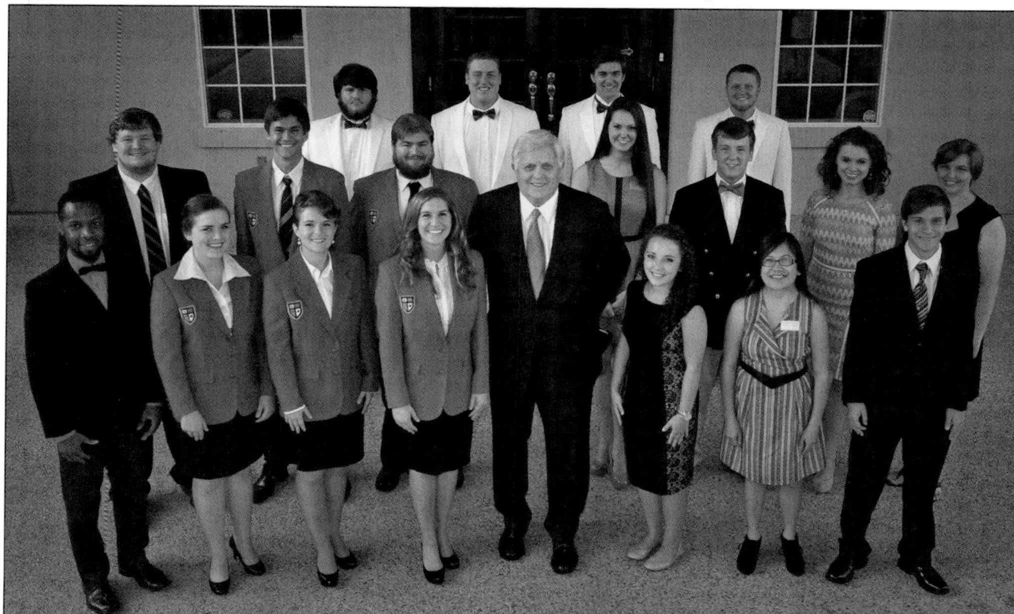

More than $3 million has been raised for scholarships over the course of six scholarship dinners beginning in 2011. Ninety percent of Carey students receive some type of financial assistance. The continued success of the dinners and the generosity of donors will allow many students, both now and in the future, the opportunity for a Christian education. Pictured with Carey students is 2014 dinner speaker Dr. Robert Khayat, chancellor emeritus of the University of Mississippi.

# Additional Acknowledgments

William Carey University has been a true love of mine since I first visited the campus in 2008. I loved the broad columns of Tatum Court, the quiet meditation areas in Chain Garden, and the wide colonnades on the Tradition campus. However, my real love of Carey grows from its people —the administrators, professors, staff members, students, and alumni—who make it a truly special place. To Dr. Tommy King, thank you for being my mentor and my friend. You made a personal investment in my success as a student and as a young professional. Thank you for your graciousness and for your fine leadership of our alma mater.

This revision would not be possible without the help of so many, including my friend, co-researcher, and editor Barbara Hamilton, a true Christian servant. Much of Carey's success in recent years would not have been possible without Barbara's strong work behind the scenes. Thanks are also due to my parents, Brandi Brewer, Shelia Brown, Jeanna Graves, Matt Gully, Regina Knight, Mia and Tom Overton, Mary Margaret Turner, and Brent Wallace, who contributed photographs to the university or provided assistance and encouragement throughout this process. I especially thank Brantley Fryfogle for his beautiful aerial photographs of the campus both before and after the storm.

Carey is forever in the debt of Milton and Donna Wheeler and the committee who assembled the 2006 first edition of this book, including Sarah Burrus, Allison Chestnut, Bennie Crockett, Jeanna Graves, Tommy King, Ralph Noonkester, Obra Quave, Lacey Walters, and Melinda Winstead. The comprehensive work assembled by this team has provided such a wonderful foundation for our university's future.

I owe a personal debt of gratitude to those family members, friends, mentors, and professors who believed in me and pushed me to always do my best, no matter the circumstances. Thank you for investing so much into my life.

Join with me in looking forward to Carey's next chapter, which I am sure will be filled with amazing stories of people "expecting great things from God and attempting great things for God."

—Joshua Wilson
Hattiesburg, Mississippi
2017

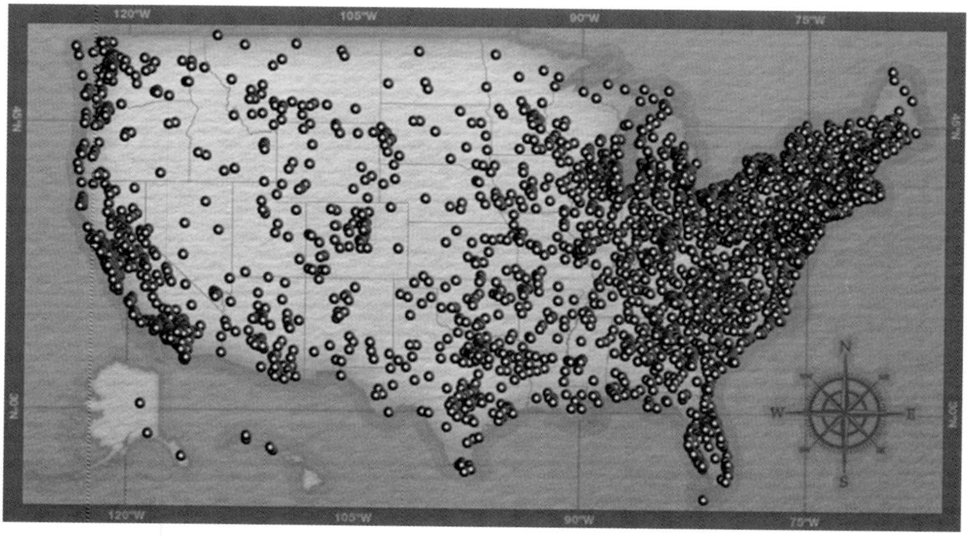